Bro & Sis Macdonald   OCT 1981

The
Doctrine and Covenants
Speaks

The
Doctrine and Covenants Speaks

By

Roy W. Doxey

Published by
Deseret Book Company
Salt Lake City, Utah

1976

Lithographed by

DESERET PRESS

in the United States of America

DEDICATION

To my mother who taught
me correct principles

PREFACE

This volume, *The Doctrine and Covenants Speaks*, represents many years of preparation and research, combined with over fifteen years of teaching the Doctrine and Covenants at Brigham Young University. Its 55 chapters were written and published singly over a number of years. Since then some of these chapters have undergone revisions, but not extensively. As to the revelations covered in this volume, in addition to material relating to the origin and development of the Doctrine and Covenants, there are discussions on Sections 1 through 72. This division of the Doctrine and Covenants at Section 72 covers slightly over one-half of the total sections in that standard work of The Church of Jesus Christ of Latter-day Saints. The second volume will contain discussions on the remaining sections through 136, received on January 14, 1847.

The Doctrine and Covenants holds a unique place among the books of scripture in this Church, the other scriptures being the Bible, The Book of Mormon, and the Pearl of Great Price. It is a modern book revealing eternal truths for the people of this generation. If these truths are followed, they will lead the Saints to the highest blessings that the Lord bestows upon his children —eternal life or exaltation. It contains the message the Lord would have this generation understand that repentance may take hold of the hearts of people throughout the world that they, too, may receive the greater blessings in store for the obedient. It is declared that the Lord's Word is to go to all people; in fact, none will escape that message, for every person's heart will be penetrated either in this life or in the world to come. (D&C 1:1-4.)

The Doctrine and Covenants begins with the revelations which brought The Church of Jesus Christ of

Latter-day Saints into existence and carries into the period of the Church's infancy up to and including a section on the martyrdom of the Prophet Joseph Smith and his brother Hyrum. Section 136 is the revelation given to Brigham Young.

To us of this year, the Lord has provided in his book of revelations: (1) the counsel of the all-wise Father whose object is to bring joy into the lives of his children today by their following instructions given to individuals, groups of persons, and the Church over a century ago; (2) a knowledge of how to live in this present world of uncertainty and insecurity; (3) the meaning of world conditions and events; (4) a philosophy of life that enables one to see God's justice and purposes for mankind; (5) a spirit of conversion to the truth-seeker which bears witness that Jesus is the Christ and of the divine mission of the Prophet Joseph Smith.

The Doctrine and Covenants breathes the spirit of truth with the divine promise:

> And if your eye be single to my glory, your whole bodies shall be filled with light, and there shall be no darkness in you; and that body which is filled with light comprehendeth all things.
>
> Therefore, sanctify yourselves that your minds become single to God, and the days will come that you shall see him; for he will unveil his face unto you, and it shall be in his own time, and in his own way, according to his own will. (D&C 88:67-68.)

A more detailed study of what one should expect from a study of The Doctrine and Covenants is found in chapter 3 of *The Doctrine and Covenants Speaks.*

Although the chapters in this book present a section-by-section discussion of The Doctrine and Covenants, one section only is not always discussed in one chapter, but one revelation may make up several chapters. An example is the material in Section 42 which contributes to five chapters. On the other hand, one chapter is written about one verse in Section 11 although the remainder of Section 11 is included with another Section to make up a chapter.

Generally, however, the chapters consist of only one section or possibly two. The arrangement of sections just noted was used to accommodate a central thesis of subject matter. Notwithstanding a theme is carried forward in each chapter, other phases of the revelations are also discussed.

In order to locate the material on each section, the reader should consult "Index by Sections of the Doctrine and Covenants" on page 565.

As to the specific contents of this book, a quick reading of chapter headings and subtitles in each chapter will provide a brief knowledge of the contents.

Although quotations appear in this book from the prophets, seers, and revelators of the dispensation, they are relatively few. If the reader desires to learn more about the teachings of the Doctrine and Covenants from the inspired men who constitute the members of the First Presidency, the Twelve Apostles, and the Patriarchs to the Church, who have the special right to teach and to declare the mind and will of the Lord, under the direction of the Prophet, Seer, and Revelator, reference is made to the author's four-volume commentary, *The Latter-day Prophets and the Doctrine and Covenants.*

The revelations in the Doctrine and Covenants witness the truth that Joseph Smith is a true prophet. There is a spirit about the revelations that evidences their truth. Joseph Smith was enlightened by the Holy Ghost and the imprint of that Spirit is upon the revelations. It is significantly true that the person who desires sincerely to know may understand by that same Spirit. So the Lord declares; so also the faithful have learned.

Therefore, why is it that ye cannot understand and know, that he that receiveth the word by the Spirit of truth receiveth it as it is preached by the Spirit of truth?

Wherefore, he that preacheth and he that receiveth, understand one another, and both are edified and rejoice together.

And that which doth not edify is not of God, and is darkness. (*Ibid.*, 50:21-23.)

The Doctrine and Covenants is a monument to the fact that Joseph Smith was chosen by the Lord to usher in the last and greatest dispensation of the gospel of Jesus Christ—the fulness of times!

It is the author's hope that *The Doctrine and Covenants Speaks* will serve to encourage more people, Latter-day Saints and others, although it is written for the Latter-day Saint especially, to become acquainted with this marvelous book of scripture—The Doctrine and Covenants.

—Roy W. Doxey

Brigham Young University
Provo, Utah
September, 1964

ABBREVIATIONS

D&C   The Doctrine and Covenants.

DHC   *Documentary History of the Church.* Also, Joseph Smith, *History of The Church of Jesus Christ of Latter-day Saints.* Period I. Edited by Elder B. H. Roberts. 6 volumes.

v.   verse

vs.   verses

p.   page

pp.   pages

         Scriptural references are abbreviated in the usual manner.

— Contents —

Chapter 1

THE LORD SPEAKS THROUGH HIS PROPHETS

In this book about the Doctrine and Covenants, we are to learn what God has revealed in this dispensation to his prophets. We should recognize that there is still need for divine direction to the leadership of The Church of Jesus Christ of Latter-day Saints, as anciently. Individually as members of the Church, we have a need for divine guidance in our lives that we may eventually become joint heirs with Christ. Acceptance of the revelations in The Doctrine and Covenants as being divine, will bring great blessings to the adherents.

The Prophet Joseph Smith instructed the brethren of the Church in 1834 in regard to the holy scriptures as follows:

We take the sacred writings into our hands, and admit that they were given by direct inspiration for the good of man. We believe that God condescended to speak from the heavens and declare His will concerning the human family, to give them just and holy laws, to regulate their conduct, and guide them in a direct way, that in due time He might take them to Himself, and make them joint heirs with His Son. But when this fact is admitted, that the immediate will of heaven is contained in the Scriptures, are we not bound as rational creatures to live in accordance to all its precepts? Will the mere admission, that this is the will of heaven ever benefit us if we do not comply with all its teachings? Do we not offer violence to the Supreme Intelligence of heaven, when we admit the truth of its teachings, and do not obey them? Do we not descend below our own knowledge, and the better wisdom which heaven has endowed us with, by such a course of conduct? For these reasons, if we have direct revelations given us from heaven, surely those revelations were never given to be trifled with, without the trifler's incurring displeasure and vengeance upon his own head, if there is any justice in heaven. . . . (*DHC* II:11.)

The Christian World and Revelation

When the clergy of Joseph Smith's day learned that Joseph professed to have had revelation from the Lord in the actual appearance of the Eternal Father and his Son Jesus Christ, there began a controversy which continues to this day. Aside from other points of difference arising from the first vision of the Prophet, the fundamental issue was the claim of Joseph Smith to revelation from God. This claim meant that the "Christian" churches had departed from the true doctrine and Church established by Jesus in the Meridian of Time.

It was contended by the adversaries of the Prophet that revelation from the Lord was neither expected nor necessary. The canon of scripture was closed—for God had spoken in the past through his Son Jesus and the apostles, and thereafter there was no need of revelation. It is not difficult at all to understand that where divine revelation was not received by the clergy who denied its necessity, they would immediately oppose such a claim as Joseph Smith put forth.

This position would take on added zeal when their own standing as ministers was set aside because of a claimed apostasy. Many were the arguments presented from the Bible in an attempt to show that revelation in a post-meridian period was not to be expected.

It is by no means an unfruitful experience to examine a few of those assumed reasons for declaring that no more scripture or revelation was necessary. In other words, how would you, as a member of the Church, meet such arguments as the following?

Arguments Advanced against Further Revelation

It is suggested that in considering these arguments against further revelation, that you first read the scripture and then the application used by those who denied that revelation would be received in our time. Next consider how you would reply to this application or interpretation. Finally, read the answer generally used by the Latter-day Saints to prove wherein the application of the clergy was out of harmony with the facts, and, therefore, false.

For I testify unto every man that heareth the words of the prophecy of this book, If any man shall add unto these things, God shall add unto him the plagues that are written in this book:

And if any man shall take away from the words of the book of this prophecy, God shall take away his part out of the book of life, and out of the holy city, and from the things which are written in this book. (Rev. 22:18-19.)

Application by "Christian" clergy:

No man has the right to add to the Bible; therefore, no further revelation (scripture) is to be expected.

Answer by Latter-day Saints:

The Bible as a collection of books did not exist when this inspired scripture was given; consequently, this injunction was not intended to include other scriptures written after the book of Revelation, such as the Gospel of John, and other parts of the New Testament. Furthermore, this admonition was given to man, and it was not intended that God could not or that he would not give further revelation. Notice in Deuteronomy 4:2, the same admonition is given concerning the writings of Moses. If the same application was made as was made for Revelation 22:18-19 by "new revelation" deniers, there would have been no inspired writings after Moses.

. . . . from a child thou hast known the holy scriptures, which are able to make thee wise unto salvation through faith which is in Christ Jesus. (2 Tim. 3:15.)

Application by "Christian" clergy:

If there was sufficient revelation to give salvation to Timothy as a child, there would be no further need for additional revelation.

Answer by Latter-day Saints:

This application would do away with the New Testament; for, again, there was not a New Testament in existence when Timothy was a child. He was acquainted with the Old Testament.

Charity never faileth: but whether there be prophecies, they shall fail; whether there be tongues, they shall cease; whether there be knowledge, it shall vanish away. (1 Cor. 13:8.)

Application by "Christian" clergy:

Prophecies and the other spiritual gifts, among which is revelation, were to cease after the days of Jesus and the apostles.

Answer by Latter-day Saints:

The next two verses (1 Corinthians 13:9-10) point out that prophecy would be unnecessary ". . . when that which is perfect is come. . . ." The day of perfection has not yet come, so these gifts are still necessary.

The absence of scriptural justification to deny new revelation is established by the accepted Christian standard of judgment—the Holy Bible. When the Lord desires to give new revelation to man, he will do so, but only in accordance with his designs. (2 Nephi 29:1-14; Alma 29:8.)

Revelation in the Past

The Latter-day Saints learned early that "Where there is no vision, the people perish. . ." (Prov. 29:18), and that "Surely the Lord God will do nothing, but he revealeth his secret unto his servants the prophets." (Amos 3:7.) It then became a matter for the early day Latter-day Saint missionaries to demonstrate from the Bible that God had always directed his people in the past. Furthermore, there were sufficient grounds for knowing that, if God's purposes for his children were to be fulfilled, new revelation from the Giver of all truth would be necessary.

One of the outstanding lessons the Latter-day Saint missionary saw in the Bible was that the Lord's servants in the Meridian of Time were directed in their ministry by revelation. In fact, Jesus had promised his disciples that the Holy Ghost would direct them after his ascension. (John 16:1-7, 13-14; 15:26.) Paul received the gospel by revelation (Galatians 1:11-12), and instructions came from the Lord by a vision and from the Holy Ghost as to when to teach the gospel and when not to teach it. (Acts 16:6; 18:9-10.)

It was also apparent that the leadership of the Church was directed in matters which affected the entire Church of Jesus Christ. An example of this may be found in the revelation to the Apostle Peter concerning the preaching of the gospel to the Gentiles. (Acts 10:19-48.) During Jesus' ministry on earth he confined his teaching to the house of Israel. (Matt. 15:24.) Paul also knew by revelation that upon the rejection of the gospel by the Jew it was to go to the Gentile. (Acts 13:46.) John the Revelator directed the Church by revelation when the seven branches of the Church in Asia required rebuke and admonition. (Rev. chapters 1-3.)

This guidance was, in part, the fulfillment of Jesus' promise concerning the Church. In conversation with his disciples Jesus asked whom men declared him to be. Various answers were given; whereupon, the Lord asked them, "But whom say ye that I am?" The reply of Peter was "Thou art the Christ, the Son of the living God." Jesus then said to Peter that "flesh and blood [man] hath not revealed it unto thee, but my Father which is in heaven." It was then that the Master declared the great truth that upon the rock of revelation, he would build his Church. (Matt. 16:13-18.)

Another reason for knowing that revelation was necessary in our times was found in the fact that the scriptures spoke of many lost or missing books which do not now form a part of the Old and the New Testaments. (Examples of these are give in 1 Chron. 29:29; 2 Chron. 33:18-19; 1 Cor. 5:9; Eph. 3:3; and Col. 4:16.)

Contending Christian Churches

The great number of divisions in Christianity which existed at the time of the Prophet Joseph Smith, each contending against the other, and new churches coming into existence, were evidence that men without revelation could not interpret the Bible correctly. The differences, which existed among the various churches and which often give rise to new organizations, were based upon this simple fact. It was pointed out that the wisdom of man's learning was not sufficient to give true doctrine. (1 Cor. 2:11, 14.) Only God could provide man with the way of eternal life and that required continuous revelation from the Lord. An outstanding example of the lack of revelation in modern Christianity was evident in that the organization of the Church of Jesus Christ as made known in the New Testament could not be duplicated by men. Although officers in the Church were mentioned, their duties and privileges were not clearly made known. Only new revelation from God could bring into being the true Church organization with saving principles and ordinances.

A New Dispensation Prophesied

The apostles of Christ had foreseen that the gospel and the Church would be lost to the world by the apostasy of the members of the Church (Isaiah 24:1-6; 2 Peter 2:1-3; Galatians 1:6-10) but gave sufficient evidence to know that revelation was not to cease forever. It was proclaimed by three New Testament writers—Peter, Paul, and John the Revelator—that subsequent to their day the Lord would usher in the greatest dispensation of the gospel. It was the Apostle Peter who said that before the second coming of Christ there would be a "times of refreshing . . . from the presence of the Lord" (Acts 3:19), which would constitute a "times of restitution [or restoration] of all things. . . ." These are Peter's inspired words:

Repent ye therefore, and be converted, that your sins may be blotted out, when the times of refreshing shall come from the presence of the Lord;

And he shall send Jesus Christ, which before was preached unto you:

Whom the heaven must receive until the times of restitution of all things, which God hath spoken by the mouth of all his holy prophets since the world began. (Acts 3:19-21.)

The word of the Lord would come in preparation for the second coming of Christ.

The second apostle of record to predict the restoration of the gospel was Paul. In his letter to the Saints at Ephesus, after reminding them of their pre-earth existence and of the mission of Jesus, he set forth the purposes of the Lord concerning the day in which we live. These are his words:

Having made known unto us the mystery of his will, according to his good pleasure which he hath purposed in himself:

That in the dispensation of the fulness of times he might gather together in one all things in Christ, both which are in heaven, and which are on earth; even in him. (Eph. 1:9-10.)

In what way does Paul's prediction relate to the latter days? This period was to be the "fulness of times," an expression which connotes a culminating or concluding period. The Lord's word was to be dispensed again in the final dispensation. Notice the similarity of thought and language of Peter's statement on the "times of restitution" before Jesus' second coming (which was to include "all things") and Paul's prophecy that Christ would "gather together in one all things in Christ. . ."

things "which are in heaven, and which are on earth." (Eph. 1:10.) In effect, what these two apostles prophesied is the same thing which the Prophet Joel said would occur "before the great and the terrible day of the Lord. . ." or the second coming of Christ. (Joel 2:28-32.)

A third prophecy, made by the Apostle John, is that of the coming of an angel in the hour of God's judgment or in the latter days preceding the second coming of Christ. This holy messenger was to bring "the everlasting gospel" which was to be preached "to every nation, and kindred, and tongue, and people." (Rev. 14:6.) Thus, the apostles Peter, Paul, and John had spoken as directed by the Spirit, and the missionaries of the new dispensation carried this message to the world.

Latter-day Saints Fulfill Prophecies

The Prophet Joseph Smith remarked at a conference of elders of the Church that "we are differently situated from any other people that ever existed upon this earth; consequently those former revelations cannot be suited to our conditions; they were given to other people, who were before us; but in the last days, God was to call a remnant, in which was to be deliverance, as well as in Jerusalem and Zion." (*DHC* II:52.) This fact was apparent to our people when they discovered that Bible prophets foresaw the time when God would raise up a people in the last days who would fulfill the prophecies spoken by them. What were some of the things to be accomplished in the Dispensation of the Fulness of Times?

New scripture was to be made known in the form of a "book" from ancient American peoples that would "speak from the dust" at a time when the religious world was in a condition of apostasy. By this book of scripture, faith in Jesus Christ would increase and bring people to understand the plan of salvation. (Read Isaiah chapter 29, especially vs. 4, 9-12, 17-19, 24.) This book was known by Ezekiel as the "stick of Joseph" and the Bible as the "stick of Judah." (Ezekiel 37:16-28.)

The prophets had made known that in the latter days Israel was to be gathered from her scattered condition. (Isa. 11:11-12; 35:4, 10; Jer. 3:12-15, 18; 16:14-16; 23:2-4, 7-8; 31:7-12; Ezek. 37:21-27.) That portion of Israel which would constitute the Latter-day Saints was to be a temple-building people (Isa. 2:2-3) and the fulfillment of the ancient prophecy of Malachi, chapter four, verses five and six, concerning the coming of Elijah would also mean new revelation subsequent to the time of Jesus' apostles.

Summary

The true ministers of the Lord in this dispensation knew that the Lord had never said by his prophets that there was to be no more revelation or scripture after the meridian dispensation. They were also assured that the Lord has (1) directed his servants by immediate revelation; (2) that the leadership of the Church was led by revelation in order to govern the Church; (3) that there was a need for further revelation because the Bible was incomplete; (4) that uninspired men were unable to interpret the Bible correctly and thereby many divisions in Christianity were created; (5) that the restoration of the gospel was prophesied; (6) that new scripture, as The Book of Mormon, was to be revealed; and (7) that Israel was to be gathered, temples were to be built, and other prophesied events were to take place as a part of the Dispensation of the Fulness of Times.

These reasons obtained from the scriptures give to us Latter-day Saints confirmation of our faith in what God has done for us in the establishment of his Church upon the earth.

Chapter 2

ORIGIN OF THE DOCTRINE AND COVENANTS

(The Doctrine and Covenants: Explanatory Introduction)

The prophesied Dispensation of the Fulness of Times opened in the spring of 1820 with the glorious revelation known as the first vision. Although this revelation is not included in the one hundred and thirty-six sections of The Doctrine and Covenants, reference to it is found in the first three paragraphs of the "Explanatory Introduction." The full account of the first vision is printed in the Pearl of Great Price. (Writings of Joseph Smith, 2:5-26.)

Value of the First Vision

As we begin a study of the revelations given to Joseph Smith, it seems most appropriate to ask ourselves this question: of what importance is the first vision in the opening of the new dispensation? In answering this question, we should keep in mind that all revelations and commandments given to men are for their salvation. What then, does the first vision contribute to the salvation of men? Here are some ideas:

First, it proved the actual existence of God our Father as a personal being. Joseph Smith saw God! "I saw two Personages, whose brightness and glory defy all description, standing above me in the air. . . ." (P.of G.P., Writings of Joseph Smith, 2:17.) No longer could men say that God does not exist because he had not revealed himself to man. A correct knowledge of God was revealed. Without this knowledge, man could not receive life eternal. (John 17:3.)

Second, it proved that Jesus is a resurrected Personage, separate and distinct from the Father.

One of them spake unto me, calling me by name and said, pointing to the other—This is My Beloved Son. Hear Him! (P.of G.P., Writings of Joseph Smith, 2:17.)

Jesus Christ is declared to be divine—the Son of God. Doubt concerning his divinity and of his resurrection is removed. Men have a firm basis for faith in Jesus as the Savior of mankind.

Third, it proved that there was an universal apostasy from the Church established by Jesus in the Meridian of Time; that no existing church was the true Church.

My object in going to inquire of the Lord was to know which of all the sects was right, that I might know which to join. No sooner, therefore, did I get possession of myself, so as to be able to speak, than I asked the Personages who stood above me in the light, which of all the sects was right—and which I should join.

I was answered that I must join none of them, for they were all wrong; and the Personage who addressed me said that all their creeds were an abomination in his sight; that those professors were all corrupt; that: "they draw near to me with their lips, but their hearts are far from me, they teach for doctrines the commandments of men, having a form of godliness, but they deny the power thereof."

He again forbade me to join with any of them; and many other things did he say unto me, which I cannot write at this time. When I came to myself again, I found myself lying on my back, looking up into heaven. When the light had departed, I had no strength; but soon recovering in some degree, I went home. And as I leaned up to the fireplace, mother inquired what the matter was. I replied, "Never mind, all is well—I am well enough off." I then said to my mother, "I have learned for myself that Presbyterianism is not true." It seems as though the adversary was aware, at a very early period of my life, that I was destined to prove a disturber and an annoyer of his kingdom; else why should the powers of darkness combine against me? Why the opposition and persecutions that arose against me, almost in my infancy? (*Ibid.*, 2:18-20.)

Fourth, it proved that men may have the assurance that sincere prayer is answered.

While I was laboring under the extreme difficulties caused by the contests of these parties of religionists, I was one day reading the Epistle of James, first chapter and fifth verse, which reads: If any of you lack wisdom, let him ask of God, that giveth to all men liberally, and upbraideth not; and it shall be given him.

Never did any passage of scripture come with more power to the heart of man than this did at this time to mine. It seemed to enter with great force into every feeling of my heart. I reflected on it again and again, knowing that if any person needed wisdom from God, I did; for how to act I did not know, and unless I could get more wisdom than I then had, I would never know; for the teachers of religion of the different sects understood the same passages if scripture so differently as to destroy all confidence in settling the question by an appeal to the Bible.

At length I came to the conclusion that I must either remain in darkness and confusion, or else I must do as James directs, that is, ask of God. I at length came to the determination to "ask of God," concluding that if he gave wisdom to them that lacked wisdom, and would give liberally, and not upbraid, I might venture. . . .

I had now got my mind satisfied so far as the sectarian world was concerned—that it was not my duty to join with any of them, but to continue as I was until further directed. I had found the testimony of James to be true—that a man who lacked wisdom might ask of God, and obtain, and not be upbraided. (*Ibid.*, 2:11-13, 26.)

In order to achieve salvation, men must "ask of God" for knowledge by which they may walk uprightly before him. (Moroni 10:3-7.) Joseph Smith's testimony concerning prayer and the reality of the future life furnish further reasons for faith in the efficacy of prayer in leading one to salvation. There is no promise that all men will receive a visitation of God the Father or of his Son Jesus Christ. These holy Personages have been seen only on a few occasions and at those times to their chosen prophets. (John 1:18; Acts 7:55-56.)

Compiling of the Revelations

The many visits of the Angel Moroni with Joseph Smith, beginning in September 1823, brought forth revelations in connection with The Book of Mormon to be studied later. This coming of the resurrected Moroni was the next step in the events which led up to the compiling of the many revelations into a volume of scripture. As also pointed out in the "Explanatory Introduction," many other revelations were received by the summer of 1830, when, "acting under Divine commandment," the Prophet "was engaged in copying and arranging the revelations received up to that time. . . ." In this work he was assisted by John Whitmer, who later became the Church historian by divine appointment. (*DHC* I:104; D&C 47:1.)

The Book of Commandments

The special priesthood conference which convened on November 1, 1831, at Hiram, Ohio, authorized the printing of 10,000 copies of the compilation of revelations to be known as the *Book of Commandments*. However, on May 1, 1832, a general council of the Church decided that 3,000 copies should be printed, and "that William W. Phelps, Oliver Cowdery, and John Whitmer, be appointed to review and prepare such revelations for the press as shall be deemed proper for publication, and print them as soon as possible at Independence, Missouri; the announcement to be made that they are 'Published by W. W. Phelps & Co. . . .'" (*DHC* I:270.) Before this (November 1831), Oliver Cowdery was appointed to "carry the commandments to Independence, Missouri, for printing. . . ." Inasmuch as he was also to take "moneys" with him, a traveling companion, John Whitmer, was to accompany him because of the protection which seemed necessary in traveling in an area where frontier conditions existed. (*Ibid.*, I:229; D&C 69.)

Destruction of the Printing Press

On the 20th of July, 1833, a mob consisting of from three to five hundred, "demanded the discontinuance of the Church printing establishment in Jackson county, the closing of the store, and the cessation of all mechanical labors. The brethren refused compliance, and the consequence was that the house of W. W. Phelps, which contained the printing establishment, was thrown down, the materials taken possession of by the mob, many papers destroyed, and the family and furniture thrown out of doors." (*Ibid.*, I:390.)

Fortunately, a few incomplete copies of the Book of Commandments survived the destruction. This book was reprinted at different times. It contains sixty-five chapters.

Approval of Doctrine and Covenants

The next date of significance in this brief history of the Doctrine and Covenants is September 24, 1834, when a committee with Joseph Smith as its head was appointed to publish the revelations. Upon the completion of its work, a General Assembly of the Church convened on August 17, 1835, at Kirtland, Ohio, "to see whether the book be approved or not by the authorities of the Church: that it may, if approved, become a law and a rule of faith and practice to the Church. . . ." The two High Councils (Kirtland and Missouri) and the quorum of the priesthood accepted and acknowledged the book as the doctrine and covenants of their faith, by a unanimous vote, and the written testimony of the Twelve Apostles was read. (*Ibid.*, II:243-246.)

Meaning of Doctrine and Covenants

This volume of revelations was printed with the title Doctrine and Covenants. It seems appropriate that the new name was given it with an increase in the number of sections from 65 to 102. The comprehensiveness of the title is indicated in the "Introduction" to the *Doctrine and Covenants Commentary*, where we learn that " 'Doctrine' means 'teaching, instruction!' . . . The word 'covenant' is a term by which God indicates the settled arrangement between Him and His people. . . . This covenant concerning the salvation of the human race, entered into in eternity, was made known to Adam, Noah, Abraham, and others, and, finally, through the Prophet Joseph, to the people of God in our day. It is the 'everlasting' covenant, because it is from eternity to eternity. The new and everlasting covenant is the Gospel of Jesus Christ." (*Doctrine and Covenants Commentary*, page xiv.)

Other Editions of The Doctrine and Covenants

Before his death, the Prophet Joseph Smith worked on another edition of The Doctrine and Covenants. (*DHC* V:264, 273.) It was printed in 1844 with 111 sections one of which was the historical account of the martyrdom of Joseph and Hyrum Smith. (It is numbered Section 135 in the current edition.)

The next important edition was the revision of 1876 when the number of sections was increased to 136. The 1921 edition is the one in current use. It contains double-column pages, with section headings, footnote references, and an index. The "Lectures on Faith" which were included in the 1835 edition are not printed in the currently used edition. In the *Doctrine and Covenants Commentary*, page xvii, one finds this statement in a footnote concerning these lectures: "These lectures were removed from the Doctrine and Covenants in the edition of 1921, not because they were called in question, for they are excellent lectures of great value on the principle of faith, but because they were not revelations. When they were received and ordered printed in the Doctrine and Covenants, it was with the understanding as expressed by Elder John Smith, 'that the lectures were judiciously arranged and compiled, and were profitable for doctrine. . .' (*DHC* II:244.) The Prophet Joseph Smith revised and prepared these Lectures himself, and they are still 'profitable for doctrine.' " The *Lectures on Faith* are available for purchase in separate form.

It should be kept in mind that not all of the revelations received by the Prophet are found in The Doctrine and Covenants.

Witnesses to The Doctrine and Covenants

Latter-day Saints are generally familiar with the testimony of the Three Witnesses and also the Eight Witnesses to The Book of Mormon. It is not so well known, however that witnesses have attested to the truth of The Doctrine and Covenants. Their testimony does not include the actual appearance of an angel, the seeing of ancient instruments and records, or having a voice declare that the record is true. But it is no less conclusive.

"The Lord has borne record to our souls, through the Holy Ghost, shed forth upon us, that these commandments were given by inspiration of God, and are profitable for all men, and are verily true . . ." (*ibid.*, I:226), was the testimony given concerning the "Book of Commandments" by the elders present at the time it was approved during the conference of the Church in November 1831. These same words appear in the "Explanatory Introduction" to each copy of The Doctrine and Covenants as the Testimony of the Twelve Apostles of the truth of this book of modern scripture.

The Holy Ghost speaks to man's spirit, and, thereby, becomes the powerful influence of conversion which is even stronger than the visible manifestation so often thought to be the convincing sign of truth. Examples of the strength of this kind of testimony are found in the experiences of the apostles of the Lord in the meridian dispensation. While with the Savior they saw him heal the sick (Matt. 15:28), cast out devils (Luke 8:29), and even raise the dead (John 11:44), and perform other mighty works. (Matt. 15:30-31.) Later, however, Peter denied being a disciple of Christ. (John 18:17, 25.) However, following Jesus' ascension and after the Holy Ghost rested upon the apostles (Acts 2), they labored in the gospel, and were imprisoned, and "many . . . were slain." (*Doctrine and Covenants Commentary*, page 41.)

As long as the recipient of the Holy Ghost abides by the commandments, that power will continue with him as a lasting possession that will not require outward manifestations to keep him in the Church.

Joseph Smith's Intregrity

The origin of The Doctrine and Covenants involves the honesty of the Prophet Joseph Smith. The Prophet well understood the great responsibility devolving upon him in speaking for the Lord in the revelations he received. One time he wrote that "it was an awful responsibility to write in the name of the Lord. . ." (*DHC* I:226.) The assurance with which he "wrote for the Lord" is well illustrated by an incident in the early history of this dispensation.

Not long after the Church was organized, the Prophet received a letter from Oliver Cowdery in which he commanded the Prophet "to erase those words," meaning a part of verse thirty-seven of Section twenty. Joseph Smith immediately wrote to Oliver Cowdery and asked:

> . . . by what authority he took upon him to command me to alter or erase, to add to or diminish from, a revelation or commandment from Almighty God. (*Ibid.*, I:105.)

In a Church which had just been organized and with so few members, if the leader had been an impostor, he could easily have compromised and changed this document to satisfy the one man and his friends who had done so much for him. For the Whitmer family had also been influenced by Oliver Cowdery to agree with him on this command to Joseph. This meant that three members of the original six who organized the Church were opposed to the Prophet Joseph Smith on this matter. But the Prophet was not an impostor. He knew he had received the will of the Lord and, although a calamity of this magnitude might conceivably have destroyed the work, it did not deter the Prophet from his course, and Oliver Cowdery and the Whitmer family soon repented of their error. (*Ibid.*, I:104, 105.)

Chapter 3

WHAT TO EXPECT FROM A STUDY OF THE DOCTRINE AND COVENANTS

(Section 1)

The title of this chapter might be changed to form a question to be answered by every reader—"What do I expect to gain from my study of The Doctrine and Covenants?" A reply to this question would undoubtedly bring many ideas. If one is thinking of subject matter or knowledge of contents alone, the reader would learn from his study that a great number of ideas are found in these revelations. The whole experience of man's earth-life is largely covered. Instruction is found, as one might expect, in how to attain spiritual salvation (sometimes called by us "entering the celestial kingdom or exaltation"). But one also discovers that these revelations are concerned with what man might consider the "temporal" things of life. From this volume of scripture, it is learned that the Lord looks upon all phases of man's earth existence as a necessary part of his journey to eternal life, or exaltation. (D&C 29:34-35.) This is very well expressed by President Joseph F. Smith in these words:

> It has always been a cardinal teaching with the Latter-day Saints that a religion that has not the power to save people temporally and make them prosperous and happy here cannot be depended upon to save them spiritually and to exalt them in the life to come. (Quoted by Albert E. Bowen, *The Church Welfare Plan*, p. 36.)

One will, therefore, find emphasis given to one's health (what one should or should not eat, as well as to the amount of sleep one should have). We discover that knowledge saves, and the value one should place upon different types of knowledge. The need to incorporate the gospel truths into one's life, in addition to the acquisition of knowledge, is emphasized so well that we are never in doubt as to the necessity of doing so. Counsel is given on what the Latter-day Saint is to do to prevent being deceived by the adversary; he learns that Satan is a personal being and also of his purposes. Above all, the student of The Doctrine and Covenants learns of the true nature of Jesus as the Savior of mankind, of his justice and mercy, and of his relationship to the inhabitants of the earth.

The Spirit of the Doctrine and Covenants

The ideas suggested thus far are only a very few of the truths to be learned as one examines the revelations section-by-section. There is almost no narrative in this book—a fact which makes it different from the other Standard Works, such as The Book of Mormon. Great truths are found on every page. To become acquainted with this volume of scripture can be one of the richest experiences of a Latter-day Saint's life. There is a spirit about a book of scripture which is readily discernible. It is the spirit of truth; the spirit that brings assurance of things divine. It comes from the Holy Ghost to bear witness of the truth. It is this spirit that the author hopes will be received by the reader. The promise is given that all may receive this blessing by their diligence. (D&C 11:22-27; 6:5-7; Alma 12:9-11.)

A Unique Book

As we study this book of scripture, we should remember that we are studying the message of the Lord Jesus Christ. This message is addressed to the people who make up the last greatest dispensation of the gospel —the fulness of times. There are many things which make The Doctrine and Covenants a unique book, but, primarily, its uniqueness arises out of the facts that it is (1) the word of Jesus Christ the Lord, and (2) it is a modern book.

A study of what the Lord himself has said concerning his message is found in Section 1. From there we shall find the Lord's answer to "What do I expect to gain from a study of The Doctrine and Covenants?"

The Superscription

As in all revelations, a knowledge of the historical background and context provides the student with essential information to understand what is intended to be obtained from the message or messages of the revelation. For purposes of this study, the reader should become familiar with the introductory material (called the "superscription" in this work) at the head of each section. Sometimes a reference to the History of the Church by Joseph Smith, known and cited in this book as the *Documentary History of the Church* (*DHC*) is given for further study about the context of the section.

The Lord's Preface

The superscription of Section 1 informs us that this revelation is known as "the Lord's Preface." (Also v. 6 in Section 1.) This revelation was given at the conference of the Church convened November 1, 1831, when the "Book of Commandments" was adopted by the priesthood assembled on that occasion. A "preface" is intended to prepare the reader with an explanation of the purpose the author had in writing the volume. It should concern itself with matters contained in the book or connected with it.

To Whom the Message Is Directed

Appropriately, the Lord introduces Section 1 with the announcement that it is he who is addressing "ye people of my church. . . ." (D&C 1:1.) But his message is not only for the Church but also "unto all men, and there is none to escape. . . ." (D&C 1:2.) Immediately one is made aware that the message of this dispensation is for everyone. In fact:

> . . . the voice of warning shall be unto all people, by the mouths of my disciples, whom I have chosen in these last days. (D&C 1:4.)

and the revelations are to be published:

> . . . unto you, O inhabitants of the earth. (*Ibid.*, 1:6.)

A Voice of Warning

What has already been given as a principal purpose of the Lord's establishing his Church upon the earth? What should we expect to gain from a study of The Doctrine and Covenants? It is a "voice of warning" unto all people. This fact was indelibly impressed upon the mind of the Prophet Joseph Smith by the Angel Moroni, who quoted several Bible prophecies indicating that certain judgments were to come in the last days and that these predictions were not yet fulfilled, but were soon to be. (P.ofG.P., Writings of Joseph Smith 2:40-41.) Following this, he informed Joseph Smith "of great judgments which were coming upon the earth, with great desolations by famine, sword, and pestilence; and that these grievous judgments would come on the earth in this generation. . . ." (*Ibid.*, 2:45.)

Later on, as the Prophet received additional revelations, the Lord made it known that the faithful of his people would be aware of the signs of the times and look forward in righteousness to Jesus' second coming. (D&C 39:21-23; 45:39-44.)

Power of Sealing the Wicked

In the performance of their duties, the Lord's servants are to possess the power to seal both on earth and in heaven. Notice that those who are sealed by this power are those who reject the gospel, and also those who rebel against the servants of the Lord after having accepted his message. (*Ibid.*, 1:8-9.) When the Lord comes he shall "recompense unto every man according to his work and measure to every man according to the measure which he has measured to his fellow man." (*Ibid.*, 1:10.)

Why This Message?

Why is the Lord's message of warning directed to the people of this generation or dispensation? The answer to this question is found in Section 1, verses 11 to 16, inclusive:

Wherefore the voice of the Lord is unto the ends of the earth, that all that will hear may hear:

Prepare ye, prepare ye for that which is to come, for the Lord is nigh;

And the anger of the Lord is kindled, and his sword is bathed in heaven, and it shall fall upon the inhabitants of the earth.

And the arm of the Lord shall be revealed; and the day cometh that they who will not hear the voice of the Lord, neither the voice of his servants, neither give heed to the words of the prophets and apostles, shall be cut off from among the people;

For they have strayed from mine ordinances, and have broken mine everlasting covenant;

They seek not the Lord to establish his righteousness, but every man walketh in his own way, and after the image of his own God, whose image is in the likeness of the world, and whose substance is that of an idol, which waxeth old and shall perish in Babylon, even Babylon the great, which shall fall.

Three reasons why this message is directed to the people of this dispensation may be found in these verses; namely, (1) to prepare the way of the Lord (*Ibid.*, 1:11), (2) because of the apostate condition of the world (*Ibid.*, 1:15), and (3) because men have set up their own gods. (*Ibid.*, 1:16.)

The God of Today

What are these gods after which men walk? Do we not know of men today who seek unrighteous dominion over their fellow men; men directed by false theories that lead people away from God's truth; the gods of vanity, greed, lust, and the whole list of vices that keep men in bondage? The word "Babylon" has come to symbolize the wickedness of the world. (Section 133:14.) Out of the world the people have been charged to come that they may not be partakers of her plagues. Eventually, the wicked world will fall, but, in preparation for that day of the Lord, there was to be a restoration of the gospel.

Results of the Lord's Message

What follows in verses 17 through 23 tells through whom the gospel was to be restored, and what could result from this great event. As you read these verses, keep in mind what the Lord promised would result from the call of Joseph Smith as the head of this dispensation. Two questions emerge from this thought: (1) does the history of the Church verify these promises of the Lord; and (2) in what part of this program have I participated?

Wherefore, I the Lord, knowing the calamity which should come upon the inhabitants of the earth, called upon my servant Joseph Smith, Jun., and spake unto him from heaven, and gave him commandments;

And also gave commandments to others, that they should proclaim these things unto the world; and all this that it might be fulfilled, which was written by the prophets—

The weak things of the world shall come forth and break down the mighty and strong ones, that man should not counsel his fellow man, neither trust in the arm of flesh—

But that every man might speak in the name of God the Lord, even the Savior of the world;

That faith also might increase in the earth;

That mine everlasting covenant might be established;

That the fulness of my gospel might be proclaimed by the weak and the simple unto the ends of the world, and before kings and rulers. (*Ibid.*, 1:17-23.)

It is worthy of observation at this point to indicate that the "others" in verse 18, unto whom the Lord "gave commandments" are those persons who were to assist the Prophet Joseph Smith in this dispensation. Many of these had already been called and received commandments by revelation. Such men as Oliver Cowdery, Sidney Rigdon, Hyrum Smith, Parley P. Pratt, Orson Pratt, and many others make up the number.

Blessings to Those Called

We discover in verses 24 through 28 what had already been accomplished and what would yet be realized in the lives of individuals who receive a call into the Lord's service. Some of these blessings are: they come to understanding; their errors are corrected; wisdom sought for is obtained; as they sin they may be chastened and repent; and strength and knowledge come through their humility. Might we today who have embarked upon a study of The Doctrine and Covenants also expect that similar blessings will accrue to us by our diligence?

Only One True Church

In continuation of the message that Joseph Smith was divinely called and others were appointed to assist him, the Lord sets forth the important fact that his Prophet has received power to translate The Book of Mormon and to bring forth "the only true and living church upon the face of the whole earth. . . ." (*Ibid.*, 1:30.) There was to be no question in the minds of the members of the Church or of the inhabitants of the world as to the position The Church of Jesus Christ of Latter-day Saints holds in the world. This proclamation by the

Lord gives added confirmation to the first vision and also to the many revelations which had already specified that there is only one way to eternal life.

Sin Is Condemned

It is further indicated that the Lord was pleased with his Church collectively, but the individual members of his Church had much to do in perfecting their lives. (Matt. 5:48.) It is evident that the Lord wanted the members of the Church to understand that membership in his kingdom does not give license to sin for he "cannot look upon sin with the least degree of allowance." (D&C 1:31), but he will forgive the repentant. (v. 32.) On the other hand, that person who does not repent, having received the light, is under the penalty of losing the Spirit of the Lord "for my Spirit shall not always strive with man. . . ." (*Ibid.*, 1:33.)

The Concluding Message

Toward the end of this great revelation which opened with the principal message of the Lord to the Church and to the inhabitants of the earth, there is a return to this fundamental purpose—the Lord desires that all men shall know of his "voice of warning" of judgments to come and that eternal life may be won by living the restored gospel of Jesus Christ. Notice how this message is reiterated in Section 1, verses 34 to 36:

. . . I the Lord am willing to make these things known unto all flesh;

For I am no respecter of persons, and will that all men shall know that the day speedily cometh; the hour is not yet, but is nigh at hand, when peace shall be taken from the earth, and the devil shall have power over his own dominion.

And also the Lord shall have power over his saints, and shall reign in their midst, and shall come down in judgment upon Idumea, or the world. (*Ibid.*, 1:34-36.)

(Notice the term "Idumea" is defined in the revelation as "the world." It is synonymous with "Babylon" in verse 16 which symbolizes the wicked world. Idumea was known as the country of Edom whose inhabitants held an inveterate enmity toward Israel.)

As one studies The Doctrine and Covenants, he knows that the gospel message brings joy into the lives of those who live its principles, while wickedness brings unhappiness. One also discovers that judgments do await the world and that one of these judgments—war—with its present-day potential for great destruction is prophesied for this dispensation. The question of whether or not the prediction that "peace shall be taken from the earth," as stated in 1831, should now be phrased "peace has been taken from the earth" is one which every Latter-day Saint should consider in the light of present conditions in the world.

Section 1, the Lord's preface to his revelations, is concluded with the definite assurance that what has been given will all be fulfilled and that the Spirit of God bears witness that "the record is true, and the truth abideth forever and ever. Amen." (*Ibid.*, 1:39.)

The Doctrine and Covenants confirms ancient truths and gives more enlightenment about the events of the immediate future and man's destiny than do other books of scripture. It contains some of the most glorious principles ever revealed to the world.

Chapter 4

THE PROPHECY CONCERNING ELIJAH THE PROPHET

(Section 2)

Section 2 is the first in chronological sequence of the revelations in The Doctrine and Covenants. It is appropriate that one of the messages of this volume of scripture should be brought to the attention of the student early in this book—the message that The Doctrine and Covenants attests to the reality of the future life by the revelations which tell of the return to the earth of resurrected beings. Section 2 was placed in The Doctrine and Covenants for the first time in the 1876 edition. It is also found in the Prophet Joseph Smith's history (*DHC* 1:12), and in the P.ofG.P. Writings of Joseph Smith 2:38-39.

In addition to attesting to the fact of the resurrection, there are two more points to be remembered from the historical background or context of this section. First, that the coming of the ancient American prophet Moroni to Joseph Smith on September 21, 1823, was the beginning of the ministry of angels in this dispensation. Second, that the misconceptions of men relative to angels were made known early to Joseph Smith.

The great importance of the reality of the resurrection will be discussed later during this study.

Ministry of Angels

The second fact—the ministry of angels—opens up a number of ideas which are important also. Although men claimed that revelation from God had ceased, there was no scriptural justification for such belief. (Chapter 1.) When people of faith have lived upon the earth, the Lord has revealed his will to them in various ways, such as by the ministry of angels. When people believe that revelation is no longer received nor necessary, such communication from the heavens is withheld. (Moroni 7:22-29, 37.) The coming of the angel Moroni was prophesied for this dispensation. (Rev. 14:6-7.)

Although the scriptures teach that angels are fellow-beings and fellow-servants of us mortals and should be thought of as those who have lived on earth and have passed on to serve as heavenly messengers, men have conceived them to be vastly different from us, for one thing, having wings as a means of locomotion.

In describing the heavenly being Moroni, Joseph Smith made known the following truths in answer to prayer for further enlightenment from God.

While I was thus in the act of calling upon God, I discovered a light appearing in my room, which continued to increase until the room was lighter than at noonday, when immediately a personage appeared at my bedside, standing in the air, for his feet did not touch the floor. He had on a loose robe of most exquisite whiteness beyond anything earthly I had ever seen nor do I believe that any earthly thing could be made to appear so exceedingly white and brilliant. His hands were naked and his arms also, a little above the wrists, so, also were his feet naked, as were his legs, a little above the ankles. His head and neck were also bare. . . . Not only was his robe exceedingly white, but his whole person was glorious beyond description, and his countenance truly like lightning. The room was exceedingly light, but not so very bright as immediately around his person.

When first I looked upon him, I was afraid but the fear soon left me. (*DHC* I:11.)

Joseph Smith was instructed many times by Moroni, who lived upon the American Continent over fourteen hundred years before, but, as a resurrected being, he came as a "fellow-servant" of those who were seeking to assist in the salvation of mankind. For this purpose was Joseph Smith commissioned by God through the reopening of the heavens in fulfillment of Bible prophecies. The modern Prophet, Joseph Smith, could testify not only that the Father and the Son, Jesus Christ, truly existed, but also that the testimony of the Bible prophets concerning the ministration of angels was true.

Elijah and Moroni

An era of faith had begun; a new dispensation of the gospel with its miracles, had been committed to man upon the earth and angels ministered once more to the Lord's appointed. Section 2 is about another angel from God who also had an important place in the Dispensation of the Fulness of Times. His coming to the earth followed that of Moroni, who spoke of Elijah in his visit to Joseph Smith. Elijah the prophet was a resurrected heavenly being as was Moroni. (D&C 133:55.) His coming was also prophesied in the Bible. (Malachi 4:5-6.)

Section 2 and Malachi 4:5-6 Compared

When Moroni visited Joseph Smith he quoted, among other prophecies, the one which closes the Old Testament, as follows:

Behold, I will reveal unto you the priesthood, by the hand of Elijah the prophet, before the coming of the great and dreadful day of the Lord.

And he shall plant in the hearts of the children the promises made to the fathers, and the hearts of the children shall turn to their fathers.

If it were not so, the whole earth would be utterly wasted at his coming. (D&C Section 2.)

A comparison of Malachi 4:5-6 shows that there are some changes in the above quoted version given by Moroni. The most significant of these is the additional fact that Elijah was to bring the priesthood to the earth. Next, the phraseology of the second sentence differs but the meaning is still preserved. And last, the penalty expressed in the last phrase of Malachi is clarified by section 2. The one point which is preserved by the same language is the expression "before the coming of the great and dreadful day of the Lord." (D&C 2:1.) This statement is highly significant because it indicates the time when Elijah would come to the earth. What does this expression mean?

It means the day when the Lord Jesus Christ comes in power and glory to take vengeance upon the wicked. It shall be a dreadful day to the unrepentant, but to the righteous it shall be a day of salvation. Before that day, however, Elijah was to come to confer the priesthood upon Joseph Smith and Oliver Cowdery as the capstone of the restoration of divine authority in the last days.

(Many of the ideas which follow come from the writings of President Joseph Fielding Smith. A collection of material on this subject is found in *Doctrines of Salvation*, Vol. II, Chapters 6-7.)

Why Elijah Restored Priesthood

Elijah was to bring priesthood to the earth. But some may ask, "Why does Elijah restore priesthood when Peter, James, and John had already brought the Melchizedek Priesthood to Joseph Smith and Oliver Cowdery?" If these three apostles had been commissioned to do so, they could have performed this function, but there is something more in the mission of Elijah than what was included in the mission of Peter, James, and John. This is what the Prophet wrote concerning Elijah:

Elijah was the last Prophet that held the keys of the Priesthood, and who will, before the last dispensation, restore the authority and deliver the keys of the Priesthood, in order that *all* the ordinances may be attended to in righteousness. It is true that the Savior had authority and power to bestow this blessing; but the sons of Levi were too prejudiced. "And I will send Elijah the

Prophet before the great and terrible day of the Lord," etc., etc. Why send Elijah? Because he holds the keys of the authority to administer in *all* the ordinances of the Priesthood; and without the authority is given, the ordinances could not be administered in righteousness. (*DHC* IV:211.) (Italics by author.)

Although Elijah, Moses, and Jesus conferred keys of authority on Peter, James, and John on the Mount of Transfiguration, the Lord had reserved Elijah for the restoration of certain keys for the salvation of man in the last dispensation. (*Ibid.*, III:387.)

Elijah's mission was one of restoring the sealing power. This power was not for the dead exclusively, but for the living also. Some have thought it was the keys of baptism for the dead, but it was not that. There were no baptisms for the dead in the days of Elijah, or before Jesus taught the gospel in the spirit world between his own death and resurrection. (1 Peter 3:18-20; 4:6.) Jesus bridged the gulf which separated the righteous in paradise from the wicked in prison. In other words, Elijah restored the fulness of the power of priesthood. This power, or the keys of the priesthood, make valid all of the ordinances of the gospel, but without this sealing power, as the Prophet Joseph Smith said, "the ordinances [of the priesthood . . .] could not be administered in righteousness."

Men who hold the priesthood may officiate by the authority they possess, but only when directed to do so by those who possess the keys of the priesthood. It is this power by which all things are bound in heaven as well as on earth that Elijah restored. Elijah had a special mission and was called to perform it. Notwithstanding Elijah's mission pertained to the living, it was more especially for the work in the temples, for the living and the dead. It is by this means that husbands and wives and children are sealed to one another.

The Wasting of the Earth

When one understands that validity is given to all ordinances of the gospel through the sealing powers of the priesthood, an understanding of the fact stated in Section 2 concerning the earth being utterly wasted at the Lord's second coming, is available. In addition, the sealing powers make possible a welding link between the fathers and the children, a work for the dead, which is essential for the salvation of the living. The "curse" spoken of by Malachi is that "the whole earth would be utterly wasted" at the Lord's coming, if the sealing power were not restored. This judgment, however, will not befall the earth because Elijah has come with this power, and the necessary keys for both the salvation of the dead and the living are in The Church of Jesus Christ of Latter-day Saints.

Salvation of the Dead

When Malachi said Elijah's mission was to "turn the heart of the fathers to the children, and the heart of the children to their fathers. . ." (Mal. 4:6), we have a thought which suggests the great work for the dead. The turning of the hearts of the fathers in the spirit world to the children on the earth, is as consistent as the fact that the living on earth seek earnestly to gather genealogical data of their deceased fathers in order that the ordinances may be performed for them in the temples of the Lord. This thought is agreeable with the angel Moroni's rendition of Malachi's prophecy where he said that "he [Elijah] shall plant in the hearts of the children the promises made to their fathers. . . ." (P.ofG.P., Writings of Joseph Smith 2:39.) The thought was suggested by Elder John A. Widtsoe that in the pre-earth life, we, who would be assigned to the earth during a time when we could accomplish a service for our kindred dead, were under a commitment to do this work because of the premortal contract to do this. Here are his words:

> In our preexistent state, in the day of the great council, we made a certain agreement with the Almighty. The Lord proposed a plan, conceived by him. We accepted it. Since the plan is intended for all men we become parties to the salvation of every person under that plan. We agreed, right then and there, to be not only saviors for ourselves but measurably, saviors for the whole human family. We went into a partnership with the Lord. The working out of the plan became then not merely the Father's work, and the Savior's work, but also our work. The least of us, the humblest, is in partnership with the Almighty in achieving the purposes of the eternal plan of salvation.
>
> That places us in a very responsible attitude towards the human race. By that doctrine, with the Lord at the head, we become saviors on Mount Zion, all committed to the great plan of offering salvation to the untold numbers of spirits. To do this is the Lord's self-imposed duty, this great labor his highest glory. Likewise, it is man's duty, self-imposed, his pleasure and joy, his labor, and ultimately his glory. ("The Worth of Souls," *The Utah Genealogical and Historical Magazine*, Oct. 1934, p. 189.)

Importance of the Dead to the Living

We learn in the scriptures that the work for the dead is of such importance to the living that they without their dead cannot be made perfect. In the language of section 128 we read:

> And now, my dearly beloved brethren and sisters, let me assure you that these are principles in relation to the dead and the living that cannot be lightly passed over, as pertaining to our salvation. For their salvation is necessary and essential to our salvation, as Paul says concerning the fathers—that they without us cannot be made perfect—neither can we without our dead be made perfect.
>
> ... For we without them cannot be made perfect; neither can they without us be made perfect. Neither can they nor we be made perfect without those who have died in the gospel also. .... (D&C 128:15, 18.)

Evidence of Prophecy Fulfilled

If a nonmember friend were to ask for evidence to support the claim of Joseph Smith and Oliver Cowdery that Elijah actually came to them and restored the keys of the priesthood, as prophesied, on April 3, 1836, in the Kirtland Temple, what would you say? President Joseph Fielding Smith has suggested the consistency of their claim because no one else in the world has testified to the return of Elijah to the earth. Their testimony becomes more reasonable when it is realized that these two men could not turn the hearts of the children to their fathers, except by the power of God. President Smith also reminds us that they did not have the power to persuade millions of people who are not members of the Church to turn their attention to their dead fathers. He sets forth evidence that organized efforts to gather genealogical data were not forthcoming until after Elijah came to the Kirtland Temple in 1836. One year after this date, Great Britain passed laws compelling the preservation of duplicate records of the dead. The New England Historical and Genealogical Society was organized in 1844, and the New York Genealogical and Biographical Society came into existence in 1869 for the purpose of compiling genealogical records.

The great increase in interest on the part of individuals in genealogy has come since 1836. Thousands of family histories have been compiled outside of this Church to aid in the great work of redeeming our dead. These efforts on the part of nonmembers of the Church bear witness that Elijah did come and restore the keys of the priesthood. The activity on the part of the members of the Church in the gathering of vital statistics with the modern methods of microfilming hundreds of thousands of records combine to bear testimony of the "spirit of Elijah" in the world.

Chapter 5

SATAN'S OPPOSITION TO THE COMING FORTH OF
THE BOOK OF MORMON

(Sections 3 and 10)

From the creation of Adam, there has been opposition to the Lord's work on the part of Satan. He has sought to destroy the souls of men by his enticings; whereas, the purposes of the Lord have been to bring about the "immortality and eternal life of man." (Moses 1:39.) When the Lord has instituted his work upon the earth, the powers of Lucifer have also been present to seek to destroy or, in any way, to hinder the Lord's purposes. This dispensation of the gospel is by no means an exception. When Joseph Smith sought the Lord in prayer to determine which of all the churches was right, the powers of darkness were present to interfere. Here are the words of Joseph Smith:

. . . I kneeled down and began to offer up the desire of my heart to God. I had scarcely done so, when immediately I was seized upon by some power which entirely overcame me, and had such an astonishing influence over me as to bind my tongue so that I could not speak. Thick darkness gathered around me, and it seemed to me for a time as if I were doomed to sudden destruction.

But, exerting all my powers to call upon God to deliver me out of the power of this enemy which had seized upon me, and at the very moment when I was ready to sink into despair and abandon myself to destruction—not to an imaginary ruin, but to the power of some actual being from the unseen world, who had such marvelous power as I had never before felt in any being—just at this moment of great alarm, I saw a pillar of light exactly over my head, above the brightness of the sun, which descended gradually until it fell upon me.

It no sooner appeared than I found myself delivered from the enemy which held me bound. . . . (P.ofG.P., Writings of Joseph Smith 2:15-17.)

Notice the words "not to an imaginary ruin, but to the power of some actual being from the unseen world. . . ." (*Ibid.*, 2:16.) Joseph Smith had come to understand, in part, the power of Satan and also the power of God on the same day. Joseph may not have known at this time that during his life many efforts would be made by evil forces to keep him from following the counsel of the Lord, but the angel Moroni cautioned him against such a temptation. (*Ibid.*, 2:46.)

Background of Sections 3 and 10

A notable example of Satan's efforts to deceive is found in the study of Sections 3 and 10 of our text. After receiving the gold plates from the angel Moroni and having translated some of the characters thereon, the Prophet was asked by Martin Harris to permit him to take the manuscript pages of translated material and show them to members of his family. Two times Martin Harris was denied the privilege to show the manuscript to others, but the third request of the Lord by Joseph Smith brought forth permission to do so. The provision was that it should be shown to only five persons and to none others. By stratagem others to whom Martin Harris showed the manuscript got it away from him, and it was never recovered. (*DHC* I:21.)

The Lord's Rebuke to Joseph

These circumstances bring us to a consideration of Section 3, which constitutes the Lord's rebuke to Joseph Smith for his part in allowing the manuscript to be lost. In the light of these conditions, the first three verses of the revelation state that the works of God cannot be frustrated, but it is the works of men that are frustrated.

It seems that at this point in the Prophet's life the Lord was teaching him an important lesson. He was to trust in the Lord, who would always uphold him, and not to fear man more than God (D&C 3:4-8.) We might well ask ourselves at this point wherein we fear "man more than God" and do not put our confidence in the Lord to assist us? Do we, for example, accept the entreaties of friends and associates and violate a commandment of the Lord in order to keep the friendship or good will of those persons? Or do we stand for the word of the Lord and his promises to us if we are faithful?

Joseph Smith's Honesty

Consider also, for a moment, the importance of this revelation in attesting to the honesty of Joseph Smith. He stood rebuked by the Lord for his part in the loss of the translated portion of the plates, but, at the same time, he made known this rebuke to his friends and to the world in allowing the revelation to become known and printed. At times people have questioned the integrity of the Prophet, but this revelation stands as a monument to the basic honesty of Joseph Smith.

After receiving Section 3, Joseph recorded that "both the plates and the Urim and Thummim were taken from me again; but in a few days they were returned to me, when I inquired of the Lord. . . ." (*DHC* I:23.) The Lord then gave to the Prophet Section 10.

Analysis of Section 10

In order for us to have a connected account of this episode in our Church history, a study should now be made of Section 10, especially verses 1 through 45. As indicated in the superscription (italicized foreword), this revelation is about the designs of wicked men to alter the manuscript in order to destroy the truthfulness of The Book of Mormon when Joseph would print as a part of that book the retranslated portion which was "lost."

Plot to Destroy the Lord's Work Revealed

Verses 1 through 3 of Section 10 refer to the gift of translation which Joseph had received with the further admonition that he was to "be diligent unto the end." (D&C 10:4.) Martin Harris is condemned by the Lord as a "wicked" man, because he was not faithful in keeping his covenant to show the manuscript to only five persons, but permitted it to get out of his hands forever. (*Ibid.*, 10:6-9.) Now comes that part of the revelation which describes the purpose of the men in altering the manuscript. (*Ibid.*, 10:10-19.) But who does the Lord say is the instigator of this plot to destroy his work. It is Satan. (*Ibid.*, 10:10, 14.) From this point on the Lord reveals to the Prophet and Martin Harris (and us) the designs of that wicked one, Satan, to destroy the Lord's work and also "that he may lead their souls to destruction." (*Ibid.*, 10:22.) (Read The Book of Mormon, 2 Nephi 28 for information on the works of Lucifer in the last days.)

Satan's Tactics

Observe the tactics of Satan in his leading men and women astray:

Yea, he stirreth up their hearts to anger against this work.

Yea, he saith unto them: Deceive and lie in wait to catch, that ye may destroy; behold, this is no harm. And thus he flattereth them, and telleth them that it is no sin to lie that they may catch a man in a lie, that they may destroy him.

And thus he flattereth them, and leadeth them along until he draggeth their souls down to hell; and thus he causeth them to catch themselves in their own snare.

And thus he goeth up and down, to and fro in the earth, seeking to destroy the souls of men. (D&C 10:24-27.)

Upon the basis of what you have already learned from this revelation, do you believe that Satan is an actual being and not an imaginary product of the mind?

The Lord's Foreordained Plan

In verses 30 to 45 the Lord informs the Prophet that he is to translate from the small plates of Nephi and not to retranslate from the plates that portion of the Nephite history which Martin Harris had lost. Foreseeing the circumstances which gave rise to the revelations known to us as sections 3 and 10, the Lord inspired Nephi and early historians to keep the additional set of plates. (The Book of Mormon, 1 Nephi 9:2-6; Words of Mormon, verses 3-7.) This part which now contains the book of Nephi to Omni, inclusive, in The Book of Mormon "is more particular concerning the things which, in my wisdom, I would bring to the knowledge of the people . . . [and] which do throw greater views upon my gospel . . ." (D&C 10:40, 45), declared the Lord. It would seem that we are more richly blessed by reason of having the translated material from the small plates of Nephi which contains ". . . the ministry and prophecies . . ." (1 Nephi 19:3; 9:4), and the "sacred" things (1 Nephi 19:6), whereas the other plates gave "a greater account of the wars and contentions and destructions of my [Nephi] people. . . ." (1 Nephi 19:4.)

What does the Lord prescribe in this revelation that Joseph Smith might do, and which we also must do, to gain a victory over Satan?

Pray always, that you may come off conqueror; yea, that you may conquer Satan, and that you may escape the hands of the servants of Satan that do uphold his work. (D&C 10:5.)

Additional Items in Sections 10 and 3

Section 10: The Nephites prayed that their brethren the Lamanites should have the gospel in the latter days (Ibid., 10:48), and that this gospel should be made known to others who should possess this land of Zion and, "that whosoever should believe in this gospel in this land might have eternal life." (Ibid., 10:50.) It was also their wish that this land should be a free land. (Ibid., 10:49-51.)

On the other hand, those upon this land who build
up churches to get gain, and do wickedly and thus build
up the kingdom of the devil shall be caused "to tremble
and shake to the center." (*Ibid.*, 10:56.)

The Lord avows that the people shall learn of the
"other sheep" of whom he spoke during his mortal ministry (John 10:16), and of the gospel which he brought
to them. This will be by The Book of Mormon which shall
"bring to light the true points of my doctrine, yea, and
the only doctrine which is in me." (D&C 10:62.) Again
we are aware of one phase of Satan's activities; namely,
to:

... stir up the hearts of the people to contention concerning
the points of my doctrine; and in these things they do err, for
they do wrest the scriptures and do not understand them. (*Ibid.*,
10:63.)

Finally, in closing this revelation, the Lord points
out what his doctrine is (*Ibid.*, 10:67), and he who declares anything less than that doctrine "is not of my
church." (*Ibid.*, 10:68.)

And now, behold, whosoever is of my church, and endureth
of my church to the end, him will I establish upon my rock, and
the gates of hell shall not prevail against them. (*Ibid.*, 10:69.)

Section 3: Notice verse 9 in which the Prophet is
reminded that he "wast chosen to do the work of the
Lord..." and compare it with 2 Nephi 3: 1-15, especially
verses 6-8, 11, 14, 15.

In Section 3:16-20, the purposes of the coming forth
of The Book of Mormon are made known: (1) The knowledge of the Savior shall come to the Lamanites, (2) That
the promises of the Lord might be fulfilled which were
made to the people upon the American continent anciently, (3) That the Lamanites might come to a knowledge of
their fathers, and (4) That the Lamanites might be saved
through their repentance. These purposes contribute to
our understanding of the purposes given on the title page
of The Book of Mormon.

Chapter 6

QUALIFICATIONS OF THOSE WHO LABOR
IN THE MINISTRY

(Sections 4 and 12)

Section 4 is the first revelation given through the Prophet to another person. Later many revelations in The Doctrine and Covenants were addressed to individuals. Some of these came in response to questions on the part of the persons concerned, or a problem existed which was clarified to Joseph Smith through revelation, as we shall see in subsequent chapters. (Chapters 7, 8, 10, 11, etc.) From the Prophet's journal or history, it is not indicated that Section 4 came either at the request of his father Joseph Smith, Senior, or because of an existing problem. Verse 3 would suggest, however, that the Prophet's father had a desire to serve in the ministry.

In a study of The Doctrine and Covenants one should, insofar as possible, know the historical background or context of the revelations to interpret properly their contents. This means not only the environment or setting but oftentimes the person or persons to whom the revelation is directed. There are also other benefits derived from such an approach, such as a better acquaintanceship with the lives of some of the men who were called into the Lord's service in this dispensation.

The Prophet's Father

The first vision and the visit of Moroni were not beyond the belief of the good man, the Prophet's father. Joseph Smith, Senior, seemed to be of a believing heart. He was the first to receive the testimony of his son concerning the visits of the angel Moroni. Undoubtedly, the

Spirit of the Lord had prepared the way that Joseph Smith might have just such a friend and confidant as his father. After Joseph had been visited three times during the one night by the angel, he rose early to work with his father in the field. This attempt to work was unsuccessful because of his exhausted condition. Upon leaving for the house, Joseph was visited by Moroni who again repeated the message of the night before. He was "commanded" to tell his father of the vision and message delivered by the angel. Upon doing so, his father said it was of God and that he should do as the angel directed him.

The Prophet's father died at the age of sixty-nine, just seventeen years after he counseled his son to do as the angel Moroni had commanded. During those years he became a member of the Church, and later he was ordained a patriarch to the Church, an office that was to continue from father to son. In this way he would fulfill the promise that he would "strengthen the church . . ." (D&C 23: 5) which was his duty forever. It was the privilege of his son Joseph to see by vision his father in the celestial kingdom. (*DHC* II:380.) It may also be of interest to know that he is referred to in The Book of Mormon in connection with the name by which his son should be known as a descendant of the Joseph who was sold into Egypt. (2 Nephi 3:14-15.)

Use of Footnote References

Section 4 commences with a thought which appears in other revelations (Sections 6:1; 11:1; 12:1; 14:1.) At this point a suggestion is offered in connection with the footnote references and their use. For instance the letter "a" by the word "marvelous" in verse 1 Section 4 refers to the first of the series of scripture references at the bottom of the page, designated by "a." As one examines each of these references, he discovers (1) the word in the reference, or (2) a similar thought expressed. The frequent use of footnote references gives a better comprehension of the meaning of the word or the thought which the Lord wishes one to know in relation to that word or thought. One should keep in mind, however, that these footnote references may not always seem to apply. This is probably true in regard to the reference Section "38: 12" of "a" which may be a typographical error.

A Marvelous Work

A dictionary definition of the word "marvelous" suggests that which causes wonder, astonishment, wonderful, exciting marvel. There is also associated with these words the idea of miracle.

Without referring to all of the footnote references, it should be noted that reference is made to Isaiah 29:14 where the Old Testament prophet foresaw the day when The Book of Mormon would be revealed to the world, and the Lord would perform a "marvelous work and a wonder." Certainly, we can understand that this ancient volume of scripture is a wonderful work as a part of the Lord's great work which was to be established on the earth in the last days. The Book of Mormon has also come to the world in a miraculous way which has created astonishment and wonder. The reference in Section 4:1 to "a marvelous work . . ." which was "about to come forth among the children of men," may refer to the coming forth of The Book of Mormon since it was to be published soon, and especially the establishment of the kingdom of God with all of the keys of the priesthood. There are other things associated with the marvelous work of the Lord in the latter days. We shall not attempt to point out all of these at this time, but only what is suggested by the footnote references under consideration. In the references Sections 95:4 and 101:95, it is made known that the Lord's "strange act" is to be brought to pass, "that I [the Lord] may pour out my Spirit upon all flesh," and "that men may discern between the righteous and the wicked. . . ." The marvelous work, or strange act, of the Lord in the last days we learn is also to convince many "of their sins, that they may come unto repentance, and that they may come unto the kingdom of my Father." (D&C 18:44.) The Book of Mormon does convince men of their sins and converts them by the Spirit of the Lord. Men learn that they must repent to receive the kingdom of the Father.

Wholehearted Service

With the Lord about to bring forth his wonderful work, it is enjoined upon each person who enters his service to "see that ye serve him with all your heart, might, mind and strength, that ye may stand blameless before God at the last day." (*Ibid.*, 4:2.) In reference to this verse, this comment is given:

Because the Lord was about to begin a marvelous work among the children of men, he needed servants who were willing to give themselves entirely to that work—"heart, might, mind, and strength"; that is, affections, will-power, reasoning faculty, and physical strength, all must be dedicated to the service of the Lord in this latter-day work. (*Doctrine and Covenants Commentary*, p. 24.)

Message to All Who Seek to Serve

Section 4 is primarily concerned with the qualifications of those who are to labor in the Lord's ministry. This would not only include Joseph Smith, Sen., but all who would seek to make a contribution to the building up of the kingdom of God upon the earth. To accomplish this work, it is necessary that they give of themselves in the manner suggested above. By the wholehearted service that one performs for others as an officer or teacher in the kingdom, he "layeth up in store that he perisheth not, but bringeth salvation to his soul." (D&C 4:4.) In what ways do you consider that your service in The Church of Jesus Christ of Latter-day Saints has contributed to your journey on the way to salvation?

Responsibilities of the Church

The mission of the Church is to save men and women. For this purpose the Lord has established his work on the earth. In this process of saving, two of the great responsibilities resting upon the Church are the preaching of the gospel, and the perfecting of the lives of the members. In both of these purposes, the Lord has wisely established as a part of his Church organization opportunities for individual service.

In the accomplishment of the general objectives of the Church, every member may make a contribution. In fact, when one enters the Church he takes upon himself the obligation of building up the kingdom of God (Church). When this covenant is entered into, the convert receives an opportunity which, if accepted, provides the means whereby he may work toward perfecting his own life.

Missionary Service

One of the most soul-satisfying experiences is to participate in advancing the Father's kingdom by performing missionary work. There are many opportunities to participate in this activity for those who qualify. Now that stake misisonary work is available to the members of the Church, one need not serve in the foreign missions to receive the happiness of being a party to the conversion of souls. All members are under the obligation of living lives that will assist others to see the light of the gospel; but this is not all, the responsibility carries over into worthy action. It is service in the kingdom that brings salvation.

The Lord has provided our unusual missionary system in which men and women may receive the opportunity to serve in preaching the gospel. The auxiliaries of the Church also provide many opportunities for service.

Service in the Auxiliaries

An example is the Relief Society of the Church as a service organization. In the great Welfare Program of the Church, we find the Relief Society making a tremendous contribution to those whom that program serves and also to the members of the society in service opportunities.

The other auxiliaries of the Church, or aids to the priesthood, provide many activity opportunities for the officers and teachers and also the members who make up the organizations. Thus, the very organizational pattern of the Church is designed to further the salvation of man. Active participation in the Church keeps one spiritually alive. It is one of the factors which increases faith and keeps testimonies strong.

Some Revelations for All

When one becomes an active agent in the ministry of the Lord, what is expected of him? Revelations numbered 4 and 12 give an answer to this question. Although they are directed to individuals, the message is for all who seek to labor in the cause of Zion. The fact that both revelations are similar suggests this point, but in Section 12 one finds that the message is intended for all having the same desire:

Now, as you have asked, behold, I say unto you, keep my commandments, and seek to bring forth and establish the cause of Zion.

Behold, I speak unto you, and also to all those who have desires to bring forth and establish this work;

And no one can assist in this work except he shall be humble

and full of love, having faith, hope, and charity, being temperate
in all things, whatsoever shall be entrusted to his care. (D&C
12:6-8.)

The revelation given to Joseph Smith, Sen., gives
additional virtues to be expected of the true ministry of
the Lord:

And faith, hope, charity and love, with an eye single to the
glory of God, qualify him for the work.

Remember faith, virtue, knowledge, temperance, patience,
brotherly kindness, godliness, charity, humility, diligence.

Ask, and ye shall receive; knock, and it shall be opened unto
you. Amen. (*Ibid.*, 4:5-7.)

Qualifications for the Ministry

A brief statement of definition and explanation of
most of the virtues mentioned in these revelations may
assist us to appreciate more fully the scope and truth
of these qualifying requirements.

Faith in its broad sense is the principle that impels
men to resolve and to act. It "becomes to us the foundation of hope, from which spring our aspirations, ambitions, and confidences for the future. . . . Faith is the
secret of ambition, the soul of heroism, the motive power
of effort." (James E. Talmage, *Articles of Faith*, p. 103.)
"The predominating sense in which the term faith is
used throughout the scriptures is that of full confidence
and trust in the being, purposes, and words of God."
(*Ibid.*, p. 96.)

Hope—Desire, with expectation of obtaining what is
desired, or belief that is obtainable. (Webster's Dictionary.)

Read Moroni 7:40-43 for Mormon's teachings on
hope.

Charity and love, with an eye single to the glory of
God. ". . . charity is the pure love of Christ. . . ." (Moroni

7:47.) This love becomes a motivating power in the lives of those who have been "born again." It becomes the offering of the true followers of Christ in return for the love the Father and the Son have bestowed upon them through the atonement wrought by the Savior. It is manifested in a keeping of the commandments, one of which is the love of mankind.

Read Moroni 7:43-46, 48 on Mormon's teachings on faith, hope, and charity. (Also 1 Corinthians 13; Colossians 3:12-15.)

Virtue—Moral practice or action; moral excellence; rectitude; morality; also chastity. (Webster's Dictionary.)

Learn the will of God, keep his commandments and do his will, and you will be a virtuous person. (*Discourses of Brigham Young*, p. 300, 1925 edition.)

. . . sincerity, "the mother of a noble family of virtues"; simplicity and purity, "the two wings with which man soars above the earth and all temporary nature. . . ."

Purity lies in the affection. It "unites with and enjoys God." It is the pure in heart that shall see God. No person of impure heart, though baptized a hundred times, can approach him. (David O. McKay, *Gospel Ideals*, pp. 14, 15.)

Knowledge — Familiarity from actual experience; practical skill, acquaintance with fact; hence, scope of information. (Webster's Dictionary.)

Add to your faith knowledge, etc. The principle of knowledge is the principle of salvation. This principle can be comprehended by the faithful and diligent; and every one that does not obtain knowledge sufficient to be saved will be condemned. The principle of salvation is given us through the knowledge of Jesus Christ. (*Teachings of the Prophet Joseph Smith*, p. 297. Also D&C 131:6; 130:18-19.)

Temperance — Moderation; self-control; calmness. (Webster's Dictionary.)

The Saints should . . . avoid excesses and cease from sin, putting far from them "the lusts of men"; and in their amusements and pastimes adopt a course that looks to the spirit as well as the letter, the intention and not the act alone, the whole and not the part, which is the meaning of moderation. In this way their conduct will be reasonable and becoming, and they shall find no trouble in understanding the will of the Lord. (Joseph F. Smith, *Gospel Doctrine*, p. 300.)

The best way to teach temperance is to keep the Word of Wisdom. (*Ibid.*, p. 301.)

Patience—Quality of being able to bear or endure pains, trials, or the like, without complaint or with equanimity; forbearance. (Webster's Dictionary.)

Now we exhort you, brethren, warn them that are unruly, comfort the feebleminded, support the weak, be patient toward all men. (1 Thess. 5:14. Also D&C 67:13; 101:38.)

Brotherly Kindness—Quality of being sympathetic, gracious, loving, affectionate. (Webster's Dictionary.)

Godliness—Purity in person and in morals is true godliness.

Humility—Humility is submission to the will of God. It is the opposite of pride and arrogance. (Mosiah 3:19.)

Diligence—Quality of being industrious; persevering effort; not careless or negligent (Webster's Dictionary. Also D&C 107:99-100.)

Virtues to Seek; Vices from Which to Repent

The foregoing virtues are goals to which all Latter-day Saints should strive. The object of gospel understanding and teaching is to bring about perfection in the lives of the true followers of the Master. The Lord performs his work through imperfect people. He does expect, as indicated above, that they who seek eternal life will seek perfection. As a practical test for each member of the

Church, we may have brought to our attention some of the things from which we should repent. In the following list one will find each one of the virtues given in Sections 4 and 12 with its accompanying antonym opposite the virtue. The opposite word, or antonym, is the vice from which we should repent.

VIRTUE	VICE
Faith	Doubt; unbelief
Charity	Selfishness, hatred
Knowledge	Ignorance
Patience	Irritability
Godliness	Irreverence
Diligence	Slothfulness; negligence
Hope	Despair, discouragement
Virtue (Chastity)	Immorality
Temperance	Excess
Brotherly kindness	Cruelty
Humility	Pride; unteachableness
Charity (love)	Hate

Chapter 7

THE THREE SPECIAL BOOK OF MORMON WITNESSES

(Sections 5, 6, 8, 9, 17)

Sections 8 and 9 of The Doctrine and Covenants are directed to Oliver Cowdery, whose acquaintanceship with the Prophet Joseph Smith began April 5, 1829. It is interesting to notice that Section 6, as also Section 3 and others, was received through the Urim and Thummim. This fact points up a use of these sacred instruments other than for the translation of ancient writings.

Oliver Cowdery Meets Joseph Smith

Oliver Cowdery had been teaching school in the New York Manchester township area where the Prophet's father's family resided. As was customary in those times, the schoolteacher lived with the families in the school district "who sent to the school," and, by this means Oliver became acquainted with the Smith family. Before this he had heard from David Whitmer, a friend, about the Prophet having received The Book of Mormon plates.

Two days after the arrival of Oliver Cowdery in Harmony township, Susquehanna County, Pennsylvania, where the Prophet was residing, the Prophet "commenced to translate the Book of Mormon, and he [Oliver] began to write for me." (P.ofG.P., Writings of Joseph Smith 2:67.) Sometime during this same month of April 1829, Joseph inquired of the Lord through the Urim and Thummim and received Section 6.

Joseph Smith Received Divine Revelation

The principal value of this revelation in our study is to learn wherein the testimony given to Oliver contributes to the fact that Joseph Smith received divine revelations. The Lord herein reveals only that which Oliver Cowdery knew before meeting Joseph, but this same information was revealed to Joseph and thus the Lord sustained him as a prophet in the eyes of Oliver.

With the foregoing facts in mind, let us turn to verses 14-18 of Section 6:

> Verily, verily, I say unto thee, blessed art thou for what thou hast done; for thou hast inquired of me, and behold, as often as thou hast inquired thou hast received instruction of my Spirit. If it had not been so, thou wouldst not have come to the place where thou art at this time.
>
> Behold, thou knowest that thou hast inquired of me and I did enlighten thy mind; and now I tell thee these things that thou mayest know that thou hast been enlightened by the Spirit of truth;
>
> Yea, I tell thee, that thou mayest know that there is none else save God that knowest thy thoughts and the intents of thy heart.
>
> I tell thee these things as a witness unto thee—that the words or the work which thou hast been writing are true.
>
> Therefore be diligent; stand by my servant Joseph, faithfully, in whatsoever difficult circumstances he may be for the word's sake. (D&C 6:14-18.)

Notice from this scripture that Oliver would not have come to visit Joseph, if it were not for the fact that his prayers had been answered. The Lord here makes known that the thoughts and intents of the heart are known to him, and that, in this case, Oliver Cowdery had received a witness that the work of translating the plates of The Book of Mormon in which Joseph Smith was employed, was of the Lord. Consequently, he is admonished to diligence in assisting Joseph.

In order that Oliver might not lose sight of the witness that had been given to him, and also that he might understand more fully that he was, in fact, helping a true prophet of the Lord, this revelation continues in verses 22 to 24 inclusive, with further confirmation:

Verily, verily, I say unto you, if you desire a further witness, cast your mind upon the night that you cried unto me in your heart, that you might know concerning the truth of these things.

Did I not speak peace to your mind concerning the matter? What greater witness can you have than from God?

And now, behold, you have received a witness; for if I have told you things which no man knoweth have you not received a witness? (*Ibid.*, 6:22-24.)

In this way, the Lord confirmed the witness Oliver had received. Notice the significant words: "If I have told you things which no man knoweth, have you not received a witness?" Joseph Smith, by revelation, now knew what only the Lord and Oliver had known previously.

In the prophet's history, we find this record of the witness given to Oliver:

After we had received this revelation, Oliver Cowdery stated to me that after he had gone to my father's to board, and after the family had communicated to him concerning my having obtained the plates, that one night after he had retired to bed he called upon the Lord to know if these things were so, and the Lord manifested to him that they were true, but he had kept the circumstance entirely secret, and had mentioned it to no one; so that after this revelation was given, he knew that the work was true, because no being living knew of the thing alluded to in the revelation, but God and himself. (*DHC* I:35.)

In addition to the testimony of Joseph Smith regarding this incident, David Whitmer, one of the three special witnesses to The Book of Mormon and while outside of the Church testified the following to Elders Orson Pratt and Joseph F. Smith:

Before I knew Joseph, I had heard about him and the plates from persons who declared they knew he had them, and swore they would get them from him. When Oliver Cowdery went to Pennsylvania, he promised to write me what he should learn about these matters, which he did. He wrote me that Joseph had told him his (Oliver's) secret thoughts, and all he had meditated about going to see him, which no man on earth knew, as he supposed, but himself, and so he stopped to write for Joseph. (*Historical Record* 6:208, May 1887.)

This circumstance resulted in the Prophet obtaining secretarial assistance which was much needed in the translation of The Book of Mormon plates. Oliver Cowdery did not return to school teaching, but remained with the Prophet to participate with him in many of the great spiritual blessings of this dispensation.

If you had the same experience as Oliver Cowdery in regard to Section 6, how would you have felt toward the Prophet and his work?

Oliver was promised that he might have the gift to translate even as Joseph Smith. (D&C 6:25.) It is further revealed that "in the mouth of two or three witnesses shall every word be established" (*ibid.*, 6:28), and that if the world accepts the word of the Lord given by the testimony of witnesses they shall be blessed. (*Ibid.*, 6: 28-31.)

Martin Harris and Section 5

We shall now turn our attention to what the Lord has said concerning the witnesses who would testify with the Prophet Joseph Smith to the truth of the gospel message. In Chapter 5 we learned that Martin Harris had received evidence of the existence of The Book of Mormon plates by receiving a translated portion of the plates which he had lost. He was still desirous to obtain further evidence, notwithstanding he had received confirmation from Professor Charles Anthon that the copied characters from the plates were true hieroglyphics. (*DHC* I:20.) As a result of this desire of Martin, the revelation now known as Section 5 was given. (*Ibid.*, 5:1.)

The Prophet was under covenant to show the plates only to those whom the Lord would designate. (*Ibid.*, 5:3.) Many times today nonmembers of the Church suggest that if they could see the gold plates, they would be convinced that Joseph Smith actually had an ancient set of records. It seems that many believe, if the plates were put on exhibit, this would be sufficient evidence to them. In this revelation the Lord does not concur with such a thought. He says:

Behold, if they will not believe my words, they would not believe you, my servant Joseph, if it were possible that you should show them all these things which I have committed unto you. (*Ibid.*, 5:7.)

The world is to have the word of the Lord through the Prophet Joseph Smith. (*Ibid.*, 5:10.) The Lord speaks through his divinely appointed servants. What he reveals does not always agree with what man thinks is true. The prophet Isaiah revealed concerning the workings of the Lord that the Lord's thoughts are not the thoughts of men, "neither are your ways my ways, saith the Lord. For as the heavens are higher than the earth, so are my ways higher than your ways, and my thoughts than your thoughts." (Isa. 55:8-9.) Rather than the plates being put on exhibit for everyone to see, there were to be three special witnesses. (D&C 5:11-15.) Joseph was not to be the only testator of the existence of the gold plates, but in this way others would also bear witness of The Book of Mormon.

And their testimony shall also go forth unto the condemnation of this generation if they harden their hearts against them. (*Ibid.*, 5:18.)

The rejection of their testimony would result in "a desolating scourge" to be poured out from time to time unless the people of the world would repent. (*Ibid.*, 5:19.) To emphasize the fact that the Lord's word is always fulfilled, he refers to the destruction of Jerusalem anciently as an example. (*Ibid.*, 5:20.)

Martin Harris was promised that he should be one of the three special witnesses to view the plates, but only on condition of humility. If he did see the plates, it was necessary that he should make it known to the world. (*Ibid.*, 5:24-28.)

Background of Section 17

As a background for our study of Section 17, which is directly connected with Section 5, a brief review of some events in the Prophet's life seems appropriate. Joseph was at this time living in Harmony township, Pennsylvania, where he had met Emma Hale whom he married on January 18, 1827. He worked at various jobs and had acquired a small farm near his father-in-law's at Harmony. By this time Oliver Cowdery had met the Prophet and the work of translating the plates was continuing. The priesthood was restored. (Chapter 8.) In June 1829, the Prophet became acquainted with Peter Whitmer of Fayette township, Seneca County, New York, who provided residence in his home for the Prophet, Emma, and Oliver. It was here that the translating of the plates was finished.

As the work of translating progressed, it was learned that there were to be three special witnesses, "provided by the Lord, to whom he would grant that they should see the plates from which this work [The Book of Mormon] should be translated. . . ." (*DHC* I:52.)

These witnesses were to bear record of what they saw and heard, as indicated in the following Book of Mormon references: Ether 5:2-4; 2 Nephi 11:3; 27:12. In response to the Prophet's inquiry of the Lord concerning those who should be the three witnesses, Section 17 was received in June 1829.

A Footnote Reference Study

Section 17 begins with a promise that these witnesses were not only to see the plates, but also the breastplate, the sword of Laban, the Urim and Thummim, and the

Liahona, also called the miraculous directors. (D&C 17: 1.) An informative experience for the reader is to consult the footnote references pertaining to each one of these items. Answers to such questions as these will result: Were the Urim and Thummim in use during the period of the Old Testament? To what extent were the Urim and Thummim used during the Nephite dispensation? What relationship is there between the breastplate and the Urim and Thummim? What is the history of the miraculous directors and the sword of Laban amongst the Nephites?

Proof That Joseph Had the Plates

The Lord made known that it would be only by faith and his power that the plates would be seen. (*Ibid.,* 17:2, 5.) In Sections 5 and 17 we discover proof that Joseph Smith actually had the plates. What do you believe this proof to be? Both of these revelations contain promises that on certain conditions, the plates could be seen. Verses 2 to 5 of Section 17 make this clear, as do also the following verses from Section 5:

And in addition to your testimony, the testimony of three of my servants, whom I shall call and ordain, unto whom I will show these things, and they shall go forth with my words that are given through you.

Yea, they shall know of a surety that these things are true, for from heaven will I declare it unto them.

I will give them power that they may behold and view these things as they are. (*Ibid.,* 5:11-13.)

No person of intelligence would make such promises in his own name or in the name of the Lord unless he could thereafter produce the plates and have their truthfulness declared from the heavens. To be unable to do these things would show him to be a fraud before those who desired to be witnesses and all men who should later learn of his deceitfulness.

The Promise of Witnesses Fulfilled

Joseph Smith did not falsify. The promises made to the three witnesses were fulfilled. Not many days after Section 17 was received, Martin Harris, David Whitmer, Oliver Cowdery, and Joseph Smith retired into the woods on the Whitmer farm and prayed that the Lord would fulfill the promises given in this revelation.

After each one of the four persons had prayed in succession without success, a second attempt was made in the same manner and with the same lack of success. Martin Harris then proposed that he withdraw from the others, as he believed his presence was the cause for their failure. He withdrew and the Prophet records that the angel showed them the plates and "we heard a voice from out of the bright light above us, saying, 'These plates have been revealed by the power of God, and they have been translated by the power of God. The translation of them which you have seen is correct, and I command you to bear record of what you now see and hear.' " (*DHC* I:54-55.) The Prophet then went to Martin Harris and while in prayer with him, the same vision was repeated, whereupon Martin Harris cried out, apparently in an ecstasy of joy, " "Tis enough; 'tis enough; mine eyes have beheld; mine eyes have beheld,' and jumping up, he shouted, 'Hosanna,' blessing God, and otherwise rejoiced exceedingly." (*Ibid.*, I:55.)

The testimony of the three witnesses to The Book of Mormon (found in the forepart of each copy of that book) verifies the divine mission of Joseph Smith. Their later experiences in and out of the Church bear solemn witness to the actuality of the things to which they bore record. Each one of these three men was excommunicated from the Church. (During the past few years evidence has been found that Martin Harris was excommunicated by a High Council Court, a fact which had not been known before. This is stated in the article, " 'publish it upon the mountains,' the Story of Martin Harris" by William H. Homer, Jr., in the *Improvement Era*, June 1955, p. 387.)

If the three witnesses had been in collusion with Joseph Smith to deceive the world, it would have been the most normal thing for them to expose the falsehood they were attempting to perpetrate. Admitting that some people live lies, the declarations they make on their deathbeds usually reveal the truth. Oliver Cowdery, David Whitmer, and Martin Harris maintained to the end of their mortal lives that an angel had appeared to them and given them a view of the plates. (Consult B. H. Roberts, *New Witness for God*, II:157, 162, 167-8.) The fact that David Whitmer never returned to the Church strengthens the validity of his testimony.

Eight additional witnesses also testified to the existence of The Book of Mormon plates. They saw and they examined the plates with their hands. (For information about the Three and Eight Witnesses, consult Preston Nibley, *Witnesses of The Book of Mormon*.)

Additional Items on Sections 6, 8, 9, and 5

Section 6: Comment upon verse 7 is given in chapter 9. We are reminded in verse 13 that to be saved in the kingdom of God "is the greatest of all the gifts of God. . . ."

In concluding this revelation, the Lord admonishes Joseph and Oliver to fear not to do good, "for whatsoever ye sow, that shall ye also reap; therefore, if ye sow good ye shall also reap good for your reward." (D&C 6:33.) This scripture is applicable to all Latter-day Saints. The thought in the last verse is a part of the account which begins with verse 32, "Verily, verily, I say unto you, as I said unto my disciples. . . ." which suggests that Joseph and Oliver were to think and ponder over the fact that Jesus is truly the Savior of the world, and that faithfulness in keeping the commandments will bring an inheritance in the kingdom of heaven. This last verse also serves to identify the Christ as the giver of the revelation.

Section 8: Oliver Cowdery is to have the gift of revelation (vs. 3, 4), which, if followed, would deliver him from his enemies. This is the same spirit by which Moses was able to bring the children of Israel through the Red Sea in safety. (v. 3.) In a world of unbelief, Latter-day Saints have greater reason to believe this miracle of the Old Testament. Notice the counsel given to Oliver in verse 10 concerning the necessity of faith. This is a truth which also applies to all Latter-day Saints.

Section 9: This revelation stresses the point that Oliver Cowdery failed to translate because he believed it unnecessary to expend effort in that attempt. The emotion or reaction described in verse 8 as a burning within one, frequently accompanies the giving of revelation or the witness of the truth. This "burning" was present with the two disciples on the road to Emmaus, who received instruction from the resurrected Jesus. (Luke 24: 13-35, especially v. 32.)

Another application of this verse is found in a sermon of Elder Melvin J. Ballard during the great depression in the United States. The principle of revelation for the benefit of the members of the Church worthy of this blessing is emphasized in the following:

You do not know what to do today to solve your financial problems, what to plant, whether to buy or sell cattle, sheep or other things. It is your privilege to study it out; counsel together with the best wisdom and judgment the Lord shall give you, reach your conclusions, and then go to the Lord with it, tell him what you have planned to do. If the thing you have planned to do is for your good and your blessing, and you are determined to serve the Lord, pay your tithes and your offerings and keep his commandments, I promise that he will fulfil that promise upon your head, and your bosom shall burn within by the whisperings of the

Spirit that it is right. But if it is not right, you shall have no such feelings, but you shall have a stupor of thought, and your heart will be turned away from that thing.

I know of nothing today that the Latter-day Saints need more than the guidance of the Holy Spirit in the solution of the problems of life. (*Conference Report*, April 1931, pp. 37-38.)

Oliver was not to translate but to continue to be Joseph's scribe.

Section 5: This appears to be the first revelation to the Prophet where it is even hinted that he might be slain (martyred) for his witness of the truth. (v. 22.)

Chapter 8

THE RESTORATION OF THE AARONIC PRIESTHOOD

(Section 13)

One of the great events in the restoration of the gospel was the conferring of the priesthood upon Joseph Smith and Oliver Cowdery. In this chapter we shall consider some of the implications of this subject.

As Latter-day Saints we know by modern revelation that in the beginning the priesthood was given to man as a necessary part of the plan of redemption. There are a number of biblical examples where men usurped authority and incurred severe punishment. (2 Chronicles 26:16-21; Acts 19:13-16.) Men who act with God's authority will be rejected in the day of judgment, declared the Savior. (Matt. 7:21-23.)

Background of Section 13

In preparation for the formal re-establishment of The Church of Jesus Christ, or kingdom of God upon the earth, the Lord sent his messengers to confer the authority necessary to effect that organization. It was while Joseph Smith and Oliver Cowdery continued the work of translation of the Book of Mormon that they went into the woods to pray and inquire of the Lord respecting baptism for the remission of sins, that was mentioned on the plates. Joseph Smith continues his account by writing:

... While we were thus employed, praying and calling upon the Lord, a messenger from heaven descended in a cloud of light, and having laid his hands upon us, he ordained us, saying:

Upon you my fellow servants, in the name of Messiah I confer the Priesthood of Aaron, which holds the keys of the ministering of angels, and of the gospel of repentance, and of baptism by immersion for the remission of sins; and this shall never be taken again from the earth until the sons of Levi do offer again an offering unto the Lord in righteousness. (D&C Section 13, See also the P. of G. P. The Writings of Joseph Smith 2:68-69.)

He said this Aaronic Priesthood had not the power of laying on hands for the gift of the Holy Ghost, but that this should be conferred on us hereafter; and he commanded us to go and be baptized, and gave us directions that I should baptize Oliver Cowdery, and that afterwards he should baptize me.

Accordingly we went and were baptized. I baptized him first, and afterwards he baptized me—after which I laid my hands upon his head and ordained him to the Aaronic Priesthood, and afterwards he laid his hands on me and ordained me to the same Priesthood—for so we were commanded.

The messenger who visited us on this occasion and conferred this Priesthood upon us, said that his name was John, the same that is called John the Baptist in the New Testament, and that he acted under the direction of Peter, James and John, who held the keys of the priesthood of Melchizedek, which Priesthood, he said, would in due time be conferred on us, and that I should be called the first Elder of the Church, and he (Oliver Cowdery) the second. It was on the fifteenth day of May, 1829, that we were ordained under the hand of this messenger, and baptized.

Immediately on our coming up out of the water after we had been baptized, we experienced great and glorious blessings from our Heavenly Father. No sooner had I baptized Oliver Cowdery, than the Holy Ghost fell upon him, and he stood up and prophesied many things which should shortly come to pass. And again, as soon as I had been baptized by him, I also had the spirit of prophesy, when, standing up, I prophesied concerning the rise of this Church, and many other things connected with the Church and this generation of the children of men. We were filled with the Holy Ghost, and rejoiced in the God of our salvation. (*DHC* I:39-42; also the P. of G. P., Writings of Joseph Smith 2:70-73.)

Jesus' Evaluation of John the Baptist

John the Baptist was considered by Jesus to be one of the greatest of the prophets. He said: "Among them that are born of women there hath not risen a greater than John the Baptist. . . ." (Matt. 11:11.) In commenting upon this statement, the Prophet Joseph Smith observed that the miracles performed by John could not have constituted his greatness, but three things pointed up John's greatness: First, he prepared "the way before the face of the Lord"; second, he was entrusted with the mission of baptizing Jesus; and third, at that time, John was the only legal administrator in the affairs of the kingdom in holding the keys of power. (*DHC* V:260-261.)

We are indebted to modern revelation for additional information about John the Baptist and the Priesthood he held. The Doctrine and Covenants, Section 13, tells of some of these powers. Section 84 makes known that his calling was to administer the "preparatory gospel" (vs. 26, 27), and that John was "baptized while he was yet in his childhood, and was ordained by the angel of God at the time he was eight days old unto this power, to overthrow the kingdom of the Jews, and to make straight the way of the Lord before the face of his people, to prepare them for the coming of the Lord, in whose hand is given all power." (D&C 84:28.) John the Baptist was a resurrected being when he restored the Priesthood. (Matt. 27:52, 53.)

An Old Testament Prophecy

Jesus often referred to the law and the teachings of the prophets. Upon one of these occasions, he applied the fulfillment of an Old Testament prophecy to the mission of John the Baptist as one who should prepare the way for the coming. As we briefly examine this prophecy, let us see how it also fulfills John's mission of restoring divine authority in the latter days:

Behold, I will send my messenger, and he shall prepare the way before me: and the Lord whom ye seek, shall suddenly come to his temple, even the messenger of the covenant, whom ye delight in: behold, he shall come saith the Lord of hosts.

But who may abide the day of his coming? and who shall stand when he appeareth? for he is like a refiner's fire, and like fuller's soap:

And he shall sit as a refiner and purifier of silver; and he shall purify the sons of Levi, and purge them as gold and silver, that they may offer unto the Lord an offering in righteousness. (Mal. 3:1-3.)

John's Twofold Mission

As indicated, this prophecy was fulfilled in part during Jesus' lifetime, for he referred to the "messenger" of this prophecy as John the Baptist who prepared the way before him. (See Matt. 11:10.) It is very clear, however, that this same messenger, John the Baptist, was also to prepare the way of Jesus Christ before his second coming. These elements in the prophecy confirm this fact: first, Jesus was to come suddenly to his temple; second, the coming of John the Baptist would occur in the last days. Otherwise, these questions would not be relevant:

But who may abide the day of his coming? and who shall stand when he appeareth? for he is like a refiner's fire, and like fuller's soap. (Mal. 3:2.)

The expression "refiner's fire" refers to the great heat required to bring ore into a fluid state making possible a separation of the precious metal from the dross with which in nature it is usually found mixed. "Fuller's soap" was used to cleanse garments and to whiten them. Thus we see that these expressions definitely refer to a burning and cleansing process, both of which are associated in the scriptures with the second coming of Jesus. (Mal. 4:1; 2 Thessalonians 2:8; and D&C 101:23-34.) Third, the sons of Levi were to offer an offering in righteousness.

To ascertain whether these three points of Malachi's prophecy were fulfilled during Jesus' mortal ministry, all one need do is ask these questions concerning that period:

(1) Did Jesus come suddenly to the temple of Herod? (2) Were the questions asked in the prophecy fulfilled in the ministry of Jesus? (3) Did the sons of Levi of that day offer an offering in righteousness?

The answer to each one of these questions would have to be answered in the negative. They could be answered only in connection with Jesus' great second coming. But before that second coming, John the Baptist was to prepare the way by bringing again to the earth the power or authority to act in the name of God. We may say today that John the Baptist has fulfilled his twofold mission: first, as the forerunner of the Savior in the meridian dispensation (Mark 1:2-4; John 1:19-23), and second, as the forerunner of Jesus' second coming by the restoration of divine authority in preparation for the re-establishment of the kingdom of God upon the earth.

In a similar way Isaiah also foretold, in his fortieth chapter, the coming of John the Baptist in the last days. (Isaiah 40:1-5; Matt. 3:12; Luke 3:2-5.)

Aaronic Priesthood to Continue

When John the Baptist conferred the Aaronic Priesthood upon Joseph and Oliver, he used words which might suggest that the priesthood so conferred would continue on the earth only until the sons of Levi would offer their prophesied offering in righteousness. This interpretation, however, cannot be held because of a recognition that as long as mortality continues there will be a need for the performance of the ordinances of the preparatory gospel with which that Priesthood is associated. This point is confirmed in Oliver Cowdery's report of this event. He said in his testimony, quoted later in this chapter, that the Priesthood would continue that the sons of Levi might offer their offering.

Sons of Levi

President Charles W. Penrose answered the question: "Who are the sons of Levi?" in this way:

Now as to the "sons of Levi," spoken of by John the Baptist in his ordination of Joseph Smith and Oliver Cowdery. (D&C 13.) They are, or will be, descendants of Levi, holding the Priesthood of Aaron, who will make the offerings predicted by the prophets to be presented to the Lord in latter days in Zion and in Jerusalem. (Malachi 3:2-4; D&C 124:38, and 128:24.) In Zion, men chosen of the Lord for the special work mentioned will be persons sanctified by the spirit unto "the renewing of their bodies." (D&C 84:32-34.) At Jerusalem they will be Levites by lineal descent, offering the sacrifices that will be required after the restoration spoken of in Zechariah 14:16-21, and many others of the prophets of old concerning 'the restitution of all things,'" [Acts 3:19-21.] (*Improvement Era* 15:952, Aug. 1912.)

Sons of Levi Offering

An explanation of the offering that is to be made by the sons of Levi in the last days is given by President Joseph Fielding Smith, as follows:

What kind of offering will the sons of Levi make to fulfil the words of Malachi and John? (Mal. 3:1-4; D&C 13; 124:39; 128:24.) Logically such a sacrifice as they were authorized to make in the days of their former ministry when they were first called. (Ezek. 43:18-27; 44:9-27.) Will such a sacrifice be offered in the temple? Eventually not in any temple as they are constructed for work of salvation and exaltation today. It should be remembered that the great temple, which is yet to be built in the city of Zion, will not be one edifice, but twelve. Some of these temples will be for the lesser Priesthood. (*History of the Church*, Vol. 1, pp. 357-359.)

When those temples are built, it is very likely that provision will be made for some ceremonies and ordinances which may be performed by the Aaronic Priesthood and a place provided where the sons of Levi may offer their offering in righteousness. This will have to be the case, because all things are to be restored. There were ordinances performed in ancient Israel in the tabernacle when in the wilderness, and after it was established at Shiloh in the land of Canaan, and later in the temple built by Solomon. The Lord has informed us that this was the case and has said that in those edifices ordinances for the people were performed. (D&C 124: 28-29.)

These temples that we now have, however, the Lord commanded to be built for the purpose of giving to the saints the blessings which belong to their exaltation, blessings which are to prepare those who receive them to "enter into his rest . . . which rest is the fulness of his glory," and these ordinances have to be performed by authority of the Melchizedek Priesthood, which the sons of Levi did not hold. (*Ibid.*, 84:24.) Now in the nature of things, the law of sacrifice will have to be restored, or all things which were decreed by the Lord would not be restored. It will be necessary, therefore, for the sons of Levi, who offered the blood sacrifice anciently in Israel, to offer such a sacrifice again to round out and complete this ordinance in this dispensation. Sacrifice by the shedding of blood was instituted in the days of Adam and of necessity will have to be restored. (Moses 5:5-8.)

The sacrifice of animals will be done to complete the restoration when the temple spoken of is built; at the beginning of the Millennium, or in the restoration, blood sacrifices will be performed long enough to complete the fulness of the restoration in this dispensation. Afterwards sacrifice will be of some other character. [3 Nephi 9:10-20.] (*Doctrines of Salvation* 3:93-94, 1956.)

Some Lessons from the Restoration of Priesthood

The Aaronic Priesthood was restored one year before the Church was organized. From the opening of this dispensation of the gospel, the Prophet Joseph Smith was being prepared for that formal organization. In addition to the numerous visits with the angel Moroni, Joseph's knowledge was greatly enhanced by the restoration of the Priesthood. As one examines the circumstances which occurred on that beautiful day of May 15, 1829, he realizes how important this event was. Let us indicate some of the truths which are suggested by the event itself. (1) The Aaronic Priesthood is the power by which baptism is performed; (2) a valid baptism must be performed by immersion; (3) baptism is for the remission of sins; (4) the ministry of angels comes through sincere faith; (5) ordination to the Priesthood is done by the laying on of hands; (6) the Aaronic Priesthood is limited in its powers; (7) the restoration of priesthood confirms the apostasy; (8) life after death is affirmed by the resurrection of John the Baptist; (9) John the Baptist acted under the direction of Peter, James, and John, the apostles, indicating the difference between the lesser and greater priesthoods, and also that all who hold the priesthood act under the direction of one who holds the keys of the priesthood; (10) the Higher Priesthood was promised. Other lessons and truths might also be obtained from this one important event—the restoration of the Aaronic Priesthood.

Oliver Cowdery's Testimony

Of the restoration of the Aaronic Priesthood, we also have the testimony of Oliver Cowdery, written September 7, 1834.

... On a sudden, as from the midst of eternity, the voice of the Redeemer spake peace to us, while the veil was parted and the angel of God came down clothed with glory and delivered the anxiously looked for message, and the keys of the Gospel of repentance. What joy! what wonder! what amazement! While the world was racked and distracted—while millions were groping as the blind for the wall, and while all men were resting upon uncertainty, as a general mass, our eyes beheld—our ears heard. As in the "blaze of day"; yes, more—above the glitter of the May sunbeam, which then shed its brilliancy over the face of nature! Then his voice, though mild, pierced to the center, and his words, " I am thy fellow-servant," dispelled every fear. We listened, we gazed, we admired! 'Twas the voice of an angel from glory— 'twas a message from the Most High, and as we heard we rejoiced, while His love enkindled upon our souls, and we were rapt in the vision of the Almighty! Where was room for doubt? Nowhere; uncertainty had fled, doubt had sunk, no more to rise, while fiction and deception had fled forever. . . .

I shall not attempt to paint to you the feelings of this heart, nor the majestic beauty and glory which surrounded us on this occasion; but you will believe me when I say, that earth, nor men, with the eloquence of time, cannot begin to clothe language in as interesting and sublime a manner as this holy personage. No; nor has this earth power to give the joy, to bestow the peace, or comprehend the wisdom which was contained in each sentence as it was delivered by the power of the Holy Spirit! Man may deceive his fellow man; deception may follow deception, and the children of the wicked one may have power to seduce the foolish and untaught, till naught but fiction feeds the many, and the fruit of falsehood carries in its current the giddy to the grave, but one touch with the finger of his love, yes, one ray of glory from the upper world, or one word from the mouth of the Savior, from the bosom of eternity, strikes it all into insignificance, and blots it forever from the mind! The assurance that we were in the presence of an angel; the certainty that we heard the voice of Jesus, and the truth unsullied as it flowed from a pure personage, dictated by the will of God, is to me, past description, and I shall ever look upon this expression of the Savior's goodness with wonder and thanksgiving while I am permitted to tarry, and in those mansions where perfection dwells and sin never comes, I hope to adore in that day which shall never cease. (*DHC* I:43, footnote from *Messenger and Advocate,* 1834.)

Not long after this event, Peter, James, and John conferred the Melchizedek Priesthood upon Joseph Smith and Oliver Cowdery, according to the promise made by John the Baptist. (D&C 27:12-13.)

Chapter 9

"HE THAT HATH ETERNAL LIFE IS RICH" (D&C 11:7)

(Sections 11:7; 14)

In their historical background, Sections 6 and 11 do not differ very much because each revelation was given to "beginners" in their understanding of the Gospel Plan. Understanding this fact will assist one to appreciate the idea in this chapter concerning the text which follows:

> Seek not for riches but for wisdom; and, behold, the mysteries of God shall be unfolded unto you, and then shall you be made rich. Behold, he that hath eternal life is rich. (D&C 11:7.)

The Church was not yet organized, but, as sincere seekers for truth, Oliver Cowdery and Hyrum Smith were anxious to understand their place in the unfolding of the marvelous work which was to be accomplished by the Lord through his servant Joseph Smith. Later the Lord made known that those associated with the Prophet had accomplished many things for themselves as well as for others. (*Ibid.*, 1:17-30.)

The Place of Wealth in the Gospel

As we study verse 7 of Section 11, it seems appropriate for us to ask if material riches should be shunned by Latter-day Saints in order to live the life demanded in the gospel. What place does wealth or property have in the Gospel Plan? Every Latter-day Saint recognizes the need for providing sufficient of this world's wealth for himself and for his family. We are under obligation to do this providing. The temporal riches of this world are provided by an all-wise Father that we might sustain ourselves.

For, behold, the beasts of the field and the fowls of the air, and that which cometh of the earth, is ordained for the use of man for food and for raiment, and that he might have in abundance. (*Ibid.*, 49:19.)

The great welfare plan, in which the Latter-day Saints participate, certainly points up the need for concern about this world's goods. This activity for those in need gives one a rich opportunity to serve his fellow man.

So important is the emphasis of The Book of Mormon upon temporal matters, that Amulek admonished those of his day to "cry [Pray] —unto" the Lord over the crops and flocks of the fields, that the people might prosper in them. (Alma 34:24, 25.)

One's temporal welfare is of such importance that President Joseph F. Smith declared:

It has always been a cardinal teaching with the Latter-day Saints that a religion that has not the power to save people temporally and make them prosperous and happy here cannot be depended upon to save them spiritually and to exalt them in the life to come. (*The Welfare Plan*, Albert E. Bowen, p. 36.)

It seems quite clear from these few ideas that riches are not to be shunned by Latter-day Saints, but rather that they have a definite place in the Lord's purposes for man. Actually, the line of separation between the temporal and the spiritual is so indefinite in the sight of the Lord that a distinction should not be attempted. (D&C 29:34-35.)

President Joseph F. Smith brings this truth to our attention in this manner:

With God all things are spiritual. There is nothing temporal with him at all, and there ought to be no distinction with us in regard to these matters. Our earthly or temporal existence is merely a continuance of that which is spiritual. Every step we take in the great journey in life, the great journey of eternity, is a step in advance or in retrogression. . . . The work we have to do here, although we call it temporal, pertains alike to our spiritual and our temporal salvation. And the Lord has just as much right to dictate, to counsel, to direct and guide us in the manipulation and management of our temporal affairs, as we call them, as he has to say one word in relation to our spiritual affairs. (*Gospel Doctrine,* p. 70.)

An Evaluation of Wealth

As stated in the *Doctrine and Covenants Commentary,* the important message to be remembered is that:

... Our Lord does not object to his people's being rich. It all depends on how they obtain wealth and how they use it. Wealth obtained by dishonesty and oppression is a curse. Wealth, used ... for the furtherance of His kingdom is a means of eternal exaltation. (p. 208.)

The riches of this earth should be a means to an end. When considered from the point of view of eternity, which is the only true criterion, riches are designed for the building up of the kingdom of God and its members. The Lord is truly the owner of all temporal possessions and we are but stewards. (D&C 104:13-17.)

What Is Wisdom?

To seek for wealth solely for the sake of satisfying one's pride, ambitions, desire for power or for worldly pleasures, or other reasons for purposes inconsistent with gospel aims, is a barrier to a Latter-day Saint's spiritual welfare. On the other hand, wisdom, which is a gift of the Holy Ghost (*ibid.,* 46:17, 18), is to be sought. Wisdom is the application of gospel principles into one's life. Knowledge without such application will lead to disappointment and loss of the "crown of righteousness."

The wise person is he who learns the will of the Lord and then does it.

Wisdom is the principal thing; therefore get wisdom: and with thy getting get understanding. (Prov. 4:7.)

O, remember, my son, and learn wisdom in thy youth; yea, learn in thy youth to keep the commandments of God. (Alma 37:35.)

As one draws close to the Lord through prayer and righteous conduct, together with study of the scriptures, there comes the power to discriminate between the true and the spurious.

Are the "Mysteries" to Be Left Alone?

What is the Lord's promise to those who seek wisdom? He has said that the "mysteries of God shall be unfolded unto you." And yet, how many of us have heard over the years the advice to leave the mysteries alone? The Prophet Joseph Smith said:

. . . Declare the first principles, and let mysteries alone, lest ye be overthrown. Never meddle with the visions of beasts and subjects you do not understand. (*Teachings of the Prophet Joseph Smith*, page 292.)

We should keep in mind that there are mysteries which should not concern us. When the Lord is willing to open some of his treasures of knowledge beyond what is already understandable, he will do so. Until then, however, let us keep within the framework which he has established. To go outside of these confines in attempting to learn of things which do not directly apply to our salvation is productive of contention and a loss of faith.

In view of this advice from the Prophet, why should the Lord promise Oliver Cowdery and Hyrum Smith that the mysteries of his kingdom would be made known to them? The answer is probably found in the fact that these men had just begun to learn about some of the Lord's purposes. Their understanding of the Lord's purposes was like that of a child. They had to grow and develop in this work.

Through Whom the "Mysteries" Are Made Known

Actually the "mysteries of God" are unfolded to men by divine revelation through the prophets. (Eph. 1:9, 10; 1 Nephi 1:1; D&C 76:12, 114.) Some of these "mysteries" are not to be made known until the people are ready to receive them. It was not until late in Joseph Smith's life that revelations concerning the temple work and ordinances relating to the dead were made known to the membership of the Church. (D&C 124, 128.) Germane to this point is Joseph Smith's statement:

> The Lord deals with this people as a tender parent with a child, communicating light and intelligence and the knowledge of his ways as they can bear it. (*DHC* V:402.)

The principle just stated applies not only to the membership of the Church as a whole, but also to the individual. As one grows in understanding of the gospel through his obedience, more is made known to him. This was true in the days of the Savior as it is today. (Matt. 13:10-13; D&C 42:65, 66.) What may be a "mystery" to one person may not be to another. It depends upon the "heed and diligence" which one gives to the words of the prophets. (Alma 12:9-11.)

Consistent with what has already been given, one can readily understand that not all of the Lord's mysteries have been revealed. In fact, great blessings of knowledge are a part of the eternal plan that is known by Latter-day Saints as eternal progression. In these words the Lord has given a promise to his faithful saints: "And to them I will reveal all mysteries, yea, all the hidden mysteries of my kingdom. . . ." (D&C 76:7.)

What Eternal Life Is

If one receives the blessing of the faithful, he will be rich, for his reward is eternal life. But what is eternal life? It is more than immortality or the enjoyment of unending conscious existence. The resurrection or immortality is for everyone who is born into mortality.

If we seek for the riches of the kingdom of God, walking in obedience to the commandments, the Lord has promised us that we shall receive the mysteries of God and then we shall receive eternal life. If, on the other hand, we seek the riches of the earth as opposed to the wisdom of following the commandments of the Lord, we shall lose the greatest of all blessings—eternal life.

Application of the Text

How does our text (*ibid.*, 11:7) apply to the members of the Church?

First, we learn that we should prepare early in life to learn the things of God.

Second, preparation for eternal life is a slow process.

When you climb up a ladder, you must begin at the bottom, and ascend step by step, until you arrive at the top; and so it is with the principles of the Gospel—you must begin with the first, and go on until you learn all the principles of exaltation. But it will be a great while after you have passed through the veil before you will have learned them. It is not all to be comprehended in this world; it will be a great work to learn our salvation and exaltation even beyond the grave. . . . (*Teachings of the Prophet Joseph Smith*, p. 348.)

Third, in the process of being saved or exalted, it is necessary that one study the gospel of Jesus Christ. (D&C 131:6; 130:18, 19.)

Fourth, we are to acquire wisdom through "study by faith," prayer, humility, and the wise application of knowledge. A testimony of the gospel is a necessary part of this process of salvation.

Fifth, among the "mysteries of God" for the faithful are the higher ordinances of the gospel. These ordinances are received in the temples of the Lord.

The necessity of receiving these sacred ordinances was expressed by the Prophet Joseph Smith in these words:

> What was the object of gathering the Jews, or the people of God in any age of the world? . . .
>
> The main object was to build unto the Lord a house whereby He could reveal unto His people the ordinances of His house and the glories of His kingdom, and teach the people the way of salvation; for there are certain ordinances and principles that, when they are taught and practiced, must be done in a place or house built for that purpose. . . .
>
> If a man gets a fulness of the priesthood of God, he has to get it in the same way that Jesus Christ obtained it, and that was by keeping all the commandments and obeying all the ordinances of the house of the Lord. . . .
>
> All men who become heirs of God and joint-heirs with Jesus Christ will have to receive the fulness of the ordinances of his kingdom; and those who will not receive all the ordinances will come short of the fulness of that glory, if they do not lose the whole. (*DHC* V:423-424; D&C 124:28, 37-61.)

Sixth, in order to obtain eternal life one must obey the leaders of the Church. Concerning this fact, Joseph Smith said:

> . . . I advise all to go on to perfection, and search deeper and deeper into the mysteries of Godliness. A man can do nothing for himself unless God direct him in the right way; and the Priesthood is for that purpose. (*Teachings of the Prophet Joseph Smith*, p. 364.)

Section 14

The superscription indicates that at the time this revelation was received the Prophet had gone to the Peter

Whitmer farm at Fayette, New York, where he completed the work of translation of The Book of Mormon.

An incident is related by David Whitmer in connection with his preparations in bringing the Prophet Joseph Smith to his father's home. It is as follows:

> Soon after this [the arrival of a letter from Oliver Cowdery] Joseph sent for me to come to Harmony to get him and Oliver, to bring them to my father's house. I did not know what to do. I was pressed with my work. I had some twenty acres to plow, so I concluded I would finish plowing and then go. I got up one morning to go to work as usual, and on going to the field, found between 5 and 7 acres of my ground had been plowed during the night. I do not know who did it, but it was done just as I would have done it myself, and the plow was left standing in the furrow. (*Doctrine and Covenants Commentary*, p. 73.)

The thesis of this chapter is taken from Section 11, verse 7—eternal life is the greatest of all God's gifts. (D&C 29:43; Moses 1:39.) In Section 14, verse 7 the Lord seems to be warning David Whitmer of the need to endure to the end. This admonition seems appropriate in view of his being a special witness to The Book of Mormon and his subsequent excommunication from the Church on April 13, 1838. (v. 8.) He was to assist in the bringing forth of the "fulness of my gospel . . . unto the house of Israel." (v. 10.)

Chapter 10

THE DESIRE TO SERVE IN THE GOSPEL PLAN

(Sections 7 and 11)

Joseph Smith, Sr., first Patriarch to the Church and father of the Prophet, said to Brigham Young: "If you will live for the blessings you desire, you will obtain them." This statement forms the basis of the title of this chapter.

Several of the revelations given before the organization of the kingdom of God upon the earth were addressed to persons who desired to learn from the Prophet how they could assist in the work committed to Joseph Smith. Among these were Joseph Smith, Senior (D&C 4), Martin Harris (who is referred to in (*ibid.*, 5), Oliver Cowdery (*ibid.*, 6, 8), Joseph Knight, Senior (*ibid.*, 12), and others.

Instructions to Hyrum Smith

Prominent among those who proved stalwart in defense of the truth was Hyrum Smith, a faithful follower of his brother Joseph. Upon learning about the Prophet's translating The Book of Mormon plates, Hyrum journeyed to Harmony Township, Pennsylvania, to obtain more information about the work in which the Prophet was then engaged. It was upon this occasion that Joseph inquired of the Lord for Hyrum. Section 11 is the answer to this request. The first nine verses of this section are the same as those addressed to Oliver Cowdery. (*Ibid.*, 6.) It seems most appropriate that the importance of the Lord's work would be emphasized to these two men who were to help the Prophet in his calling. Both of them apparently had similar desires. Notice verses 8 and 14 of Section 11:

Verily, verily, I say unto you, even as you desire of me so it shall be done unto you; and, if you desire, you shall be the means of doing much good in this generation.

Verily, verily, I say unto you, I will impart unto you of my Spirit, which shall enlighten your mind, which shall fill your soul with joy;

And then shall ye know, or by this shall you know, all things whatsoever you desire of me, which are pertaining unto things of righteousness, in faith believing in me that you shall receive. (*Ibid.*, 11:8, 13-14.)

As you read these verses and reflect on the promises made therein, what would you give to receive similar blessings? These verses point out the means by which men may receive the Lord's help in realizing their good desires. In the context to verse 14, Hyrum is informed that he is to put his trust "in that Spirit which leadeth to do good—yea, to do justly, to walk humbly, to judge righteously. . . ." (*Ibid.*, 11:12.) If he will do this the righteous desires of his heart will be given to him, but this will also require that faith be expressed in the Lord, which is the basis of a fulfillment of the things which should fill his soul with joy. (*Ibid.*, 11:13.)

Revelations to Others

At other times in this dispensation men sought through the Prophet to learn how their desires might be realized. The Lord on one of these occasions (August, 1831) reminds his people that "those who desire in their hearts, in meekness, to warn sinners to repentance, let them be ordained unto this power." (*Ibid.*, 63:57.)

We are reminded in another revelation that as "a pattern in all things" that "ye may not be deceived" by Satan, men may be contrite and their language meek, yet to be acceptable to the Lord they must obey the ordinances of the gospel. (*Ibid.*, 52:14-16.)

One of the distinguishing characteristics of the true follower of the Master is the sustaining of those in authority over him. The upholding of the leadership of the kingdom of God arises out of the truth that our leaders, both local and general, are the Lord's representatives. (*Ibid.*, 84:35-38.) To another group of elders the Lord made known the way by which they could obtain the kingdom. His words are, "And if ye desire the glories of the kingdom, appoint ye my servant Joseph Smith, Jun., and uphold him before me by the prayer of faith." (*Ibid.*, 43:12.) This meant not only by an upraised hand and even by prayer, but by actual material support when necessary.

Book of Mormon Contribution

One of the informative and significant changes found in the Sermon on the Mount as given in The Book of Mormon, deals with the granting of the desire to partake of the blessings of the kingdom of God. Notice the contribution of the Nephite scripture:

Therefore if thou bring thy gift to the altar, and there rememberest that thy brother hath ought against thee;
Leave there thy gift before the altar, and go thy way; first be reconciled to thy brother, and then come and offer thy gift. (Matt. 5:23-24.)
Therefore, if ye shall come unto me, or shall desire to come unto me, and rememberest that thy brother hath ought against thee—
Go thy way unto thy brother, and first be reconciled to thy brother, and then come unto me with full purpose of heart, and I will receive you. (3 Nephi 12:23-24.)

Before one can claim the fulness of reward, one must seek reconciliation with those who have anything against him. It is well to notice that the injured or "presumed" injured party is to go to the one who is responsible for the injury or hurt. (Matt. 18:15-17.) This admonition does not absolve the latter from also seeking to make the reconciliation which will bring forth the promised blessings. (D&C 64:8-11.)

Calls to the Ministry

As we consider the revelation given to Hyrum Smith (*ibid.*, 11), we learn that righteous desires will be granted but that they may not come immediately. Hyrum sought to preach the gospel, but the time had not yet arrived for him to do this. In fact, the Lord informed him that he must be patient in this desire, saying "you need not suppose that you are called to preach until you are called." (*Ibid.*, 11:15.) This is an important principle in relation to the gospel. The author remembers one non-Mormon minister who cited Sections 4:3 and 6:4 to justify his own "call" to the ministry as being taught in Latter-day Saint scriptures. However, these revelations were given before the restoration of divine authority and the organization of the Church. Hyrum Smith and all others at that time were informed of the necessity of receiving a call from the Lord when the time was appropriate, through his Prophet upon the earth.

Many today in the Church have reason to ponder over these significant ideas found in the revelation to Hyrum Smith. One who truly desires to serve the Lord should make preparations by living close to the Lord in keeping his commandments with all his might, mind, and strength. (*Ibid.*, 11:20.) Part of this preparation is the learning of what the Lord requires of one by studying his scriptures. (*Ibid.*, 11:22.) There is strong confirmation in verse 25 to the truth that when the Lord does call people to serve him in some capacity in building up the kingdom on the earth, the revelation thus received should not be denied but readily accepted as the word of the Lord. How many of us find ourselves in a condition where, without justification, we do not respond to the call of the Lord's servants and thus bring upon ourselves the penalty of rejecting his revelations?

Examples from the Past

For those who have the desire to serve the Lord and

faithfully keep his commandments and seek to bring
forth and establish the cause of Zion (*ibid.*, 11:6), the
Lord has promised rich rewards. (*Ibid.*, 11:7.) (See
Chapter 9.)

These rewards are given to those who desire them
sufficiently to live the law which will bring forth the
greatest blessings. The kind of desire which the Lord requires of his children is that of strength and ardor of
feeling that motivate them to act in accordance with his
law. There are many examples in the scriptures of those
who were prompted by a desire great enough to call forth
the blessings of heaven. It seems that the case of the first
Nephi, son of Lehi, illustrates this principle very well.
He was rewarded of the Lord because of his "great desire" founded upon a faith which was genuine. (1 Nephi
2:16.) The Lord softened his heart that he might believe
even greater things because of his diligence. His life
might be considered one of a consuming desire to know
the truth and then to follow the voice of the Spirit.

Enos, grandson of Father Lehi, was rewarded with
the desire of his heart because of his faith. (Enos 9, 12-
17.) An Old Testament example of fulfilled desire on
the part of Judah during the reign of King Asa may
also be cited. (2 Chronicles 15:15.)

Is the Office All-Important?

Opportunities to serve in the Church usually come
to all who have the desire. These calls to serve may seem
to be minor at times, but one should keep in mind that
his or her contribution, regardless of the position one
holds, moves the kingdom forward. Individual blessings
are received as one remains actively engaged in the
Lord's work. Important to an understanding of the kind
of desire that one should have in connection with service
in the Church, are these words of President Brigham
Young:

If I find a man, as I do once in a while, who thinks that he ought to be sustained in a higher position than he occupies, that proves to me that he does not understand his true position, and is not capable of magnifying it. Has he not already the privilege of exhibiting all the talents he has—of doing all the good he is capable of in this kingdom? Is he curtailed in the least, in anywise or place, in bringing forth his wisdom and powers, and exhibiting them before the community, and leading out? No, not in the least. Are any of you infringed upon or abridged in the least? Is there a sister who has not the privilege of exhibiting all the talent and power she will, or is capable of, for the benefit of her sisters and her children? Are the sisters deprived of any liberty in displaying their taste and talent to improve the community? (*Journal of Discourses* 7:161-162.)

A person's exaltation in the celestial kingdom is not dependent on the position he may hold in the Church, but upon how well he incorporates the principles of righteousness into his life and, at the same time, accepts the responsibilities of membership in the kingdom of God.

If the motivation behind one's desire for position is prompted by ambition to exalt oneself, there is lacking the necessary qualification to serve in righteousness. Martin Harris' desire to become one of the three witnesses to The Book of Mormon is a good case in point. (D&C 5:23-25.) When the apostles James and John desired to exalt themselves by occupying positions on the right and left of Jesus in the Father's kingdom, the Lord gently reprimanded them and, at the same time, denied their desire. (Mark 10:35-41; Matt. 2:20-24.)

Desires of the Living to Aid Their Dead

As one considers further thoughts relative to one's desire in the gospel plan, he learns that the basis of the doctrine of salvation for the dead is desire on the part of the dead to receive the saving ordinances of the gospel. Basically, the ordinances for the dead administered in the temples are for those who have died "without a knowledge of the gospel." (D&C 128:5.) Their desires for salvation will be realized when they have accepted the gospel in the spirit world and when the ordinances are performed in their behalf by the living. In other words, the desires of men's hearts go to judgment as well as their works. (Alma 29:4-5; 41:3-6.) This is indicated in a revelation to the Prophet Joseph Smith not found in The Doctrine and Covenants. On January 21, 1836, in the Kirtland Temple the "voice of the Lord" came as he beheld in vision the celestial kingdom:

> All who have died without a knowledge of this Gospel, who would have received it if they had been permitttd to tarry, shall be heirs of the celestial kingdom of God; also all that shall die henceforth without a knowledge of it, who would have received it with all their hearts, shall be heirs of that kingdom, for I, the Lord, will judge all men according to their works, according to the desire of their hearts. (*DHC* II:380.)

We may also see wherein the desires of the living in behalf of their deceased relatives are realized in this doctrine as their hearts are turned toward their dead in the spirit world.

Death of Righteous from War

One of the comforting assurances received in this life by parents who have lost sons or daughters as the result of war is based upon this concept stated in the revelation given to the Prophet. Such faithful members of the Church will be rewarded according to their desires— the blessings of the exaltation will be made available to them. This fact was stated by the First Presidency during World War II, when many of our righteous young men and women were called to the other side. Among other things, the general conference message of the First Presidency said:

> In this terrible war now waging, thousands of our righteous young men in all parts of the world and in many countries are subject to a call into the military service of their own countries.

Some of these, so serving, have already been called back to their heavenly home; others will almost surely be called to follow. But "behold," as Moroni said, the righteous of them who serve and are slain: "do enter into the rest of the Lord, their God," and of them the Lord has said ". . . those that die in me shall not taste of death, for it shall be sweet unto them." (D&C 42:46.) Their salvation and exaltation in the world to come will be secure. That in their work of destruction they will be striking at their brethren will not be held against them. (*Conference Report*, April 6, 1942, p. 95.)

Section 7

We now have an opportunity to examine a revelation in which the desires of one of the Lord's apostles mentioned in the New Testament are clarified. Joseph Smith and Oliver Cowdery could not agree as to whether or not the following account stated definitely that John the Beloved was promised that he would continue to live in mortality until the second coming of Jesus:

Then Peter, turning about, seeth the disciple whom Jesus loved following; which also leaned on his breast at supper, and said, Lord, which is he that betrayeth thee?

Peter seeing him saith to Jesus, Lord, and what shall this man do?

Jesus saith unto him, if I will that he tarry till I come, what is that to thee? follow thou me.

Then went this saying abroad among the brethren, that that disciple should not die: yet Jesus said unto him, He shall not die; but, if I will that he tarry till I come, what it that to thee? (John 21:20-23.)

By the use of the Urim and Thummim Joseph Smith saw a parchment written by John wherein his desire was granted to have power over death that he might continue to bring souls unto Jesus. The Doctrine and Covenants, Section 7:6 states definitely that John became a ministering angel, and that his ministry was not to end until the Savior comes in his glory. His mission is to "prophesy before nations, kindreds, tongues and people."

(*Ibid.*, 7:3.) Nephi foresaw this mission of John. (Nephi 14:18-27.)

As one who has power over death and yet a mortal in other ways, John is known as a translated being. In reference to the work of such beings, the Prophet Joseph Smith once said:

Translated bodies cannot enter into rest until they have undergone a change equivalent to death. Translated bodies are designed for future missions. (*DHC* IV:425.)

From 3 Nephi, Chapter 28, we learn about the three Nephites, who were given their desire to function in a capacity similar to that of the Apostle John. They were given the privilege to continue their mortal lives until the second coming of Christ. During this time they would minister for the salvation of scattered Israel. They did not have pain, but only sorrow for the sins of the world. Prisons could not keep them nor could they be destroyed. These are some of the powers of the translated being.

In addition to John's assisting in the restoration of the Melchizedek Priesthood in this dispensation, we have evidence that during the time of Joseph Smith, he was actively engaged in bringing souls unto Jesus. During the June 1831 general conference of the Church, it is recorded that:

The Spirit of the Lord fell upon Joseph in an unusual manner, and he prophesied that John the Revelator was then among the Ten Tribes of Israel who had been led away by Shalmaneser, king of Assyria, to prepare them for their return from their long dispersion, to again possess the land of their fathers. (*DHC* 1:176.)

Again in this revelation (D&C 7) we have an example of fulfilled desires in righteousness. The Lord promised the Apostle Peter that his good desire to come speedily unto him at the allotted time for man to die was granted. (*Ibid.*, 7:4, 5, 8.)

Chapter 11

THE WORTH OF SOULS

(Sections 15, 16, and 18)

The first two revelations for study in this chapter are identical, but they were given to different persons. The message thus given was of great importance to those two sons of Peter Whitmer, into whose home the Prophet Joseph Smith, Emma, his wife, and Oliver Cowdery were received in June 1829. (*DHC* I:48, 49.) John and Peter Whitmer, Jr., to whom Sections 15 and 16 were given, and especially the former, became zealous friends of Joseph Smith and assistants in the work. It was their desire to learn from the Lord what was of most worth to them in life. (D&C 16:4.) The answer of the Lord was definite and clear:

> And now, behold, I say unto you, that the thing which will be of the most worth unto you will be to declare repentance unto this people, that you may bring souls unto me, that you may rest with them in the kingdom of my Father. Amen. (*Ibid.*, 15:6.)

The Church had not been formally organized at this time, but The Book of Mormon was translated and, within a year, it was to be printed that it might become in the beginning of this dispensation an effective missionary tool in bringing people to repentance.

Notwithstanding the fact that the Whitmer brothers were given the charge to declare repentance, they would be under the same commandment given to Hyrum Smith, that a formal call to the ministry was necessary before they could preach. (*Ibid.*, 11:15.) It seems evident from the historical context in which Sections 15 and 16 are given, that this call to preach repentance means preaching the gospel of Jesus Christ in calling people to repentance and not just including the principle of repentance as a part of the gospel.

A Unique Missionary System

With these ideas in mind, we are shown how the Lord was preparing men to assist in what later has come to be one of the most unusual missionary systems in the world.

The missionary work of the Church has been carried on regardless of the cost involved. Sacrifices of many kinds have been made by loyal, devoted men and women of this Church. The missionary system has demanded great sacrifices. The expenditure of funds by the missionaries, their families, and the Church has been in the hundreds of millions of dollars. Many missionaries have given their lives, whereas others have shortened their lives, through exposure, hardship, and disease.

The loving service of the wives and mothers of these missionaries has been shown through the decades since this system was inaugurated. In many instances they have taken upon themselves the added responsibility of additional work in the home and on the farm. Widows have, in many cases, provided for their missionary sons and daughters. Added to this sacrifice is the separation of loved ones from their homes. All of these contributions emphasize the service rendered by a devoted people to a divine charge.

The results of this service in the Church and to the missionary system have been great. The building up of the kingdom of God has been furthered as hundreds of thousands from many nations have been brought into the Church. The contribution of these converts in service and material means has compensated the Church many times over, for this contribution has increased the missionary effort, the building of temples, chapels, and, in general, the entire work of building up Zion. At the same time these converts have, in many instances, found new freedoms, opportunities to rear their posterity under conditions more favorable to living the Gospel Plan. Into the communities of the Saints, a greater understanding of people from all parts of the world is brought by the returning missionaries. An increased understanding and respect for mankind has developed among the Saints by this unique system.

The individual benefits to the missionaries in this undertaking have been manifold. Impetus to greater educational aims, the desire to give further service to mankind, and increased abilities in personal relationships, together with other personal benefits, have been realized.

The giving of self and loved ones to a cause which has as its basis a divine mandate to preach repentance and to gather of Israel from the four quarters of the earth, is done because of a personal conviction that the gospel is true.

In 1835, the Prophet Joseph Smith declared his deep respect and love for mankind in the following statement:

> The servants of God will not have gone over the nations of the Gentiles, with a warning voice, until the destroying angel will commence to waste the inhabitants of the earth, and as the prophet hath said: "It shall be a vexation to hear the report." I speak thus because I feel for my fellow men; I do it in the name of the Lord, being moved upon by the Holy Spirit. Oh that I could snatch them from the vortex of misery, into which I behold them plunging themselves, by their sins; that I might be enabled by the warning voice, to be an instrument of bringing them to unfeigned repentance, that they might have faith to stand in the evil day! (*DHC* II:263.)

Section 18—The Worth of Souls

In laying the foundation of the Lord's work in the last days, with stress upon the teaching of the gospel, the Lord gave a revelation, in June 1829, addressed to

Joseph Smith, Oliver Cowdery, and David Whitmer. (D&C 18.) Especially pertinent to the objective of this chapter are verses 10-16 of this revelation:

Remember the worth of souls is great in the sight of God;

For, behold, the Lord your Redeemer suffered death in the flesh; wherefore he suffered the pain of all men, that all men might repent and come unto him.

And he hath risen again from the dead, that he might bring all men unto him, on conditions of repentance.

And how great is his joy in the soul that repenteth!

Wherefore, you are called to cry repentance unto this people.

And if it so be that you should labor all your days in crying repentance unto this people, and bring, save it be one soul unto me, how great shall be your joy with him in the kingdom of my Father!

And now, if your joy will be great with one soul that you have brought unto me into the kingdom of my Father, how great will be your joy if you should bring many souls unto me! (*Ibid.*, 18:10-16.)

Have you ever considered that you are of great worth in the sight of God? We are confronted directly with the fact that our Redeemer Jesus Christ suffered death of body, and in doing so he suffered "the pain of all men. . . ." (*Ibid.*, 18:11.) Here we are brought to the realization that our Elder Brother underwent severe pain in order that we "might repent and come unto him." (*Ibid.*, 18:11.) This is not the first time that the Lord has made known that by his suffering the resurrection is brought to pass and eventually a judgment. Jacob, The Book of Mormon prophet, said:

And he cometh into the world that he may save all men if they will hearken unto his voice; for behold, he suffereth the pains of all men, yea, the pains of every living creature, both men, women, and children, who belong to the family of Adam.

And he suffereth this that the resurrection might pass upon all men, that all might stand before him at the great and judgment day. (2 Nephi 9:21-22.)

The resurrection of the body saves men from "devil, and death, and hell. . . ." (2 Nephi 9:19.) In order that men might be saved in the celestial kingdom, they must comply with the principles and ordinances of the gospel. This gives to them a release from the bondage of sin and brings them into spiritual life with God. If they do not repent, then they receive a lesser portion of the salvation which they have earned by their obedience to terrestrial or telestial laws. (D&C 88:21-24.)

In other words, men must be obedient to the gospel commandments, which are made efficacious for men through the suffering and death of the Savior. Expressed in scripture this principle is that Jesus "bringeth about means unto men that they may have faith unto repentance." (Alma 34:15.)

We are of great worth in the sight of God as shown by the great suffering of Jesus in making the atonement for us.

And he hath risen again from the dead, that he might bring all men unto him, on conditions of repentance.

And how great is his joy in the soul that repenteth! (D&C 18:12-13.)

Why the Lord's Joy Is Great

One of the reasons for the "worth of souls in the sight of God" is the fact that men and women are spirit sons and daughters of God. It is not very difficult for a Latter-day Saint to understand the soul's worth when he remembers this parent-child relationship. God is perfect. His love is divine and, therefore, it is greater than that of any human being. It has been said that mother love comes nearest to the divine of any love which is known to man. Great as this love is, God's love is infinitely greater and more constant. John the apostle set forth the fact:

For God so loved the world, that he gave his only begotten Son, that whosoever believeth in him should not perish, but have everlasting life. (John 3:16.)

Jesus also loved men, his spirit brothers and sisters, with such a perfect love that he willingly did his Father's bidding and suffered death for them.

That soul which repents and follows the path of righteousness finds in his own heart a love for the Father and the Son that helps him to draw closer to them in appreciation for their love. It is in this way that "joy" of the Lord is great. The soul that repents adds to the Lord's glory in that eternal life is made possible for the obedient. (Moses 1:39.)

Joy by Service

Man as an authorized servant of the Lord is commanded "to cry repentance unto this people." (D&C 18:14), and if one's entire life is spent in this work, and he brings but one person unto the Lord, how great will be his joy with him in God's kingdom. If, however, there are many souls brought to repentance, his joy will be even greater. (*Ibid.*, 18:15-16.)

The Motivation of Missionary Work

These thoughts bring to our attention the need for a missionary system based upon a sincere love for man. The real motivation in this work is the love for the souls of men. There will grow in man such a love, if man will allow the Spirit of the Lord to develop that sentiment. When the missionary is prompted by love for his fellow men, all of his energies are directed to the missionary work. Then he realizes the joy in bringing only one soul unto him while greater joy comes in the many who are brought unto the Lord. One of the miracles of missionary work is the mighty change which is wrought in the hearts of the missionaries as a result of the zeal they develop in this work.

Consistent with what has preceded in this meaningful revelation, the Lord makes his will known: "And if you have not faith, hope, and charity, you can do nothing": (*Ibid.*, 18:19.) Missionaries are not to have the spirit of contention which is of the devil. (3 Nephi 11: 29, 30.) They are to oppose all evil, however. (D&C 18: 20.) The necessity of taking upon himself the name of Christ by being baptized and enduring to the end is clearly made known. (*Ibid.*, 18:22.) There is no other way that one can be saved in the kingdom of the Father. (*Ibid.*, 18:23-25.)

The Calling of the Twelve

In this same revelation, it is stated that there are to be Twelve Apostles, whose calling is to "declare my gospel, both unto Gentile and unto Jew." (*Ibid.*, 18:26.) These brethren are to receive their appointment because they sincerely desire to take upon them the name of the Lord. (*Ibid.*, 18:26-28.) Oliver Cowdery and David Whitmer were called to search out the Twelve who are to be known by "their desires and their works. . . ." (*Ibid.*, 18: 37-38; also Chapter 10.) In fulfillment of this revelation, the Prophet later said that the Lord had revealed that the Three Witnesses were to select the Twelve.

As to why Martin Harris may not have been included in Section 18, the following from Elder B. H. Roberts is instructive:

I think it was designed from the first that the Three Witnesses should choose the Twelve Special Witnesses of the name and mission of the Lord Jesus Christ—the Twelve Apostles; but at the time the revelation of June, 1829 [Section 18], was given, making known that Twelve Apostles would be called, and designating Oliver Cowdery and David Whitmer as the ones to choose them, Martin Harris was out of favor with the Lord, and I suggest that it was for that reason doubtless that his name was omitted at that time. The evidence that Martin Harris was wavering about that time in his adherence to the Prophet and the work of God is found in Doctrine and Covenants, sec. xix, given in the month of June, 1829; in which revelation Martin Harris is sharply reproved for such wavering; for his covetousness; for hesitating to dispose of his land to meet the obligations entered into with the printer. He is commanded to repent of all these things, which, happily he did; but evidently not before the revelation concerning the choosing of the Twelve (Doctrine and Covenants, sec. xviii) was given, for which reason doubtless his name is not there associated with those of his fellow Witnesses when they were designated to choose the Twelve Apostles. (*DHC* II:186-187, footnote.)

The duties of the Twelve, as given in Section 18, are to ordain men to Priesthood offices, declare the gospel, baptize, and to testify of the truth as revealed. (D&C 18: 31-36.)

In concluding Section 18, dealing with the worth of the human soul and the calling of the Twelve, it is declared that a marvelous work will be performed by the Lord through his servants in this dispensation "unto the convincing of many of their sins, that they may come unto repentance, and that they may come unto the kingdom of my Father." (*Ibid.*, 18:44.)

Chapter 12

A MESSAGE FROM HIM WHO IS ETERNAL

(Section 19)

Revelations in The Doctrine and Covenants are better understood if information is known concerning their historical background. Although Section 19 is one of the most important doctrinal revelations received by the Prophet, we do not have specific information about its origin. In other sections of this book of scripture, we have become acquainted with some facts about Martin Harris to whom this revelation was addressed through the Prophet Joseph Smith. It is apparent from the revelation that the Lord felt the necessity to call Martin to repentance at this time. (vs. 13, 20.) Although he had received the blessing of being one of the Three Witnesses, it appears that he had yet to learn obedience and to be reminded of the suffering which comes from nonrepentance. (v. 15.) The reference in the last part of verse 20 to the time when the Lord withdrew his Spirit from Martin, which caused him to suffer, may have reference to the time when the translated portion of the Book of Mormon was lost. (D&C Sections 3 and 10.)

Important Doctrinal Teachings

Although Section 19 has much to say to and about Martin Harris, it is a revelation, among many others, which emphasizes important doctrinal teachings. At the outset there is revealed the truth that Jesus is the Redeemer of the world, the Great I AM or Jehovah, as he was known in the Old Testament. (v. 1.) Because he did the will of the Father in becoming the Atoner for mankind, Jesus is able to destroy Satan and his works at the end of the world. (vs. 2, 3.)

There follows in this revelation the familiar scriptural standard of judgment: namely, that all men will be judged according to their works. (*Ibid.*, 19:3; Rev. 20:13.) But verses 4 through 12 make known an important doctrinal concept of the character of God. The importance of this doctrine is best indicated in the historical background in which it was given. When one knows the beliefs of Joseph Smith's period concerning hell and punishment, he is prepared to understand how the modern Prophet's theological teachings paved the way for a far nobler understanding of God than that conceived by an apostate world. It was not that Joseph Smith had discovered these theological teachings in the Bible, but rather that the Lord revealed them to him. There is another phase of this subject which is important to realize. It is that a change has come about in the Christian world relative to the doctrine of hell and punishment that, sometimes, makes it difficult for some Latter-day Saints of this generation to appreciate fully the message given by the Savior in the First Vision. Some may find it difficult to understand why the Lord would say to the inquiring boy Joseph Smith that he must join none of the churches:

> ... for they were all wrong, and the personage who addressed me said that all their creeds were an abomination in His sight: that those professors were all corrupt; that "they draw near to me with their lips, but their hearts are far from me; they teach for doctrines the commandments of men: having a form of godliness, but they deny the power thereof." (*DHC* 1:6.)

"Christian" Doctrine Changed

That a decided change has come during the past century in Christian thinking relative to hell and punishment is well expressed by George Harris in *A Century's Change in Religion*. He says that everlasting punishment is seldom mentioned in the pulpit now (1914); that "hell" is seldom uttered. The concept of a morally ruined man has come to be considered as the character being debased, rather than of extreme physical suffering. He states that the unquenchable fire, the worm that does not die, are believed to mean corrosion and decay.

The "Abominable" Doctrine

But when did this new thought arise? Several decades after the days of Joseph Smith, even as late as the last quarter of the nineteenth century, theologians were teaching a doctrine which was an abomination in the Lord's sight. Just what was that doctrine?

Some ideas held then and to some extent today were brought to the attention of people in England as well as the United States by the Dean of Canterbury in a series of sermons delivered in Westminster Abbey, November and December 1877. In the Preface of his book *Eternal Hope*, Dr. F. W. Farrar states that the common view is (1) that at death there is passed upon every impenitent sinner an irreversible doom to endless tortures, either material or mental, of the most awful and unspeakable intensity; and (2) that this doom awaits the vast majority of mankind.

In further exposition of these common teachings, the Dean said in one of his five sermons:

What the popular notion of hell is, you, my brethren, are all aware. Many of us were scared with it, horrified with it, perhaps almost maddened by it in our childhood. It is that, the moment a human being dies—at whatever age, under whatever disadvantages—his fate is sealed hopelessly and forever; and that if he die in unrepented sin, that fate is never-ending agony, amid physical tortures the most frightful that can be imagined; so that, when we think of the future of the human race, we must conceive of "a vast and burning prison, in which the lost souls of millions and millions writhe and shriek for ever, tormented in a flame that never will be quenched." You have only to read the manuals, you have only to study the pictures published, though but rarely, by members of our own Church, and more frequently by Roman Catholics on the one hand, and some sections of Non-conformists on the other, to see that such has been and is the common belief of Christendom. (*Ibid.*, pp. 55-57.)

To illustrate the horrible concept of hell as taught in an earlier day, Dean Farrar quotes several examples, among which is this one from Jonathan Edwards:

The world will probably (!) be converted into a great lake or liquid globe of fire, in which the wicked shall be overwhelmed, which shall always be in tempest, in which they shall be tossed to and fro, having no rest day or night, vast waves or billows of fire continually rolling over their heads, of which they shall ever be full of a quick sense, within and without; their heads, their eyes, their tongues, their hands, their feet, their loins and their vitals shall for ever be full of a glowing, melting fire, enough to melt the very rocks and elements. Also they shall be full of the most quick and lively sense to feel the torments, not for ten millions of ages, but for ever and ever, without any end at all. . . . (*Ibid.*, p. 57.)

An apostate "Christian" world had gone astray in fostering such teachings concerning eternal punishment and hell (spirit world). It had lost a true understanding of the relationship of God and mankind as a parent-child relationship. The understanding of the character of God was perverted by a false concept of his plan for his children. People eventually revolted against this position by even denying the existence of and the power of Satan in the world. (2 Nephi, Chapter 28.)

The Lord's Answer

The revelation given for Martin Harris sets forth the Lord's answer to the abominable doctrine described above as a preparation for the preaching of the true doctrine of Christ in this dispensation. Verses 4 through 12 of The Doctrine and Covenants, Section 19 follow:

And surely every man must repent or suffer, for I, God, am endless.

Wherefore, I revoke not the judgments which I shall pass, but woes shall go forth, weeping, wailing and gnashing of teeth, yea, to those who are found on my left hand.

Nevertheless, it is not written that there shall be no end to this torment, but it is written *endless torment.*

Again, it is written *eternal damnation;* wherefore it is more express than other scriptures, that it might work upon the hearts of the children of men, altogether for my name's glory.

Wherefore, I will explain unto you this mystery, for it is meet unto you to know even as mine apostles.

I speak unto you that are chosen in this thing, even as one, that you may enter into my rest.

For, behold, the mystery of godliness, how great is it! For, behold, I am endless, and the punishment which is given from my hand is endless punishment, for Endless is my name. Wherefore—

Eternal punishment is God's punishment.

Endless punishment is God's punishment.

How do these scriptures give one a concept of punishment and hell which brushes aside the accumulated error of many centuries? In order for man to escape the suffering caused by the misuse of his free agency, he must repent. Punishment for the unrepentant is in accordance with the demand of justice. (vs. 15-19; Alma 34:14-16.) But the Lord declares that there is an end to "endless torment." (D&C 19:6.) In explanation of the use of "endless" and "eternal" in connection with punishment, the Lord explains in verse 7 that these adjectives are more expressive than others to "work upon the hearts of the children of men, altogether for my name's glory." (*Ibid.*, 19:7.) Then the Lord proceeds to explain further that since these expressions are his name, one should understand that it is his punishment that is administered because of wrongdoing without repentance and, therefore, it is not to be endured forever. (*Ibid.*, 19:10-12, 6.) In other words, as you read the terms "endless punishment" and "eternal damnation" substitute the word "God's" for "endless" and "eternal" (v. 10). In making this substitution the expressions mean that the punishment one receives following the death of the body is "God's punishment," and "it is not written that there shall be no end to this torment." (v. 6.)

Repentance Commanded

We are immediately informed in the revelation (*ibid.*, 19:15-19) that if one does not repent, ... one's sufferings will be sore, even so much that one presently would not know of their intensity. A comparison is made with the sufferings of the Savior. However, there is an end! There is release! Provision is made in the true gospel of Jesus Christ that the blood of Jesus redeems and cleanses men of sin if they will repent. The Plan provides that this is possible in the spirit world for all except the few who become sons of perdition because they have lost the power of repentance. (*Ibid.*, 76:40-48; Matt. 12:31, 32; Alma 12:16-18.) The repentant dead, however, will be redeemed and come from the prison house (spirit world) as heirs of salvation in one of the kingdoms of glory.

Hell and Punishment

Is there a hell? The modern scriptures answer in the affirmative. (D&C 76:84-85, 106.) Where is this hell? It is the spirit world—the intermediate state between death and the resurrection. (Alma 40:11-14; Luke 16:19-31.)

The punishment meted out to the wicked, corrupt, and unrepentant of this earth is not the kind taught by an apostate religious world. What did the Prophet Joseph Smith say was the punishment of the wicked? Here is his answer:

There is no pain so awful as that of suspense. This is the punishment of the wicked; their doubt, anxiety and suspense cause weeping, wailing and gnashing of teeth. (*DHC* V:340.)

The great misery of departed spirits in the world of spirits, where they go after death, is to know that they come short of the glory that others enjoy and that they might have enjoyed themselves, and they are their own accusers. (*Ibid.*, V:425.)

Recapitulation

Summary: Whereas an apostate world taught the abominable doctrine that the fire of hell is material and that its agonies are physical agonies; that there is an everlasting damnation of suffering for all who die in a state of sin; and that the vast majority of mankind receive this condemnation, the Lord revealed that eternal punishment means God's punishment, and "it is not written that there shall be no end of this torment." (D&C 19:6.) But there is a hell and there is a punishment that men may eventually be prepared to enjoy a heaven commensurate with their deeds and desires. (Chapter 10.)

Voluntary Suffering of Jesus

Reference has already been made to verses 15 through 19 of Section 19 concerning the great suffering of the Lord in bleeding at every pore, in suffering both body and spirit, and then giving his life that man might be redeemed from his sins. Although some phases of the atonement of Jesus and his suffering were considered in Chapter 11, this revelation does express the magnitude of the cost involved in that atonement. It is probably sufficient here to remind ourselves that when we know the extent of the suffering of Jesus, we should appreciate more fully the love which he and the Father have for us in providing by the atonement an opportunity to escape from an endless misery, as subjects of Satan. (2 Nephi 9:6-27, especially vs. 7-9, 21; Alma 42:14-15; Luke 22:44; Mosiah 3:7.)

It would be impossible for anyone to describe adequately the great suffering of Jesus as he took upon himself the sins of mankind. President John Taylor has given us a description of Jesus' suffering

> The suffering of the Son of God was not simply the suffering of personal death; for in assuming the position that He did in making an atonement for the sins of the world He bore the weight, the responsibility, and the burden of the sins of all men, which, to us, is incomprehensible. . . .
>
> Groaning beneath this concentrated load, this intense, incomprehensible pressure, this terrible exaction of Divine justice, from which feeble humanity shrank, and through the agony thus experienced sweating great drops of blood, He was led to exclaim, "Father, if it be possible, let this cup pass from me." He had wrestled with the superincumbent load in the wilderness, He had struggled against the power of darkness that had been let loose upon him there; placed below all things, His mind surcharged with agony and pain, lonely and apparently helpless and forsaken, in his agony the blood oozed from His pores. Thus rejected by His own, attacked by the powers of darkness, and seemingly forsaken by His God, on the cross He bowed beneath the accumulated load, and cried out in anguish, "My God, why hast thou forsaken me!" When death approached to relieve Him from His horrible position, a ray of hope appeared through the abyss of darkness with which He had been surrounded, and in a spasm of relief, seeing the bright future beyond, He said, "It is finished! Father, into thy hands I commend my spirit." (*Mediation and Atonement*, pp. 146-147.)

Two Plans

The benefits of the atonement for personal salvation arise out of our obedience to the laws and commandments of the gospel. The forgiveness of sins comes to us by this obedience to the ordinances of the gospel and by enduring to the end, walking in obedience to the commandments. (3 Nephi 27:13-21; D&C 18:22.)

When we contemplate the great love which God has for mankind in providing redemption through the plan of life and salvation, we may also exclaim with Lehi's son Jacob, as recorded in 2 Nephi, chapter 9:

O the wisdom of God, his mercy and grace!...
O how great the goodness of our God!...
O how great the plan of our God!...
O the greatness and the justice of our God!
O the greatness of the mercy of our God, the Holy One of Israel!...
O how great the holiness of our God!... (2 Nephi 9:8 ff.)

On the other hand, there is the cunning plan of the evil one. In Jacob's exhortation, he reminds his brethren to:

... remember the awfulness in transgressing against that Holy God, and also the awfulness of yielding to the enticings of that cunning one. Remember, to be carnally-minded is death, and to be spiritually-minded is life eternal. (*Ibid.*, 9:39.)

Do you feel as Jacob felt in expressing this gratitude to God for the Gospel Plan? Do his expressions of joy also express your sincere feeling for what the Lord has done in restoring light and truth through the Prophet Joseph Smith?

Additional Instructions to Martin Harris

In Section 19, the Lord informs Martin Harris that there are some things which are fundamentals of the gospel not yet to be taught to the world, but repentance is the principal message. (vs. 21, 31, and 32.) Some matters were too advanced for those who were yet babes in gospel understanding. The Lord, therefore, set forth what an earlier prophet had counseled concerning food suited for children contrasted with meat which is suited for those of "full age." (Hebrews 5:12-14.)

Significant in Section 19 is the statement that The Book of Mormon is the Lord's word:

... to the Gentile, that soon it may go to the Jew, of whom the Lamanites are a remnant, that they may believe the gospel, and look not for a Messiah to come who has already come. (D&C 19:27.)

A definition or clarification of an expression found in many scriptures is given in this revelation. As an example John the Baptist prepared the way of the Lord by declaring that Jesus would follow him and "baptize you with the Holy Ghost and with fire." (Luke 3:16.) Nephi taught by revelation that through the acceptance of the gospel, there:

> ... cometh the baptism of fire and of the Holy Ghost; and then can ye speak with the tongue of angels, and shout praises unto the Holy One of Israel. (2 Nephi 31:13.)

Jesus used this expression in addressing the Nephites. (3 Nephi 19:18-20.) Martin Harris is told to:

> ... declare repentance and faith on the Savior, and remission of sins by baptism. and by fire, yea, even the Holy Ghost. (D&C 19:31.)

In other words, water baptism plus the baptism of the Holy Ghost, or "fire," after repentance and faith, cleanse and purify in remitting sins. (2 Nephi 31:17.)

In closing one of the great revelations in The Doctrine and Covenants, the Lord addresses questions to Martin Harris which may be asked of many today.

> Pray always, and I will pour out my Spirit upon you, and great shall be your blessing—yea, even more than if you should obtain treasures of earth and corruptibleness to the extent thereof.
> Behold, canst thou read this without rejoicing and lifting up thy heart for gladness?
> Or canst thou run about longer as a blind guide?
> Or canst thou be humble and meek, and conduct thyself wisely before me? Yea, come unto me thy Savior. Amen. (D&C 19:38-41.)

Chapter 13

THE CHURCH ORGANIZED IN THE LAST DISPENSATION

(Sections 20:1-36; 21)

Many events had transpired in the life of Joseph Smith and some of his co-workers by April 6, 1830. Both the Father and the Son Jesus Christ had appeared to Joseph ten years before this date. The angel Moroni had declared "the fulfillment of the prophets—the book to be revealed. . . ." (D&C 128:20.) To Moroni had been committed the keeping and revealing of the record of the stick of Ephraim. (*Ibid.*, 27:5.) Many times this angelic personage had instructed the Prophet in the work assigned him, and finally, in March 1830, The Book of Mormon was available for purchase. The two Priesthoods —Aaronic and Melchizedek—had been restored that man might represent the Lord again.

The commandment of the Lord to Joseph Smith and Oliver Cowdery to ordain each other elders in the Church was given in the chamber of Peter Whitmer, Senior, where Joseph Smith and Oliver Cowdery were living. These ordinations could not be performed, however, until:

. . . our brethren, who had been and who should be baptized, assembled together, when we must have their sanction to our thus proceeding to ordain each other, and have them decide by vote whether they were willing to accept us as spiritual teachers or not. . . ." (*DHC* I:61.)

This commandment was given, according to Elder B. H. Roberts, in or before June 1829. Reference to it was made by the Prophet in his letter to the saints in Nauvoo, Illinois, under date of September 6, 1842, in this manner:

And again, the voice of God in the chamber of old Father Whitmer, in Fayette, Seneca County. . . . (D&C 128:21.)

The fulfillment of the command to ordain each other occurred on April 6, 1830, when the brethren were present to approve of this action, together with the formal reorganization of the Church of Jesus Christ on the earth. (*DHC* I:60-61, footnote.)

The Church Organized

In introducing Section 20 "A Revelation on Church Government" (*ibid.*, I:64), the Prophet wrote that the Lord had given many instructions relative to duties and responsibilities devolving upon him and his fellow-laborers, and that the instructions given therein were obtained "by the spirit of prophecy and revelation. . . ." (*Ibid.*, I: 64.)

With six persons (Joseph Smith, Jun., Oliver Cowdery, Hyrum Smith, Peter Whitmer, Jun., Samuel H. Smith, and David Whitmer) present at the Peter Whitmer farm on the day appointed by the following commandment, The Church of Jesus Christ of Latter-day Saints came into existence:

The rise of the Church of Christ in these last days, being one thousand eight hundred and thirty years since the coming of our Lord and Savior Jesus Christ in the flesh, it being regularly organized and established agreeable to the laws of our country, by the will and commandments of God, in the fourth month, and on the sixth day of the month which is called April. (D&C 20:1.)

Following prayer, the brethren present consented to the proposition that the organization be effected, and that Joseph Smith and Oliver Cowdery be approved as the First and Second Elders, respectively, of "The Church of Jesus Christ of Latter-day Saints." With these ordinations taken care of:

We then took bread, blessed it, and brake it with them; also wine, blessed it, and drank it with them. We then laid our hands on each individual member of the Church present, that they might receive the gift of the Holy Ghost, and be confirmed members of the Church of Christ. The Holy Ghost was poured out upon us to a very great degree—some prophesied, whilst we all praised the Lord, and rejoiced exceedingly. (*DHC* I:78.)

Although apparently nine persons had received baptism by April 6th, this ordinance had been performed for the remission of sins, and with the kingdom of God now established by divine commandment, they were again baptized that they would become members of the kingdom of God. (John 3:5; *DHC* I:76, footnote.) On this memorable day, which will yet be acknowledged in the annals of modern history as an epoch-making event, others were baptized and some were ordained to offices of the priesthood. How celestial beings must have rejoiced, as the followers of Satan raged, in contemplation of what this event meant in the salvation of the living, and the eventual release of the spirit dead from their state of bondage! This was a day prophesied of centuries before the birth of Jesus. (Daniel 2:44.) It was one of the great events of the "restitution of all things, which God hath spoken by the mouth of all his holy prophets since the world began" (Acts 3:21), "the dispensation of the fulness of times . . ." wherein God would "gather together in one all things in Christ, both which are in heaven, and which are on earth; even in him." (Eph. 1:10.)

The Day the Savior Was Born

In consideration of the foregoing facts, would it seem at all inconsistent that when the day was appointed for this event it would be on the anniversary date of the Savior's birth—April 6th? And, also, as President Joseph F. Smith one time suggested, the anniversary date of the Lord's crucifixion? (Quoted in YMMIA Manual 1899-1900, *Dispensation of the Fulness of Times*, Part I, published 1899, page 45.)

Joseph Smith and Youthful Weaknesses

It is apparent from the Prophet's journal that the reference in verse 5 to his being "entangled again in the vanities of the world" (D&C 20:5) refers to certain weaknesses of youth and the foibles of human nature, but he was not guilty of any great malignant sins. Joseph declares that it was never in his nature to commit such sins.

> But I was guilty of levity, and sometimes associated with jovial company, etc., not consistent with that character which ought to be maintained by one who was called of God as I had been. (*DHC* I:9.)

Then Section 20 recounts that by Joseph humbling himself, an angel (Moroni) ministered unto him "whose countenance was as lightning, and whose garments were pure and white above all other whiteness." (D&C 20:6.) Joseph was given commandments which inspired him and he was given power to translate The Book of Mormon. (*Ibid.*, 20:6-8.)

The Fulness of the Gospel

The Book of Mormon is declared to contain the "fulness of the gospel of Jesus Christ," a statement which appears in other places in the revelations. (*Ibid.*, 20:9; 27:5; 42:12; 135:3.) What does this expression mean in connection with The Book of Mormon? There seems to be some confusion in the minds of some members of the Church concerning the meaning of this point. Fulness of the gospel does not have reference to a fulness of knowledge, but that there is sufficient knowledge available for salvation. The Lord has placed considerable stress in his scriptures regarding the necessity of having saving knowledge. (*Ibid.*, 131:6; 88:77, 78.) Included with saving knowledge, there is the necessity for the Priesthood and its keys to be present in order to make effective the principles and ordinances for salvation. Where the keys of the Priesthood and the knowledge are, there is the fulness of the gospel.

Some Purposes of The Book of Mormon

What does this revelation, Section 20, declare to be a purpose of The Book of Mormon? It is to prove to the world "that the holy scriptures are true." (*Ibid.*, 20:11.) In this way, the Lord answers the argument of some who have said that because they cannot see anything new in The Book of Mormon there is no reason for there being another book of scripture. In reality, The Book of Mormon has the function of being a witness for the ancient scriptures (Bible) and also in witnessing that Jesus is the Christ. According to this revelation, the Nephite scriptures are also in the world that men may know that to other people the Lord has given his guidance by revelation. (*Ibid.*, 20:9-12.)

The world shall be judged by the teachings of the Book of Mormon, for this volume of scripture constitutes a witness for the Lord's work in this generation, and because there are witnesses for it. (See verse 13.) If people will accept it for what it is "and work righteousness . . ." the promise is made that they shall receive a crown of eternal life, while those who reject it will stand condemned before the Lord. (*Ibid.*, 14-15.)

Fundamental Book of Mormon Teachings

With these purposes indicated and the testimony of Joseph Smith and Oliver Cowdery given (*ibid.*, 20:16, 35, 36), the Lord makes known some fundamental truths revealed in The Book of Mormon. (*Ibid.*, 20:17-34.) As these teachings are set forth below, notice the order in which they are given. The quotation from The Doctrine and Covenants is given first and then a Book of Mormon reference.

1. The existence, eternal nature, and creative power of God.

By these things we know that there is a God in heaven, who is infinite and eternal, from everlasting to everlasting the same unchangeable God, the framer of heaven and earth, and all things which are in them. (*Ibid.*, 20:17.)

In all scripture the existence of God is assumed. There is one place in The Book of Mormon, however, where the existence of God is argued. It is in the discussion between Alma and Korihor the anti-Christ. (Alma 30:37-45.)

2. The creation of man in God's image and likeness.

And that he created man, male and female, after his own image and his own likeness, created he them. . . . (D&C 20:18.)

Behold, this body, which ye now behold, is the body of my spirit; and man have I created after the body of my spirit; and even as I appear unto thee to be in the spirit will I appear unto my people in the flesh. (Ether 3:16.)

3. Man should love, serve, and worship the only living and true God and no other being.

And gave unto them commandments that they should love and serve him, the only living and true God, and that he should be the only being whom they should worship. (D&C 20:19.)

And now, ye remember that I said unto you: Thou shalt not make unto thee any graven image, or any likeness of things which are in heaven above, or which are in the earth beneath, or which are in the water under the earth.

And again: Thou shalt not bow down thyself unto them, nor serve them. . . . (Mosiah 13:12-13.)

4. The fall of man came by transgression of God's commandments.

But by the transgression of these holy laws man became sensual and devilish, and became fallen man. (D&C 20:20.)

. . . the devil has power over them [the wicked]; yea, even

that old serpent that did beguile our first parents, which was the cause of their fall; which was the cause of all mankind becoming carnal, sensual, devilish, knowing evil from good, subjecting themselves to the devil.

Thus all mankind were lost; and behold, they would have been endlessly lost were it not that God redeemed his people from their lost and fallen state. (Mosiah 16:3-4.)

5. Because of the fall, Jesus' sacrifice was made as foretold in scriptures.

Wherefore, the Almighty God gave his Only Begotten Son, as it is written in those scriptures which have been given of him. (D&C 20:21.)

... and when the day cometh that the Only Begotten of the Father, yea, even the Father of heaven and of earth, shall manifest himself unto them in the flesh, behold, they will reject him, because of their iniquities, and the hardness of their hearts, and the stiffness of their necks.

Behold, they will crucify him; and after he is laid in a sepulchre for the space of three days he shall rise from the dead with healing in his wings; and all those who shall believe on his name shall be saved in the kingdom of God. Wherefore, my soul delighteth to prophesy concerning him, for I have seen his day, and my heart doth magnify his holy name. (2 Nephi 25: 12-13.)

6. Jesus, though tempted, sinned not.

He suffered temptations but gave no heed unto them. (D&C 20:22.)

Know ye not that he was holy? But notwithstanding he being holy, he showeth unto the children of men that, according to the flesh he humbleth himself before the Father, and witnesseth unto the Father that he would be obedient unto him in keeping his commandments. (2 Nephi 31:7.)

7. Jesus was crucified, resurrected, and ascended into heaven.

He was crucified, died, and again the third day;
And ascended into heaven, to sit down on the right hand of the Father, to reign with almighty power according to the will of the Father. . . . (D&C 20:23-24.)

And it came to pass that the Lord spake unto them saying:

Arise and come forth unto me, that ye may thrust your hands into my side, and also that ye may feel the prints of the nails in my hands and in my feet, that ye may know that I am the God of Israel, and the God of the whole earth, and have been slain for the sins of the world. (3 Nephi 11:13-14.)

8. Salvation in the kingdom of God is dependent upon acceptance of the gospel and endurance in faith to the end.

That as many as would believe and be baptized in his holy name, and endure in faith to the end, should be saved—

And we know that all men must repent and believe on the name of Jesus Christ, and worship the Father in his name, and endure in faith on his name to the end, or they cannot be saved in the kingdom of God. (D&C 20:25, 29.)

And he commandeth all men that they must repent, and be baptized in his name, having perfect faith in the Holy One of Israel, or they cannot be saved in the kingdom of God.

And if they will not repent and believe in his name, and be baptized in his name, and endure to the end, they must be damned; for the Lord God, the Holy One of Israel, has spoken it. (2 Nephi 9:23-24.)

9. Salvation is for faithful believers who lived before as well as after the earthly ministry of Jesus.

Not only those who believed after he came in the meridian of time, in the flesh, but all those from the beginning, even as many as were before he came, who believed in the words of the holy prophets, who spake as they were inspired by the gift of the Holy Ghost, who truly testified of him in all things, should have eternal life.

As well as those who should come after, who should believe in the gifts and callings of God by the Holy Ghost, which beareth record of the Father and of the Son. . . . (D&C 20:26-27.)

For he is the same yesterday, today, and forever; and the way is prepared for all men from the foundation of the world, if it so be that they repent and come unto him.

For he that diligently seeketh shall find; and the mysteries of God shall be unfolded unto them, by the power of the Holy

Ghost, as well in these times as in times of old, and as well in times of old as in times to come; wherefore, the course of the Lord is one eternal round. (1 Nephi 10:18-19.)

10. The Father, Son, and Holy Ghost are one God. "They are one in essence, in purpose, in spirit, in attributes, in power, and glory, but they are, nevertheless, three personages." (*Doctrine and Covenants Commentary*, p. 103.)

Which Father, Son, and Holy Ghost are one God, infinite and eternal, without end. Amen. (D&C 20:28.)

And after this manner shall ye baptize in my name; for behold, verily I say unto you that the Father, and the Son, and the Holy Ghost are one; and I am in the Father, and the Father in me, and the Father and I are one. (3 Nephi 11:27.)

11. Justification and sanctification through the grace of Jesus Christ are just and true.

And we know that justification through the grace of our Lord and Savior Jesus Christ is just and true;

And we know also, that sanctification through the grace of our Lord and Savior Jesus Christ is just and true, to all those who love and serve God with all their mights, minds, and strength. (D&C 20:30-31.)

Nevertheless they did fast and pray oft, and did wax stronger and stronger in their humility, and firmer and firmer in the faith of Christ, unto the filling their souls with joy and consolation, yea, even to the purifying and the sanctification of their hearts, which sanctification cometh because of their yielding their hearts unto God. (Helaman, 3:35.)

12. Despite grace, man may fall from God.

But there is a possibility that man may fall from grace and depart from the living God;

Therefore let the church take heed and pray always, lest they fall into temptation;

Yea, and even let those who are sanctified take heed also. (D&C 20:32-34.)

Verily, verily, I say unto you, ye must watch and pray always, lest ye be tempted by the devil, and ye be led away captive by him. (3 Nephi 18:15.)

Following these great truths concerning the plan of salvation, there is further testimony given relative to these fundamental Book of Mormon teachings. (D&C 20:35-36.)

(Note: the remaining part of Section 20 will be discussed in the next chapter.)

Section 21

At the time the Church was organized, the Lord gave this revelation. (Section 21.) It sets forth the important fact that a record or history is to be maintained, and also defines the duties and responsibilities of the Prophet Joseph Smith. Briefly stated, the titles given to him at this time are important in that they show functions which may be exercised by the one who is the Lord's prophet on the earth. (D&C 21:1.) The seer is one who "sees" or has visions. He is declared to be a revelator and a prophet. (Mosiah 8:13-18.) The prophet speaks for the Lord by divine appointment; consequently the Lord declares that Joseph Smith's word "ye shall receive, as if from mine own mouth, in all patience and faith." (D&C 21:5.)

In commenting upon this verse President Joseph Fielding Smith has written:

This is the word which the Lord gave to Israel in relation to Moses. It is just as true in the case of any other person who is sustained as the mouthpiece of the Almighty. Later in speaking of his inspired servants the Lord said: "And whatsoever they shall speak when moved upon by the Holy Ghost shall be scripture, shall be the will of the Lord, shall be the mind of the Lord, shall be the word of the Lord, shall be the voice of the Lord, and the power of God unto salvation." [Ibid., 84:4.] (Church History and Modern Revelation, series 1, p. 100, 1947.)

If we accept the words of the Prophet by waiting on the Lord in exercising faith, we shall be blessed that the "gates of hell" shall not prevail against us. (D&C 21: 5-6, 9.) By divine inspiration one who speaks for the Lord may also translate.

In continuing the revelation, Joseph Smith is declared to be the First Elder of the Church and Oliver Cowdery the Second. (*Ibid.*, 21:10-11.) Interesting items are found in verse 12 wherein Oliver Cowdery is designated as the "first preacher of the church. . . ." (*Ibid.*, 21:12.) He gave the first public discourse in this dispensation. He also became a missionary to the Lamanites or the "Jews" as the Indians were sometimes named in the revelations. (*Ibid.*, 32; 28:8.)

Chapter 14

THE RESPONSIBILITIES OF THE MEMBERS
OF THE CHURCH

(Sections 22; 20:37-84; 26)

In chapter 13 we considered teachings relative to the "fulness of the gospel" as they are contained in The Book of Mormon. In addition, the Lord had commanded the organizing of his Church on April 6, 1830. Inasmuch as only the first part of Section 20 was considered in chapter 13, we shall now examine related revelations and the rest of this revelation. As we do so, let us keep in mind that with the organizing of the kingdom of God upon the earth, there were many things to be made known as to exactly how the Church should function. There are numerous revelations yet to be studied which point out many phases of how the Lord's Church is to carry on its manifold purposes. This is also true with regard to the duties of those who constitute the membership of the organization. In other words, the Lord did not make everything known at one time, but as circumstances demanded, further light and information came through revelations to the Prophet.

Section 22

One of the first questions to arise in this newly organized Church, was concerning the important ordinance of water baptism. It seems that some people who had been baptized into sectarian churches were desirous of uniting with the Church without rebaptism. (*DHC* I:79; and superscription of Section 22.) In the minds of some, apparently, it was believed that the important factor about baptism was that it be performed by immersion. There are so many "Christians" today who feel, as in Joseph Smith's day, that authority to administer this ordinance is unnecessary, or that any clergyman is authorized by God to perform it.

In order that there may be no question, the Lord made known in Section 22 that there is only one baptism and that is the one administered under the "new and everlasting covenant . . ." (D&C 22:1), which is the gospel of Jesus Christ as restored through the Prophet Joseph Smith. (*Ibid.*, 66:2.) The "dead works" of men for salvation in the kingdom of God are futile and although "a man should be baptized an hundred times it availeth him nothing. (*Ibid.*, 22:2.) Divine law from the beginning prescribed only one "gate" into the kingdom of God, and that through an authorized baptism. (*Ibid.*, 22:1-4; 2 Nephi 31:17; Moses 7:64-68.)

Requirements for Baptism

Another question to arise in this newly organized Church, was the important matter of what should be required of those who came into the fold of Christ. With definite emphasis upon the need to be born of water and of the Holy Ghost, as set forth in The Book of Mormon, just published, the Lord stated in plainness what is required of the prospective member of his Church.

Notice carefully the thirty-seventh verse of Section 20 which reads as follows:

And again, by way of commandment to the church concerning the manner of baptism—All those who humble themselves before God, and desire to be baptized, and come forth with broken hearts and contrite spirits, and witness before the church that they have truly repented of all their sins, and are willing to take upon them the name of Jesus Christ, having a determination to serve him to the end, and truly manifest by their works that they have received of the Spirit of Christ unto the remission of their sins, shall be received by baptism into his church. (D&C 20:37.)

These instructions require a high degree of performance. For example, does not the Lord expect a prospective member of the kingdom to observe the Sabbath day in the manner the Lord has revealed through his living oracles? What about being honest in business transactions and, especially, with the Lord in regard to the payment of tithing, also in keeping the Word of Wisdom and other similar requirements?

If one believes what the Lord revealed as requisites to receive a "remission of sins," then there should not be any question concerning these matters. One is expected and one should come before the Lord with a "broken heart and contrite spirit" (*ibid.*, 59:8) sorrowing for past sins and in true humility seeking forgiveness, "and witness before the church that they have truly repented of all their sins. . . ." (*Ibid.*, 20:37.) The Church member, before whom this convert comes to be received into fellowship, should also have a determination to serve Jesus Christ to the end.

Responsibility of Mothers

Although under a patriarchal order, the father presides in the family in giving counsel and instruction, the great responsibility of the mother is to rear the children in light and truth. It is a well-known fact that the influence of the mother upon her children is very great. The fact that she is with the children so much during their formative years, and even later, gives her a greater opportunity to influence the children in the home. When the teaching of the children comes from both parents, as it should, the double impact upon the child is apparent. Both parents have this responsibility even in matters relating to areas of Church government and administration which normally are best known by the father. An example of this subject matter is found in our text from The Doctrine and Covenants, Section 20.

All the leaders of the Church have given emphasis to the need of teaching in the home. Among these was President Joseph F. Smith, who, in the following quotation, places the responsibility upon both parents.

> Another great and important duty devolving upon this people is to teach their children, from their cradle until they become men and women, every principle of the gospel, and endeavor, as far as it lies in the power of the parents, to instil into their hearts a love for God, the truth, virtue, honesty, honor and integrity to everything that is good. That is important for all men and women who stand at the head of a family in the household of faith. Teach your children the love of God, teach them to love the principles of the gospel of Jesus Christ. Teach them to love their fellowmen, and especially to love their fellow members in the Church that they may be true to their fellowship with the people of God. Teach them to honor the priesthood, to honor the authority that God has bestowed upon his Church for the proper government of his Church. (*Gospel Doctrine*, pp. 292-293.)

The Necessity of Study and Its Application

But how shall we teach our children from their cradles until they become men and women, if we are not informed on these important truths? With an understanding of light and truth, the maturity of years often provides wisdom and judgment which give to parents an influence that may be exercised in behalf of their posterity, young and old.

There is no one in the Church who is exempt from teaching his children the restored gospel. So emphatic is the Lord concerning this matter, that, in 1833 he rebuked the members of the First Presidency composed of Joseph Smith, Frederick G. Williams, and Sidney Rigdon, because of their failure to comply completely with this admonition. (D&C 93:40-48.)

In addition to the need, perhaps this rebuke by the Lord was to be an object lesson for all members of the Church relative to their own responsibilities. There comes a time, however, as indicated concerning the Prophet in verse 48 of Section 93, when the members of a family stand condemned, if they do not give heed to the righteous teachings of the parents.

A Statement of Truths

What do we find in the remaining part of Section 20 which provides opportunities for study in an understanding of Church administration, duties of members, and the law by which we are governed? Here are the elements of this basic revelation which may be referred to as the "constitution" of the kingdom of God.

1. The duties of the elders of the Church are (*ibid.*, 20:38-45):

> To baptize.
> To ordain other elders, priests, teachers, and deacons.
> To administer the sacrament.
> To confirm baptized persons into the Church by the laying on of hands and giving of the Holy Ghost.
> To teach, expound, exhort, and watch over the Church.
> To take the lead of all meetings and conduct them as they are led by the Holy Ghost.

2. The duties of the priests of the Church are (*ibid.*, 20:46-52):

> To preach, teach, expound, exhort, baptize, and administer the sacrament.
> To visit the house of each member and exhort the family to pray vocally and in secret and attend to all family duties.
> To ordain other priests, teachers, and deacons.
> To take the lead of meetings when no elder is present.
> To assist the elders if occasion requires it.

3. The teachers of the Church should (*ibid.*, 20:53-56):

> Watch over and strengthen the Church always.
> See that there is no iniquity in the Church—neither hardness with each other, nor lying, backbiting, nor evil speaking.

See that the Church meets together often and that all the members do their duty.

Take the lead of meetings in the absence of the elder or priest.

4. The deacons of the Church should (*ibid.*, 20:57-59):

Assist teachers with their duties when the occasion arises.

Warn, expound, exhort, teach, and invite all to come unto Christ.

5. Law of common consent (*ibid.*, 20:60-67):

a. Every elder, priest, teacher, and deacon is to be ordained according to the gifts and callings of God unto him by the power of the Holy Ghost.

b. Conferences of the Church are to meet once in three months or from time to time, and these conferences are to do whatever Church business is necessary at the time.

c. Elders are to receive their license from other elders by vote of the Church or from conferences, and each priest, teacher, deacon may receive license to perform his duties from an elder, or by a conference of the Church.

d. No person may be ordained to an office in the Church where there is an organized branch without the vote of that branch, but where there is no branch, a presiding elder, high councilor, high priest, or elder may ordain him.

e. Every president of the High Priesthood, bishop, high councilor, and high priest is to be ordained by the direction of a high council at general conference.

6. Duties of Church members (*ibid.*, 20:68-71):

a. All ordinances performed in the Church must be done in order. The members shall manifest to all that they are worthy to belong to the Church.

b. Every member having children should bring them to the elders for a blessing.

c. No one can be received into the Church of Christ until he has arrived at the age of accountability before God and is capable of repentance.

7. Ordinances (*ibid.*, 20:72-79):

a. Immersion is the only mode of baptism, and it must be performed by a person who has authority of Jesus Christ to baptize.

b. The Church should meet together often to partake of the sacrament in remembrance of the Lord. The manner of administering the sacrament is given in Section 20.

8. Records (*ibid.*, 20:80-84):

a. Any member of the Church found in transgression is to be dealt with as the scriptures direct. It is the duty of the stakes, wards, or branches to keep a record of those who have been excommunicated that their names may be blotted out, and also of all members.

b. All members of the Church who move from one locality to another are to take a letter certifying that they are regular members and in good standing in the Church.

Opportunities for Mothers

An understanding of the above truths will help us to realize that as parents in Zion who have had our children baptized, our responsibility to instruct and prepare them for useful service is not ended. President Heber J. Grant once said that it was folly for parents to imagine that their children will grow up with a knowledge of the gospel without teaching. Parents are not justified when they leave the teaching of their children to the auxiliaries of the Church. The amount of time children are in these organizations per week is small. The great opportunities for teaching the gospel are in the home. A testimony comes and grows by faith arising from true knowledge and diligence in keeping the commandments. If parents know the gospel they can govern themselves and teach correct principles to their children.

Common Consent

One of the great principles in governing the kingdom of God in all dispensations of the gospel is the law of common consent. Whenever that kingdom has been organized on the earth it has never been a democracy, as such, but one of the elements of democracy is this principle. The members do not legislate their own laws by which they are governed, nor do they elect their officers. Revelation from the Law Giver, Jesus Christ, is the means of governing his kingdom. Common consent means that by the united voice of the Church certain actions pertaining to its operations are submitted to the members. As verses 60 through 67 of Section 20 point out, general Church business and ordinations to offices are performed by common consent. Elders of the Church act only under direction of those who are empowered to direct them because of the right given to them by the approval of the members. That the vote of the Church is necessary to make valid the privilege to hold office is brought out clearly in other revelations. (*Ibid.*, 41:9; 51:12; 124:124-144.)

A good example of the operation of this law was the occasion of the organization of the Church on April 6, 1830. A rereading of Chapter 13 will indicate how Joseph Smith and Oliver Cowdery were accepted by those present to be their teachers, and whether or not there was agreement to organize the Church upon that eventful day.

Section 26

One of the shortest revelations in The Doctrine and Covenants is Section 26. Nevertheless, it is important in the fact that again the Lord emphasizes

And all things shall be done by common consent in the Church, by much prayer and faith, for all things you shall receive by faith.

When we exercise our rights under the law of common consent, it is to be done "by much prayer and faith. ..." If one lives by prayer and in faith, one should be entitled to the Holy Ghost that his judgments may be in accordance with the will of our Lord. Every true Latter-day Saint has the right to that Spirit, if he will but live for it.

The fact that the Prophet Joseph Smith was directed in the governing of the Church and that he relied upon the Lord "by much prayer and faith . . ." is given confirmation in the last part of verse 1 of Section 26. Concerning the conference to be held in the West, together with other matters, the Prophet is told that "it shall be made known what you shall do." (*Ibid.*, 26:1.)

Chapter 15

THE SACRAMENT

(Sections 27:1-4; 20:75-79)

Under date of August 1830, the Prophet Joseph Smith recorded the following circumstance which resulted in his receiving the first four verses in Section 27. The remaining part of this revelation was written in the following month of September 1830. (*DHC* I:106.)

According to the history of the Church, Newel Knight and his wife came to visit the Prophet and his wife at Harmony Township, Pennsylvania. Inasmuch as neither Newel Knight's wife nor Emma had been confirmed members of the Church, it was deemed advisable that in the religious service where this confirmation would be performed, the Sacrament of the Lord's supper would be administered. In order to prepare for this, the Prophet wrote that "I set out to procure some wine for the occasion, but had gone only a short distance when I was met by a heavenly messenger, and received the following revelation":

Listen to the voice of Jesus Christ, your Lord, your God, and your Redeemer, whose word is quick and powerful.

For, behold, I say unto you, that it mattereth not what ye shall eat or what ye shall drink when ye partake of the sacrament, if it so be that ye do it with an eye single to my glory—remembering unto the Father my body which was laid down for you, and my blood which was shed for the remission of your sins.

Wherefore, a commandment I give unto you, that you shall not purchase wine neither strong drink of your enemies;

Wherefore, you shall partake of none except it is made new among you; yea, in this my Father's kingdom which shall be built up on the earth. (D&C 27:1-4.)

Obedient to this commandment, wine of their own making was prepared, and the confirmations attended to in the meeting. Of the occasion, the Prophet stated that:

> The Spirit of the Lord was poured out upon us, we praised the Lord God, and rejoiced exceedingly. (*DHC* I:108.)

Revelation to Explain Problems

From the information provided in the above account, it is clear that the Prophet did not specifically make a request of the Lord concerning the Sacrament. The heavenly being communicated the message because of the circumstances which were present, principally that the enemies of the Prophet might well take opportunity to harm him. There are other revelations in The Doctrine and Covenants where there is no indication that the Prophet had made a specific request for enlightenment on the problem or information received. The idea suggested by this fact is that the Lord did not always wait, as it were, for his Prophet to make a request for guidance and the direction of the kingdom, but that revelations were given when the need was present. Some might suggest that the Prophet received revelations only because he was aware of a specific need. This point of view does not seem to be consistent with the fact that the Church is literally the kingdom of God and the Law Giver of the kingdom knows the direction his kingdom should go. The Lord knows the end from the beginning. This truth is the basis of prophecy, as well as the fact that the Lord operates by law and, thereby, man may have security by faith in his word. An example of these thoughts is this verse from the "Lord's Preface" to The Doctrine and Covenants:

> Search these commandments, for they are true and faithful, and the prophecies and promises which are in them shall all be fulfilled.
> What I the Lord have spoken, I have spoken, and I excuse not myself; and though the heavens and the earth pass away, my

word shall not pass away, but shall all be fulfilled, whether by mine own voice or by the voice of my servants, it is the same.

For behold, and lo, the Lord is God, and the Spirit beareth record, and the record is true, and the truth abideth forever and ever. Amen. (D&C 1:37-39.)

It certainly is true that the Prophet was a prayerful man and one who was constantly desirous of receiving divine help in his grave responsibilities. He was an instrument through whom the Lord did work that his purposes would be accomplished in behalf of his children. (2 Nephi 3:6-15.) Problems in connection with the building up of the kingdom on the earth were many and the Prophet did go before the Lord with these problems and questions; but the Lord does not leave his work to man who by reason alone would give direction to the Church.

Sacramental Prayers

Although Latter-day Saints may be present in two meetings of the Church each Sunday when the Sacrament is administered and they hear the sacramental prayers spoken, it is well to study them and benefit from that analysis. They are recorded in Moroni chapters 4 and 5, as well as The Doctrine and Covenants as follows:

O God, the Eternal Father, we ask thee in the name of thy Son, Jesus Christ to bless and sanctify this bread to the souls of all those who partake of it, that they may eat in remembrance of the body of thy Son, and witness unto thee, O God, the Eternal Father, that they are willing to take upon them the name of thy Son, and always remember him and keep his commandments which he has given them; that they may always have his Spirit to be with them. Amen.

O God, the Eternal Father, we ask thee in the name of thy Son, Jesus Christ to bless and sanctify this wine to the souls of all those who drink of it, that they may do it in remembrance of the blood of thy Son, which was shed for them; that they may witness unto thee, O God, the Eternal Father, that they do always remember him, that they may have his Spirit to be with them. Amen. (D&C 20:77, 79.)

Meaning of the Sacrament

From both revelations—Sections 20 and 27—quoted above, one's attention is drawn to the fact that the Sacrament serves the purpose of keeping the true follower of Jesus in remembrance of the atonement made by the Savior. His body and blood were offered voluntarily that mankind might be rescued from the power which Satan would have over all human beings in keeping them in misery forever. (2 Nephi 9:5-27.) As repeatedly stated, however, the cleansing, remitting of sins for entrance into the kingdom of God comes by strict obedience to the full gospel plan. (2 Nephi 9:18, 21; Alma 34:15, 16; D&C 29:17; 76:40-44, 50-53.)

After all is said concerning the mission of Jesus on this earth, the fundamental reason for his mortal life was to become the Savior of men. All gospel principles and ordinances are related to the atonement of Jesus Christ.

The sacrifices instituted in the very beginning were intended to be a memorial or type of sacrifice of Jesus, that the people of God might be kept in remembrance of what he would do for them in the Meridian of Time.

As President John Taylor wrote:

As from the commencement of the world to the time when the Passover was instituted, sacrifices had been offered as a memorial or type of the sacrifice of the Son of God; so from the time of the Passover until that time when He came to offer up Himself, these sacrifices and types and shadows had been carefully observed by Prophets and Patriarchs; according to the command given to Moses and other followers of the Lord. (*The Mediation and Atonement*, page 125.)

When Jesus met with his disciples to eat the Passover, he also ate the Sacrament of the Lord's Supper; for, as President Taylor said:

. . . the two ceremonies centered in Him, He was the embodiment of both. . . . in view of what was almost immediately to take place, He instituted the Sacrament of the Lord's Supper in commemoration of this great crowning act of redemption . . . and now we, after the great sacrifice has been offered, partake of the Sacrament of the Lord's Supper in remembrance thereof. Thus this act was the great connecting link between the past and the future. . . . (*Ibid.*, pp. 124-125.)

The Sacrament, an Emblem

The bread and wine (water) of the Sacrament of the Lord's Supper are declared in scripture to be "the emblems of the flesh and blood of Christ. . . ." (D&C 20: 40.)

Other Purposes of the Sacrament

Unlike baptism—which is performed once for each person to remit sins and to enter the Church—the sacrament is to be taken often. (*Ibid.*, 20:75.) We can see in this commandment the wisdom of the Lord for the repetitive act of partaking of these sacred emblems, because it allows the member to reflect frequently upon what the Savior has done for him.

We are reminded of covenants made when we entered the waters of baptism which put every sincere member of the Church on the way to becoming sanctified or Godlike. It is for this purpose the Lord has provided an opportunity for his people to renew their covenants. What are these covenants? We have already considered one of them—that we will always remember the Savior. The remaining two covenants, as indicated in the sacramental prayers, are that we will take upon us the name of Jesus Christ, and that we will always keep his commandments which he has given us. These two covenants mean that we will be called by his name and never bring shame upon that name, and that we will obey all of his commandments.

The Promised Blessing

The sacramental prayers end with these words: "that they may always have his Spirit to be with them." (*Ibid.*, 20:77.) But is it the partaking of the Sacrament which brings this promised blessing? No, it is the keeping of the commandments, including the observance of the commandment to partake of the Sacrament often.

The Sacrament Meeting

The importance of the commandment to meet together often to partake of the bread and water of the Sacrament emphasizes the need for all Latter-day Saints to attend the Sacrament meetings. The Lord has specifically stated that a proper observance of the Sabbath day includes attendance at this meeting. (*Ibid.*, 59:8-12.)

Those who regularly absent themselves from partaking of the Sacrament find it easier to commit sin, and to criticize the leadership of the Church. If this course is continued they may lose the spirit of the Lord and depart from the faith.

In keeping with the purpose of the Sacrament meeting, the First Presidency, consisting of President George Albert Smith, J. Reuben Clark, Jr., and David O. McKay, under date of May 2, 1946, answered these two questions for presidents of stakes and bishops of wards: Should music be played during the administration of the Sacrament? To whom should the Sacrament first be given in a meeting?

Their answers follow:

There is no objection to having appropriate music during the preparation of the emblems, but after the prayer is offered, perfect silence should prevail until the bread and the water have been partaken of by the full congregation. . . . The Sacrament should be first given to the presiding authority in the meeting. This may be the bishop, perhaps one of the stake presidency, or one of the visiting General Authorities. . . . When the Sacrament is given first to the presiding authority, those officiating may pass the Sacrament consecutively to members of the Church who are sitting on the rostrum and in the audience.

The importance of and the proper attitude to be maintained during the administration of the Sacrament were emphasized by the First Presidency in this way:

. . . careful consideration of the institution and purpose of the Sacrament will lead to the conclusion that anything which detracts the partaker's thought from the covenants he or she is making is not in accordance with the ideal condition that should exist whenever this sacred, commemorative ordinance is administered to the members of the Church.

Reverence for God and for sacred things is fundamental in pure religion. Let every boy and girl, every man and woman in the Church, manifest this principle by maintaining perfect order by self-communion whenever and wherever the Sacrament is administered. (*The Church News*, May 11, 1946.)

Sacrament for Church Members

It should be self-evident to all that since the Sacrament is a covenant-renewal opportunity for the partaker, only those who have entered into a covenant relationship with the Lord are eligible to receive these sacred emblems.

When the resurrected Savior met with his disciples upon the American Continent, he commanded that they partake of the Sacrament. Upon their obedience to his command, Jesus said:

And this shall ye always do to those who repent and are baptized in my name; and ye shall do it in remembrance of my blood, which I have shed for you, that ye may witness unto the Father that ye do always remember me. And if ye do always remember me ye shall have my Spirit to be with you. . . .

And now behold, this is the commandment which I give unto you, that ye shall not suffer any one knowingly to partake of my flesh and blood unworthily, when ye shall minister it;

For whoso eateth and drinketh my flesh and blood unworthily eateth and drinketh damnation to his soul; therefore if ye know that a man is unworthy to eat and drink of my flesh and blood ye shall forbid him.

Nevertheless, ye shall not cast him out from among you, but ye shall minister unto him and shall pray for him unto the Father, in my name; and if it be that he repenteth and is baptized in my name, then shall ye receive him, and shall minister unto him of my flesh and blood. (3 Nephi 18:11, 28-30.)

Children and the Sacrament

The Lord has said that children are not accountable to him until they are eight years of age. (D&C 68:25-28.) This means that they are blameless before him; they are of the kingdom of heaven. (Matt. 19:14.) Children are already members of the Lord's kingdom and therefore they are worthy to receive the Sacrament.

Worthiness and the Sacrament

As indicated already, worthiness to partake of the sacramental emblems requires that one be a member of The Church of Jesus Christ of Latter-day Saints. Worthiness includes cleanliness in thought and action, absence of enmity toward fellow man and a desire to do the will of our Father and to keep all of his commandments.

The Prophet in this dispensation as instructed by the Lord has admonished that those who partake of this ordinance should be worthy. (D&C 46:4.) In verse 69 of Section 20, we learn that previous to the partaking of the Sacrament, the members shall manifest before the Church, and also before the elders, by a Godly talk and conversation, that they are worthy of it, that there may be works of faith agreeable to the holy scriptures—walking in holiness before the Lord.

Forgiveness of Sins

Mistakenly, some members of the Church seem to believe that by partaking of the Sacrament one receives

forgiveness of sins. On the contrary, forgiveness is received upon the principle of genuine repentance. A purpose of the Sacrament is to allow the Church member to
self-examine himself that he may strive diligently to overcome his feelings and weaknesses. Partaking of the Sacrament does not remit sins, but it will give spiritual
strength to worthy members who are sincerely endeavoring to live the commandments. Brigham Young said:

> It is one of the greatest blessings we could enjoy, to come
> before the Lord, and before the angels, and before each other, to
> witness that we remember that the Lord Jesus Christ has died
> for us. This proves to the Father that we remember our cove-
> nants, that we love his Gospel, that we love to keep his command-
> ments, and to honor the name of the Lord Jesus upon the earth.
> (*Discourses of Brigham Young*, 1941 Edition, page 172.)

Water or Wine?

This chapter began with a quotation from Section
27:1-4 wherein the Lord revealed by an angel that:

> . . . it mattereth not what ye shall eat or what ye shall drink
> when ye partake of the sacrament, if it so be that ye do it with
> an eye single to my glory. . . . (D&C 27:2.)

To the Saints of the latter days, the Lord has spoken
authorizing the use of water in place of wine. This revelation is a good example of the functioning of continuous
revelation in a divinely directed organization. Consistent
with the principle is the following comment:

> The New Testament churches used wine diluted with water.
> In our day the Lord has commanded the use of pure water in-
> stead of adulterated wine, and this is by no means contrary to the
> Scriptures. In their accounts of the institution of the Sacrament,
> Matthew, Mark, Luke, and Paul—the latter having received his
> information of the Lord Himself (1 Cor. 11:23) make it clear
> that it is the eating of the broken bread and the partaking of the
> common Cup—the contents are not once mentioned—that con-
> stitute the essential elements of the sacrament. Compare 1 Cor.
> 11:26. (*Doctrine and Covenants Commentary*, page 134.)

Pertinent to the thinking of Latter-day Saints about alcoholic beverages because of the Word of Wisdom (D&C 89:5-6), this comment is appropriate:

The Lord in His infinite wisdom, directed the Saints not to buy wine or any other strong drink, of enemies, and consequently not to use wine in the Sacrament, unless they themselves had made it; and then it should be "new wine." Dr. F. W. Farrar says that "new wine" (Luke 5:37) means unfermented wine, or "must"—a beverage which improves with age; it is "a rich and refreshing, but non-intoxicating beverage." (*Doctrine and Covenants Commentary*, page 134.)

Chapter 16

"MAGNIFY THINE OFFICE"

(Sections 23 and 24)

One purpose of this chapter is to show that although revelations were directed to certain individuals as members of the Church and also to one nonmember, the application of the truths in the revelations may be made to others. These two revelations also provide an opportunity for us to become acquainted, insofar as we can, with some of the people who were called into the Lord's service in the beginning of this dispensation.

Introduction

Although consisting of only seven verses, Section 23 of The Doctrine and Covenants contains words of admonition and counsel to five persons, one of whom was not a member of the Church. It is worthy of notice that the four members of the Church are declared by the Lord to be "under no condemnation." (verses 1, 3, 4, and 5.) On the other hand, Joseph Knight, Senior, the non-member, is not given this assurance, nor is he told that he is condemned. As we would look upon this circumstance today with what is given in verse 7 to Brother Knight, who became a member of the Church two months later, we can see where he would come under condemnation if he had not affiliated with the true Church. A revelation was directed to Joseph Knight, Senior, almost one year earlier. (Section 12.) This good man had given material assistance to the Prophet Joseph Smith and did believe that Joseph actually had the Book of Mormon plates. He had desires to assist in the work at that time. Conditions had changed during the year, and the kingdom of God had begun to function on the earth under divine command. This fact made a most significant difference in the message the Lord gave to Mr. Knight in April 1830. He again sought divine counsel through the Prophet Joseph Smith. In addition to being told of the need for prayer in his life, both vocal and secret, this counsel was given:

And, behold, it is your duty to unite with the true church, and give your language to exhortation continually, that you may receive the reward of the laborer. Amen. (D&C 23:7.)

Reasons for Being a Member of the Church—Reflection

What answer would the Latter-day Saint give to the thought expressed to Joseph Knight, Senior, that it was his "duty" to become a member of the kingdom of God? With an understanding of the gospel, the member of the Church might suggest these reasons:

1. I am a child of God in the spirit and, as his child, in my limited understanding, I am duty-bound to accept his counsel.
2. Jesus our Lord gave himself that I might live amid conditions which provide the use of my highest potentialities.
 a. Jesus suffered intensely, giving his life, that I might be saved from a fate which is described as remaining in misery with the father of lies. (2 Nephi 9:9.)
 b. Jesus offered this atonement for me that I might through faithfulness receive "all that the Father hath."
3. From modern scriptures, especially, I have received God's truth which gives me opportunity to know more about *how* I may receive blessings in this life and also in the life to come.
4. I have received the gift of the Holy Ghost which has given to me knowledge (assurance) that The Church of Jesus Christ of Latter-day Saints is the only true and living Church upon the face of the earth.
5. The fulness of the gospel has provided opportunities for service to my fellow men, for personal development, and many other joys and satisfactions in life.

Under each one of the above truths, and others which might be listed, there are many reasons for its being my duty to accept the blessings which can come only by being a member of the kingdom of God.

Why It Is a Duty to Join the Church

If, however, you were now to present reasons why Joseph Knight or a nonmember should become a member of the Church on the basis of "duty," what, in addition to the above reasons, would you suggest?

It is my duty to accept The Church of Jesus Christ of Latter-day Saints because:

1. It has been restored to the earth after a long period of apostasy when it was no longer present among men.
2. God has commanded that all men repent and accept the message as revealed in the restored gospel.
3. The gospel, as restored, is the same gospel as taught by Jesus and, later, by his apostles, as given in the Bible.
4. The teachings of The Church of Jesus Christ of Latter-day Saints are reasonable and consistent, with the reopening of the heavens by direct revelation.
5. Evidence of modern scriptures verifies the truth of other scriptures.
6. The fruits of the gospel, as restored, have brought joy and happiness into the lives of its adherents.

Other reasons might be given under each one of the foregoing to confirm, either by scripture or otherwise, the validity of those general reasons. If one who has not become affiliated with The Church of Jesus Christ of Latter-day Saints were to acknowledge the truth of the above statements or even of some of them, he would be duty bound to accept membership in this Church.

Message to Oliver Cowdery

In connection with the Lord's counsel to the members of the Church mentioned in Section 23, it is well to consider, briefly, the facts made known concerning each one.

Oliver Cowdery is told to "beware of pride, lest thou shouldst enter into temptation." (verse 1.) Despite the great opportunities that had already come to Oliver in being with the Prophet Joseph Smith when the Aaronic and Melchizedek priesthoods were restored, and, later, when additional keys of the priesthood were brought back to the earth, as well as other privileges in assisting to build up the kingdom of God on the earth, Oliver permitted pride to enter his heart with a consequent loss of membership in the kingdom. (*DHC* 3:16-18.) Although Oliver Cowdery returned to the Church, the great blessings that he once enjoyed were not returned to him. However, he died in full fellowship in the kingdom, true to his testimony of The Book of Mormon.

Hyrum Smith, the Prophet's brother, received the blessing that his calling was to strengthen the Church continually. By revelation the Lord called him to be a counselor in the First Presidency in 1837. Later he was appointed Patriarch to the Church. (D&C 124:91-96.)

The office of Patriarch to the Church is hereditary and is received by the eldest sons born in the lineage of Joseph Smith, Senior. (*Ibid.*, 107:40.) In connection with the call of Hyrum Smith to be Patriarch to the Church, we again learn of the power of prophecy possessed by Joseph Smith. This revelation states to Hyrum that ". . . thy duty is unto the church forever, and this because of thy family. . . ." (*Ibid.*, 23:3.)

Samuel H. Smith

Samuel H. Smith strengthened the Church during his ministry as the first missionary of this dispensation until his death on July 30, 1844. How well this revelation was fulfilled is borne out in the life of Samuel as recorded in Church publications. (*Doctrine and Covenants Commentary*, pp. 120-121; *L.D.S. Biographical Encyclopedia*,

I. pp. 278-282.) In keeping with the prophetic spirit of this revelation, Patriarch Joseph Smith, Senior, on his deathbed gave this blessing to his son Samuel:

Samuel, you have been a faithful and obedient son. By your faithfulness you have brought many into the Church. The Lord has seen your diligence, and you are blessed, in that he has never chastised you, but has called you home to rest; and there is a crown laid up for you, which shall grow brighter and brighter unto the perfect day.

When the Lord called you, he said, "Samuel, I have seen thy suffering, and heard thy cries, and beheld thy faithfulness; thy skirts are clear from the blood of this generation." Because of these things I seal upon your head all the blessings which I have heretofore pronounced upon you; and this my dying blessing, I now seal upon you. Even so. Amen. (*History of Joseph Smith by His Mother, Lucy Mack Smith*, p. 310.)

The following excerpt from his obituary notice appearing in the *Times and Seasons* brings to our attention the quality of devotion and attributes of character of this good man.

The exit of this worthy man, so soon after the horrible butchery of his brothers, Joseph and Hyrum, in Carthage jail, is a matter of deep solemnity to the family, as well as a remediless loss to all. If ever there lived a good man upon the earth, Samuel H. Smith was that person. His labors in the Church from first to last; carrying glad tidings to the eastern cities, and finally his steadfastness as one of the Witnesses to the Book of Mormon, and many saintly traits of virtue, knowledge, temperance, patience, godliness, brotherly kindness and charity, shall be given of him hereafter, as a man of God. (*L. D. S. Biographical Encyclopedia* I:282.)

The Prophet's Father

Joseph Smith, Senior, received a blessing similar to that given to his son Hyrum.

Behold, I speak a few words unto you, Joseph; for thou also art under no condemnation, and thy calling also is to exhortation, and to strengthen the church; and this is thy duty from henceforth and forever. Amen. (D&C 23:5.)

Specifically, the Patriarchal office was conferred upon Joseph Smith, Senior, and it was to continue in his lineage as indicated above, and thus forever the Church would be strengthened. One experience in his life does show how his calling was to exhortation. A mission to members of his own family, to whom he bore a strong testimony of the truth of The Book of Mormon, eventually resulted in all of that large family coming into the Church, except one brother and a sister. On one occasion he was unjustifiably put into a "dismal dungeon" where he declared that he ". . . was not the first man who had been imprisoned for the truth's sake; and when I should meet Paul in the Paradise of God, I could tell him that I, too, had been in bonds for the Gospel which he had preached. . . ." (*History of Joseph Smith by His Mother Lucy Mack Smith*, page 185.) When he was released, thirty days later, he baptized two persons whom he had converted.

Section 24 and the Prophet

As indicated in the superscription of Section 24, persecution of the Prophet became intense shortly after the organization of the Church. He was brought before the court on two separate charges and acquitted both times. (See *DHC* I:86-90.) Notwithstanding the bitterness of mobs against the Prophet, there were many times when words of consolation were given and other things occurred to strengthen his faith and cheer the hearts of his followers. One such instance is given by the Prophet shortly before this revelation (Section 24) was received. The wife of Newel Knight had a dream which enabled her to say that Oliver Cowdery and Joseph Smith would visit them that day. That day found the fulfillment of this dream. The Prophet recorded ". . . and thus was our faith much strengthened concerning dreams and visions in the last days, foretold by the ancient Prophet Joel." (*DHC* I:101.)

Verse 1 of Section 24 is to be understood in view of the persecutions of the Prophet and Oliver, while verse 2 points out that they must continue to exercise the principle of repentance in their lives.

Important for this lesson is the significant admonition to Joseph, ". . . Magnify thine office. . . ." (verse 3.) At this time the Prophet returned to his small farm at Harmony, Pennsylvania, where he began his labors in sowing his fields. This was not the calling of the Prophet, however, for he was commanded to perform the calling which he had received by divine appointment, "And in temporal labors thou shalt not have strength, for this is not thy calling" (verse 9) "but devote all thy service in Zion." (verse 7.) The three branches of the Church mentioned in verse 3 were to sustain him, and blessings instead of a cursing were to be theirs. By this temporal assistance, the Prophet would be able to have sufficient to magnify his office ". . . and to expound all scriptures, and continue in laying on of the hands and confirming the churches" [branches]. (verse 9.)

"Magnify Thine Office"

When the Prophet Joseph Smith was told to magnify his calling, the Lord was definite that he had a calling to which he should give his time and talent. In The Church of Jesus Christ of Latter-day Saints the members have many opportunities for service because of the nature of its organization. These privileges range from callings as teachers in the auxiliaries to offices of leadership. In each calling, regardless of what it may be, there are definite responsibilities which pertain to that calling. Every converted member of the Church desires to make his or her contribution to the kingdom of God. In what way may this be done? One definite way is to magnify one's calling as a member of the kingdom and in his specific calling in the Church.

How to Magnify One's Calling

What does it mean to "magnify" a calling? Basically, to magnify means to enlarge or make great. As applied to a calling in the Church, one does not enlarge the office, but, by faithfully carrying out the duties of the calling, one "makes" or "enlarges" the office in the eyes of the membership. In this sense, then, the dictionary definition which says to "cause to be held in greater esteem or respect" may be applied.

The important thing for us is to know wherein the Lord, through his prophets, indicated that an office was being magnified. Some ideas concerning this fact should be considered under these points:

1. Worthiness of life.
   Sections 4 and 12 (See Chapter 6.)
2. Study the scriptures and information relative to the calling.

This counsel addressed to missionaries was given that they might magnify their calling. (D&C 88:78-80.)

And as all have not faith, seek ye diligently and teach one another words of wisdom; yea, seek ye out of the best books words of wisdom; seek learning, even by study and also by faith. (*Ibid.*, 88:118.)

3. Unselfish devotion.

Now, my beloved brethren, I, Jacob, according to the responsibility which I am under to God, to magnify mine office with soberness, and that I might rid my garments of your sins, I come up into the temple this day that I might declare unto you the word of God. (Jacob 2:2.)

4. Follow the leaders placed over us.

In speaking to the Relief Society, the Prophet Joseph Smith said:

... that it was the folly and nonsense of the human heart for a person to be aspiring to other stations than those to which they are appointed of God for them to occupy; that it was better for individuals to magnify their respective callings, and wait patiently till God shall say to them, "Come up higher." (*DHC* 4: 603.)

5. Obtain the Spirit and keep it.

And the Spirit shall be given unto you by the prayer of faith; and if ye receive not the Spirit ye shall not teach. (D&C 42:14.)

When a Latter-day Saint prepares himself for service in the various ways mentioned above and strives to magnify his calling in the kingdom of God, the Lord will magnify him. (Joshua 3:7; 1 Chron. 29:25.) Paul felt that the works which were done through the priesthood magnified the name of the Lord. (Acts 19:13-17.) This same apostle considered that by his life of worthiness Jesus was magnified in him. (Philippians 1:20.)

Chapter 17

THE REVELATION TO EMMA HALE SMITH

(Section 25)

Section 25 is the only revelation in The Doctrine and Covenants that is directed to a woman. The revelation is prophetic in calling Emma Hale Smith to a position of honor and responsibility. It also admonishes her to a life of consecrated devotion to duties demanded by reason of her position as the Prophet's wife.

The first verse of the section points out that "all those who receive my gospel are sons and daughters of my kingdom." (D&C 25:1.) Although this fact is made known in many subsequent revelations (*Ibid.*, 34:3; 35: 2; 45:8), it is significant in this revelation because Emma had been baptized during the last week of June 1830, and confirmed a member of the Church in August. In the meantime (July 1830) she was the subject of this revelation. Verse eight of Section 25 points out that Emma was yet to receive the Holy Ghost by the laying on of hands. The latter circumstance forms a part of the background of Section 27. (See Chapter 15.) By reason of Emma's becoming a member of the kingdom of God and enjoying the blessings of the Holy Ghost, she would be prepared to fulfill some of the specific duties indicated in this revelation.

Emma Hale (born July 10, 1804) became the wife of Joseph Smith on January 18, 1827. They were married for approximately seventeen and one-half years before the martyrdom of the Prophet. There followed three and one-half years of widowhood, when she married (Major) Lewis Crum Bidamon with whom she lived until her death on April 30, 1879.

When the Saints moved West under the direction of the Twelve Apostles with Brigham Young as their President, Emma Smith did not accompany them. She did not continue in the faith for which her husband and his brother Hyrum gave their lives as martyrs.

There were born to Joseph and Emma nine children. The first three, two of whom were twins, died at birth; one other child was born dead and another died at the age of fourteen months. The other four grew to adulthood. Of these children eight were sons, and the only girl was one of the twins who died at birth. Their last child was born after the Prophet's martyrdom. After the death of their twins, they adopted the motherless twins of John Murdock, one of whom, a boy, died at one day less than eleven months of age, only a few days after the Prophet was tarred and feathered by a mob at Hiram, Ohio. (*DHC* I:265.)

Emma has been described as a woman of exceptional intelligence, refinement, and culture. She was neat in appearance and an immaculate housekeeper. Into her home came such visitors as Stephen A. Douglas and Josiah Quincy, Mayor of Boston, not to mention the great many faithful Latter-day Saints who also came to visit the Prophet.

As the wife of the Prophet, Emma was called upon to undergo many hardships because of the persecutions the Prophet underwent. There were times when the Prophet was imprisoned, in exile, on missions, and discharging his many duties in organizing and directing the Church. Persecution drove the Smith family from one place to another so that their children were born in four different states. It was during some of these trials and persecutions that Section 25 was received. (I am indebted to the research of Raymond T. Bailey for much of the foregoing material.)

The Lord's Counsel to Emma

Her first duty, Emma was told in Section 25, was to be a comfort to her husband in his afflictions by giving "consoling words, in the spirit of meekness." (D&C 25:5.) Where the Prophet was to go she was to be with him, and in the absence of Oliver Cowdery to act as his secretary or scribe. (*Ibid.*, 25:6.)

In the fourth verse the Lord admonished Emma to murmur not concerning things which she had not seen. This counsel may arise out of the fact that she and also the "world" were not to see The Book of Mormon plates, which the Lord declared was his wisdom. Regardless of how people may feel about the ways of the Lord, if we accept him as an all-wise Being, we will recognize, as did Isaiah, that his ways are not always the ways of man nor are his thoughts the thoughts of men. (Isaiah 55: 8-9.) This revelation sets forth a principle which is indicated in other scriptures; namely, that the Lord calls imperfect people into his service, although he does require that they show forth fruits of repentance.

An Elect Lady

Verse three states that Emma is "an elect lady, whom I have called." The way in which this honor was to come to her is indicated in verse seven:

And thou shalt be ordained under his hand to expound scriptures, and to exhort the church, according as it shall be given thee by my Spirit. (D&C 25:7.)

When the Relief Society of the Church was organized on Thursday, March 17, 1842, Emma's call as an "elect lady . . ." was fulfilled. Of this expression, the Prophet Joseph Smith said on that occasion:

I assisted in commencing the organization of "The Female Relief Society in Nauvoo" in the Lodge Room. Sister Emma

Smith, President, and Sister Elizabeth Ann Whitney and Sarah M. Cleveland, Counselors. I gave much instruction, read in the New Testament, and Book of Doctrine and Covenants, concerning the Elect Lady, and showed that *the elect meant to be elected to a certain work, &c.*, and that the revelation was then fulfilled by Sister Emma's election to the Presidency of the Society, she having previously been ordained to expound the Scriptures. Emma was blessed, and her counselors were ordained by Elder John Taylor. (*DHC* IV:552, 553.) (Italics, the author's.)

In her capacity as President of the Relief Society, Emma certainly could expound the scriptures and exhort the women of the Society to good works by the inspiration of the Holy Ghost.

The term "ordained" as used in this revelation and in the days of the Prophet was used synonymously with "set apart." Today, we "ordain" male members of the Church to an office in the priesthood, and we "set apart" men and women to offices and callings in the Church. And so with Emma, she was as we would say today, set apart to her callings by the priesthood who rule in the kingdom of God.

The Priesthood Rules

The Apostle Paul is reported in the New Testament to say that a woman is not to "speak" in the Church. According to the Prophet Joseph Smith, as given in the inspired version of the Bible, Paul's counsel was that women should not "rule" in the Church, "but to be under obedience," that is, they are under the direction of the Priesthood authorities and receive their instructions from them. (1 Cor. 14:34-35.) This principle was stated by the Prophet to the members of the Relief Society the month following their organization:

You will receive instructions through the order of the Priesthood which God has established, through the medium of those appointed to lead, guide and direct the affairs of the Church in this last dispensation; and I now turn the key in your behalf in the name of the Lord, and this Society shall rejoice, and knowledge and intelligence shall flow down from this time henceforth; this is the beginning of better days to the poor and needy, who shall be made to rejoice and pour forth blessings on your heads. (*DHC* IV:607.)

We have an example of the Priesthood directing the affairs of the Church in the circumstances that led to the organization of the Society. Notwithstanding certain sisters had drawn up a constitution to organize a society, it is reported by Sarah M. Kimball:

In the spring of 1842, a maiden lady (Miss Cook) was seamstress for me, and the subject of combining our efforts for assisting the Temple hands came up in conversation. She desired to be helpful, but no means to furnish. I told her I would furnish material if she would make some shirts for the workmen. It was then suggested that some of the neighbors might wish to combine means and efforts with ours, and we decided to invite a few to come and consult with us on the subject of forming a Ladies' Society. The neighboring sisters met in my parlor and decided to organize. I was delegated to call on Sister Eliza R. Snow and ask her to write for us a constitution and by-laws and submit them to President Joseph Smith prior to our next Thursday's meeting. She cheerfully responded, and when she read them to him he replied that the constitution and by-laws were the best he had ever seen. "But," he said, "this is not what you want. Tell the sisters their offering is accepted of the Lord, and He has something better for them than a written constitution. Invite them all to meet me and a few of the brethren in the Masonic Hall over my store next Thursday afternoon, and I will organize the sisters under the priesthood after a pattern of the priesthood." He further said, "This Church was never perfectly organized until the women were thus organized." (*The Relief Society Magazine*, vol. VI, March 1919, page 129.)

The Prophet's Counsel to the Relief Society

Pertinent to the subject matter of this revelation and to the Relief Society is the counsel given by the prophet in some of the later meetings of the Society he attended. In addition to the important truth that the sisters, with their officers presiding over them, were to be directed by the Priesthood authorities, the following counsel was given by Joseph Smith:

He spoke of the disposition of many men to consider the lower offices in the Church dishonorable, and to look with jealous eyes upon the standing of others who are called to preside over them; that it was the folly and nonsense of the human heart for a person to be aspiring to other stations than those to which they are appointed of God for them to occupy; that it was better for individuals to magnify their respective callings, and wait patiently till God shall say to them, "Come up higher. . . ."

He exhorted the sisters always to concentrate their faith and prayers for, and place *confidence in their husbands,* whom God has appointed for them to honor, *and in those faithful men whom God has placed at the head of the Church to lead His people*; that we should arm and sustain them with our prayers. . . .

. . . you must put down iniquity, and by your good examples, stimulate the Elders to good works; if you do right, there is no danger of your going too fast.

He said he did not care how fast we run in the path of virtue; resist evil, and there is no danger. . . .

This is a charitable Society, and according to your natures; it is natural for females to have feelings of charity and benevolence. You are now placed in a situation in which you can act according to those sympathies which God has planted in your bosom. . . .

You must not be contracted, but you must be liberal in your feelings. Let this Society teach women how to behave towards their husbands, to treat them with mildness and affection. When a man is borne down with trouble, when he is perplexed with care and difficulty, if he can meet a smile instead of an argument or a murmur—if he can meet with mildness, it will calm down his soul and soothe his feelings; when the mind is going to despair, it needs a solace of affection and kindness. (*DHC* IV:603-607.) (Italics, the author's.)

. . . put a double watch over the tongue: no organized body can exist without this at all. All organized bodies have their peculiar evils, weaknesses and difficulties, the object is to make those not so good reform and return to the path of virtue that they may be numbered with the good, and even hold the keys of power, which will influence to virtue and goodness—should chasten and reprove, and keep it all in silence, not even mention them again; then you will be established in power, virtue, and holiness, and the wrath of God will be turned away.

. . . search yourselves—the tongue is an unruly member— hold your tongues about things of no moment. . . .

I do not want to cloak iniquity—all things contrary to the will of God, should be cast from us, but don't do more hurt than good, with your tongues—be pure in heart. Jesus designs to save the people out of their sins. (*Ibid.*, V. 20.)

The First Latter-day Saint Hymnal

Another assignment given to Emma Smith was that of making a selection of sacred hymns for the Church.

And it shall be given thee, also, to make a selection of sacred hymns, as it shall be given thee, which is pleasing unto me, to be had in my church.

For my soul delighteth in the song of the heart; yea, the song of the righteous is a prayer unto me, and it shall be answered with a blessing upon their heads. (D&C 25:11-12.)

In accordance with this call, Emma made a selection of hymns which appeared in two volumes. W. W. Phelps was appointed to revise and arrange them for printing. The first hymnal was published in 1835, with ninety selections, and the second in 1841, with three hundred forty selections.

The first hymnal classified the selections as mourning hymns, evening hymns, farewell hymns, hymns on baptism, on the Sacrament, on marriage, and miscellaneous. The authors of the words of many of these hymns were Latter-day Saints. The principal contributor was William W. Phelps who wrote many well-known Latter-day Saint hymns. Parley P. Pratt was another contributor to this volume. Among some of the songs included in Emma's compilation are favorites of many in the Church today. Some of these are: "The Spirit of God like a Fire Is Burning"; "Redeemer of Israel"; "Gently Raise the Sacred Strain"; "Earth with Her Ten Thousand Flowers"; "How Firm a Foundation, Ye Saints of the Lord"; "He Died! The Great Redeemer Died!" and "I Know That My Redeemer Lives."

The Lord revealed that the songs which would be pleasing unto him would be those that came from the heart. The song of the righteous is indeed a prayer unto the Lord, for those who live his laws are truly the righteous of the earth.

Brother George D. Pyper once wrote concerning the hymns selected by Emma Smith:

It is said that the character of a people may be judged by the songs they sing. If this be true then an examination of those selected by Emma Smith prove that the Latter-day Saints were a reverential, peace-loving, worshipful, God-fearing people. After a hundred years it is acknowledged that the songs selected for that first Latter-day Saint Hymn book are among the best of all Christian hymns. (*Stories of Latter-day Saint Hymns*, by George D. Pyper, page 195.)

My Voice Is unto All

In closing the revelation to Emma Smith, the Lord stated a principle which has application to Emma and also to every person in The Church of Jesus Christ of Latter-day Saints.

Keep my commandments continually, and a crown of righteousness thou shalt receive. And except thou do this, where I am you cannot come.

And verily, verily, I say unto you, that this is my voice unto all. Amen. (D&C 25:15-16.)

Chapter 18

"THOU SHALT NOT COMMAND HIM WHO IS AT THY HEAD"

(Sections 28; 43:1-7; 27:5-18)

It is important that every member of The Church of Jesus Christ of Latter-day Saints understands the principles set forth in Sections 28 and 43. These revelations make known an important aspect of revelation. The dispensation in which we live is a period during which Jesus said that many ways would be used to "deceive the very elect, who are the elect according to the covenant." (Pearl of Great Price, Joseph Smith 1:22.) If there are any people on the earth whom Satan is desirous of deceiving, it is those who have become members of the kingdom of God. It is our opportunity to learn in this chapter how the Lord's covenant people may be able to detect false revelators.

Hiram Page and Section 28

Hiram Page, a member of the Church, had in his possession a stone which he claimed aided him in receiving revelation about certain things, among which was the upbuilding of Zion. Prior to an appointed conference of the Church for September 1830, the Prophet Joseph decided that it was necessary to ask the Lord concerning the purported revelations of Hiram Page. It seems that the Whitmer family and Oliver Cowdery were believing much of what Brother Page was claiming as revelation. If we keep in mind these facts, we will understand why the Lord declares, in verse 11 of Section 28, that Oliver Cowdery is to take "Hiram Page, between him and thee alone, and tell him that those things which he hath written from that stone are not of me and that Satan deceiveth him." (D&C 28:11.)

Why should not Hiram Page receive revelation for the Church? The verse which follows (verse 12) informs us that it was not his privilege because he had not been appointed, "neither shall anything be appointed unto any of this church contrary to the church covenants." (*Ibid.*, 28:12.) In verse 13, the further fact is made known that all things must be done in order. The Church of Jesus Christ of Latter-day Saints, or the kingdom of God, is the perfect organization, for it is the divine way in which mankind may work out its salvation, the most important work which should have man's attention in this life.

The Lord's Mouthpiece

During the meeting at which the Church was organized, a revelation was received setting forth an important truth relative to Joseph Smith as the leader of the Church and how that organization might prosper:

Wherefore, meaning the church, thou shalt heed unto all his words and commandments which he shall give unto you as he receiveth them, walking in all holiness before me;

For his word ye shall receive, as if from mine own mouth, in all patience and faith.

For by doing these things the gates of hell shall not prevail against you; yea, and the Lord God will disperse the powers of darkness from before you, and cause the heavens to shake for your good, and his name's glory. (*Ibid.*, 21:4-6.)

It is apparent in these scriptures that the Lord wanted the Church, in the very beginning, to understand that the Prophet was the mouthpiece of the Lord and that by obedience to that leadership the Church would prosper. Darkness would not prevail. With this truth known, those who have become the truly faithful covenanted of the Lord will exercise patience and faith in following the counsel of the Lord's anointed.

One Revelator of the Church

If the prophet, seer, and revelator of the Church is the mouthpiece of the Lord, then who else may speak for the Lord's Church?

In Section 28, Oliver Cowdery, although sustained as the second elder of the Church, was told that he should be heard by the Church in whatsoever he should teach by the Comforter concerning the revelations and commandments which had already been given. (Verse 1.)

But, behold, verily, verily, I say unto thee, no one shall be appointed to receive commandments and revelations in this church excepting my servant Joseph Smith, Jun., for he receiveth them even as Moses. (*Ibid.*, 28:2.)

This fact—no one but the Prophet is to receive revelation for the Church—is emphasized further by the Lord by informing Oliver that:

And if thou art led at any time by the Comforter to speak or teach, or at all times by the way of commandment unto the church, thou mayest do it.

But thou shalt not write by way of commandment, but by wisdom;

And thou shalt not command him who is at thy head, and at the head of the church;

For I have given him the keys of the mysteries, and the revelations which are sealed, until I shall appoint unto them another in his stead. (*Ibid.*, 28:4-7.)

Background of Section 43

There was another occasion when it was necessary for the Lord to make known further information about this principle of revelation for the Church. It came about by these circumstances—a woman, by the name of Hubble, "came making great pretensions of revealing commandments, laws and other curious matters." (*DHC*

1:154.) Here, again, we learn that the adversary was seeking to disturb the minds of the Saints.

Joseph Smith and Revelation

In this revelation (Section 43), the Lord again states that Joseph Smith was "appointed unto you to receive commandments and revelations." (D&C 43:2.)

And this ye shall know assuredly—that there is none other appointed unto you to receive commandments and revelations until he be taken, if he abide in me. (*Ibid.*, 43:3.)

In other words, as long as the Prophet remained faithful, he was recognized as the Lord's mouthpiece. But this was not all. There is an unusual thought expressed in the next verse which definitely clarifies and strengthens the principle of who is to receive revelation for the Church. It is stated in this way:

But verily, verily, I say unto you, that none else shall be appointed unto this gift except it be through him; for if it be taken from him he shall not have power except to appoint another in his stead. (*Ibid.*, 43:4.)

Does this scripture mean that if Joseph Smith were to become unfaithful to his high calling and thus lose the privilege to act as the Lord's prophet, he could still "appoint another in his stead?" The answer is *yes*.

The revelation continues in reminding the Saints that these truths are being given in order that "you may not be deceived. . . . And this shall be the law unto you, that ye receive not the teachings of any that shall come before you as revelations or commandments . . . that you may know they are not of me." (*Ibid.*, 43:5, 6.)

In other words, only one may receive revelation for the Church, and that is the prophet, seer, and revelator— in this case, Joseph Smith. At this particular time during the life of Joseph Smith, provision was made for the continuation of the keys of the Priesthood on the earth by the process just mentioned. This provision does not operate today in the Church, for the Lord provided another way when the Quorum of the Twelve Apostles was organized in 1835.

Joseph Smith and Keys of the Priesthood

In order that we may not misunderstand, it is important that we know that two years later the Lord declared to the Prophet Joseph Smith:

Verily I say unto you, the keys of this kingdom shall never be taken from you, while thou art in the world, neither in the world to come;

Nevertheless, through you shall the oracles be given to another, yea, even unto the church. (*Ibid.*, 90:3-4.)

The fact made known here concerning the faithfulness of Joseph Smith as the Prophet of this dispensation was foreknown by Joseph, the son of Jacob (Israel), and also to Lehi as recorded in The Book of Mormon. (2 Nephi 3:3-15, especially vs. 6-8.)

The explanation of the quotation from Section 90 is best expressed in the following words:

In a revelation given in February 1831, the Lord declared that Joseph Smith was the only one appointed to receive revelation and commandments for the Church "until he be taken, if he abide in me," but should the Prophet fail this gift would be taken from him and given to another. (D&C 43:3-4.) Now in March 1833, after the Prophet had been tried and proved, the Lord said that the keys, through which direction, commandment and revelation come, "shall never be taken from you, while thou art in the world, neither in the world to come." Yet when the Prophet should be taken the "oracles" would be given to another, "even to the church." Therefore after the martyrdom the keys remained and were in possession of the Church and exercised through the presiding council, which at that time was the council of the Twelve Apostles, and in the Church the oracles are found and will continue unto the end of time. (*Doctrine and Covenants Commentary*, p. 577.)

Keys of the Priesthood to be Continued

In what way has the Lord provided for the continuation of the keys of Priesthood bestowed by angelic personages, as Peter, James, and John; Moses; Elijah, and others? By ordination the Twelve have all the authority that was given to the Prophet Joseph Smith. Every key and every authority given to him are conferred upon each new apostle as he is ordained, but he does not use all of those powers and authority as a member of the Twelve. The authority is inherent in him sometime to become President of the Church. The only man on the earth who can exercise all of these keys and powers at once is the President of the Church. Consequently, when a President of the Church dies, the apostles, having already received the keys and authority conferred upon Joseph Smith, set apart the newly appointed President of the Church, empowering him to exercise all of those keys and powers as President of the Church.

Summary—One Revelator

In the revelations studied in this chapter we have learned that there are certain ways by which the members of the Church may know the person to receive revelation for the Church. Attempts have been made by some to deceive the Latter-day Saints into believing that a revelation has been given to another person than the President of the Church for the benefit of the entire Church membership. The two revelations studied in this lesson set forth the three standards by which a Latter-day Saint may judge any person claiming revelation for the Church.

1. He must be *called* by revelation through the proper authority or Priesthood of God. (D&C 28:2-6; 43:2.)
2. He must be *approved* by the membership of the Church as the President of the Church. (*Ibid.*, 28:12-13; 43:7.)

3. He must be *set apart* by those who possess the authority. (*Ibid.*, 28:7; 43:7.)

These criteria or standards also apply in the appointment of any officer in The Church of Jesus Christ of Latter-day Saints. An example of this is given in the revelation appointing Edward Partridge as the first bishop unto the Church. (*Ibid.*, 41:9.)

In the event that someone either in the Church or from the outside, as some have done, were to present a revelation to a member of this Church as coming from God for the instruction of the Church, the member would immediately be able to apply these three standards to the person claiming the revelation. No person in the kingdom of God should be deceived, for the Lord has spoken plainly on this matter in these two revelations as well as in other ways. It should ever be remembered that God's house is a house of order, and this is one way by which the Lord maintains the necessary orderly procedure. (*Ibid.*, 132:7-8.)

With this information before us, it is pertinent to keep in mind the truth spoken by President Joseph F. Smith concerning the foregoing points and also the limitations put upon individual members of the Church in receiving revelation for their own guidance.

It is not the business of any individual to rise up as a revelator, as a prophet, as a seer, as an inspired man, to give revelation for the guidance of the Church, or to assume to dictate to the presiding authorities of the Church in any part of the world, much less in the midst of Zion, where the organizations of the priesthood are about perfect, where everything is complete, even to the organization of a branch. It is the right of individuals to be inspired and to receive manifestations of the Holy Spirit for their personal guidance to strengthen their faith, and to encourage them in works of righteousness, in being faithful and observing and keeping the commandments which God has given unto them; it is the privilege of every man and woman to receive revelation to this end, but not further. . . .

And thus his priesthood will ever be found to be composed

of the right men for the place, of men whose backs will be fitted for the burden, men through whom he can work and regulate the affairs of his Church according to the counsels of his own will. And the moment that individuals look to any other source, that moment they throw themselves open to the seductive influences of Satan, and render themselves liable to become servants of the devil; they lose sight of the true order through which the blessings of the Priesthood are to be enjoyed; they step outside of the pale of the kingdom of God, and are on dangerous ground. Whenever you see a man rise up claiming to have received direct revelation from the Lord to the Church, independent of the order and channel of the priesthood, you may set him down as an impostor. (*Gospel Doctrine*, pp. 41-42.)

Historical Setting of Section 27

Reference may be made to Chapter 15 on the Sacrament for historical material on Doctrine and Covenants, Section 27. In that chapter only the first four verses of this revelation were considered. The revelation was given to the Prophet Joseph Smith by an angel. The Prophet said concerning this revelation, "the first four paragraphs of which were written at this time [August 1830], and the remainder in the September following." (*DHC* 1:106.)

Other Dispensations and the Fulness of Times

The Prophet is told in the following verses from The Doctrine and Covenants, Section 27, of the time when he and others will dine with our Lord on our earth. In this message we should notice its relationship to the great events of the past and of the present dispensation, especially the source from whence Joseph Smith received authority and information.

Behold, this is wisdom in me; wherefore, marvel not, for the hour cometh that I will drink of the fruit of the vine with you on the earth, and with Moroni, whom I have sent unto you to reveal the Book of Mormon, containing the fulness of my everlasting gospel, to whom I have committed the keys of the record of the stick of Ephraim;

And also with Elias, to whom I have committed the keys of bringing to pass the restoration of all things spoken by the mouth of all the holy prophets since the world began, concerning the last days;

And also John the son of Zacharias, which Zacharias he (Elias) visited and gave promise that he should have a son, and his name should be John, and he should be filled with the spirit of Elias;

Which John I have sent unto you, my servants, Joseph Smith, Jun., and Oliver Cowdery, to ordain you unto the first priesthood which you have received, that you might be called and ordained even as Aaron;

And also Elijah, unto whom I have committed the keys of the power of turning the hearts of the fathers to the children, and the hearts of the children to the fathers, that the whole earth may not be smitten with a curse;

And also with Joseph and Jacob, and Isaac, and Abraham, your fathers, by whom the promises remain;

And also with Michael, or Adam, the father of all, the prince of all, the ancient of days;

And also with Peter, and James, and John, whom I have sent unto you, by whom I have ordained you and confirmed you to be apostles, and especial witnesses of my name, and bear the keys of your ministry and of the same things which I revealed unto them;

Unto whom I have committed the keys of my kingdom, and a dispensation of the gospel for the last times; and for the fulness of times, in the which I will gather together in one all things, both which are in heaven, and which are on earth. (D&C 27:5-13.)

This account gives, among other things, a resumé of the way by which Joseph Smith was called and received his ordination to the Priesthood as indicated in this chapter. It also refers to the greatness of this dispensation by the Apostle Paul who prophesied that the Lord:

... hath purposed in himself: That in the dispensation of the fulness of times he might gather together in one all things in Christ, both which are in heaven, and which are on earth; even in him. (Ephesians 1:9-10.)

Blessings Await You

Would you like to receive the great blessing of being with the Savior and of meeting and conversing with the great persons of the past and the prophets of our own dispensation who have also made their contribution to the advancement of the Lord's work? The possibility of your being in this great assemblage is suggested in Doctrine and Covenants, Section 27, verse 14:

And also with all those whom my Father hath given me out of the world.

This is a wonderful promise given to the Saints of the latter days. But how shall this great blessing come to us? The remainder of the revelation gives the answer. It is necessary to

. . . take upon you my whole armor, that ye may be able to withstand the evil day, having done all, that ye may be able to stand. (*Ibid.*, 27:15.)

In taking upon oneself the full armor of the Lord is meant to be armored with "truth," "righteousness," "faith," the "Spirit," and then we shall have "peace" and eventual "salvation."

Chapter 19

SOME FUTURE EVENTS

(Section 29:1-29)

In the Prophet Joseph Smith's history, he does not provide us with information about the reason for receiving Section 29 of the Doctrine and Covenants except that it was given prior to the conference beginning September 26, 1830. The Church had been organized more than five months before this. We know that at the first time the angel Moroni visited the Prophet considerable emphasis was given by that holy messenger to what would transpire in the latter days. In his second appearance during the night of September 21-22, 1823, the Prophet said:

... he informed me of great judgments which were coming upon the earth, with great desolations by famine, sword, and pestilence; and these grievous judgments would come on the earth in this generation. ... (*DHC* I:14.)

That part of Section 29 which is reserved for this chapter deals, in general, with some of these judgments and events associated with them. In many revelations to be studied in this book, we learn about future events, one of the important contributions of the Doctrine and Covenants.

Chapter Divisions

For this chapter the revelation is divided into these parts: (1) introduction and the gathering of the elect (verses 1-8); (2) second coming of Jesus and the millennium (vs. 9-11); (3) the judgment (v. 12); (4) the first resurrection (v. 13); (5) signs preceding the second coming of Jesus (vs. 14-21); (6) events following the millennium. (Vs. 22-29.)

It seems needless to say that all of these subjects will not be given extensive discussion in this chapter, for they are found in subsequent revelations.

The Gathering of the Saints

Attention is drawn immediately in this revelation, as well as in others, to the fact that this divine message comes from our Redeemer who has atoned for our sins. Because Jesus has offered himself as the Savior, there is reason for his bringing together "as many as will hearken to my voice and humble themselves before me." (D&C 29:2.) The allusion to a hen gathering her chickens under her wings in verse 2 reminds one of the Savior's sorrow concerning those of Jerusalem who would not come into his fold because of wickedness. (Matt. 23:37.)

In the Dispensation of the Fulness of Times the Lord again calls upon all who will humble themselves in mighty prayer to respond to his call. Only those who hearken to his voice will make up his people. (D&C 45:28-29.) In the introduction to this revelation, however, the Lord directs his message to those who have already received the gospel; for, "your sins are forgiven you, therefore ye receive these things." (*Ibid.*, 29:3.)

This is a thought which we should keep in mind. Those who have become members of the kingdom of God and who truly humble themselves in the manner suggested receive great knowledge and guidance. And thus the six elders who were present when the revelation was given and who were chosen to declare the gospel were to be instructed in matters of great importance concerning the latter days. These elders, if they did not succumb to the adversary's temptings (v. 2) would enjoy the blessing of:

... Whatsoever ye shall ask in faith, being united in prayer according to my command, ye shall receive.

And ye are called to bring to pass the gathering of mine elect; for mine elect hear my voice and harden not their hearts. (*Ibid.*, 29:6-7.)

Faith, unity, prayer, and righteous living continue to bring success to the missionaries as they proclaim the gospel courageously.

As one studies these few verses (1-8), he discovers that there are two aspects to the principle of gathering. The first is being gathered out of the world into the kingdom of God, and this, it seems, is the phase of the gathering the Church is now in principally. Nephi saw this period of the latter days in vision:

And it came to pass that I, Nephi, beheld the power of the Lamb of God, that it descended upon the saints of the church of the Lamb, and upon the covenant people of the Lord, who were scattered upon all the face of the earth; and they were armed with righteousness and with the power of God in great glory.

. . . there were wars and rumors of wars among all the nations and kindreds of the earth.

. . . then, at that day, the work of the Father shall commence, in preparing the way for the fulfilling of his covenants, which he hath made to his people who are of the house of Israel. (1 Nephi 14:15, 17.)

In the second phase of the principle of gathering, Israel is to be gathered in unto one place. (D&C 29:8; 45:64-71.) The eventual center place for the gathering of the elect of the Lord will be in the New Jerusalem, indicated by revelation as the western part of Missouri.

In the meantime, there have been other gathering places where the Saints have been brought together to work out certain purposes of the Lord in these latter days. As already indicated by prophecy, that with the growth of the Church in the world, many places of gathering are appointed and may probably yet be appointed. This fact was revealed in a subsequent revelation, as follows:

Zion [New Jerusalem] shall not be moved out of her place, not withstanding her children are scattered.

They that remain, and are pure in heart, shall return, and come to their inheritances, they and their children, with songs of everlasting joy, to build up the waste places of Zion—

And all these things that the prophets might be fulfilled.

And, behold, there is none other place appointed than that which I have appointed; neither shall there be any other place appointed than that which I have appointed, for the work of the gathering of my saints—

Until the day cometh when there is found no more room for them; and then I have other places which I will appoint unto them, and they shall be called stakes, for the curtains or the strength of Zion.

Behold, it is my will, that all they who call on my name, and worship me according to mine everlasting gospel, should gather together and stand in holy places;

And prepare for the revelation which is to come, when the veil of the covering of my temple, in my tabernacle, which hideth the earth, shall be taken off, and all flesh shall see me together. (*Ibid.*, 101:17-23.)

The Lord declared that those who enter his Church are gathered out of the world. In the early part of the dispensation in which we live, calls were made upon the members to come together to work out the purposes of the Lord in Ohio, Missouri, Illinois, and then in the western part of the United States. The kingdom of God has flourished in its growth and power bringing about the continuing fulfillment of Nephi's prophecy that the Saints, though scattered among the nations, are armed with righteousness and the power of God. These Saints remain in the missions of the Church building up the work of the Lord in their places of conversion exercising their power in affecting for good the lives of their associates. Moreover stakes are continually being formed from mission areas.

The Second Coming of Jesus (D&C 29:9-11)

From the revelation quoted above (*ibid.*, 101), we learn a purpose of the gathering of the Saints—to prepare for the second coming of the Savior. This purpose is given in Section 29 verse 8 "to prepare their hearts and be prepared in all things against the day when tribulation and desolation are sent forth upon the wicked." There follows the plainly stated fact that the day is coming soon when all the wicked shall burn as stubble, in order that when the Lord comes he will dwell in righteousness with men on earth for the thousand years of the millennium.

The Twelve and Judgment (D&C 29:12)

It should be evident to all that the coming of Jesus in great power marks the beginning of the millennial period of peace and righteousness. (verse 11.) Preparation for that period is now going on.

Associated with the Redeemer at his coming will be the Twelve Apostles "which were with me in my ministry at Jerusalem." (*Ibid.*, 29:12.) These apostles will come clothed with robes of righteousness and with crowns upon their heads to judge the "whole house of Israel, even as many as have loved me and kept my commandments, and none else." (*Idem.*) After having proved themselves, the Twelve will receive their blessing as indicated.

Does this mean that included with the Twelve will be Judas, the betrayer of the Lord? It seems not. All this revelation states is that the Twelve who will come with the Lord will be those "which were with me in my ministry at Jerusalem." (*Idem.*) In order to fill the vacancy in that quorum, the remaining eleven apostles met and, under divine guidance, selected Matthias. He qualified as an apostle of that dispensation because he "companied with us all the time that the Lord Jesus went in and out among us, Beginning from the baptism of John, unto that same day that he was taken up from us." (Acts 1:21-22.) Matthias will come as a member of the Twelve in filling the office "from which Judas by transgression fell." (Acts 1:15-26.)

The power of judgeship will extend beyond those of Jesus' mortal ministry to include other branches of Israel led into other parts of the world, as the Nephite Twelve. (1 Nephi 12:9-10.)

The Resurrection (D&C 29:13)

In this verse we learn that at the second coming of Christ there will be a resurrection of those who "died in me":

For a trump shall sound both long and loud, even as upon Mount Sinai, and all the earth shall quake, and they shall come forth—yea, even the dead which died in me, to receive a crown of righteousness, and to be clothed upon, even as I am, to be with me, that we may be one. (*Ibid.*, 29:13.)

Who are those "which died in me"? This does not apply only to those who, it has been said, will judge the house of Israel—the Twelve. The crown of righteousness will also be received by those who faithfully kept the commandments, and they will be one with Jesus their Redeemer. This fact is indicated in other revelations, two of which are:

And the saints that are upon the earth, who are alive, shall be quickened and be caught up to meet him.
And they who have slept in their graves shall come forth, for their graves shall be opened; and they also shall be caught up to meet him in the midst of the pillar of heaven—
They are Christ's, the first fruits, they who shall descend with him first, and they who are on the earth and in their graves, who are first caught up to meet him; and all this by the voice of the sounding of the trump of the angel of God. (*Ibid.*, 88:96-98.)

And the graves of the saints shall be opened; and they shall come forth and stand on the right hand of the Lamb, when he shall stand upon Mount Zion, and upon the holy city, the New Jerusalem; and they shall sing the song of the Lamb, day and night forever and ever. (*Ibid.*, 133:56.)

Signs of the Times (D&C 29:14-21)

But, before the coming of the Savior, bringing with him the Twelve, the resurrected Saints, and the ushering in of his millennial reign, certain signs will be seen and known, in order that the nearness of Jesus' coming may be known to those who watch for that event.

These events of the last days, are said to consist of certain phenomena which are observed in the heavens, as well as in the earth beneath. (*Ibid.*, 29:14.) In that day there shall be "weeping and wailing among the hosts of men; And there shall be a great hailstorm sent forth to destroy the crops of the earth." (*Ibid.*, 29:15-16.)

In connection with these events heralding the Lord's coming, it would seem that all Latter-day Saints would desire and obey the counsel of their divinely appointed leaders by sustaining them in their office, not only by the upraised hand, but also by following that counsel. For example, we have been given counsel concerning the Church Welfare Program instituted by the Lord for the welfare of his people. We are admonished to participate in welfare projects that surpluses might be available to the Saints when in need. All too often, those who do contribute their time, talents, and means, are those who are already making contributions in many other ways in building up the kingdom of God. Is there not in the Welfare Program an opportunity for all to make a contribution which will redound to their temporal and eternal welfare?

And it shall come to pass, because of the wickedness of the world, that I will take vengeance upon the wicked, for they will not repent; for the cup of mine indignation is full; for behold, my blood shall not cleanse them if they hear me not. (*Ibid.*, 29:17.)

We are informed in the above verse that, because of the wickedness of the world, and it is well to notice that the world will not repent, vengeance will come to the inhabitants of the earth. The rebellious, those who harden their hearts in wickedness, must suffer. As the time draws near to the end of this dispensation, men may believe that they can seek refuge in the blood of Christ and be saved, but the Lord here declares that "the cup of mine indignation is full; for behold, my blood shall not cleanse them if they hear me not." (*Ibid.*, 29:17.)

"Wherefore, I the Lord God will send forth [judgments in the form of] flies . . . which . . . shall eat their flesh." (*Ibid.*, 29:18.) We may believe that diseases and plagues are indicated in verses 18 through 20 causing the conditions described there. All the abominations of the wicked world will not continue when Christ comes. "And the great and abominable church . . . shall be cast down." (*Ibid.*, 29:21.)

Events Following the Millennium (D&C 29:22-29)

When the Savior comes to reign upon the earth as Lord of Lords and King of Kings, the period of peace and righteousness will be ushered in. Conditions existing on the earth during the millennium are to be considered in a future chapter, but this revelation informs us of certain things to happen after the period of the millennium.

The first of these events is that men will deny their God:

And again, verily, verily, I say unto you that when the thousand years are ended, and men again begin to deny their God, then will I spare the earth but for a little season. (*Ibid.*, 29:22.)

Many persons will have been born during this period, which raises a question concerning the people who will have lived on the earth during the millennium. Will they be tempted by Satan and tried because they will not have had the same kind of trial as did those who lived before the millennium?

Brother Orson Pratt has said concerning this:

When the period called the Millennium has passed away, Satan will again be loosed. Now the query arises, Will Satan have power to deceive those who have lived on the earth, and have fallen asleep for a moment, and have received their immortal bodies? No, he will not. When they have passed through their probation, and have received their immortal bodies, Satan will have no power over them. Thus generation after generation will pass away, during the Millennium, but by and by, at the close of that period, unnumbered millions of the posterity of those who lived during the Millennium will be scattered in the four quarters of the earth, and Satan will be loosed, and will go forth and tempt them, and overcome some of them, so that they will rebel against God; not rebel in ignorance or dwindle in unbelief, as the Lamanites did; but they will sin wilfully against the law of heaven, and so great will the power of Satan be over them, that he will gather them together against the Saints and against the beloved city, and fire will come down out of heaven and consume them. (*Journal of Discourses* 16:322.)

With the earth being spared for a "little season":

And the end shall come, and the heaven and the earth shall be consumed and pass away, and there shall be a new heaven and a new earth.

For all old things shall pass away, and all things shall become new, even the heaven and the earth, and all the fulness thereof, both men and beasts, the fowls of the air, and the fishes of the sea;

And not one hair, neither more, shall be lost, for it is the workmanship of mine hand. (D&C 29:23-25.)

The final resurrection will come after the events spoken of in Section 29 of the Doctrine and Covenants and in Revelation, Chapter 20.

Then after the foregoing events—the loosing of Satan at the end of the millennium and the "little season" occur—there shall be the last resurrection of the dead called forth by Michael or Adam.

The closing event following the millennium is revealed by the Lord:

> And the righteous shall be gathered on my right hand unto eternal life; and the wicked on my left hand will I be ashamed to own before the Father;
>
> Wherefore I will say unto them—Depart from me, ye cursed, into everlasting fire, prepared for the devil and his angels.
>
> And now, behold, I say unto you, never at any time have I declared from mine own mouth that they should return, for where I am they cannot come, for they have no power. (*Ibid.*, 29:27-29.)

The extreme ends of salvation, eternal life (Godhood) for the righteous and everlasting condemnation for the wicked, are indicated in the foregoing verses. Notice how the Lord places the wicked (sons of perdition) in the place prepared for the devil and his angels from whence they shall not return, for they have no power. Subsequent revelations, to be studied, give us information concerning the grades of salvation intermediate between these two extremes.

Chapter 20

SPIRITUAL CREATIONS

(Section 29:30-50)

Understood in relationship to the material of Chapter 19, we shall see that this chapter dealing with some first principles of the plan of salvation, has a very definite bearing upon man's present and eternal welfare.

Spiritual and Temporal Existence

In Chapter 19 we learned, among other things, about a judgment to come upon the righteous and the wicked. Verse 30 of Section 29 points out that we should remember that all of the blessings for the righteous and the condemnation upon the wicked have not been made known.

Most important for our consideration is the fact stated in verses 31 and 32:

> For by the power of my Spirit created I them; yea, all things both spiritual and temporal—
> First spiritual, secondly temporal, which is the beginning of my work; and again, first temporal, and secondly spiritual, which is the last of my work. (D&C 29:31-32.)

When the Lord revealed that his creations were both spiritual and temporal and that the spiritual was first, a most significant truth was given. At this early period in the restoration of the gospel, the faithful members of the Church were being told something about their life before this earth was organized. About three years later (1833), the Lord also made known that Jesus was the Firstborn of his children and the rest of the human race was in the beginning with the Father. (*Ibid.*, 93:21, 23.)

Jesus Is Our Elder Brother

Because Jesus was the Firstborn in the spirit, or the eldest of God's children, he is our Elder Brother. It seems imperative that, as Latter-day Saints, we understand the greatness of the Redeemer as compared with the rest of our Father's spirit children. This difference is brought out by the following statement of the First Presidency and the Council of the Twelve issued June 30, 1916, as follows:

There is no impropriety, therefore, in speaking of Jesus Christ as the Elder Brother of the rest of human kind. That He is by spiritual birth Brother to the rest of us is indicated in Hebrews: "Wherefore in all things it behoved him to be made like unto his brethren, that he might be a merciful and faithful high priest in things pertaining to God, to make reconciliation for the sins of the people." (Hebrews 2:17.) Let it not be forgotten, however, that He is essentially greater than any and all others, by reason (1) of His seniority as the oldest or firstborn; (2) of His unique status in the flesh as the offspring of a mortal mother and of an immortal, or resurrected and glorified, Father; (3) of His selection and fore-ordination as the one and only Redeemer and Savior of the race; and (4) of His transcendent sinlessness.

Jesus Christ is not the Father of the spirits who have taken or yet shall take bodies upon this earth, for He is one of them. He is The Son, as they are sons or daughters of Elohim. (James E. Talmage, *Articles of Faith*, pp. 472-473.)

Man's Pre-Earth Life

Whereas, the Christian world teaches that the individual's first creation, or birth, was temporal without a spiritual life before entry into this mortal world, the gospel of Jesus Christ in its fulness gives a true understanding of man's divine origin.

The doctrine of man's spiritual creation is explained in a statement issued by the First Presidency composed of Joseph F. Smith, John R. Winder, and Anthon H. Lund:

Adam, our great progenitor, "the first man," was, like Christ, a pre-existent spirit, and like Christ he took upon him an appropriate body, the body of a man, and so became a "living soul." The doctrine of the pre-existence,—revealed so plainly, particularly in latter days, pours a wonderful flood of light upon the otherwise mysterious problem of man's origin. It shows that man, as a spirit, was begotten and born of heavenly parents, and reared to maturity in the eternal mansions of the Father, prior to coming upon the earth in a temporal body to undergo an experience in mortality. It teaches that all men existed in the spirit before any man existed in the flesh, and that all who have inhabited the earth since Adam have taken bodies and become souls in like manner. ("The Origin of Man," *Improvement Era*, Vol. XIII, November 1909, page 80.)

Animal and Plant Creation

Not only was man created in the spirit first, but also the rest of God's creations. The revelations speak of this spiritual creation as including vegetation and animal. How clearly this is spoken of in these verses:

And every plant of the field before it was in the earth, and every herb of the field before it grew. For I, the Lord God, created all things, of which I have spoken, spiritually, before they were naturally upon the face of the earth. For I, the Lord God, had not caused it to rain upon the face of the earth. And I, the Lord God, had created all the children of men; and not yet a man to till the ground; for in heaven created I them; and there was not yet flesh upon the earth, neither in the water, neither in the air. (Pearl of Great Price, Moses 3:5.)

... that which is spiritual being in the likeness of that which is temporal; and that which is temporal in the likness of that which is spiritual; the spirit of man in the likeness of his person, as also the spirit of the beast, and every other creature which God has created. (D&C 77:2.)

Creations Are Eternal

From the scriptures we learn some important truths relative to the creations of God: (1) they constitute an *organizing* of already existing *eternal* material (*ibid.*,

131:7); and (2) that his creations will therefore continue to exist as a part of the resurrection. (See *ibid.*, 29:23-25.) These truths are pointed out in the statement made by the First Presidency in this way:

> By His almighty power He organized the earth, and all that it contains, from spirit and element, which exist co-eternally with Himself. He formed every plant that grows, and every animal that breathes, each after its own kind, spiritually and temporally —"that which is spiritual being in the likeness of that which is temporal, and that which is temporal in the likeness of that which is spiritual." He made the tadpole and the ape, the lion and the elephant; but He did not make them in His own image, nor endow them with Godlike reason and intelligence. Nevertheless, the whole animal creation will be perfected and perpetuated in the Hereafter, each class in its "distinct order or sphere," and will enjoy "eternal felicity." That fact has been made plain in this dispensation. [D&C 77:3.] ("The Origin of Man," *Improvement Era*, Vol. XIII, November 1909, page 81.)

Spiritual and Temporal

Basic to much of Latter-day Saint teachings concerning how the spirit sons and daughters of God should understand the way they should live in mortality is found in these verses:

> Speaking unto you that you may naturally understand; but unto myself my works have no end, neither beginning; but it is given unto you that ye may understand, because ye have asked it of me and are agreed.
>
> Wherefore, verily I say unto you that all things unto me are spiritual, and not at any time have I given unto you a law which was temporal; neither any man, nor the children of men; neither Adam, your father, whom I created.
>
> Behold, I gave unto him that he should be an agent unto himself; and I gave unto him commandments, but no temporal commandment gave I unto him, for my commandments are spiritual; they are not natural nor temporal, neither carnal nor sensual. (D&C 29:33-35.)

An understanding of many of the revelations which follow in these chapters is devoted to the proper interpretation of the foregoing truth. Commandments to build houses, sell or retain property, and other similar activities will engage our attention later. These activities are the basis of many of the accomplishments of our people and also for what may be done in the future. These statements from some of our leaders of the past express the Latter-day Saint point of view:

Brigham Young:

With God, and also with those who understand the principles of life and salvation, the Priesthood, the oracles of truth and the gifts and callings of God to the children of men, there is no difference in spiritual and temporal labors—all are one. If I am in the line of my duty, I am doing the will of God, whether I am preaching, praying, laboring with my hands for an honorable support; whether I am in the field, mechanic's shop, or following mercantile business, or wherever duty calls, I am serving God as much in one place as another; and so it is with all, each in his place, turn and time. (*Journal of Discourses* 13:260.)

Joseph F. Smith:

You must continue to bear in mind that the temporal and the spiritual are blended. They are not separate. One cannot be carried on without the other, so long as we are here in mortality.
. . .
The Latter-day Saints believe not only in the gospel of spiritual salvation, but also in the gospel of temporal salvation.
. . .
The work that we are engaged in is not designed to be limited by the spiritual necessities of the people alone. It is the purpose of God in restoring the gospel and the Holy Priesthood not only to benefit mankind spiritually, but also to benefit them temporally. (*Gospel Doctrine,* pp. 208-209.)

Adam and the Devil

In continuation of our study of "first things" as they are made known in this important revelation, we have our attention drawn again to the pre-earth life.

The "origin" of Satan's rebellion, the number of the spirits who followed him, the fact of free agency as a principle in the pre-existence, the eventual home of the devil's miserable horde, and the place of his operations in the lives of us mortals are all indicated in these verses:

And it came to pass that Adam, being tempted of the devil— for, behold, the devil was before Adam, for he rebelled against me, saying, Give me thine honor, which is my power; and also a third part of the hosts of heaven turned he away from me because of their agency;

And they were thrust down, and thus came the devil and his angels;

And, behold, there is a place prepared for them from the beginning, which place is hell.

And it must needs be that the devil should tempt the children of men, or they could not be agents unto themselves; for if they never should have bitter they could not know the sweet—(D&C 29:36-39.)

Adam and the Fall

It should be apparent to all Latter-day Saints that basic to an understanding of the purpose of life is an acceptance of the account given in the scriptures that Adam was a real historical person, and of the rebellion of Satan. (Abraham 3:23-35; Moses 4:1-4.) Adam's place in the plan of salvation is such an important one that it was formulated in the heavens before the foundations of the earth were laid. It seems that Adam's place in the divine plan was necessary that there be an opportunity for making possible the union of the spirit of man and a mortal body. What is called the fall of Adam is but a means of giving further opportunities for the progression of the spirit sons and daughters of God. We obtain knowledge from this modern revelation of what happened to Adam as a result of his partaking of the forbidden fruit and also of the effect of that act upon his posterity. It is declared that Adam "became subject to the will of the Devil, because he yielded unto temptation" and:

Wherefore, I, the Lord God, caused that he should be cast out from the Garden of Eden, from my presence, because of his transgression, wherein he became spiritually dead, which is the first death, even that same death which is the last death, which is spiritual, which shall be pronounced upon the wicked when I shall say: Depart, ye cursed.

But, behold, I say unto you that I, the Lord God, gave unto Adam and unto his seed, that they should not die as to the temporal death, until I, the Lord God, should send forth angels to declare unto them repentance and redemption, through faith on the name of mine Only Begotten Son.

And thus did I, the Lord God, appoint unto man the days of his probation—that by his natural death he might be raised in immortality unto eternal life, even as many as would believe;

And they that believe not unto eternal damnation; for they cannot be redeemed from their spiritual fall, because they repent not;

For they love darkness rather than light, and their deeds are evil, and they receive their wages of whom they list to obey. (D&C 29:41-45.)

With these scriptures before us, we see that in yielding to temptation Adam became subject to two penalties: (1) spiritual death, or banishment from the presence of God, and (2) temporal death, or separation of his spirit and mortal body.

In the process of time Adam died the temporal death. By breaking the commandment, he became mortal and subject to sin; therefore, he could no longer remain in the presence of God.

So it is with us, Adam's posterity, we die the temporal death, and we also become spiritually dead when we transgress God's commandments at the age of accountability, which is eight years. In order that Adam and his posterity might know of the way they might become spiritually alive and become prepared to enter into the Lord's presence, revelations were given to Adam by angels. The gospel plan was available to them that they might exercise faith in Jesus, the Only Begotten of the Father. Through the atonement wrought by the Savior, man is rescued from the grave to immortality, or resurrection; and if he has been faithful to the covenants received in the gospel, he may enter into his exaltation, or eternal life. But for those who do not repent, either in this life or in the spirit world, they must remain spiritually dead.

In this revelation, it is pointed out that those that believe not will go to eternal damnation and cannot be redeemed from their spiritual fall, because they do not repent.

This is called the second death, and is not to be understood as a separation of spirit and body after being resurrected.

Children and the Fall

Death of the body comes to all by reason of the fall of Adam. Death is as essential as is birth in the eternal plan. (Moses 6:59.) "It hath passed upon all men, to fulfil the merciful plan of the great Creator." (2 Nephi 9:6.) Many who travel through life suffer pain, sorrow, and the vicissitudes of our mortality. Often the mortal body becomes decrepit and worn out. At times there seems to be little reason for continued existence, but in the plan of our Eternal Father there is reason.

The problem which is often brought to parents' attention so forcefully is the death of a little child or the inability to bring a child into mortal life after once the biological processes of growth have begun. These are problems for which we do not yet have full and complete answers. We do know, as believers in the scriptures, that the Lord has declared little children to be blameless before him. They come into this life innocent. (D&C 93:38.) Therefore, the fall of Adam does not affect their relationship to their salvation before the Lord. The Lord has also made known that:

But behold, I say unto you, that little children are redeemed from the foundation of the world through mine Only Begotten;

Wherefore, they cannot sin, for power is not given unto Satan to tempt little children, until they begin to become accountable before me;

For it is given unto them even as I will, according to mine own pleasure, that great things may be required at the hand of their fathers. (*Ibid.*, 29:46-48; cf., 74:7.)

The atonement of Jesus Christ redeems little children whereby they do not need the ordinance of baptism for their salvation. (Moroni 8:11-20.)

Those parents who lose a child before the age of accountability, or eight years (*ibid.*, 68:25), may be assured as to their salvation in the celestial kingdom. Concerning this, the Lord made known to Joseph Smith "that all children who die before they arrive at the years of accountability, are saved in the celestial kingdom of heaven." (*DHC* 2:381.) If one will keep before him the truth that the most important thing in life for those little ones, and for us, is life itself, the taking of a mortal body whereby there is assured a resurrection of the body joined with the spirit eternally, much of the sting of death is removed.

Prenatal Death

Closely associated with the problem of life and its importance in the plan of salvation is the time when the spirit enters the body, whether before birth or when the breath of life is taken at birth. If the spirit enters the body before birth, then we would believe that the resurrection will come to the so-called "stillborn."

In an article by the First Presidency, consisting of Joseph F. Smith, Anthon H. Lund, and Charles W. Penrose, we find this statement:

True, it is that the body of man enters upon its career as a tiny germ or embryo, which becames an infant, *quickened at a certain stage by the spirit* whose tabernacle it is, and the child, after being born, develops into a man. ("The Origin of Man," *Improvement Era,* Vol. XIII, November 1909, page 80. Italics by author.)

In other words, the answer to the problem is indefinite, and no attempt was made by the First Presidency to answer whether the spirit enters the body before or after birth. On the other hand, opinions have been expressed, and they should be known as opinions, but, in the main they express hope and encouragement to parents.

Mentally Retarded Persons

The revelation we are studying ends with these words:

And, again, I say unto you, that whoso having knowledge, have I not commanded to repent?

And he that hath no understanding, it remaineth in me to do according as it is written. And now I declare no more unto you at this time. Amen. (D&C 29:49-50.)

Those persons who are deficient mentally, having not understanding, seem to be in the same relationship as children—blameless before God. As children, they do not require the ordinance of baptism for their salvation, but they are in the hands of the all-wise Father. They apparently are in the class who are "without the law." Of these the prophet Mormon wrote to his son Moroni:

For behold that all little children are alive in Christ, and also all they that are without the law. For the power of redemption cometh on all them that have no law; wherefore, he that is not condemned, or he that is under no condemnation, cannot repent; and unto such baptism availeth nothing. (Moroni 8:22.)

Unto whom much is given, much is required, but unto whom little is given, little is required, is the letter and the spirit of the scriptures.

Chapter 21

LESSONS IN OBEDIENCE

(Sections 30 and 31)

A conference of the Church was appointed for September 1830, but just prior to this assemblage the Prophet Joseph Smith and others had gone to stay with the Whitmers at Fayette township, New York. As we have learned from Chapter 18, Hiram Page claimed to receive revelations for the Church. When the Prophet learned about Brother Page and his seer stone, it brought sorrow to him because of the influence which Satan had upon some of the members of the Church in deceiving them. Because of these conditions, revelations numbered 28 and 29 were received.

When the September conference convened, the subject of the seer stone was discussed. It developed that Brother Page and those who had been influenced by him recognized that only one person was empowered to receive revelation for the Church. They, therefore, renounced the purported revelations and harmony was restored. It was at the conclusion of this conference that the two revelations pertaining to this chapter were received—Sections 30 and 31.

In What Do You Place Your Trust?

The short revelation numbered Section 30 is directed to the three sons of Peter Whitmer, Senior, at whose home the Prophet was staying. Before this time, the Lord had made known that these men — David, Peter, and John—had a calling to make known the truths of the everlasting gospel. This opportunity to participate in the Lord's work was to be of utmost worth to them in

bringing souls unto the Lord. (Sections 14, 15, and 16.)
The time had now come when they were to "declare repentance unto this generation." (Section 30:4, 5, 9-11.)

It appears that the revelation to David Whitmer
(verses 1-4) constitutes a rebuke for his following Hiram
Page with his purported revelations. The words of the
Lord to David may also be pertinent to us as a lesson in
obedience. Consider yourself as being taught by the Lord
in these words:

> . . . you have feared man and have not relied on me for
> strength as you ought.
>
> But your mind has been on the things of the earth more
> than on the things of me, your Maker, and the ministry where-
> unto you have been called; and you have not given heed unto my
> Spirit, and to those who were set over you, but have been per-
> suaded by those whom I have not commanded. (D&C 30:1-2.)

As a member of the Church, wherein have you
trusted in man rather than trusted implicitly in the
word of the Lord? How often have you, as a worker in
the Church, considered the things of the earth (world)
to be of more importance than the work of your Maker?
Have you given heed to the Spirit and to those who have
been placed over you, or have you been influenced by
other considerations, be it men, women, or the material
things of life? If so, how thankful we should be for the
principle of repentance, a part of which is the resolution
to do better. What lesson does this provide for us? We
must lay a secure foundation on the principles of truth
with the knowledge that deviation from the course of the
Lord leads to lost privileges and blessings.

Lesson from the Life of Thomas B. Marsh

To understand Section 31 of The Doctrine and Covenants we should know something about Thomas B.
Marsh to whom this revelation was directed.

The life story of Brother Marsh affords us an opportunity to learn several lessons. In addition to the important principle of obedience, we learn lessons of the necessity to follow the leadership of those over us in the Church, and that any person may depart from the truth, the consequences of which bring sorrow. Furthermore, repentance may not always restore one to his former standing in the kingdom of God.

For a period of about eight years Brother Marsh was a devoted member of the Church, but in a year of apostasy, when several of the leading brethren became disaffected, he was excommunicated (in 1839). In 1857 at Florence, Nebraska, he was rebaptized and came to Utah where he spent his last days.

Spirit of Apostasy

Shortly after Thomas B. Marsh was baptized, the Lord gave a revelation, Section 31, directed to him through the Prophet Joseph Smith. Of special interest to us are verses nine and twelve which read as follows:

Be patient in afflictions, revile not against those that revile. Govern your house in meekness, and be steadfast. . . .

Pray always, lest you enter into temptation and lose your reward. (*Ibid.*, 31:9, 12.)

This counsel is prophetic in view of Brother Marsh's apostasy. Elder George A. Smith in a general conference address tells the following reason for this apostasy:

When the Saints were living in Far West, the wife of Marsh and Sister Harris agreed to exchange milk, in order to enable each of them to make a larger cheese than they could do separately. Each was to take the other the "strippings" as well as the rest of the milk. Mrs. Harris performed her part of the agreement, but Mrs. Marsh kept a pint of "strippings" from each cow. When this became known the matter was brought before the Teachers, and these decided against Mrs. Marsh. An appeal was taken to the Bishop. He sustained the Teachers. If Marsh had obeyed the Revelation and governed his house in humility and with steadfastness, he would have righted the wrong done, but instead of doing so, he appealed to the High Council. Marsh, who at the time was President of the Twelve, possibly thought that the Council would favor him, but that body confirmed the Bishop's decision. He was not yet satisfied, but appealed to the First Presidency, and Joseph, the Prophet, and his two Counsellors consented to review the case. They approved the finding of the High Council. Was Marsh satisfied then? No. With the persistency of Lucifer himself, he declared that he would uphold the character of his wife, "even if he had to go to hell for it." (*Doctrine and Covenants Commentary*, p. 167.)

Follow Leadership

Concerning this circumstance, Elder Heber C. Kimball told a Salt Lake congregation that about the time Brother Marsh was preparing to leave the Church, he received a personal revelation consisting of from three to five pages, which he read to Brothers Kimball and Brigham Young.

In it God told him what to do, and that was to sustain brother Joseph and to believe that what brother Joseph said was true. But no; he took a course to sustain his wife and oppose the Prophet of God, and she led him away. . . .

We told him that if he would listen to that revelation he had received, he would be saved; but he listened to his wife, and away he went. (*Journal of Discourses*, 5:28, 29.)

The seriousness of Marsh's apostasy is indicated in the further comment made by Brother George A. Smith upon the occasion mentioned above.

The then President of the Twelve Apostles, the man who should have been the first to do justice and cause reparation to be made for wrong, committed by any member of his family, took that position, and what next? He went before a magistrate and swore that the "Mormons" were hostile to the State of Missouri. That affidavit brought from the government of Missouri an exterminating order, which drove some 15,000 Saints from their homes and habitations, and some thousands perished through suffering the exposure consequent on this state of affairs. (*Doctrine and Covenants Commentary*, p. 167.)

Man May Fall from Grace

In a short autobiography, Brother Marsh wrote that after he had apostatized he went to Richmond, Missouri, where he met David, John, and Jacob Whitmer and Oliver Cowdery, who had all apostatized:

> I enquired seriously of David if it was true that he had seen an angel, according to his testimony as one of the witnesses of the Book of Mormon. He replied as sure as there is a God in heaven, he saw the angel according to his testimony in that book. ... I interrogated Oliver Cowdery in the same manner, who answered similarly. (*Millennial Star,* Vol. 26, page 406.)

It will be remembered that Thomas B. Marsh, as one of the members of the first Quorum of the Twelve, was a testator to the truth of the book of Doctrine and Covenants. A general assembly of the Church was held in Kirtland, Ohio, on August 17, 1835, to take into consideration the work of a committee appointed to compile the revelations into a book. This action was taken "to see whether the book be approved or not by the authorities of the Church: that it may, if approved, become a law and rule of faith and practice to the Church." During the course of the meetings Brother W. W. Phelps read the written testimony of the Twelve, as it appears in the "Explanatory Introduction" to The Doctrine and Covenants. (The minutes of this assembly comprise chapter 18 of the *Documentary History of the Church*, Volume II.)

Notwithstanding the great manifestation which came to the three special witnesses of The Book of Mormon and the Lord bearing record to the souls of the witnesses to The Doctrine and Covenants through the Holy Ghost shed forth upon them, some of these witnesses apostatized and were excommunicated. It is not our pres ent purpose to suggest all of the reasons why men having such testimonies do depart from the truth, but the important thing for us is to learn lessons from the experiences of those who have become apostate.

When The Church of Jesus Christ of Latter-day Saints was organized, the Lord declared that a person might fall away from the truth.

And we know that all men must repent and believe on the name of Jesus Christ, and worship the Father in his name, and endure in faith on his name to the end, or they cannot be saved in the kingdom of God.

But there is a possibility that man may fall from grace and depart from the living God;

Therefore let the church take heed and pray always, lest they fall into temptation;

Yea, and even let those who are sanctified take heed also. (D&C 20:29, 32-34.)

From What Do Men Fall?

And so it has been. But from what do men fall away? Here is Brigham Young's answer:

Everything that there is good, pure, holy, god-like, exalting, ennobling, extending the ideas, the capacities of the intelligent beings that our Heavenly Father has brought forth upon this earth.

What will the apostate receive in exchange? Continuing, President Young said:

I can comprehend it in a very few words. These would be the words that I should use: death, hell and the grave. That is what they will get in exchange. We may go into the particulars of that which they experience. They experience darkness, ignorance, doubt, pain, sorrow, grief, mourning, unhappiness; no person to condole with in the hour of trouble, no arm to lean upon in the day of calamity, no eye to pity when they are forlorn and cast down; and I comprehend it by saying death, hell and the grave. This is what they will get in exchange for their apostasy from the Gospel of the Son of God. (*Journal of Discourses* 16: 160.)

When Brother Marsh returned to the Church, he bore witness that his period of apostasy was one of misery and affliction. He stated:

. . . let no one feel too secure; for, before you think of it, your steps will slide. You will not then think nor feel for a moment as you did before you lost the Spirit of Christ; for when men apostatize, they are left to grovel in the dark. (*Journal of Discourses* 5:206.)

Follow a Straight Course

But what is it that leads members of the Church from the truth? In the case of Brother Marsh, it seemed such a small thing in what his wife did, but he, as he confessed later, was a very "stiffnecked man." Many times it is the small, inconsequential thing that leads one away, as President Young one time put it:

Very trifling affairs are generally the commencement of their divergence from the right path. If we follow a compass, the needle of which does not point correctly, a very slight deviation in the beginning will lead us, when we have traveled some distance, far to one side of the true point for which we are aiming. (*Journal of Discourses* 12:125.)

On the other hand, if we adhere to the commandments of the Lord, keeping a steady course on the straight way to eternal life, we shall secure to ourselves joy and happiness in this life and the crown of righteousness in the life to come. In this connection, The Book of Mormon prophet, Alma, counseled his son Helaman by making reference to the compass or director which worked according to their fathers' faith in God, as follows:

Therefore, they tarried in the wilderness, or did not travel a direct course, and were afflicted with hunger and thirst, because of their transgressions.

And now, my son, I would that ye should understand that these things are not without a shadow; for as our fathers were slothful to give heed to this compass (now these things were temporal) they did not prosper; even so it is with things which are spiritual.

For behold, it is as easy to give heed to the word of Christ, which will point to you a straight course to eternal bliss, as it was for our fathers to give heed to this compass, which would point unto them a straight course to the promised land.

And now I say, is there not a type in this thing? For just as surely as this director did bring our fathers, by following its course, to the promised land, shall the words of Christ, if we follow their course, carry us beyond this vale of sorrow into a far better land of promise. . . .

See that ye look to God and live. . . . (Alma 37:42-45, 47.)

What else is there which leads people from the kingdom of God? As in the case of Thomas B. Marsh, it was an unwillingness to follow the leadership of the Church, but to become a law unto himself. When men and women feel that they can flaunt the laws of God and thereby become independent of the counsel of their leaders in the Church, whether it be the bishop, stake president, or the General Authorities, they set for themselves a course of action, which, if not repented of, will lead to loss of the Spirit of the Lord and eventual apostasy.

Notice how this rejection of the counsel of those over Brother Marsh lost for him the Spirit of the Lord in the case mentioned above by Elder George A. Smith. The loss of the Spirit brought blindness to him, and he spent his time in looking for the evil:

. . . and then, when the Devil began to lead me, it was easy for the carnal mind to rise up, which is anger, jealousy, and wrath. . . . I thought I saw a beam in Brother Joseph's [Smith] eye, but is was nothing but a mote, and my own eye was filled with the beam . . . and as Brother Heber [Kimball] says, I got mad, and wanted everybody else to be mad. I talked with Brother Brigham and Brother Heber, and I wanted them to be mad like myself; and I saw they were not mad. . . . Brother Brigham, with a cautious look, said, "Are you the leader of the Church, Brother Thomas?" I answered, "No." "Well then," said he, "Why do you not let that alone?" (*Journal of Discourses* 5:207.)

Contrast—Obedience and Disobedience

On the other hand, if Thomas B. Marsh had applied the admonition given him years before in the revelation from which this part of our chapter is taken (Section 31: 9, 12), and, when the time of deviation from the straight course of the gospel plan began, if he had repented, great would have been his blessings. Sometimes a contrast sharpens one's understanding of such possibilities. About the same period when Brother Marsh apostatized, Elder Parley P. Pratt partook of the spirit of apostasy. In relating his own experience, we may also learn a lesson:

About this time, [1837], after I had returned from Canada, there were jarrings and discords in the Church at Kirtland, and many fell away and became enemies and apostates. There were also envyings, lyings, strifes and divisions, which caused much trouble and sorrow. By such spirits I was also accused, misrepresented and abused. And at one time, I also was overcome by the same spirit in a great measure, and it seemed as if the very powers of darkness which war against the Saints were let loose upon me. But the Lord knew my faith, my zeal, my integrity of purpose, and he gave me the victory.

I went to brother Joseph Smith in tears, and, with a broken heart and contrite spirit, confessed wherein I had erred in spirit, murmured, or done or said amiss. He frankly forgave me, prayed for me and blessed me. Thus, by experience, I learned more fully to discern and to contrast the two spirits, and to resist the one and cleave to the other. And, being tempted in all points, even as others, I learned how to bear with, and excuse, and succor those who are tempted. (*Autobiography of Parley P. Pratt*, 1874 Edition, pp. 183-184.)

Summary

How does one lose a testimony of the gospel? It does not come abruptly, but, in most instances, gradually. We may well consider the masterful way in which the late Elder John A. Widtsoe answered this question:

> Starvation of a testimony usually begins with failure to keep properly in touch with divine forces, to pray. Then, desire to learn and to live the gospel law soon weakens. Sacred covenants are forgotten. Study of the gospel is set aside for some other study or activity. There is less and less participation in the life of the Church. Eyes are blurred so that the laws of life are forgotten.
>
> There are many attacks by the evil one upon a weakening testimony. Commonly, a feeling of superiority, ending in ambition for office, overshadows all else and leads to testimony starvation. Personal ambition has always been a destructive force in human lives. Sometimes, and closely related to the feeling of superiority, are false interpretations of scripture. These rise to such magnitude, though at variance with accepted, revealed doctrine, that they endanger the spiritual life of the individual. The various cults that arise, like mushrooms, from time to time, are but variations of this manner of destroying a testimony. They can always be recognized, for they are in opposition to some principle or regulation of the Church.
>
> Most frequently, however, the loss of a testimony is due to finding fault with one's fellow believers, and with the leadership of the Church. Every action of bishop, stake president, or General Authority seems wrong to such unfortunate people. Their vision distorts the world and all in it.
>
> The dying testimony is easily recognized. The organizations and practices of the Church are ignored; the radio takes the place of the sacrament meeting; golf or motion pictures, the Sunday worship; the cup of coffee, instead of the Word of Wisdom; the cold, selfish hand instead of helpfulness, charity for the poor, and the payment of tithing.
>
> Soon, the testimony is gone, and the former possessor walks about, somewhat sour and discontented, and always in his heart, unhappy. He has lost his most precious possession, and has found nothing to replace it. He has lost inward freedom, the gift of obedience to law. ("What Does It Mean to Have a Testimony?" *Improvement Era*, May 1945, pp. 273, 280.)

Chapter 22

AND THE KINGDOM GREW

(Sections 32, 33, and 34)

Before the Church was organized in this dispensation, the Lord revealed that the field was white already to harvest and that to those who thrust in their sickle with their might, rich treasures would accrue in the saving of souls in the kingdom of God. Concurrent with this promise The Book of Mormon was translated and published to the world as a new witness for Jesus as the Savior. The Lord had made known, early in this dispensation, that it was his purpose to bring The Book of Mormon information of the Nephites and Lamanites to their descendants. (D&C 10:48-51.) In addition, this divine record indicated great promises and blessings for the descendants of Lehi. (2 Nephi 30:5; 3 Nephi 5:22, 23; 21:26.)

Appointment of Missionaries to the Lamanites

By the time the conference of September 26, 1830, convened, there was considerable interest shown toward the Lamanites on the part of some of the elders present. Before this conference, however, the Lord by revelation had called Oliver Cowdery on a mission to this people. (D&C 28:8-10.) Peter Whitmer, Jun. and Ziba Peterson assigned to accompany him. (*Ibid.*, 30:5-6)

Conversion of Parley P. Pratt

Parley P. Pratt had accepted the gospel only one month before this time (October 1830). His conversion to the gospel in receiving a testimony of the truth of The Book of Mormon is typical of the manner in which the kingdom of God has grown. In his own words, we read:

I opened it with eagerness, and read its title page. I then read the testimony of several witnesses in relation to the manner of its being found and translated. After this I commenced its contents by course. I read all day; eating was a burden, I had no desire for food; sleep was a burden when the night came, for I preferred reading to sleep.

As I read, the spirit of the Lord was upon me, and I knew and comprehended that the book was true, as plainly and manifestly as a man comprehends and knows that he exists. My joy was now full, as it were, and I rejoiced sufficiently to more than pay me for all the sorrows, sacrifices and toils of my life. I soon determined to see the young man who had been the instrument of its discovery and translation. (*Autobiography of Parley P. Pratt*, 1874 Edition, page 38.)

The strength of his conversion was so great that he traveled to Palmyra, New York, the home of the Smith family, for further information. Hyrum Smith, the Prophet's brother, who had already been promised that he would have "the power of God unto the convincing of men" (D&C 11:21), and Parley P. Pratt remained up almost all of the night discussing the claims of The Church of Jesus Christ of Latter-day Saints. After leaving the Smith home the following morning, he continued his account:

This discovery greatly enlarged my heart, and filled my soul with joy and gladness. I esteemed the Book, or the information contained in it, more than all the riches of the world. Yes; I verily believe that I would not at that time have exchanged the knowledge I then possessed, for a legal title to all the beautiful farms, houses, villages and property which passed in review before me, on my journey through one of the most flourishing settlements of western New York. (*Autobiography of Parley P. Pratt*, 1874 Edition, p. 40.)

Sidney Rigdon a Convert

The Prophet Joseph Smith wrote in his history of the Church (*DHC*) that soon after the appointment of the brethren to this Lamanite mission, they journeyed west-

ward preaching in the various villages through which
they traveled. In the vicinity of Kirtland, Ohio, their missionary efforts among the white people brought immediate results. Brother Pratt had been a preacher for the
organization known as "Disciples of Christ" or "Campbellites" before his conversion to the true gospel. It was
because of his activities in that organization that he
stopped over to visit with friends belonging to that
church. Among these people was Sidney Rigdon, who
presided over one of these same churches. The missionary
practice followed today of presenting The Book of Mormon to missionary contacts was done in this case. Sidney
Rigdon indicated that, although he believed the Bible to
be a revelation from God, he did not feel the same way
about The Book of Mormon. This being the first time,
however, that he had seen the book he would read it with
the purpose of determining whether or not it was of God.

By permission of Mr. Rigdon, the missionaries were
given the opportunity to preach to his congregation.
When this was done, Mr. Rigdon told his people that
what they had heard was of such an extraordinary character that it required their most serious consideration.
These missionaries converted a number of Mr. Rigdon's
parishioners. Within two weeks, and after careful reading of The Book of Mormon, together with prayer, Mr.
Rigdon was fully convinced of the truth of the work.

The Lamanite Mission by Parley P. Pratt

Parley P. Pratt has given us our best first-hand account of the Lamanite mission with its successes among
the white people in Ohio especially, as well as the work
accomplished among the Lamanites. (*Autobiography of
Parley P. Pratt*, pp. 49-50.)

In and around the Kirtland region the interest in the
message of the missionaries was so high that people
thronged by night and day so that the missionaries hardly
had time for rest.

Meetings were convened in different neighborhoods, and multitudes came together soliciting our attendance; while thousands flocked about us daily; some to be taught, some for curiosity, some to obey the gospel, and some to dispute or resist it. (*Ibid.*, p. 50.)

In two or three weeks from the time of their arrival in that region, the missionaries had baptized one hundred and twenty-seven, and before long it had increased to one thousand. Simeon Carter, who is mentioned in some revelations later, upon reading The Book of Mormon, walked fifty miles to Kirtland where he was baptized and ordained an elder. He returned to his home and within a short time a branch of the Church was organized there with sixty members.

The missionaries continued their journey farther west preaching to both whites and Indians until they reached the western frontier in Jackson County, Missouri.

Brother Pratt relates that this was about fifteen hundred miles from where they started, most of which was traveled by foot over a period of four months. The missionaries had preached the gospel to tens of thousands of people, including two nations of Indians. This was the first mission of the Church west of New York State. During this time many hundreds of people were converted to the true Church.

Just west of Independence, Missouri, was the settlement of the Delaware Indians whose interest in The Book of Mormon increased day by day until nearly the whole tribe began to become responsive to its message. The excitement thus created came to the attention of sectarian missionaries and Indian agents who ordered the Latter-day Saint missionaries from the area. "Thus ended our first Indian Mission," wrote Brother Pratt, "in which we had preached the gospel in its fulness, and distributed the record of their forefathers among three tribes, viz.: the Cattaraugus Indians, near Buffalo, New York, the Wyandots of Ohio, and the Delawares west of Missouri." (*Ibid.*, p. 61.)

Thus the kingdom of God grew, with the greatest success among the Gentiles. The Book of Mormon was one of the principal means which gave the truth-seeker a testimony that the gospel of Jesus Christ had been restored.

In the true missionary spirit, Brother Pratt continued:

> We trust that at some future day, when the servants of God go forth in power to the remnant of Joseph, some precious seed will be found growing in their hearts, which was sown by us in that early day. (*Idem.*)

Today's Activities

Since 1830 our people have taken the message of The Book of Mormon to the descendants of Father Lehi. In recent years a renewed effort has been made to proselyte the Indians in the United States. One of the first tribes to be contacted in the eastern states was the Catteraugus tribe near Buffalo. Because of this missionary work among these Indians, a branch of the Church presided over by a Lamanite convert on that reservation, is in operation. A Church-owned chapel was dedicated there in 1957.

The Book of Mormon was a new volume of scripture and a powerful converter of men, and it was the means by which many of the missionaries and investigators learned of great fundamental teachings of the gospel of Jesus Christ. (See Chapter 13.)

Section 33

In The Doctrine and Covenants, Section 33, Ezra Thayer and Northrop Sweet were called to preach the gospel. (verse 2.) In calling these brethren to this work, the revelation provides us with an understanding of the reason for the growth of the kingdom of God and the need for participation in missionary activities.

There was an urgent need in the beginning of this dispensation for people to know that the world religiously had become corrupted. A great apostasy or falling away from the teachings of the Savior had made its inroads into every part of the Lord's vineyard.

And my vineyard has become corrupted every whit; and there is none which doeth good save it be a few; and they err in many instances because of priestcrafts, all having corrupt minds. (D&C 33:4; see also 2 Nephi 26:29.)

The importance of this evaluation of the world, when given, and as an evidence for the truth of the restored gospel, is well stated in the following comment on this verse:

Many object to the teachings of the gospel on the subject of the deviation from the original pattern. They take exception to the picture of total corruption presented but this only confirms the truth of the gospel. We have in holy writ successive portraits of human nature taken at various times. One was taken before the deluge: "All flesh had corrupted his way upon the earth." (Gen. 6:12.) Another is presented by Eliphaz, in Job: "Man, which drinketh iniquity like water." (Job 15:16.) David viewed the conditions in this light: "The Lord looked down from heaven upon the children of men, to see if there were any that did understand, and seek God. They are all gone aside; they are all together become filthy; there is none that doeth good, no, not one." (Psalm 14:2, 3.) Paul, in his day, repeats this and draws a terrible picture of man outside the influence of the gospel. (Rom. 3:10-18.) "There is," he says, "no fear of God before their eyes." The picture presented in the Revelations given in our day has the same features. "They [the sects] were all wrong. . . ." My vineyard has been corrupted, every whit." Let the reader compare these statements with those quoted from the Bible, and he will feel convinced that they originated in the same source—the Foundation of truth. The purpose of God in presenting these pictures is to call men to repentance. Even those who are doing good, according to the best of their understanding, err in many respects because of "priestcraft." (*Doctrine and Covenants Commentary*, p. 173.)

The need for a restoration of the gospel of Jesus Christ arose out of the fact of a departure from the truth; consequently, the Church was called out of the wilderness, or apostasy. It was this apostasy from the gospel and the restoration that John saw in vision. (Rev. 12:1-6; 14: 6-7.)

The Eleventh Hour

The Dispensation of the Fulness of Times is referred to in this (Section 33 of The Doctrine and Covenants) and other revelations as "the eleventh hour, and the last time that I shall call laborers into my vineyard." (D&C 34:3. See also D&C 43:28; 95:4.)

The prediction that the Lord would gather his elect from the nations of the earth in this last time is fully affirmed by the number who have come into the gospel net. It is worthy to notice that the "elect" of the Lord are those who believe in him and hearken unto his voice. (See verse 6.) The gatherers in this important activity are the missionaries who are always counseled to work devotedly in thrusting in their sickles and "reap with all your might, mind, and strength." (*Ibid.*, 33:7.) This counsel is as pertinent today as in other dispensations of the gospel, and the rewards to the gatherers are as sure.

The Rock of Revelation

The kingdom of God grew as people accepted the gospel—faith, repentance, baptism in water for the remission of sins and the receiving of the Holy Ghost. There is no other way to hearken to the voice of the Redeemer and to be saved. The gospel of Jesus Christ and its organization, the Church, is founded upon the "rock" of revelation. Men and women know of the truth of the gospel by the power of revelation to their souls. Continuance in the true faith insures to them that the "gates of hell," the powers of Satan in the spirit world, will not hold them from their eternal reward because they have won the victory by overcoming evil on the earth. (*Ibid.*, 33: 10-13.)

What was to make the kingdom of God, the Church, grow in this dispensation? A knowledge of the great apostasy whereby the Lord's vineyard became corrupted in its every part; the restoration of the gospel and Church in the last days; the revelation of the Lord given to men whereby they might know of these facts, and The Book of Mormon as a source of knowledge of that gospel and of its truth.

Section 34 and a Prophetic Element

With the conversion of Parley P. Pratt, many able men came into the Church through his preaching. Among these was his brother Orson Pratt, one of the most ardent missionaries that this dispensation has seen. Joining the Church at the age of nineteen, he immediately set out to visit the Prophet Joseph Smith, who was residing about 200 miles away. Many converts to the true Church of this period sought counsel from the Prophet. The prophetic nature of many of the revelations given through Joseph Smith is well-known among Latter-day Saints.

In Section 34 we find a revelation part of which has been literally fulfilled, if we are thinking of the element of prophecy. Although short in length, it is deep in meaning.

Orson Pratt, A Missionary

Orson Pratt is told that he is blessed because he has accepted the gospel (verse 4), but more blessed is he because he is now called to preach the gospel (verse 5):

To lift up your voice as with the sound of a trump, both long and loud and cry repentance unto a crooked and perverse generation, preparing the way of the Lord for his second coming. (*Ibid.*, 34:6.)

Important indeed is this prophetic element in the quoted verse concerning Brother Pratt's call to proclaim the gospel "both long and loud." If there was ever a man in this dispensation who served faithfully and devotedly in the missionary work in building up the kingdom on the earth, it was Orson Pratt. Over a period of fifty years it is said that he traveled more miles, preached more sermons, studied and wrote more upon the gospel and science than any other man in the Church. It would be reasonable to believe that this revelation (Section 34) served as a factor in his achieving this tremendous record. The Lord declared:

... lift up your voice and spare not ... therefore prophesy, and it shall be given by the power of the Holy Ghost.

And if you are faithful behold, I am with you until I come. (*Ibid.*, 34:10-11.)

Brother Pratt's missionary work included at least eleven missions to the eastern part of the United States, with seven different missions to Great Britain and Europe. Hundreds of people came into the fold of Christ through these efforts. One of his difficult missionary assignments was in Scotland where he labored for nine months raising up a branch of more than two hundred members. True to the call which came in 1830 by this revelation (Section 34), he knew that he was preparing the way for the Lord for his second coming. His literary works, which were many, emphasized the need for preparing oneself for the glorious coming of the Savior. (*Ibid.*, 34:7-9.)

It was Orson Pratt who arranged the text of The Book of Mormon and The Doctrine and Covenants in chapters and verses, with footnotes and references as published in 1876-1879.

In this chapter we have seen how the kingdom of God grew by the Lord raising up men equipped to labor with all their might, mind, and strength in a field that was white already to harvest. They had a message which bore the stamp of divine approval and which, by the Spirit of the Lord, was carried into the hearts of men. One instrumentality by which this was done, as it is to-day, was The Book of Mormon.

Chapter 23

A TRIAL OF FAITH

(Sections 35, 39, and 40)

The persons to whom the revelations comprising this chapter were addressed were formerly ministers in the "Christian" clergy. One of these we were introduced to in the last chapter.

Sidney Rigdon, Forerunner

Sidney Rigdon was at one time in the Reformed Baptist Church and later one of the leaders in the "Disciples of Christ" Church in Ohio, from which so many converts came, beginning in 1830. When Sidney Rigdon and Edward Partridge, also a former member of the latter organization and a convert to the gospel of Jesus Christ, visited the Prophet Joseph Smith in December 1830, a revelation was received in which some interesting thoughts are given concerning Brother Rigdon.

Behold, verily, verily, I say unto my servant Sidney, I have looked upon thee and thy works. I have heard thy prayers, and prepared thee for a greater work.

Thou are blessed, for thou shalt do great things. Behold thou wast sent forth, even as John, to prepare the way before me, and before Elijah which should come, and thou knewest it not.

Thou didst baptize by water unto repentance, but they received not the Holy Ghost;

But now I give unto thee a commandment, that thou shalt baptize by water, and they shall receive the Holy Ghost by the laying on of the hands, even as the apostles of old. (D&C 35:3-6.)

As this revelation points out, there was a considerable difference between the work performed by Sidney Rigdon as one who was not a member of the true Church of Jesus Christ and the service to which he was being called. Although he baptized with water unto repentance, that baptism was not effective for salvation; for "they received not the Holy Ghost." It is necessary for salvation that one receive both baptisms, water and spirit, which, in reality, are only one baptism. (John 3:5; Eph. 4:5.)

When Nephi, by vision, learned the reasons for Jesus' being baptized and the necessity of teaching the Nephites (and us) the place of baptism in the plan of salvation, he counseled:

> Wherefore, do the things which I have told you I have seen that your Lord and your Redeemer should do; for, for this cause have they been shown unto me, that ye might know the gate by which ye should enter. *For the gate by which ye should enter is repentance and baptism by water; and then cometh a remission of your sins by fire and by the Holy Ghost.* (Italics by author.)
>
> And then are ye in this straight and narrow path which leads to eternal life; yea, ye have entered in by the gate. . . . (2 Nephi 31:17-18.)

In order for one to receive the remission of sins, it is essential that he receive the baptism of the Holy Ghost as well as water baptism.

Preparation for Gospel Restoration

In view of the Lord's statement that Sidney Rigdon was as John the Baptist in preparing for a greater work, may we consider that there were many others, who, at different periods, also prepared the way for the establishment of the true gospel on the earth? As Latter-day Saints we believe that when the time came for the restoration of the gospel in its fulness, everything was in readiness. The Lord had preserved this land of America that it might be the place where his latter-day work would be established. Book of Mormon prophets had seen in vision the time when this land "choice above all other lands" was being prepared. (*Ibid.*, 1:3-9; 10:10-14, 19; Ether 13:1-6.)

In Nephi's vision, the "man among the Gentiles" believed by us to be Columbus, "who was separated from the seed of my brethren by the many waters" (1 Nephi 13:12), was wrought upon by the Spirit of God to perform his mission of discovery. Other Gentiles were also to come to this land out of captivity, until a mighty Nation founded upon principles of freedom would be raised up under the providence of God. (*Ibid.*, 13:13-19.)

In the meantime, other leaders were performing a work of preparation—a preparation of the minds of men whose descendants would benefit from their noble labors. The discovery of the printing press; the removal of the shackles of ignorance was a slow process, but, in time, it brought about conditions which permitted men to think for themselves.

Religiously, men benefited from these improved conditions, but the gospel of Jesus Christ was not restored until full preparation had been made. President John Taylor places before us the attitude of Latter-day Saints in some of these matters:

Who are we? The children of our Heavenly Father. Who are the world, as we sometimes denominate those that are not of our Church? The children of our Heavenly Father. . . .

Now outside the Gospel, outside of revelation, outside of any special communication from the Lord, all men, more or less, everywhere have certain claims upon their Heavenly Father, who is said to be the God and Father of the spirits of all flesh . . . and whenever and wherever there was no knowledge of life and immortality there was no Gospel. But outside of that there have been many good influences in the world. Many men in the different ages, who, in the midst of wickedness and corruption, have tried to stop the current of evil, have placed themselves in the catalogue of reformers. . . . The many reformers that existed in former ages have been men many of whom have been sincerely desirous to do the will of God, and to carry out His purposes, so far as they knew them. And then there are thousands and tens of thousands of honorable men living to-day in this nation, and other nations, who are honest and upright and virtuous, and who esteem correct principles and seek to be governed by them, so far as they know them. . . .

Men may be desirous to do right; they may be good, honorable and conscientious; and then when we come to the judgment pertaining to these things we are told that all men will be judged according to the deeds done in the body, and according to the light and intelligence which they possessed.

I will take, for instance, the position of the reformers, going no further back than Luther and Melancthon; and then you may come to Calvin, Knox, Whitfield, Wesley, Fletcher, and many others; men who have been desirous in their day to benefit their fellow-men; who have proclaimed against vice, and advocated the practice of virtue, uprightness and the fear of God. But we all, who have contemplated these subjects, know that those men never did restore the Gospel as it was taught by our Lord and Savior Jesus Christ; neither did they see or comprehend alike in biblical matters; they groped, as it were, in the dark with a portion of the Spirit of God. They sought to benefit their fellowman; but not having that union with God that the Gospel imparts, they were unable to arrive at just conclusions pertaining to those matters. Hence one introduced and taught one principle, and another introduced and taught another; and they were split up and divided, and the spirit of antagonism was found at times among them; and with all their desires to do good, they did not, and could not restore the Gospel of the Son of God, and none among them were able to say, Thus saith the Lord. And that is the condition of the religious world to-day. . . . (*Journal of Discourses* 23:369-371.)

A Minister Makes a Covenant

As we now turn our attention to another clergyman, James Covill, (D&C 39), who had served in the Baptist ministry for about forty years, we are informed by the Prophet Joseph Smith that he came to him "and covenanted with the Lord that he would obey any command that the Lord would give to him through me, as His servant." (*DHC* I:143.)

Sons and Daughters of God

Several times in revelations we have studied, the Savior has made known the way we may become his sons and daughters. For example, Section 34 begins with

"My son Orson. . ." and later after giving the reasons for this introduction, states: "Wherefore you are my son." (D&C 34:3.) Why was this recent convert to the Church so addressed? Why was James Covill, a nonmember, told that Jesus Christ is the light and life of the world and that, in the Meridian of Time (the time of the earthly ministry of Jesus), Jesus was not received?

> But to as many as receive me, gave I power to become my sons; and even so will I give unto as many as will receive me, power to become my sons.
> And verily, verily, I say unto you, he that receiveth my gospel receiveth me; and he that receiveth not my gospel receiveth not me. (*Ibid.*, 39:4-5.)

The answer is the same for everyone who qualifies in the same way that Brother Pratt qualified. All who accept "the only true and living church upon the face of the earth" become sons or daughters of the "Lord God." Jesus Christ, as your Redeemer, "so loved the world that he gave his own life, that as many as would believe might become the sons of God." (*Ibid.*, 34:3.)

> Christ is our Redeemer. Redemption means deliverance by means of ransom. There is a deliverance from guilt (Eph. 1:7; Col. 1:14) ; from the power and dominance of sin, through the sanctifying influence of the Holy Spirit (1 Peter 1:18) ; and from death through the resurrection. (Rom. 8:23.) There is, finally, a deliverance from all evil. (Eph. 1:14; 4:30; 1 Cor. 1:30; Titus 2:14.) All this is the work of Christ, through obedience to the gospel. (*Doctrine and Covenants Commentary*, page 177.)

Jesus is our Savior when we accept him in the waters of baptism and by confirmation of the Holy Ghost. This is what James Covill is told as a nonmember. (D&C 39: 4-6.) Jesus' atonement for individual exaltation is of no force until the person completes his repentance through the ordinances of the gospel. (*Ibid.*, 29:17; 42:1.) As we become the sons and daughters of Jesus, so also, he becomes our Father. (See Chapter 20 for discussion on this point.)

Rich Rewards Promised

James Covill, the clergyman, was informed that the Lord had looked upon him and his works and, at that time, his heart was right before him. (*Ibid.*, 39:7-8.) There had been times in the past, however, when the things of the world had brought sorrow into Mr. Covill's life. Notice the important fact made known in verse 6 that if this man would accept Jesus as his Savior, the Holy Ghost, which he had not received, would give him the "peaceable things of the kingdom." It would seem from the circumstances which brought this clergyman to the Prophet, that he was not at peace. There were unanswered questions and difficulties which had not been resolved in his mind.

In applying this idea to us who are members of the kingdom, how may we receive peace of mind? A function of the Holy Ghost is to give to the son or daughter of Jesus Christ a sense of security, peace, and joy. This satisfaction comes by having the influence of the Holy Spirit through living the laws of the gospel, just as James Covill was promised "a blessing so great as you never have known" (*Ibid.*, 39:10) by his adherence to the same laws.

A greater work in teaching the fulness of the gospel than the work in which he had formerly engaged was before Covill, predicated upon his obedience. His contribution would be to assist in moving the kingdom forward that, eventually, Zion might come. (*Ibid.*, 39:11-13.) How many of us have before us this objective? Do our works make such contributions?

Our forefathers were gathered from out of the world that they might eventually receive eternal life. Mr. Covill was promised that he could participate in this great undertaking of gathering Israel from the nations to "be gathered unto me [Jesus] in time and in eternity." (*Ibid.,* 39:22.) Those who are gathered are to look forth for the signs of the Lord's coming. As we continue steadfast in his work, our knowledge and testimony of him will increase. (*Ibid.,* 39:23.)

The Rejection of a Covenant

Notwithstanding that great blessings were promised James Covill upon his acceptance of the true gospel, he did not have sufficient faith in the Redeemer to accept his counsel. The day of his deliverance from the sorrows of the world was at hand (*ibid.,* 39:10), provided he would be obedient. But Covill returned to his former principles and people, and of him the Lord said:

> Behold, verily I say unto you, that the heart of my servant James Covill was right before me, for he covenanted with me that he would obey my word.
> And he received the word with gladness, but straightway Satan tempted him; and the fear of persecution and the cares of the world caused him to reject the word.
> Wherefore he broke my covenant, and it remaineth with me to do with him as seemeth me good. Amen. (*Ibid.,* 40:1-3.)

James Covill was a covenant breaker. It is apparent that his former weaknesses gained ascendancy over the gladness which came into his heart, and he succumbed to fear. It was a fear of persecution and the cares of the world. Unmindful of the beatitude of promised blessings to those who are persecuted for righteousness' sake (for their reward was to be an inheritance in the kingdom of heaven), Covill's actions were not motivated to this extent. (Matt. 5:10-12.) The fear that he might not be able to provide for himself temporally, also was a factor in his rejection of the gospel.

Blessings Predicated upon Obedience

Judgment of all such individuals is in the hands of the Lord. There have been many in the world who have come to the threshold of the kingdom of God but who have succumbed to similar fears. Concerning such an one who was in the same profession as James Covill, we have the comment of President Joseph F. Smith. An ordained minister in the "English Church" for fifty-five years wrote to his Latter-day Saint relatives that:

I preach three sermons every week and execute other ministerial duties, but I never preach anything contrary to the doctrines of "Mormonism," not designedly but necessarily, because I see the fundamentals of Holy Scripture are the same as those restored by what people call "Mormonism."

He then posed this question:

What is to become of such as me, who believes this about you, and yet are tied and bound by circumstances such as mine?

The President of the Church wrote:

In answer to the question, "What is to become of such as me?" let it be said that every person will receive his just reward for the good he may do and for his every act. But let it be remembered that all blessings which we shall receive, either here or hereafter, must come to us as a result of our obedience to the laws of God upon which these blessings are predicated. Our friend will not be forgotten for the kindness he has extended to the work and the servants of the Lord, but will be remembered of Him and rewarded for his faith and for every good deed and word. But there are many blessings that result from obeying the ordinances of the gospel, and acknowledging the priesthood authorized by the Father and restored to The Church of Jesus Christ of Latter-day Saints, that cannot be obtained, until the person is willing to comply with the ordinances and keep the commandments revealed in our day for the salvation of mankind. The true searcher will see and understand this truth and act upon it, either in this world or in the world to come, and not until then, of course, may he claim all the blessings. The earlier he accepts, the earlier will he obtain the blessings, and if he neglects to accept the laws, in this world, knowing them to be true, it is reasonable to suppose that disadvantages will result that will cause him deep regret. (*Improvement Era*, November 1912, 71-72.)

"Unto Whom Much Is Given Much Is Required"

One is reminded of the truth given by the Lord when he said that "unto whom much is given much is required" (D&C 82:3) and as greater light is made known and as one sins against that light, condemnation results. This thought is pertinent:

Ye call upon my name for revelations, and I give them unto you; and inasmuch as ye keep not my sayings, which I give unto you, ye become transgressors; and justice and judgment are the penalty which is affixed unto my law.

Therefore, what I say unto one I say unto all: Watch for the adversary spreadeth his dominions, and darkness reigneth. (*Ibid.*, 82:4-5.)

In accordance with this thought, how many who have entered the kingdom of God have found that they were not deeply rooted in gospel teachings and faith in the Redeemer so that they succumbed to the fears of the world? Are any of us as the seeds in the parable of the sower where the word of God has not taken sufficient root, and "the care of this world, and the deceitfulness of riches, choke the word," and seeds become barren? Or, on the other hand, are seeds sown on the "good ground" which beareth the fruit of the gospel in our lives? (Matt. 13:18-23.)

How many of us may fall away from the principles of the gospel because of fear of persecution? In the early part of the dispensation persecution was many times physical. Today, however, it may be, as it was then also, the tauntings of associates or "friends." The use of names having strong unchristian implications or inferences of overzealousness may be examples of a type of persecution which has mental or psychological effect. In common expression it may be expressed as "Don't be fanatical about your religion!" or "Why be so straight-laced?" Aside from the usual meaning of inflicting loss and injury, persecution means to harass, to pursue with persistent solicitations or to annoy.

Additional Items from Section 35

Beginning with verse 7 of Section 35, we learn that by faith great things are to be manifest in the latter days, including the working of miracles. (D&C 35:7-11.) In harmony with what has already been given in this chapter, the Lord makes known that those who do "good" in his sight, are "those who are ready to receive the fulness of my gospel" (*ibid.*, 35:12) and that those who constitute the "poor and the meek" (*ibid.*, 35:15) of the earth shall have the gospel preached unto them, and they shall be looking forth for the time of my coming, for it is nigh at hand." (*Ibid.*, 35:15; see D&C 35:12-18.) The faithful members of the kingdom of God will make contributions to the building of that kingdom and eventually "Zion shall rejoice upon the hills," probably having reference to the home of the Saints in the West. (*Ibid.*, 35:19-24.) By the power of God, latter-day Israel will be saved in the Lord's kingdom, and all who belong to the Savior should lift up their hearts and be glad. (*Ibid.*, 35:25-27.)

Chapter 24

THE GREAT I AM

(Sections 36, 37 and 38)

The revelation (D&C Section 38), which will command our attention principally in this chapter, was given at the beginning of the year 1831. The Church had been organized for about nine months. It was a year during which a large number of revelations were received for the development of the growing kingdom of God. Many commandments during this period were given for the temporal as well as the spiritual welfare of the Saints.

The Great I Am

Section 38 opens with some important truths regarding the Savior. Other books of scripture give affirmation of those truths but this revelation provides us with a clear understanding of Jesus' position in the plan of salvation before his mortal birth.

> Thus saith the Lord your God, even **Jesus Christ, the Great I Am**, Alpha and Omega, the beginning and the end, the same which looked upon the wide expanse of eternity, and all the seraphic hosts of heaven, before the world was made;
>
> The same which knoweth all things, for all things are present before mine eyes;
>
> I am the same which spake, and the world was made, and all things came by me.
>
> I am the same which have taken the Zion of Enoch into mine own bosom; and verily, I say, even as many as has believed in my name, for I am Christ, and in mine own name, by the virtue of the blood which I have spilt, have I pleaded before the Father for them. (*Ibid.*, 38:1-4.)

In verse one we find the title to this chapter—The Great I Am. This title or name of the Christ is related in meaning to Jehovah, a name which the Jews regarded as sacred to the extent of not saying it. They substituted the Hebrew name Adonai (Ăd-ō-ni), meaning "the Lord."

The use of the title I Am is found in other scriptures and is definitely associated with Jesus in this and other revelations. (*Ibid.*, 29:1; 39:1.) Certain Jews at the time of the Master criticized him and declared themselves to be of Abraham's lineage, and thereby believed themselves preferred above others. The Savior used this expressive statement in declaring his divine calling: "Verily, verily, I say unto you, Before Abraham was, I am." (John 8: 58.) In effect, the Lord was saying that before Abraham was, he was Jehovah, or the Being that gave revelation to the prophets.

Seraphic Hosts

In this revelation (Section 38), the Redeemer is said to have surveyed the wide expanse of eternity and also to have seen "The seraphic hosts of heaven, before the world was made." (D&C 38:1.) Those who compose the seraphic hosts are seraphs or angels without wings, however, for when wings or flying is associated with such personages, the language is symbolic and conveys the meaning of the power of motion, movement.

Jesus as Creator

As one continues to read this revelation, he is immediately impressed with the additional point that Jesus is truly the Creator of this earth and that all things came by him. (*Ibid.*, 38:3.) His work with the children of men in this world has not been confined to what we sometimes call the New Testament or meridian period, but, from the very beginning, he is the Lord of the Old Testament dispensations. Notice how verse 4 points this up:

I am the same which have taken the Zion of Enoch into mine own bosom; and verily, I say, even as many as have believed in my name, for I am Christ, and in mine own name, by the virtue of the blood which I have spilt, have I pleaded before the Father for them. (*Ibid.*, 38:4.)

For those who obediently follow the Master's way of life, the benefits of his atonement are available, while, on the other hand, those who become hardened in their lives look forward to a "judgment of the great day, which shall come at the end of the earth." (*Ibid.*, 38:5.) In the meantime, however, the hardened or "wicked" unrepentant remain in chains of darkness in the spirit world. (*Ibid.*, 38:6, and Alma 40:11-14.)

The same Jesus who was born in the Meridian of Time gave commandments and revelations to the prophets of the Old Testament. The Book of Mormon brings out clearly that it was Jesus Christ who spoke to the prophets before the time of his birth into mortality. (1 Nephi 19: 10; 3 Nephi 11:10, 14.) Important in this regard are the words of the resurrected Jesus to the Nephites:

Behold, I am he that gave the law, and I am he who covenanted with my people Israel; therefore, the law in me is fulfilled for I have come to fulfill the law; therefore it hath an end. . . .

Behold, I have given unto you the commandments; therefore keep my commandments. And this is the law and the prophets, for they truly testified of me. (3 Nephi 15:5, 10.)

God Is Perfect

That God is perfect is acclaimed in scripture. (Matt. 5:48; D&C 93:21, 26.) Revelation 38 makes known concerning the Lord's knowledge of all things.

The same which knoweth all things, for all things are present before mine eyes. (D&C 38:2.)

In Section 88, verse 41, the Lord also makes known his characteristic of being all-knowing.

From the "Lectures on Faith" prepared for use in the School of Elders, during the winter of 1834-35, there are some meaningful passages concerning the perfection of God in all things. These two quotations are important:

... God is the only supreme governor and independent being in whom all fulness and perfection dwell; who is omnipotent [all-powerful], omnipresent [everywhere present] and omniscient [all-knowing]; without beginning of days or end of life; and that in him every good gift and every good principle dwell. . . .

... Without the knowledge of all things, God would not be able to save any portion of his creatures; for it is by reason of the knowledge which he has of all things, from the beginning to the end, that enables him to give the understanding to his creatures by which they are made partakers of eternal life; and if it were not for the idea existing in the minds of men that God had all knowledge it would be impossible for them to exercise faith in him. ("Lectures on Faith," Lecture 2, paragraph 2; Lecture 4, paragraph 11.)

God is not relatively perfect, but his perfection is absolute. Latter-day Saints have recognized that our knowledge of the Lord and our relationship to him are known by what he has revealed on these matters. Men may believe ideas which are not in the revealed word of God, but these notions are but the products of their own thinking and not from him who knoweth all things. (2 Nephi 9:20, 28-29.)

The Latter-day Saint finds in modern revelations great comfort, strength, and a security such as that experienced by Ammon of The Book of Mormon:

Now have we not reason to rejoice? Yea, I say unto you, there never were men that had so great reason to rejoice as we, since the world began; yea, and my joy is carried away, even unto boasting in my God; for he has all power, all wisdom, and he is a merciful Being, even unto salvation, to those who will repent and believe on his name.

Now if this is boasting, even so will I boast; for this is my life and my light, my joy and my salvation, and my redemption from everlasting wo. Yea, blessed is the name of my God, who has been mindful of this people, who are a branch of the tree of Israel, and has been lost from its body in a strange land; yea I say, blessed be the name of my God, who has been mindful of us, wanderers in a strange land. (Alma 26:35-36.)

"I Am in Your Midst"

Continuing in Section 38, we learn:

But behold, verily, verily, I say unto you that mine eyes are upon you. I am in your midst and ye cannot see me;

But the day soon cometh that ye shall see me, and know that I am; for the veil of darkness shall soon be rent, and he that is not purified shall not abide the day. (D&C 38:7-8.)

Here again, the Lord gives further assurance to his Saints that there is reason to rejoice for "I am in your midst and ye cannot see me." As one remains true to the faith, the Spirit whispers to his soul that this is the work of God, and that he is directing it through his appointed servants. He has not always made himself visibly manifest, but the time will come when he shall withdraw the veil separating himself from us, and we shall then behold him. The comforting assurance that he is with his Church and people abounds in the soul of every true Latter-day Saint.

One may be reminded of the vision of the Prophet Joseph Smith in the Kirtland Temple in 1836, when he said:

I saw the Twelve Apostles of the Lamb, who are now upon the earth, who hold the keys of this last ministry, in foreign lands, standing together in a circle, much fatigued, with their clothes tattered and feet swollen, with their eyes cast downward, and Jesus standing in their midst, and they did not behold Him. The Savior looked upon them and wept. (*DHC* 2:381.)

As of them, so today, the Savior is continuing to direct his Church on the earth.

When the Lord at his coming shall be seen, it is said that the purified will abide that day. Those who have accepted the Savior as their Redeemer are declared in this revelation to be "clean." As to the world at large, the powers of darkness prevail upon the earth because of the great apostasy which will bring destruction to the tares or the wicked. (D&C 38:10-12.) Notwithstanding the saints are "clean," there are those among them who are not taking full advantage of their privileges in receiving greater blessings. Although the Lord is mindful of their weaknesses, he will extend his mercy to them. (*Ibid.*, 38: 14.)

Section 37

In this short revelation given in December of the year 1830, the Lord makes known that the Prophet and Sidney Rigdon were to discontinue their present activities in "translating" or revising the Bible until they go to the Ohio valley. The membership of the Church was commanded also to "assemble together at the Ohio." This is the first time that a place of gathering was indicated for the Church as a whole. We have already learned of the growth of the kingdom in that area. (See Chapter 22.)

A Promise of the Future

Returning to Section 38, we learn that the Lord reveals his intentions concerning the temporal welfare of the Saints. It is evident that not only the Prophet Joseph Smith but the poor among the Saints had prayed for the time when the condition of those in need might be improved. Taking cognizance of their condition, the revelation reads:

And for your salvation I give unto you a commandment, for I have heard your prayers, and the poor have complained before me, and the rich have I made, and all flesh is mine, and I am no respecter of persons.

And I have made the earth rich, and behold it is my footstool, wherefore, again I will stand upon it.

And I hold forth and deign to give unto you greater riches, even a land of promise, a land flowing with milk and honey, upon which there shall be no curse when the Lord cometh;

And I will give it unto you for the land of your inheritance, if you seek it with all your hearts. (D&C 38:16-19.)

What are the promises of the Lord to his people who cry unto him for relief from a lack of the things of this earth? The day will come, when the Lord stands upon the earth, that his people shall inherit it and receive all of the bounteous blessings that the earth will provide. By what means will these blessings come to the Saints? Here is a commentary upon this question:

God's design was to give to His gathered people great riches, even a land of promise, "upon which there shall be no curse [of destitution] when the Lord cometh."

The Lord promises to give His Saints such a land, if they will seek it with all their hearts. It cannot be obtained except through diligent, God-directed effort. (*Doctrine and Covenants Commentary*, p. 204.)

Notice in verse 20 how the promised land is to be:

. . . for the inheritance of your children forever, while the earth shall stand, and ye shall possess it again in eternity, no more to pass away. (*Ibid.*, 38:20.)

Were the Saints to wait until some long period ahead for the relief of the poor among them? No, certain members of the Church in the New York area were to "look to the poor and the needy, and administer to their relief that they shall not suffer." (*Ibid.*, 38:34-35.)

The commandment had gone forth that the members were to go to the Ohio, where the law of the Lord would be given his people. (*Ibid.*, 38:32.) The keeping of this law would bring great spiritual blessings as well as temporal. It is the Lord's purpose to provide for his Saints in his own way and not after the manner of the world. An explanation of that law of the Lord is spoken of in the revelations to be studied in this book. There are yet great blessings to be received by the Lord's people.

As we return to a study of the future as envisioned in this revelation, it is apparent that there were questions among the members in 1831 concerning the laws of the land, and what the Saints might expect. When the Savior comes to inaugurate his reign, he shall be the ruler of the earth, and then men shall truly be free.

> But, verily I say unto you that in time ye shall have no king nor ruler, for I will be your king and watch over you.
>
> Wherefore, hear my voice and follow me, and you shall be a free people, and ye shall have no laws but my laws when I come, for I am your lawgiver, and what can stay my hand. (*Ibid.*, 38:21-22.)

From the Great I Am, who is our Creator and Redeemer, we are asked the question (38:22): "What can stay my hand?" The voice of the Spirit to each Latter-day Saint verifies the all-perfection of God and his designs for his people. The answer to this question is given in many scriptures:

> How long can rolling waters remain impure? What power shall stay the heavens? As well might man stretch forth his puny arm to stop the Missouri river in its decreed course, or to turn it up stream, as to hinder the Almighty from pouring down knowledge from heaven upon the heads of the Latter-day Saints. [*Ibid.*, 121:33.] (See also D&C 76:3; Matt. 24:35.)

Be One in Purpose and Action

Following the assurance that the time will come when a righteous reign of law will begin with the second coming of Christ, the Lord informs us that each person is to esteem his brother as himself and to "practise virtue and holiness before me." (D&C 38:24.) When men so esteem their brothers, then they will have come, in a large

measure, to the objective of the accomplishment of the
Lord's purposes by following this important truth: "I
say unto you, be one; and if ye are not one ye are not
mine." (*Ibid.*, 38:27.) Unity in faith and oneness in
action have been the objectives of the Church in all dispensations. The necessity of unity in The Church of Jesus
Christ is strongly expressed in Jesus' words as he prayed
to the Father that his apostles might "be one, as we are."
Furthermore, it was his desire that all those who would
believe on him:

> . . . may be one; as thou, Father, art in me, and I in thee,
> that they also may be one in us: that the world may believe that
> thou hast sent me. (John 17:21.)

As the Saints of this dispensation become unified in
the building up of the kingdom of God upon the earth, to
which they are committed, then the world will more
readily believe in the Christ and in the restoration of the
gospel. Are not people attracted to the standard of righteousness by the fruits of the gospel as they are observed in
the lives of the members of the Church? This was the prophetic understanding of Ezekiel who saw the gathering of
Israel in our dispensation, and who saw that the unbe-
liever should "know that I am the Lord, saith the Lord
God, *when I shall be sanctified in you before their eyes.*"
(Ezekiel 36:23. Italics are the author's. See Ezekiel 36:
21-24.)

So important is the need for unity among the members of the Priesthood of the Church and also the other
members, that President J. Reuben Clark, Jr., of the
First Presidency has often admonished the Church to
come more fully to a oneness of action:

> We are all bound together as one, and insofar as we fail, as
> individuals, to carry on the work which we are supposed to do,
> we are to that extent hindering the carrying on of the work of
> the Lord and to that extent we are responsible for the lack or

fullness of growth that may occur on account of our failure. (*Conference Report,* September 29, 30, and October 1, 1950, page 171.)

The Civil War

Consistent with the theme of this revelation regarding the Lord's concern for his people, another important part of the future is called to their attention. The first intimation of the coming American Civil War is indicated in this manner:

Ye hear of wars in far countries, and you say that there will soon be great wars in far countries, but ye know not the hearts of men in your own land.

I tell you these things because of your prayers; wherefore, treasure up wisdom in your bosoms, lest the wickedness of men reveal these things unto you by their wickedness, in a manner which shall speak in your ears with a voice louder than that which shall shake the earth; but if ye are prepared ye shall not fear. (D&C 38:29-30.)

Important in understanding this portent of things to come is this comment from the *Doctrine and Covenants Commentary,* page 208:

In the United States the opinion prevailed that internal troubles such as those from which France, Belgium, Poland, and some other countries suffered, could not arise in the great Republic. The people generally did not know what was in the hearts of men, but the Lord knew, and He gave in this paragraph, the first intimation that there would be civil war in the United States. . . .

If they [the Saints] were wise, they would prepare themselves by gathering to one place. As a matter of fact the Saints did, in due time, go to the valleys of the Rocky Mountains, and in those impregnable "chambers" they were effectively secluded "for a little moment, until the indignation be overpast." (Isa. 26:20.)

Seek the Riches of Eternity

After the Lord counseled his people to care for the needs of the poor (D&C 38:35), reference is made to the time when his servants will be endowed with power from on high and sent forth to the nations. (*Ibid.*, 38:38.) Not many years later, when the Church was assembled in Ohio, a great pentecostal feast was enjoyed at the dedication of the Kirtland Temple and the manifold blessings accruing to the Church membership therefrom. (*Ibid.*, Section 110.)

Significantly, this revelation draws to an end with the admonition that:

... if ye seek the riches which it is the will of the Father to give unto you, ye shall be the richest of all people, for ye shall have the riches of eternity; and it must needs be that the riches of the earth are mine to give; but beware of pride, lest ye become as the Nephites of old. (*Ibid.*, 38:39.)

This stern reminder of the Nephite period and the destruction of their civilization and people is one to be remembered. Examples of the results of pride and other evils as emphasized by Nephite historians who saw them either in vision or who witnessed the destructions are worthy of careful consideration. (2 Nephi 26:10; 3 Nephi 6:15; Moroni 8:27.)

To the members of the Church who dedicate so much of their time and effort to the assistance of those in need, the words of Jacob will give encouragement to continue and further to assure their own eternal welfare.

Think of your brethren like unto yourselves, and be familiar with all and free with your substance, that they may be rich like unto you.

But before ye seek for riches, seek ye for the kingdom of God.

And after ye have obtained a hope in Christ ye shall obtain riches, if ye seek them; and ye will seek them for the intent to do good—to clothe the naked, and to feed the hungry, and to liberate the captive, and administer relief to the sick and the afflicted. (Jacob 2:17-19.)

Section 36

The short revelation numbered thirty-six was addressed to Edward Partridge, who later became "a bishop to the Church." (D&C Section 41.) It was during the month of December 1830, that he was baptized. In this revelation he is called to preach the gospel boldly. (*Ibid.*, 41:1, 3.) By his receiving the Holy Ghost, Brother Partridge was to be taught "the peaceable things of the kingdom." (*Ibid.*, 36:2.) As a missionary is called to bring people to repentance, so this recent convert to the Church was to speak peace to the souls of men who would thus be rescued from the evils of the world. (*Ibid.*, 36:6.)

We have in this revelation the first indication that temples were to be constructed in this dispensation. The Lord says, "I will suddenly come to my temple." (*Ibid.*, 36:8.) Edward Partridge was present in the Kirtland Temple when the Savior accepted it as his own. (*Ibid.*, Section 110.)

Chapter 25

A PROMISE FULFILLED

(Sections 41; 42:1-17)

From our history of the Church and other sources, we learn of events in the Ohio valley to which the Saints had been instructed to gather. From Section 38 we learned that when the Saints gathered to the Ohio, they would receive the law of the Lord. With the great increase in Church membership in that area, it is clear that many problems would arise. This condition would make necessary the presence of the Prophet Joseph Smith to direct the activities of the growing kingdom of God.

The Prophet's first visit to Kirtland brought forth an event which is an example of the seeric powers possessed by Joseph Smith. Briefly, it is recorded that in company with his wife Emma, Sidney Rigdon, and Edward Partridge (the latter two having been converted as a result of the Lamanite mission, see Chapter 22), the Prophet walked into the store operated by Whitney and Gilbert. He approached Newel K. Whitney and said: "Newel K. Whitney! Thou art the man!" whereupon, Mr. Whitney replied: "You have the advantage of me. . . . I could not call you by name as you have me." The Prophet then said, "I am Joseph the Prophet. . . . You've prayed me here, now what do you want of me?" (*DHC* I:146.)

An indication of how the Lord prepared the way of the first missionaries into the Ohio valley and the visit of the Prophet later is told in the experience of Mr. and Mrs. Whitney. As members of the Campbellite faith, they desired to know how they might obtain the gift of the Holy Ghost.

One night, says Mother Whitney, it was midnight—my husband and I were in our house at Kirtland, praying to the Father

to be shown the way when the Spirit rested upon us a cloud
overshadowed the house. It was as though we were out of doors.
The house passed away from our vision. We were not conscious
of anything but the presence of the spirit and the cloud that was
over us. We were wrapped in the cloud. A solemn awe pervaded
us. We saw the cloud and felt the Spirit of the Lord. Then we
heard a voice out of the cloud saying, "Prepare to receive the
Lord, for it is coming." At this we marveled greatly, but from
that moment we knew that the word of the Lord was coming to
Kirtland. (Jenson, Andrew: *L. D. S. Biographical Encyclopedia*
I:223.)

Conditions in Kirtland

The Prophet learned when he arrived in Kirtland
that some very strange things had been developing in
that branch of the Church. Let us keep in mind that the
members there, all recent converts, had been associated
with other churches, consequently theological ideas and
practices were understood by them differently. In the
words of Elder George A. Smith, it is reported that "a
society that had undertaken to have a community of
property" and had been called "the Morley family" being
"located on a farm owned by Captain Isaac Morley . . .
had not yet been instructed in relation to their duties."
These members developed some "extravagant and wild
ideas." The Prophet Joseph Smith taught the people the
true order of the Church which resulted in the apostasy
of some members who continued to be deceived. Among
these was Wycom Clark, who "got a revelation that he
was to be the prophet—that he was the true revelator"
and with a few others organized the "Pure Church of
Christ." (*Journal of Discourses* 11:3-4.)

Section 41

A knowledge of these conditions helps us to understand the following verses which introduce this section,
the first revelation received in Kirtland:

Hearken and hear, O ye my people, saith the Lord and your God, ye whom I delight to bless with the greatest of all blessings, ye that hear me; and ye that hear me not will I curse, that have professed my name, with the heaviest of all cursings.

Hearken, O ye elders of my church whom I have called, behold I gave unto you a commandment, that ye shall assemble yourselves together to agree upon my word;

And by the prayer of your faith ye shall receive my law, that ye may know how to govern my church and have all things right before me. (D&C 41:1-3.)

Notice the emphasis put upon the law of common consent; namely, that the brethren were to ". . . assemble . . . together to agree upon my word." As they came together for this purpose they were to meet ". . . by the prayer of your faith . . ." in order to be prepared for the law which had been promised earlier. (*Ibid.*, 38:32.) It was only a few days later that this promise was fulfilled when the Lord gave Section 42, which is known as "The Law of the Church."

In continuation of preparation for this event, the Saints are advised that:

He that receiveth my law and doeth it, the same is my disciple; and he that saith he receiveth it and doeth it not, the same is not my disciple, and shall be cast out from among you;

For it is not meet that the things which belong to the children of the kingdom should be given to them that are not worthy, or to dogs, or the pearls to be cast before swine. (*Ibid.*, 41:5-6.)

These words bring out clearly who is the true disciples of the Lord. He who professes to believe and to be the followers of the Christ is deceiving himself and also those who follow him when there is no acceptance of what the Lord reveals as his law. There were members of the Church in Kirtland who considered themselves true disciples, as there have been since the days of Joseph Smith. Unless members continue to obey the law of the Lord, they are not disciples, and a judgment awaits them. (John 8:31-32; Matt. 7:21-23.) On the other hand, the promise is given that the Spirit will be with the true believer. (Ether 4:10-12.)

With the growth of the kingdom, the Lord called Edward Partridge to be the first bishop in this dispensation. In this call by revelation, there are established the important steps in all calls to service in the Church. This procedure is: first, the call by the authorized servant of the Lord; second, appointment "by the voice of the Church"; and third, ordination by those in authority. As pointed out in a former chapter, these three steps also constitute a key against the claims of those who seek to deceive Latter-day Saints. (See Chapter 18.)

Bishop Partridge was to devote his entire time to the office of bishop. His work as bishop was to be confined to those things "as it shall be appointed unto him in my [the Lord's] laws in the day that I shall give them." (D&C 41:10.) This thought is important to remember: when one receives an office in the Church, he is to function only within the calling he has received. Compliance with this important principle maintains order in the kingdom and prevents disharmony, regret, and in some cases, even apostasy.

In closing this revelation, the members of the Church are informed of the necessity to obey the words given; otherwise, they will be answered upon their souls in the day of judgment. (*Ibid.*, 41:12.) President Brigham Young had this to say about such a situation:

> Those who do not profess to know anything of the Lord are far better off than we are, unless we live our religion, for we who know our Master's will and do it not, will be beaten with many stripes; while they who do not know the Master's will and do it not will be beaten with few stripes. This is perfectly reasonable. (*Journal of Discourses* 16:111.)

The Promised Law (Section 42)

Including this and the next four chapters, there is an opportunity to examine the important teachings of the law of the Church. Although there are different ways that this revelation might be divided, it seems that this division is a practical one: the law of preaching the gospel (D&C 42:4-17); the law of moral conduct (*ibid.*, 42:18-29); the law of consecration (*ibid.*, 42:30-42); the law of administration to the sick (*ibid.*, 42:43-52); the law of sundry duties (*ibid.*, 42:53-69); the law of remuneration of services (*ibid.*, 42:70-73); and the law concerning transgressors. (*Ibid.*, 32:74-93.)

Introduction to the Law

The Church is told to hearken obediently to the instructions given in this revelation. (*Ibid.*, 42:1-4.) The twelve elders in whose presence this revelation was given, are to go forth to teach the gospel by the power of the Spirit. The preaching or dissemination of the gospel may be called the law of preaching the gospel.

The Law of Preaching the Gospel

Missionaries of the Church are to travel "two by two." The reasons for doing this are apparent when one considers that the testimony of two or three witnesses is the Lord's way of making known his marvelous work. There is also protection, both moral and physical, afforded the missionaries against those who would seek to do them harm.

In the sixth verse of this revelation, the elders are told that they are to declare "my word like unto angels of God." (*Ibid.*, 42:6.) In this same year of 1831, the Lord reminded the elders that:

And now, verily saith the Lord, that these things might be known among you, O inhabitants of the earth, I have sent forth mine angel flying through the midst of heaven, having the everlasting gospel, who hath appeared unto some and hath committed it unto man, who shall appear unto many that dwell on the earth.

And this gospel shall be preached unto every nation, and kindred, and tongue, and people.

And the servants of God shall go forth, saying with a loud voice: Fear God and give glory to him, for the hour of his judgment is come;

And worship him that made heaven, and earth, and the sea, and the fountains of waters. (*Ibid.,* 133-36-39.   Italics are the author's.)

When one compares these verses with what was proclaimed by the Apostle John in foretelling the restoration of the gospel by an angel (Rev. 14:6-7), the part in italics by the writer suggests that the divinely commissioned missionaries are to carry the angel's message to the world. This message becomes more meaningful when it is understood that when the elders speak by the Holy Ghost they are speaking with the "tongue of angels." (Cf. 2 Nephi 32:2-3; 31:11-14.)

Ordination Necessary

In order to preach the gospel and officiate in the ordinances thereof, the person must be ordained by one having the proper authority, and he is known to hold such authority. (D&C 42:11.) Those who go forth representing the Lord are to teach the principles of the gospel as contained in the books of scripture available at the time— the Bible and The Book of Mormon. Later The Doctrine and Covenants and the Pearl of Great Price came into existence as books of scripture. Experience has shown that the Bible and The Book of Mormon are better adapted for missionary use. Occasionally the Lord has pointed out that the world is to receive the milk of the gospel first and later the stronger teachings which have been compared to meat. (*Ibid.,* 19:22.) Again, there is suggested that The Book of Mormon contains the "fulness of the gospel." The meaning of this expression is simply that it implies (a) sufficient knowledge for salvation, and (b) the necessity of the Priesthood. (Chapter 13.)

The missionaries are not only to proclaim the gospel from these books of scripture, but they are to observe the "covenants and church articles to do them." (*Ibid.*, 42:13.) By this it is meant that other sources of truth, as contained in later revelations through prophets, are to be practiced as well as taught. The teaching by the missionary is to be done under the influence of the Spirit. (*Ibid.*, 42:13.) If this is done, there will be given sufficient to influence the investigator, and the missionary will not be led astray in what he teaches.

The Prayer of Faith

There follows in this revelation the statement of a great truth for both the set apart missionary as well as the teacher in the auxiliary organizations of the Church.

And the Spirit shall be given unto you by the prayer of faith; and if ye receive not the Spirit ye shall not teach. (*Ibid.*, 42:14.)

In The Church of Jesus Christ of Latter-day Saints, where so many members have an opportunity to teach the gospel, there seems to be reason for knowledge of and emphasis upon this truth.

To receive any blessings from the Lord the necessity of exercising faith in Him is a truism. The Prophet Joseph Smith learned this as a lad when he read the words of James that if one lacked wisdom, he was to ask of God. "But let him ask in faith, nothing wavering. For he that wavereth is like a wave of the sea driven with the wind and tossed." (James 1:6.) The faith required is that of full trust in the Lord, recognizing from the depths of one's soul that the desired result will follow.

Prayers for divine assistance sometimes are words expressed in prayer language, but they lack faith intended in the expression "prayer of faith," which we are admonished will bring the blessing of the Lord. An example of this contrast is found in the case of the Zoramites in The Book of Mormon. Their set prayer was meaningless because it was uttered to gain the favor of men and for religious ritual only. (Alma 31:15-22, 34-38.)

Some of the essentials in obtaining the "prayer of faith" and to receive the influence of the Holy Ghost were given by President Brigham Young, as follows:

Let us be humble, fervent, submissive, yielding ourselves to the will of the Lord, and there is no danger but that we shall have His Spirit to guide us. (*Journal of Discourses* 13:155.)

But what is there to say about the growth of faith necessary for one who wants to exercise the "prayer of faith"? Alma spoke of the need to "arouse your faculties, even to an experiment... and exercise a particle of faith, yea, even if ye can no more than desire to believe, let this desire work in you, even until ye believe...." (Alma 32:27.)

But what if the individual does not feel the need to pray at a given time for the assistance of the Lord? The following gleanings from President Brigham Young are pertinent to obtaining the spirit of prayer:

It matters not whether you or I feel like praying, when the time comes to pray, pray. If we do not feel like it, we should pray till we do. . . . You will find that those who wait till the Spirit bids them pray, will never pray much on this earth. (*Discourses of Brigham Young*, p. 44.)

Receive the Spirit

Every member of this Church may have the privilege of enjoying the Holy Ghost, which is the Spirit referred to in the admonition before us. (D&C 42:14.) The Spirit will be received to the degree that the member of the Church is diligently seeking to keep the commandments of the Lord. Worthiness of life, coupled with prayer and faith, will bring forth the Spirit. (*Ibid.*, 63: 64.)

The Spirit and Teaching

Why should a person have the Spirit of the Lord to teach, as admonished in our text? (*Ibid.*, 42:14.) The Lord has specifically informed us that we are to have his Spirit. Fundamentally, the person having the Spirit will be able to distinguish between the truth and error. Is not the Holy Ghost the giver of truth? (John 14:15-17.) To some of the missionaries of this dispensation a reminder was given that they should preach by the Spirit of truth:

> Verily I say unto you, he that is ordained of me and sent forth to preach the word of truth by the Comforter, in the Spirit of truth, doth he preach it by the Spirit of truth or some other way?
>
> And if it be by some other way it is not of God. (D&C 50:17-18.)

To those who receive the word of truth, is it received by that same Spirit— truth, or in some other way, is another question the Lord asks these missionaries. (*Ibid.*, 50:19.) If the teacher and the hearer receive the Lord's word under the influence of his Spirit both are enlightened and rejoice together. (*Ibid.*, 50:22.)

But what if the member of the Church, as a teacher in an auxiliary organization or in the capacity of the member who tells others, members or nonmembers, of the gospel, does not feel adequately prepared of the Spirit? Certainly, no one may have all of the knowledge necessary, nor the fulness of the Spirit to accomplish the call at hand.

This feeling of inadequacy may also be present among many who are called to preach the gospel as missionaries. In a revelation given to two missionaries, there is found this encouraging word: "declare the things which ye have heard, and verily believe, and know to be true." (*Ibid.*, 80:4.) However, those who do have the responsibility of teaching are under the definite obligation to prepare themselves in knowledge and also to have the Holy Ghost.

Source of Knowledge

The law of preaching the gospel is concluded with these words:

And all this ye shall observe to do as I have commanded concerning your teaching, until the fulness of my scriptures is given.

And as ye shall lift up your voices by the Comforter, ye shall speak and prophesy as seemeth me good;

For, behold, the Comforter knoweth all things, and beareth record of the Father and of the Son. (*Ibid.*, 42:15-17.)

Although the Lord had not yet made known many important principles and ordinances of the gospel by the year 1831, this was not to prevent the missionaries from preaching the gospel. They were to go on their missions relying upon the Holy Ghost for guidance. More revelation was forthcoming that the Lord's representatives might also more effectively teach the plan of salvation. An example of the way in which the Spirit directed some of the early brethren in their activities is related by President George Q. Cannon:

I remember hearing related Brother Parley P. Pratt's first interview with the Saints at Fayette, Seneca County, where the Church was organized. . . . On that occasion he was called upon to speak; the Prophet Joseph was not present at the time. He brought forth from the prophecies of Isaiah, Jeremiah, Ezekiel, and other prophets, abundant proofs concerning the work which the Lord had established through His servant Joseph. A great

many of the Latter-day Saints were surprised that there were so
many evidences existing in the Bible concerning this work. The
Church had then been organized some five months, but the members had never heard from any of the Elders these proofs and
evidences which existed in the Bible. (*Doctrine and Covenants
Commentary,* pp. 238-39.)

Chapter 26

THE LAW OF MORAL CONDUCT

(Sections 42:18-20, 79, 84, 85)

In the last chapter, the background for the study of Section 42 was given. By way of reminder, we learned that not long after the Prophet Joseph Smith arrived in Kirtland, Ohio, the Lord gave to him, as promised earlier (D&C 38:32; 41:3), his law to the Church. The first part of this law is known as that of preaching the gospel. (*Ibid.*, 42:4-17.)

"Historical" Background

In the world today there are at least two points of view concerning the origin of the Ten Commandments: first, that they are simply the crystallization of moral laws which have developed out of the experiences of an evolving civilization, which belief arises out of the notion that man evolved from a lower form of animal, known as organic evolution; and second, that this formation of a code of moral laws was the work of Moses.

As far as Latter-day Saints are concerned, the gospel teaches us that in the beginning the Lord gave commandments to Adam by revelation. One of the unique teachings of the restored gospel is that the gospel of Jesus Christ was upon the earth before the time of Jesus' mortal ministry. Included in this concept is the fact that God revealed his will to man and that man did not "make" the laws of salvation. In the plan of salvation are the Ten Commandments, which do form the basis of the laws governing civilized people. Did the Ten Commandments come into being for the first time on Mount Sinai through the prophet Moses? No, the Lord provided laws and commandments for the salvation of his children in the gospel of Jesus Christ from the beginning. (*Ibid.*, 20: 17-19.)

Section 42 and Moral Law

In Section 42 some of the great moral commandments are given; but the reader should not consider that all of the laws pertaining to moral conduct in the Doctrine and Covenants are found in this revelation. For our present consideration, however, the following laws are included in this chapter: "*Thou shalt not kill* (*ibid.*, 42: 18-19, 79), *steal* (*ibid.*, 42:20, 84-85), *lie* (*ibid.*, 42:21, 86), *commit adultery* (*ibid.*, 42:23-25, 74-75), *speak evil of thy neighbor* (*ibid.*, 12:27, 88), and *thou shalt love thy wife* (*ibid.*, 42:22.)

That more laws of moral conduct than the foregoing are a part of the gospel is made plain in these two verses:

Thou knowest my laws concerning these things are given in my scriptures; he that sinneth and repenteth not shall be cast out. (*Ibid.*, 42:28.)

And if he or she do any manner of iniquity, he or she shall be delivered up unto the law, even that of God. (*Ibid.*, 42:87.)

The Single Standard

The single standard of morality is defined as a law which applies to both sexes; whereas, the double standard of morality means that the male or the female may have a different rule of conduct from the other. In this revelation the Lord repeatedly emphasizes the single standard of conduct as his law to the Church. This is done by the use of "he or she" or "man or woman," particularly in verses 80 to 92. An example of this is given in verse 87, quoted above.

"I Speak unto the Church"

As the *Doctrine and Covenants Commentary* (page 222) points out, the laws of moral conduct are given especially to the Church, as the Ten Commandments were given to ancient Israel. A distinction may be made, according to this same source, among various laws given to man.

Some are binding because of peculiar conditions or relations that may exist, and cease to be binding with the end of those conditions. New conditions require new laws, Israel in a settled condition in Canaan needed many rules and regulations which would have been inapplicable to their national life while in the wilderness. Laws regarding property, marriage, etc., belong to this class. (*Doctrine and Covenants Commentary*, pp. 222-223.)

These may be classified as statutes. (*Ibid.*, pp. 222-223.) On the other hand, there are moral laws which are permanent. Concerning them, it is said:

Some laws are binding because they are founded on the nature and attributes of God. If God is love, it is our duty to love Him and teach others. If He is just, merciful, pure, it is our duty to conform our lives to the divine standards of justice, mercy, and holiness. And from this springs another class of laws which are founded on the permanent relations of men in their present state of existence. They are called the moral laws to distinguish them from statutes, which are founded on temporary relations of man to man which may vary from time to time and in different countries. Moral laws are permanent. (*Ibid.*, 223.)

An example is taken from an address by President J. Reuben Clark, Jr., of a temporary law which prohibits the Israelites from eating sea foods "that have not fins and scales. . . ." (Lev. 11:10.) A possible reason for this prohibition, President Clark points out, may have been because of the perishability of certain sea foods which would have generated poison harmful to the body, because of a lack of a means of food preservation. With our modern means of refrigeration and rapid transportation, there is no law against the use of this particular food. The Lord is concerned today, as anciently, with the health of his people.

Thus the law that God's people must be clean and healthy has not changed, but the rule prescribed to secure obedience to the law has changed with the change in the manner of living. (*Ibid.*, p. 224.)

"Thou Shalt Not Kill"

As explained by Elder Harold B. Lee of the Council of the Twelve, the reason for the injunction of the Lord against taking human life, has its basis in the plan instituted in the heavens before the earth came into existence. Every person is a spirit child of God for whom the Lord has planned to bring to pass his immortality and, if faithful, an eternal life. (Moses 1:39.) Satan and his spirit followers rebelled against that plan and thus have sought to destroy all mortals by enticing them to commit sins. On the other hand, the Advocate of man with the Father is Jesus our Redeemer who gave his life that man might be able to repent and, eventually by man's faithfulness, receive eternal glory.

One of the most serious of all sins and crimes against the Lord's plan of salvation is the sin of murder or the destruction of human life. It seems clear that to be guilty of destroying life is the act of "rebellion" against the plan of the Almighty by denying an individual thus destroyed in mortality, the privilege of a full experience in this earth-school of opportunity. It is in the same category as the rebellion of Satan and his hosts and therefore it would not be surprising if the penalties to be imposed upon a murderer were to be of similar character as the penalties meted out to those spirits which were cast out of heaven with Satan. ("The Sixth Commandment," *The Ten Commandments Today*, p. 88.)

As scriptural examples to indicate the nature of the penalties imposed, Elder Lee suggests the case of (a) Cain (Genesis 4:6-12), and (b) David in plotting the death of Uriah; and also the crucifixion of the Savior by the Jews. The Prophet Joseph Smith as recorded in his history, discusses the case of David by stating that the murderer, one who sheds innocent blood, cannot have forgiveness.

> David sought repentance at the hand of God carefully with tears, for the murder of Uriah; but he could only get it through hell: he got a promise that his soul should not be left in hell. . . .
> . . . and the Priesthood that he [David] received, and the throne and kingdom of David is to be taken from him and given to another. . . . (*DHC* 6:253.)

Concerning certain Jews, who, it appears, assented to the crucifixion of Jesus, the Prophet said Peter did not say to them ". . . Repent and be baptized . . . for the remission of sins. . . ." (Acts 2:38.) See also *DHC* VI: 253.)

In commenting upon the commandment against taking human life, the *Doctrine and Covenants Commentary* quotes Jesus' injunction against this crime, (Matt. 5:21-22), and of his condemnation of anger "without a cause."

> There is a difference between the anger that is but malice or thirst for revenge, and the emotion that is felt in the presence of injustice and wrong. It is malice that is forbidden. To take the life of a fellow-being in order to gratify malice is the highest crime one human being can commit against another. . . . This commandment prohibits dueling, because dueling is but manslaughter, actual or potential. It prohibits suicide, which is self-murder. It condemns unjustifiable wars, which are but wholesale murders. There have been wars which are justifiable from the standpoint of one side of the contesting parties, but when the nations have courts of arbitration there will be no justification for any war, any more than there is for murder. The moral law must be applied to nations as well as individuals. "He that killeth shall die." (v. 19.) (*Doctrine and Covenants Commentary*, p. 224.)

Military Service and Killing

Is the Latter-day Saint who is called into the military service of his country guilty of murder as he takes human life while in that service?

During World War II, the First Presidency addressed a message to the members of the Church at the 112th annual general conference, in which they considered this question. After quoting from the modern revelations concerning war, the following appears:

When, therefore, constitutional law, obedient to these principles, calls the manhood of the Church into the armed service of any country to which they owe allegiance, their highest civic duty requires that they meet that call. If, hearkening to that call and obeying those in command over them, they shall take the lives of those who fight against them, that will not make of them murderers nor subject them to the penalty that God has prescribed for those who kill, beyond the principle to be mentioned shortly. For it would be a cruel God that would punish His children as moral sinners for acts done by them as the innocent instrumentalities of a sovereign whom He had told them to obey and whose will they were powerless to resist. . . .

In this terrible war now waging, thousands of our righteous young men in all parts of the world and in many countries are subject to a call into the military service of their own countries. Some of these, so serving, have already been called back to their heavenly home; others will almost surely be called to follow. But "behold," as Moroni said, the righteous of them who serve and are slain "do enter into the rest of the Lord their God," and of them the Lord has said "those that die in me shall not taste of death, for it shall be sweet unto them." (D&C 42:46.) Their salvation and exaltation in the world to come will be secure. That in their work of destruction they will be striking at their brethren will not be held against them. That sin, as Moroni of old said, is to the condemnation of those who "sit in their places of power in a state of thoughtless stupor," those rulers in the world who in a frenzy of hate and lust for unrighteous power and domination over their fellow men, have put into motion eternal forces they do not comprehend and cannot control. God, in His own due time, will pass sentence upon them. (*Conference Report*, pp. 94-96.)

Penalty for Murder

As part of the moral law, the Lord revealed in this dispensation:

And now, behold, I speak unto the church. Thou shalt not kill; and he that kills shall not have forgiveness in this world, nor in the world to come.

And again, I say, thou shalt not kill; but he that killeth shall die. (D&C 42:18-19.)

The Church of Jesus Christ of Latter-day Saints accepts capital punishment for this offense against God and the law of the land.

And it shall come to pass, that if any persons among you shall kill they shall be delivered up and dealt with according to the laws of the land; for remember that he hath no forgiveness; and it shall be proved according to the laws of the land. (*Ibid.*, 42:79.)

"Thou Shalt Not Steal"

Thou shalt not steal; and he that stealeth and will not repent shall be cast out. . . .

And if a man or woman shall rob, he or she shall be delivered up unto the law of the land.

And if he or she shall steal, he or she shall be delivered up unto the law of the land. (*Ibid.*, 42:20, 84-85.)

The essence of the moral law of the gospel of Jesus Christ is summed up in the words of the Savior that his disciple will love God and his neighbor as himself. (Matt. 22:37-39.) In a modern revelation, the Lord has again brought to the attention of his people that they are to follow this commandment. After expressing the fact that one should love the Lord "with all thy heart, with all thy might, mind, and strength; and in the name of Jesus Christ thou shalt serve him," it continues, "Thou shalt love thy neighbor as thyself. Thou shalt not steal neither commit adultery, nor kill, nor do anything like unto it." (D&C 59:5-6.)

It should not be difficult for one to understand that if there is love in one's heart for his fellow men, he will not steal, commit adultery, neither kill nor do anything that would injure his fellow man. The association of these three crimes with the love of God and neighbor in the modern revelation assuredly points up their importance in the sight of the Lord. Dishonesty in any of its forms, if uncontrolled or unregulated by divine fiat and if accepted by man as the foundation of a civilized people, would lead to a state of chaos in civilization.

The Nephites at one point in their history were told that their iniquity in casting out the prophets and thus disregarding the law of God would bring destruction upon them. Samuel, the Lamanite, prophesied of the time when the riches of the wicked Nephites would be lost because of a disregard for the property rights of others. Of the nation, the prophet said they would lament over their losses in a time of need. (Helaman 13:33-36.)

The fulfillment of this prophecy came toward the end of the Nephite nation during the time of Mormon when "no man could keep that which was his own, for the thieves, the robbers, and the murderers, and the magic art, and the witchcraft which was in the land." (Mormon 2:10.)

Types of Stealing

Ordinarily, a person thinks of stealing as involving the taking of someone else's property without realizing the consequences of this act before the law of the land. The types of stealing and the penalties imposed by the laws of the State of Utah which do not differ very much from most States, are summarized by Elder W. Cleon Skousen, former Salt Lake City Police Chief, as follows:

Many people are astonished when they discover how severe the punishment can be for thievery. The reason the penalty is so severe is because stealing strikes at the very foundation of a community. It is lawless indifference to the property rights of others. There can be no security when homes and stores are frequently raided by thieves. And there can be no safety on a highway where hijackers and road-robbers operate.

Because the criminal code in each state lays great stress on the seriousness of stealing, it is thought it may be of interest to list some of the different kinds of thievery mentioned by the state statutes.

1. Robbery. This kind of stealing consists of taking property from a person or from his immediate presence by means of force or fear. Robbery usually involves the use of a knife, a gun, or explosives. Therefore the penalty is very severe. [In Utah, for example, the penalty is five years to life.] (Utah Penal Code, 76-51-2.)

2. Grand Larceny. This consists of stealing something which is worth more than $50 or stealing something (regardless of value) from a person or from his presence; for example, it would be grand larceny if a pickpocket took $75 from a person's pocket. However, if the victim happened to catch the pickpocket and the pickpocket pulled a gun in order to get money, then the crime would be robbery, because the victim would have been subjected to force or fear. Grand larceny also includes the theft of certain domestic animals (regardless of value), such as horses and cattle. The penalty for grand larceny in Utah is one to ten years and a fine of from $50 to $1,000. (Utah Penal Code, 76-38-6.)

3. Petit [Pronounced Petty] Larceny. This includes other types of stealing not listed under grand larceny, such as shoplifting, chicken stealing, taking a bicycle, etc. These will usually come under petit larceny. The penalty in Utah is imprisonment in the county jail up to six months and a fine up to $300. (Utah Penal Code, 76-38-7.)

4. Burglary. This consists of breaking into a building, an automobile, trailer, railroad car, etc., for the purpose of stealing something or otherwise committing a felony. This type of crime may create a wave of hysteria in a community, particularly where burglaries are committed in banks, stores, or wealthy residences, and nitroglycerine or other explosives are used to open safes or storage vaults. As with robbery, this is considered a very serious type of crime and therefore carries a severe penalty. In burglaries of the above type the penalty is twenty-five to forty years (Utah Penal Code, 76-9-4), and daytime burglaries which does not involve explosives carries a penalty of one to twenty years (Utah Penal Code, 76-9-4), and day-time burglaries which do not involve explosives carry a penalty of six months to three years. (Utah Penal Code, 76-9-6.)

5. Forgery. This usually consists of getting money by altering the amount of a check or putting a false signature on it. There

are many other kinds of forgery, but this is the one about which we hear the most. The penalty for this offense is one to twenty years.

6. Fraud. This is a method of stealing which might be described as obtaining something of value or gaining a particular advantage by deceitfully misrepresenting the true facts. There are many kinds of frauds, such as writing checks on a bank where the check writer has no account, or he may have an account but writes a check for a much larger sum than he has in the bank. The penalty for this kind of stealing may go as high as fourteen years in the state penitentiary. (Utah Penal Code, 76-20-11.) The fraud of burning property to collect insurance carries a penalty of one to ten years. (U. S. Penal Code, 76-33-1.)

7. Confidence Games. This is a special kind of fraud where the victim is told that he can make a fortune overnight by following certain instructions. The usual procedure is to ask some person with outstanding financial ability to participate in the scheme. The operators take his money and disappear before he realizes that he has been duped. Even experienced businessmen are occasionally taken in by these schemes. Members of the Church are cautioned never to deal with strangers who claim to have a marvelous scheme for getting rich quickly. If the scheme had any merit, the operator would take it to his friends. He would not be around selling such a "sure thing" to strangers. These people always say their schemes are "very secret," and the victim is cautioned against discussing it with anyone because they say others might try to "cut in on the deal" if the word got around.

The penalty for stealing by means of a confidence game may go as high as ten years in the state penitentiary. (Utah Penal Code, 76-20-17.)

8. Extortion and Blackmail. This kind of stealing is usually done by writing a threatening letter, or otherwise inducing a victim to "pay off" because of force or fear. In Utah the penalty may be as much as three years. (Utah Penal Code, 76-19-3.) However, if the mails were used to make a threat of extortion, the crime is a federal violation which carries a penalty up to twenty years in prison and $5,000 fine. (U. S. Code, Title 18, Section 876.)

9. Embezzlement. This is a kind of stealing where a person appropriates money or property which has been entrusted to him. If the value of the property is over $50, then the penalty is one to ten years with a fine of $50 to $1,000. (Utah Penal Code, 76-17-

11.) If the value of the property is less than $50, the penalty is the same as that described for petit larceny.

10. Impersonation. This type of stealing is getting money, property, or some special advantage by pretending to be an officer or a person with special authority. In Utah the penalty for this violation may be as high as one year in the county jail and a fine of $1,000. If a federal officer is impersonated, the penalty may be three years imprisonment and $1,000 fine. (U.S. Code, Title 18, Sections 912-913.)

11. Kidnapping. The stealing of either children or adults is one of the most vicious of all crimes. Sometimes the person is kidnapped for ransom, sometimes for a revengeful beating, sometimes for a life of vice and debauchery. After the kidnapping and slaying of the Lindbergh baby in 1932, the United States Congress passed a law against kidnapping which permits the jury to recommend the death sentence where the kidnapped victim has been injured or killed. (U. S. Code, Title 18, Section 1201.) Almost immediately the number of kidnappings for ransom fell off sharply.

12. Plagiarism. This is stealing someone else's writings, ideas or creative work and claiming it to be one's own. The penalty depends upon the damages suffered by the victim. However, this may also be a violation of the Federal Copyright Law. In that event the penalty is up to one year imprisonment and a one thousand dollar fine. (U. S. Code, Title 17, Section 104.)

13. Espionage. This is stealing information which will endanger the security of the nation. In peacetime the penalty may be as high as twenty years. In wartime, the crime of espionage is particularly serious and the court may impose the death sentence. (U. S. Code, Title 18, Section 791-797.) (*Skousen, Cleon*, "The Eighth Commandment," *The Ten Commandments Today*, pp. 126-129.)

"Will a Man Rob God?"

In the book of Malachi we learn that one who withholds tithes and offerings from the Lord is guilty of robbing God. "Will a man rob God? Yet ye have robbed me. But ye say, wherein have we robbed thee? In tithes and offerings. Ye are cursed with a curse: for ye have robbed me, even this whole nation." (Mal. 3:8-9.)

If we consider this stern rebuke in the light of the

above discussion on stealing, what must we conclude concerning the tithing obligations placed upon us by the Lord? Would we not be in a similar situation as David on the occasion of the Prophet Nathan's visit? It was David who condemned himself unknowingly when Nathan approached him about a situation where one man was taking advantage of another man, at which time David became angry and said that the erring man "shall surely die." In the end, David was informed that he was the erring man. (2 Samuel 12:1-14.) We also are guilty when we condemn stealing, and in the same instant say we love the Lord and yet rob him of tithes. Is it possible that we could love our brethren and yet steal from them? Can we therefore without impunity, say we love the Lord and yet rob him at the same time?

Chapter 27

THE LAW OF MORAL CONDUCT (Continued)

(Section 42:21-26, 80-83, 86)

While conducting a conference of the Church at Fayette, New York, during the month of January 1831, the Prophet Joseph Smith received the Lord's promise that when he got to the Ohio valley the law to the Church would be given. Upon the Prophet's arrival in Kirtland, Ohio, the following month of February, the Prophet received the great revelation which included more of the Lord's will than the immediate problem before the Saints at the time; that is, the need to care for the relief of the poor and needy. The responsibility of the Church to carry the gospel to the world and the manner in which this should be done formed the basis of the first part of the law. (Chapter 25.)

A major part of the law to the Church is concerned with the relations of people who are interested in living lives which conform to the law of the Lord. These basic laws of moral conduct are necessary for a civilized people. An introduction to this law was given in the last chapter.

"Thou Shalt Not Lie"

The liar is strongly condemned in many scriptures of ancient and modern origin. The revelation under discussion is emphatic in denouncing this vice. (D&C 42: 21, 86.)

What is a lie? A dictionary definition is as follows: "To utter a falsehood with an intention to deceive, or with an immoral design; to say or do that which is designed to deceive another when he has a right to know the truth, or when morality requires a just representation. To cause an incorrect impression; to present a misleading appearance."

The Father of Lies

Lying is the opposite of truth. Those who indulge in lying, the speaking of untruths, are being deceived by the father of lies, the devil, who, from the beginning, sought to destroy God's work. In denouncing the false beliefs and practices of certain Jews, Jesus said:

Ye are of your father the devil, and the lusts of your father ye will do. He was a murderer from the beginning, and abode not in the truth, because there is no truth in him. When he speaketh a lie, he speaketh of his own: for he is a liar, and the father of it.

And because I tell you the truth, ye believe me not. (John 8:44-45.)

Satan's Plan

It is Satan's plan to deceive all people who will succumb to his influence. The half-truth is used as a means of deception. As President George Q. Cannon once explained concerning Mother Eve being deceived by the devil, he:

. . . told the truth in telling that, but he accompanied it with a lie as he always does. He never tells the complete truth. He said that they should not die. The Father had said that they should die. The devil had to tell a lie in order to accomplish his purposes; but there was some truth in his statement. Their eyes were opened. They had a knowledge of good and evil just as the Gods have. They became as Gods; for that is one of the features, one of the peculiar attributes of those who attain unto that glory—they understand the difference between good and evil. (*Journal of Discourses*, 26:190-191.)

Those who tell half-truths or untruths; in short, they who falsify are aiding and abetting the cause of the devil. They bring themselves into bondage, and, depending upon the purpose of the lie in reference to others, they may lead the deceived from the paths of honesty and virtue. It would seem obvious that the lie is one of the most powerful tools in the hands of Satan and those who perpetuate his designs to bring about the destruction of the souls of men.

Should a Latter-day Saint foster the kingdom of the devil by imitating the plans of the evil one?

Slave to a Lie

Do members of the kingdom of God realize that the lie brings eventual sorrow and regret into their own lives? Is it clear that when one follows this practice, he is bringing himself into a bondage which counteracts the very purpose of his earth-existence?

How much easier it is to tell the truth and be free from any enemy of salvation. When the Prophet Joseph Smith said that salvation consists of a man's being placed beyond the power of his enemies, meaning the enemies of his progression, such as dishonesty, greediness, lying, immorality, and other vices, he was saying that man is in bondage to these vices.

Joseph Smith and Salvation

Salvation is nothing more nor less than to triumph over all our enemies and putting them under our feet. And when we have power to put all enemies under our feet in this world, and a knowledge to triumph over all evil spirits in the world to come, then we are saved, as in the case of Jesus, who was to reign until He had put all enemies under his feet, and the last enemy was death. (*DHC* 5:387.)

As long as man is a captive to habits and vices that restrict or limit his power to act as a free agent, he will not receive salvation. But, wherein does the individual place himself in such a position of bondage by lying? He binds himself by making the lie a part of himself to the extent that he is no longer free from the falsehood. It has been said that to be a successful liar, it is necessary to remember not only the lie but the person to whom it is told. In doing this the person immediately loses his freedom to that extent. The necessity of remembering the lie, makes a deeper impression upon the liar, requiring that it become a part of his life.

The Truth Shall Make You Free

On the other hand, "the truth shall make you free." (John 8:32.) The truth-teller need not fear the consequences of his actions—he is free indeed. When the lie is spoken, it is almost always discovered and the loss of a friend and character debasement follow. When confronted with the temptation to lie or deceive, one should think of the consequences—possible loss of friends, sorrow, and regret. What self-respecting person would knowingly place himself in this position?

The adversary sought to destroy the work of the Lord in bringing forth The Book of Mormon by a planned attempt to use the loss of the translated portion from the gold plates to his advantage. The plan was to change that part which had been translated and then "expose" the Prophet Joseph Smith by showing that his retranslation was incorrect. This plan, however, was foiled by the translation of the small plates of Nephi which covered the same period of history. Of Satan it is said in the revelation disclosing this deception that:

Yea, he stirreth up their hearts to anger against this work.

Yea, he saith unto them: Deceive and lie in wait to catch, that ye may destroy; behold, this is no harm. And thus he flattereth them, and telleth them that it is no sin to lie that they may catch a man in a lie, that they may destroy him.

And thus he flattereth them, and leadeth them along until he draggeth their souls down to hell; and thus he causeth them to catch themselves in their own snare.

And thus he goeth up and down, to and fro in the earth, seeking to destroy the souls of men. (D&C 10:24-27.)

Korihor, the anti-Christ, in learning of the power of Alma, became convinced that he (Korihor) had been deceived, and then confessed his guilt in deceiving some Nephites. Alma records that ". . . the devil will not support his children at the last day, but doth speedily drag them down to hell." (Alma 30:60.)

Punishment of the Liar

Severe rebukes of the liar are mentioned many places in scripture. Solomon said that the Lord hates "a lying tongue" (Proverbs 6:17), and a "false witness that speaketh lies, and he that soweth discord among brethren." (*Ibid.*, 6:19.)

"Wo unto the liar, for he shall be thrust down to hell." (2 Nephi 9:34.) Concerning those who will eventually make up the telestial kingdom, it is revealed that:

These are they who are liars, and sorcerers, and adulterers, and whoremongers, and whosoever loves and makes a lie.

These are they who suffer the wrath of God on earth.

These are they who suffer the vengeance of eternal fire.

These are they who are cast down to hell and suffer the wrath of Almighty God, until the fulness of times, when Christ shall have subdued all enemies under his feet, and shall have perfected his work. (D&C 76:103-106; cf. 63:17.)

"Thou Shalt Not Commit Adultery"

As heretofore pointed out, the law of moral conduct applies to both sexes. This is the single standard of conduct. This fact is indicated clearly in making known the procedure of excommunication from the Church as the penalty for this sex sin.

And if any man or woman shall commit adultery, *he* or *she* shall be tried before two elders of the church, or more, and every word shall be established against him or her by two witnesses of the church, and not of the enemy; but if there are more than two witnesses it is better.

But *he* or *she* shall be condemned by the mouth of two witnesses; and the elders shall lay the case before the church, and the church shall lift up their hands against *him* or *her*, that they may be dealt with according to the law of God.

And if it can be, it is necessary that the bishop be present also.

And thus ye shall do in all cases which shall come before you. (*Ibid.*, 42:80-83. Italics by author.)

Because of the Lord's setting forth the single standard of conduct as his law, it is not inconsistent, nor is it a changing of the scriptures from their intended meaning, to insert the words shown in brackets below.

Thou shalt love thy wife [husband] with all thy heart, and shalt cleave unto her [him] and none else.

And he that looketh upon a woman [man] to lust after her [him] shall deny the faith, and shall not have the Spirit; and if he [she] repents not he [she] shall be cast out.

Thou shalt not commit adultery; and he [she] that committeth adultery, and repenteth not, shall be cast out.

But he [she] that has committed adultery and repents with all his [her] heart, and forsaketh it, and doeth it no more, thou shalt forgive;

But if he [she] doeth it again, he [she] shall not be forgiven, but shall be cast out. (*Ibid.*, 42:22-26.)

The penalty for adultery is severe because in the category of sins, it is classed next to murder. (Alma 39: 5-9.) President Joseph Fielding Smith of the Council of the Twelve has written the following in comment upon verses 22 to 26 of Section 42 quoted above:

Now this revelation was given before the endowment was made known. Since that time when a man is married in the temple, he takes a solemn covenant before God, angels, and witnesses that he will keep the law of chastity. Then if he violates that covenant it is not easy to receive forgiveness. I call your attention to this statement by the Prophet Joseph Smith: "If a man commit adultery, he cannot receive the celestial kingdom of God. Even if he is saved in any kingdom, it cannot be the celestial kingdom."

Of course, a man may, according to the Doctrine and Covenants, 132:26, receive forgiveness, if he is willing to pay the penalty for such a crime: that is he "shall be destroyed in the flesh, and shall be delivered unto the buffetings of Satan unto the day of redemption," which is the time of the resurrection. We cannot destroy in the flesh, so what the Lord will require in lieu thereof, I do not know. (*Doctrines of Salvation* II:93-94.)

From what the Lord has revealed about repentance or forgiveness of this sin, as great as it is, there is forgiveness for the Church member upon his or her true repentance. It may be forgiven when the member of the Church has not received the light and understanding of the temple ordinances, but even then the second offense will surely bring the casting out of the offender from the Church. For the person who may have committed this act before membership in the Church, upon his or her sincere repentance and the acceptance of baptism the remission of sins is received. Salvation in the kingdom of God comes to him or to her who endures to the end. (3 Nephi 30; 1 Cor. 6:9-11.)

An Heinous Practice

Elder Harold B. Lee draws attention to a practice directly related to this subject:

There is, however, another heinous practice, the sin of abortion, or the destruction of unborn children by illegal operations, which lies somewhere a close kin to the crime of destroying human life and certainly to be condemned under the subject heading of this chapter, "Thou shalt not kill!"

Against this deplorable practice the leaders of the Church have declared from the beginning. This serious sin against the Lord's plan is committed by two groups of individuals: first, those who, having committed their first great error in yielding to sexual sin, seek to cover their sins after gratifying their lusts, by committing an even more heinous crime before the law of the land and against the law of God; and, second, by those having entered into the sacred relationships of the married state but who, rather than accept the responsibilities of parenthood, yield to this awful practice by which they forfeit their rights to wonderful blessings which otherwise could have been theirs. ("The Sixth Commandment," *The Ten Commandments Today*, pp. 91-92.)

Love Thy Husband

"Thou shalt love thy wife [husband] with all thy heart, and shalt cleave unto her [him] and none else." (D&C 42:22.) When the Lord instituted marriage in the beginning, it was the intention that husband and wife should remain true to each other. They were to "be one flesh" (Genesis 2:24; see also Mark 10: 6-9; Ephesians 5:31) and to be faithful to each other, as the word "cleave" denotes.

Two ideas from the Apostle Paul bring together an emphasis which the Lord intends in this same connection:

Nevertheless neither is the man without the woman, neither the woman without the man, in the Lord.

For as the woman is of the man, even so is the man also by the woman; but all things of God. (1 Cor. 11:11-12.)

Husbands, love your wives, even as Christ also loved the church, and gave himself for it. . . .

Nevertheless let everyone of you in particular so love his wife even as himself; and the wife see that she reverence her husband. (Ephesians 5:25, 33.)

Safeguard against Sin

As the reader remembers the New Testament Sermon on the Mount, he will recognize the common element in Matthew 5:27-28, and part of Section 42:22-26 of The Doctrine and Covenants given above. When the resurrected Savior instructed the Nephites, however, he gave them this admonition which seems to reinforce and further clarify the meaning of the New Testament scripture, as also the modern revelation. Jesus emphasized in those instructions that control of thought, feelings, and desires is necessary as a safeguard against adultery.

Behold, it is written by them of old time, that thou shalt not commit adultery;

But I say unto you, that whosoever looketh on a woman [man], to lust after her [him], hath committed adultery already in his [her] heart.

Behold, I give unto you a commandment, that ye suffer none of these things to enter into your heart;

For it is better that ye should deny yourselves of these things, wherein ye will take up your cross, than that ye should be cast into hell. (3 Nephi 12:27-30.)

Is not this instruction in harmony with the words of the prophet-king Benjamin and later by Amulek (see Alma 12:14), when Benjamin counseled his people, as follows?

And finally, I cannot tell you all the things whereby ye may commit sin; for there are divers ways and means, even so many that I cannot number them.

But this much I can tell you, that if ye do not watch yourselves, and your *thoughts*, and your *words*, and your *deeds*, and observe the commandments of God, and continue in the faith of what ye have heard concerning the coming of our Lord, even unto the end of your lives, ye must perish. And now, O man, remember, and perish not. (Mosiah 4:29-30. Italics by author.)

Vulgarity of thought, word, and desire may well lead to the deed. "For as he thinketh in his heart, so is he. . . ." (Proverbs 23:7.)

Results of Unchaste Thoughts

Transgression begins in the mind, prompted by obscene pictures, salacious literature, immodesty of dress, and other forms of lewdness. Impure thoughts thus engendered, unless repented of, encourage apostasy. Three consequences of this thought-transgression are mentioned in the text under consideration (D&C 42:22-26), (1) a denial of the faith; (2) a loss of the Spirit; and (3) to be cast out of the Church. Included in these consequences is (4) that fear will come to the transgressor as he realizes that his unrepentance has brought upon him the condemnation of those who love him most in this life and also the wrath of God. (*Ibid.*, 63:16.)

Honest Hearts Produce Honest Actions

Admonitions against breaking the law of moral conduct are of great importance. Although breaking the laws against stealing and lying are more common than adultery and the taking of human life, none of these offenses against the Lord should be taken lightly. When one is genuinely converted to the gospel of Jesus Christ, it will be recognized that the breaking of a commandment is wrong in itself. Some people feel that they can commit sin as long as no one knows about the sin. The foundation of such a belief is based upon an idea contrary to the teachings of the gospel. Falling into the error of the Pharisees should not be an indulgence of the Latter-day Saint. Out of the heart proceed evil thoughts and deeds. (Matt. 15:11-20, especially 18-19.)

The Ideal Home

Love in the home is expressed in other ways in addition to the one on which emphasis has been placed thus far in this chapter. One of these ways is consideration for the feelings of the wife and husband, as expressed by President David O. McKay, in a general conference:

I cannot imagine a man's being cruel to a woman. I cannot imagine her so conducting herself as to merit such treatment.

Perhaps there are women in the world who exasperate their husbands but no man is justified in resorting to physical force or in exploding his feelings in profanity. There are men, undoubtedly, in the world who are thus beastly, but no man who holds the Priesthood of God should so debase himself. (*Conference Report,* October 1951, p. 181.)

Where confidence and love between husband and wife exist, there is the basis of the ideal home. In the words of President Joseph F. Smith, we learn:

A home is not a home in the eye of the gospel, unless there dwell perfect confidence and love between the husband and the wife. Home is a place of order, love, union, rest, confidence, and absolute trust; where the breath of suspicion of infidelity cannot enter; where the woman and the man each have implicit confidence in each other's honor and virtue. (*Gospel Doctrine,* p. 302.)

Chapter 28

THE LAW OF CONSECRATION

(Section 42:30-42, 53-55, 70-73)

When the law to the Church was promised, we learned that there was considerable poverty among the Saints. The Lord informed the Prophet Joseph Smith that when that law was revealed, his plan for caring for the poor would be given. (D&C 38:15-22, 32, 41.) Although this is not the only subject matter of this great revelation, it is an important part of Section 42, and the subject of many later revelations.

Up to this time our study of this revelation has included the laws of preaching the gospel and of moral conduct. As we have indicated, the living of the moral law is fundamental in "working out one's salvation." When a person becomes acquainted with the law of consecration, it is apparent that, as a basis for living this law, the moral teachings of the gospel are directly related to the successful operation of the law of consecration.

Man's Struggle

The basic wants of man are known to be food, clothing, and shelter. In order for a man to obtain these for himself and family, he has to struggle with his environment as the principal factor in accomplishing this purpose. When the law was promised, the Lord revealed that he had made the earth rich and that the Saints would partake of those riches. (*Ibid.*, 38:16-20.) After the law of consecration was given, the Lord also made known that he would provide for his people in his own way. Furthermore, that every man is a steward in his sight and that ample riches of the earth are available for man. (*Ibid.*, 104:13-14, 17.)

Several systems or plans for giving security to man have been devised. The Lord, however, has revealed that pertaining to his Saints there is a way which will give security in accordance with the way in which his plan is lived.

And it is my purpose to provide for my saints, for all things are mine.

But it must needs be done in mine own way. . . . (*Ibid.*, 104: 15-16.)

The Lord's Way in the Past

There are two instances in the scriptures where the Lord's people lived the law given to them to the extent that there was neither rich nor poor among them. The first of these was in the days of righteous Enoch and his people. Although there were wars and contentions among the people of other lands, Enoch's people lived the laws of God to the degree that they were blessed exceedingly.

The fear of the Lord was upon all nations, so great was the glory of the Lord, which was upon his people. And the Lord blessed the land, and they were blessed upon the mountains, and upon the high places, and did flourish.

And the Lord called his people ZION, because they were of one heart and one mind, and dwelt in righteousness; and there was no poor among them. (Moses 7:17-18.)

Following the visit of the resurrected Christ to the Nephites on the American Continent, a reign of righteousness was inaugurated and continued for about 165 years. The record of this period is an informative one because it makes known the means by which their happy condition was achieved. (4 Nephi 2-3, 15-16.)

The New Testament example of a similar instance of having "all things common" is not as clear as the latter

account. The record states that there was some division
of property among the Saints in the meridian dispensation. (Acts 2:41-47.)

In addition to the all-important condition of morality
which existed among the members of the Church in
these earlier dispensations, we discover another principle
which the Lord informed our own dispensation was
necessary for the successful living of the Lord's law. It
is given in Section 38, as follows: "I say unto you, be
one; and if ye are not one ye are not mine." (D&C 38:27.)

"All Things Common"

In commenting upon the practice of the New Testament Saints having "all things common," Elder Albert E.
Bowen furnishes the following observation based upon
the commentaries of others:

> In relation to the matter of their having all things in com-
> mon it is interesting to note that the Primitive Church apparently
> did not long continue the practice. Gibbon relates that the rule
> was early relaxed so as to permit of individual undertakings and
> was finally supplanted by the law of tithing. (I Gibbon, *Decline
> and Fall*, p. 416-417.) In this connection Dummelow's Bible Com-
> mentary, p. 824, says: "The Church of Jerusalem recognized the
> principle of private property. A disciple's property really was his
> own, but he did not SAY it was his own; he treated it as if it were
> common property. The Anabaptist principle that private property
> is unlawful finds no support in the Acts. The communism was
> voluntary. (*The Welfare Plan*, pp. 15-16.)

In the thinking of some people of our own times.
there is an association of the law of consecration with
having things in common to the extent that they believe it
is in agreement with communism of today. In 1838, the
Prophet Joseph Smith set down in print some questions
which were most frequently asked him, as he said, in
order to save himself the trouble of repeating them over
and over again. Among these was the one: "Do the Mormons believe in having all things in common?" His an-

swer was, "No." (*DHC* 3:23.) As indicated in Chapter 25 on the background of Section 41 (the first revelation received by the Prophet in Kirtland, Ohio), some members of the Church in that place had been organized in an effort to live as the early Christians are said to have lived, having all things common. Concerning the Kirtland branch, the Prophet wrote:

The branch of the Church in this part of the Lord's vineyard, which had increased to nearly one hundred members, were striving to do the will of God, as far as they knew it, though some strange notions and false spirits had crept in among them. With a little caution and some wisdom, I soon assisted the brethren and sisters to overcome them. The plan of "common stock," which had existed in what was called "the family," whose members generally had embraced the everlasting Gospel, was readily abandoned for the more perfect law of the Lord; and the false spirits were early discerned and rejected by the light of revelation. (*Ibid.*, 1:146-147.)

As we shall see in our brief discussion of the law of consecration, it is neither communistic nor communal.

The Law of Consecration

The Lord's way of providing for the poor required that the individual consecrate or give to the Church all of his property. This was to be done by deed or legal title.

And behold, thou wilt remember the poor, and consecrate of thy properties for their support that which thou hast to impart unto them, with a covenant and a deed which cannot be broken. (D&C 42:30.)

Following this introduction to the law of consecration, the revelation continues with these words:

And inasmuch as ye impart of your substance unto the poor, ye will do it unto me; and they shall be laid before the bishop of my church and his counselors, two of the elders, or high priests, such as he shall appoint or has appointed and set apart for that purpose.

And it shall come to pass, that after they are laid before the bishop of my church, and after that he has received these testimonies concerning the consecration of the properties of my church, that they cannot be taken from the church, agreeable to my commandments, every man shall be made accountable unto me, a steward over his own property, or that which he has received by consecration, as much as is sufficient for himself and family. (*Ibid.*, 42:31-32.)

Again, emphasis is given to the consecration as belonging to the Church, but the donor is to become a steward over that which he has consecrated or properties which may not have belonged to him. As noted in the verses above, the standard or measure of one's stewardship is "as much as is sufficient for himself and family." In Section 51, Edward Partridge, and those chosen by him, are to "appoint unto this people their portions, every man equal according to his family, according to his circumstances and his wants and needs." (*Ibid.*, 51:3.) Although this and other revelations point out that men are to be equal under the law of consecration, the words just quoted describe the manner in which the men are to be equal. In pointing up this fact, President J. Reuben Clark, Jr., Counselor in the First Presidency, says:

Obviously, this is not a case of "dead level" equality. It is "equality" that will vary as much as the man's circumstances, his family, his wants and needs, may vary. (*Conference Report*, October 4, 1942, p. 55.)

If, however, there would arise a difference of opinion between the agent of the Church and the member, over the amount to be received as a stewardship, the Prophet Joseph Smith wrote the following to Bishop Edward Partridge:

. . . every man must be his own judge how much he should receive and how much he should suffer to remain in the hands of the Bishop. I speak of those who consecrate more than they need for the support of themselves and their families.

The matter of consecration must be done by the mutual consent of both parties; for to give the Bishop power to say how much every man shall have, and he be obliged to comply with the Bishop's judgment, is giving to the Bishop more power than a king has; and upon the other hand, to let every man say how much he needs, and the Bishop be obliged to comply with his judgment, is to throw Zion into confusion, and make a slave of the Bishop. The fact is, there must be a balance or equilibrium of power, between the Bishop and the people, and thus harmony and good will may be preserved among you.

Therefore, those persons consecrating property to the Bishop in Zion, and then receiving an inheritance back, must reasonably show to the Bishop that they need as much as they claim. But in case the two parties cannot come to a mutual agreement, the Bishop is to have nothing to do about receiving such consecrations; and the case must be laid before a council of twelve High Priests, the Bishop not being one of the council, but he is to lay the case before them. (*DHC* I:364-365.)

From the foregoing and other places yet to be noted, it should be clear to all that the principle of free agency is an important part of this order. The difference between this law and that of communism, as known today, lies in man's freedom to act. This fact and another one in connection with this law is further indicated in the answer to this and a related question: Is it intended that the donor of property in receiving a stewardship have legal title to the stewardship received from the Church? The revelation answering this question states:

And let my servant Edward Partridge, when he shall appoint a man his portion, give unto him a writing that shall secure unto him his portion, that he shall hold it, even this right and this inheritance in the church, until he transgresses and is not accounted worthy by the voice of the church, according to the laws and covenants of the church, to belong to the church.

And if he shall transgress and is not accounted worthy to belong to the church, he shall not have power to claim that portion which he has consecrated unto the bishop for the poor and needy of my church; therefore, he shall not retain the gift, but shall only have claim on that portion that is deeded unto him. (D&C 51:4-5.)

Not only was the person to consecrate his property to the Church by legal deed and thus surrender all claim to the property, but the stewardship received as a member of the order was to be his own. Private property is a fundamental part of the operation of the law of consecration. But what if the member of this order is no longer worthy to continue in the Church, is the property deeded to him his own or that of the Church? From the foregoing revelation the answer is that he has claim on the stewardship deeded to him. This answer also points up the fact of free agency in that a person may leave the order and yet still retain his property.

The Bishop's Storehouse

As a member of the order produces surpluses from his stewardship or there are residues arising from the original consecration beyond what the donor has consecrated to the Church, provision is made in the revelations for the use of these portions. (D&C 42:33-34.)

Not only were these residues to be used for the poor, but also for the building up the kingdom of God upon the earth, as the revelation indicates:

And for the purpose of purchasing lands for the public benefit of the church, and building houses of worship, and building up of the New Jerusalem which is hereafter to be revealed. (*Ibid.*, 42:35.)

In a later revelation, the Lord makes known that children are to be maintained from the parents' stewardship, but if the time should come that they are unable to provide a stewardship for their children of age, the Lord's storehouse is to provide for them. It also indicates:

And the storehouse shall be kept by the consecrations of the church; and widows and orphans shall be provided for, as also the poor. (*Ibid.*, 83:6.)

Law of Remuneration

Provision is made in verses 70 through 73 of Section 42 for those who labor in a full-time capacity for the Church to have their families supported out of the general funds of the Order.

The law of remuneration is that those who administer in spiritual affairs must have their stewardships and labor for their living, "even as the members." This is wisdom. For in that position they are absolutely independent and can preach the truth without fear. Those who administer in temporal affairs and give their entire time to public business are to have a just remuneration. If they were to earn a living for themselves, they could not give all their time and energy to the community. (*Doctrine and Covenants Commentary*, p. 234.)

Summary

The law of consecration, also known as the United Order (not to be confused with the Orders operated between 1877 and 1884 in the West), required that the donor of property consecrate his wealth by legal title to the agent (bishop) of the Church. In return, the consecrator would receive a stewardship, also called an inheritance, by legal title or deed, which secured his inheritance by law. If he left the Order, this stewardship would be his own; thus, the law of consecration was not communistic because of the principles of free agency and private property. The surplus arising from the "working" of the stewardship, beyond the circumstances and wants and needs of the family, would be placed in the bishop's storehouse for the care of the poor, widows, orphans, and the building up of Zion. Additional stewardships would also come, in part, from this source.

History of the United Order

In the spring of 1831, members of the Church from New York State began arriving in the Kirtland, Ohio, area. A branch of the Church from Colesville, New York, settled at Thompson, Ohio, where they were given the privilege of organizing themselves according to the law of consecration. (D&C 51:15.) That this branch of the Church was to remain in Ohio for only a short time is evident from the revelation, for they were to receive another commandment about their location at some future time. (*Ibid.*, 51:16.) In the meantime, however, they were to act as though they were to be in Ohio "for years." (*Ibid.*, 51:17.) It was only a matter of months until the faithful members of this branch were commanded to gather in Missouri. (*Ibid.*, 56:5-7.) It was during the time of the saints sojourn in Jackson County, Missouri, that further attempts were made to live this law.

The United Order Discontinued

By revelation the Lord set the law of consecration in abeyance until such time as the saints would again be established in Missouri to build up the city of Zion. (*Ibid.*, 105:34.) One reason for the failure of this law to remain in force, as reported in *The Evening and Morning Star*, was that "There has not been enough consecrated to plant the poor in inheritances." A reason for this condition was that many, before coming to Zion, had given their property away, and sacrificed some, resulting in their not having property which could be made available for consecration. (*DHC* I:381.) It should also be remembered that, due to other weaknesses of the Saints, they did not measure up to the standards necessary to live this law. (D&C 101:6-8; 105:2-6.) The persecution of the Church in Missouri shortened the time when the law of consecration was in force among the saints.

Although some members in Illinois, the place of gathering after the expulsion of the saints from Missouri, felt that the law of consecration should be lived, the

Prophet Joseph Smith said to the Iowa High Council at a meeting at Montrose:

> . . . that it was the will of the Lord that we should desist from trying to keep it; and if persisted in, it would produce a perfect defeat of its object, and that he assumed the whole responsibility of not keeping it until proposed by himself. (*DHC* 4:93.)

Revocation of Commandments

Does the Lord command or give his people the privilege of living a law and then revoke that command? The word of the Lord is definite in this regard, as evidenced in the modern revelation. (D&C 56:1-4.) An example from the New Testament may be appropriately referred to when the Lord commanded his disciples not to take purse and scrip (baggage), but subsequently, when circumstances and conditions were different, he counseled them to take purse and script. (Luke 22:35-36; Mt. 10:9-10.) Another example in our dispensation when conditions released the saints from compliance to a command was the building of the temple in Jackson County, Missouri. Due to circumstances, the persecution of the saints, this commandment was also placed in abeyance. (D&C 124:49-51.)

Conversion Necessary

It is evident from the revelations already referred to in this chapter that obedience to the law of consecration requires that the members of the Church live on a high moral plane, keeping the commandments to the extent that they are able to eliminate greed, selfishness, dishonesty, and other barriers to living the great commandment—to love one's neighbor as oneself.

The testimony of the gospel is a necessary step in the

accomplishment of this purpose, but there remains the fact that one must still, as a member of the Church, be "born again." (Alma, chapter 5.)

The Welfare Plan

Over two decades ago, by revelation to the leadership of the Church, there was inaugurated the Welfare Plan. Conditions at that time brought into existence a program designed to meet the circumstances of the times. Through the years since 1936, this program has made great advances in the accomplishment of the objectives which brought it into being. The existence of the "bishop's storehouse," originally a part of the law of consecration, is known to all Latter-day Saints. The accumulated stocks of food, clothing, and other materials in these buildings for the use of faithful members of the Church in need, have demonstrated the complete justification for such a plan.

To some in the Church, however, there is another reason for the Welfare Program other than to take care of the present needs of the people. Appropriate to this lesson are the remarks made in a General Conference by President J. Reuben Clark, Jr., of the First Presidency, when he compared the Welfare Plan with the law of consecration.

We have all said that the Welfare Plan is not the United Order and was not intended to be. However, I should like to suggest to you that perhaps, after all, when the Welfare Plan gets thoroughly into operation—it is not so yet—we shall not be so very far from carrying out the great fundamentals of the United Order.

In the first place I repeat again, the United Order recognized and was built upon the principle of private owernship of property; all that a man had and lived upon under the United Order, was his own. Quite obviously, the fundamental principle of our system today is the ownership of private property.

In the next place, in lieu of residues and surpluses which were accumulated and built upon the United Order, we, today, have our fast offerings, our Welfare donations, and our tithing, all of which may be devoted to the care of the poor, as well as for the carrying on of the activities and business of the Church. After all, the United Order was primarily designed to build up a system under which there should be no abjectly poor, and this is the purpose, also, of the Welfare Plan.

In this connection it should be observed that it is clear from these earlier revelations, as well as from our history, that the Lord had very early to tell the people about the wickedness of idleness, and the wickedness of greed, because the brethren who had were not giving properly, and those who had not were evidently intending to live without work on the things which were to be received from those who had property. (D&C 56:16-20.)

Furthermore, we had under the United Order a bishop's storehouse in which were collected the materials from which to supply the needs and the wants of the poor. We have a bishop's storehouse under the Welfare Plan, used for the same purpose.

As I have already indicated, the surplus properties which came to the Church under the Law of Consecration, under the United Order, became the "common property" of the Church (D&C 82:18) and were handled under the United Order for the benefit of the poor. We have now under the Welfare Plan all over the Church, ward land projects. In some cases the lands are owned by the wards, in others they are leased by the wards or lent to them by private individuals. This land is being farmed for the benefit of the poor, by the poor where you can get the poor to work it.

We have in place of the two treasuries, the "Sacred Treasury" and "Another Treasury," the general funds of the Church.

Thus you will see, brethren, that in many of its great essentials, we have, as the Welfare Plan has now developed, the broad essentials of the United Order. Furthermore, having in mind the assistance which is being given from time to time and in various wards to help set people up in business or in farming, we have a plan which is not essentially unlike that which was in the United Order when the poor were given portions from the common fund. (*Conference Report*, October 3, 1942, pp. 57-58.)

Chapter 29

THE LAW OF ADMINISTRATION TO THE SICK

(Section 42:43-52)

The introduction of Section 42 of The Doctrine and Covenants has been given in other chapters. In general, the receiving of this revelation arose out of the Lord's recognition of the poverty of some saints. The law concerning this condition and the promises of the Lord that the earth is to bring forth its fulness for the benefit of his people " in the due time of the Lord" is provided in this revelation. We have already learned that there are other laws mentioned in this revelation, one of which is the subject of this chapter.

Objective of This Chapter

Although reference is made to the working of miracles, including healings, in other revelations yet to be studied, this chapter will be limited in subject matter to some of the principles of adminstration to the sick. All of the ramifications of this important subject are not to be discussed in this chapter.

Some Aspects of This Ordinance

The healing of a person's infirmity, disease, or the correction of some impediment such as in speech, use of legs or arms, have always been a part of the gospel of Jesus Christ. One of the most direct references to the practice of administering to the sick during the meridian dispensation is that given in the New Testament, as follows:

Is any sick among you? Let him call for the elders of the church; and let them pray over him, anointing him with oil in the name of the Lord:

And the prayer of faith shall save the sick, and the Lord shall raise him up; and if he have committed sins, they shall be forgiven him.

Confess your faults one to another, and pray one for another, that ye may be healed. The effectual fervent prayer of a righteous man availeth much. (James 5:14-16.)

There are several factors to be noted in James' counsel concerning this ordinance. One of these is that the Lord provided in his plan such an ordinance as administration to the sick by the elders of the Church. In other places in the New Testament are found references to the laying on of the hands for this purpose. The Savior said that his believers should "lay hands on the sick, and they shall recover." (Mark 16:18.) In our own dispensation, the Prophet Joseph Smith has told us that the sign of the healing of the sick is the laying on of hands. (*DHC* IV: 555.)

The use of oil is indicated by James as a part of the ordinance of administration to the sick. In the call and commission to the Twelve Apostles, it is recorded by Mark that Jesus,

... called unto him the twelve, and began to send them forth by two and two; and gave them power over unclean spirits. ...

And they went out, and preached that men should repent.

And they cast out many devils, and anointed with oil many that were sick, and healed them. (Mark 6:7, 12-13.)

After asking this question "Can not the Lord hear prayer and heal the sick just as well without laying on of hands and anointing with oil as with?" Elder Orson Pratt said:

He could have thrown down the walls of Jericho without the children of Israel walking around them and blowing rams' horns; but the Lord has a form, then why not comply with it, and leave the event with him. (*Journal of Discouses* 16:290.)

A frequently raised question arising out of James' instructions is this one answered by President Joseph Fielding Smith:

"James says when a man administers to a sick person he has power to remit his sins; how does the elder get power to remit sins?"

It is not the elder who remits or forgives the sick man's sins, but the Lord. If by the power of faith and through the administration by the elders the man is healed it is evidence that his sins have been forgiven. It is hardly reasonable to think that the Lord will forgive the sins of a man who is healed if he has not repented. Naturally he would repent of his sins if he seeks for the blessings by the elders. (Smith, Joseph Fielding, "Your Question," *The Improvement Era*, August 1955, p. 607.)

The Lord Speaks to Us

From the law of the Lord:

And whosoever among you are sick, and have not faith to be healed, but believe, shall be nourished with all tenderness, with herbs and mild food, and that not by the hand of an enemy.

And the elders of the church, two or more, shall be called, and shall pray for and lay their hands upon them in my name; and if they die they shall die unto me, and if they live they shall live unto me. (D&C 42:43-44.)

The elders of The Church of Jesus Christ of Latter-day Saints are to administer to the members of the kingdom of God in this dispensation by the "prayer of faith" and the power of the Priesthood. Rather than restricting or limiting the operations of the Priesthood of God, the fulness of times is the period when greater evidence of the power of the Lord is to be manifest. This dispensation is the time for gathering together in one all dispensations of times to culminate in the salvation of mankind. In the beginning of this dispensation, the Lord said in his preface to The Doctrine and Covenants that he had established the gospel upon the earth "That faith also might increase in the earth; That mine everlasting covenant might be established." (D&C 1:21-22.)

Medical Aid?

Throughout the law of administration to the sick, as given in Section 42, emphasis is placed upon the principle of faith in bringing about a restoration to health. (D&C 42:48-51.) It does not follow, however, that Latter-day Saints believe that the use of medicine and the skill of the surgeon are not to be used. In commenting upon verses 43 and 44 of this revelation, the *Doctrine and Covenants Commentary*, p. 232, gives the following information:

The Latter-day Saints believe in the healing virtue of the prayer of faith, but they do not proscribe the use of "herbs and mild food," nor the aid of a physician. In the month of November, 1842, Brigham Young was seriously ill. In his diary the Prophet Joseph notes that, "He was suddenly and severely attacked by disease, with strong symptoms of apoplexy," and then he adds, "We immediately administered to him by laying on of hands and prayer, accompanied with the use of herbs." (*History of the Church*, Vol. 5, p. 126.)

Under date of December 26th, 1842, the Prophet writes:

"General Law gave me in custody of Doctor Richards, with whom I visited Sister Morey, who was severely afflicted. We prescribed Lobelia for her, among other things, which is excellent in its place." (*Ibid.*, p. 209.) (*Doctrine and Covenants Commentary*, p. 232.)

Revelation Continued

In continuing this law the Lord reveals some important truths relative to the Latter-day Saints' attitude toward the dead and also the blessing awaiting the faithful of his kingdom:

Thou shalt live together in love, insomuch that thou shalt weep for the loss of them that die, and more especially for those that have not hope of a glorious resurrection.

And it shall come to pass that those that die in me shall not taste of death, for it shall be sweet unto them;

And they that die not in me, wo unto them, for their death is bitter.

And again, it shall come to pass that he that hath faith in me to be healed, and is not appointed unto death, shall be healed.

He who hath faith to see shall see.

He who hath faith to hear shall hear.

The lame who hath faith to leap shall leap.

And they who have not faith to do these things, but believe in me, have power to become my sons; and inasmuch as they break not my laws thou shalt bear their infirmities. (D&C 42:45-52.)

Death is a part of the eternal plan of the Father. Jacob taught that death "hath passed upon all men, to fulfill the merciful plan of the great Creator." (2 Nephi 9: 6.) The Prophet Joseph Smith spoke of death as the last enemy to be overcome. (*DHC* 5:387-388.) The ancient prophets heralded the day when the bands of death would be broken by the resurrection of the body from the grave. Thus, there would be no victory in the grave. Life would be endless. The removal of death by the resurrection was proclaimed as a grand objective of the atonement of Christ. Sorrow would depart from the land in the realization that no longer would there be a parting of loved ones. (2 Nephi 9:19; Mosiah 15:20; 16:9; I Cor. 15:53-55; D&C 63:49.)

They That Die Not Unto the Lord

A scene of mourning is depicted in The Book of Mormon account of the great destruction upon this continent when the Savior was crucified. (3 Nephi 8:23-25.) Following this destruction a voice was heard, crying: "Wo, wo, wo unto this people; wo unto the inhabitants of the whole earth except they shall repent; for the devil laugheth, and his angels rejoice, because of the slain of the fair sons and daughters of my people." (*Ibid.*, 9:2.) But for what reason was there rejoicing on the part of the devil and his cohorts? The scripture continues, "and it is because of their iniquity and abominations that they are fallen." (*Ibid.*, 9:2.) So strongly did the Nephites feel against the necessity of taking the lives of the Lamanites in the days of Helaman and Moroni (the great general and prophet) that they sorrowed in sending so many "out of this world into an eternal world, unprepared to meet their God." (Alma 48:22-25.) Mormon's lamentation over the fallen Nephites in the last great battle with the Lamanites reminds one of the eternal truth that all must stand before the judgment-seat of Christ where every man will be rewarded according to justice and mercy. (Mormon 6:16-22.)

"Death Shall Be Sweet Unto Them"

When death strikes in a family, it is natural to weep for the loss thus sustained. The extent of such mourning, among Latter-day Saints, however, may also be determined by the circumstances. President John Taylor had this to say at a funeral service:

It is proper to sorrow; it is proper to show respect for the departed. It is proper that our sympathies should be drawn out; it is proper that we should assemble together to attend to appropriate funeral services, as we are now doing, that we may reflect upon our lives and upon the uncertainty thereof, and upon death and the results that may follow after; and that we consider the Gospel of the Son of God, and reflect upon our position, etc. . . . We, above all other people upon the face of the earth, ought to be free from outward show, and from the appearance of sorrow and mourning, having had planted within us the germs of immortality and eternal life; inasmuch as when we get through with the affairs of this world, we not only expect, but we know that we will inherit eternal lives in the celestial kingdom of God. And knowing this, it would not be for us to mourn as people without any hope. (*Journal of Discourses* 22:255.)

In quoting the words of President Joseph F. Smith, the *Doctrine and Covenants Commentary* (p. 232) gives the following statement which applies to the expressions from the text of our chapter "and if they die they shall die unto me" (D&C 42:44) and "Those that die in me shall not taste of death, for it shall be sweet unto them" (D&C 42:46):

That which we call death is merely the slumber and rest of this mortal clay, and that only for a little season, while the spirit, the life, has gone to enjoy again the presence and society of those from whence it came, and to whom it is joy again to return. And this will be the condition of the righteous until the morning of the resurrection, when the spirit will have power to call forth the lifeless frame to be united again, and they both become a living soul, an immortal being, filled with the light and power of God. . . .

What reason have we to mourn? None, except that we are deprived for a few days of the society of one whom we love. (*Journal of Discourses* 19:265.)

Faith To Be Healed

The scriptures teach us that where faith is present, blessings follow. Miracles are performed by this principle. (Mark 16:17-18.) Jesus said to the woman healed by him, "thy faith hath made thee whole." (Mt. 9:22.) On the other hand, no mighty miracles were performed by Jesus in "his own country" because of the unbelief of the people, who knew him as the carpenter; yet "he laid his hands upon a few sick folk, and healed them." (Mark 6:5.) Upon one occasion Paul healed a lame man because he had faith to be healed. (Acts 14:8-10.)

Are All of Faith to be Healed?

From an informative sermon by Elder Spencer W. Kimball of the Council of the Twelve, this thought is expressed on this question and the subject of pain, sorrow, and punishment:

Now, we find many people critical when a righteous person is killed, a young father or mother is taken from a family, or when violent deaths occur. Some become bitter when oft-repeated prayers seem unanswered. Some lose faith and turn sour when solemn administrations by holy men seem to be ignored and no restoration seems to come from repeated prayer circles. But if all the sick were healed, if all the righteous were protected and the wicked destroyed, the whole program of the Father would be annulled and the basic principle of the Gospel, free agency, would be ended.

If pain and sorrow and total punishment immediately followed the doing of evil, no soul would repeat a misdeed. If joy and peace and rewards were instantaneously given the doer of good, there could be no evil—all would do good and not because of the rightness of doing good. There would be no test of strength, no development of character, no growth of powers, no free agency, only satanic controls.

Should all prayers be immediately answered according to our selfish desires and our limited understanding, then there would be little or no suffering, sorrow, disappointment or even death, and if these were not, there would also be an absence of joy, success, resurrection, eternal life and Godhood. (Kimball, Spencer W.: "Tragedy or Destiny," address to the Brigham Young University Student Body, December 6, 1955, pp. 4-5.)

Elder Kimball continues in pointing out that death is a part of life's experiences:

Everyone must die. Death is an important part of life. Of course, we are never quite ready for the change. Not knowing when it should come, we properly fight to retain our life.

Why are we so afraid of death? We pray for the sick—we administer to the afflicted—we implore the Lord to heal and reduce pain and save life and postpone death, and properly so, but is eternity so frightful? So awful?

The Prophet Joseph Smith confirmed:

"The Lord takes many away even in infancy, that they may escape the envy of man and the sorrows and evils of this present world; they were too pure, too lovely, to live on this earth; therefore, if rightly considered, instead of mourning we have reason to rejoice as they are delivered from evil and we shall have them again. The only difference between the old and the young dying is, one lives longer in heaven and eternal light and glory than the other, and is freed a little sooner from this miserable world." (*Ibid.*, p. 8.)

"Appointed unto Death"

In commenting upon the Lord's statement that "he that hath faith in me to be healed, and is not appointed unto death, shall be healed." (D&C 42:48), Brother Kimball states in the source already quoted:

If not "appointed unto death" and sufficient faith is developed, life can be spared. But if there is not enough faith many die before their time. It is evident that even the righteous will not always be healed and even those of great faith will die when it is according to the purpose of God. Joseph Smith died in his thirties as did the Savior. Solemn prayers were answered negatively. . . .

"If he is not appointed unto death!" That is a challenging statement.

I am confident that there is a time to die. I am not a fatalist. I believe that many people die before "their time" because they are careless, abuse their bodies, take unnecessary chances, or expose themselves to hazards, accidents and sickness. . . . (Kimball, Spencer W.: "Tragedy or Destiny," address to the Brigham Young University Student Body, December 6, 1955, pp. 6, 9.)

In confirmation of some of these ideas, Elder Kimball refers to the scripture in Job 22:15-16; Ecclesiastes 3:1-2, 7:17, with the stated belief that "we die prematurely but seldom exceed our time very much though there are exceptions." As an exception, reference is made to King Hezekiah of Judah. (2 Kings 20:1-6.) Examples from The Book of Mormon bearing out the fact that efforts were made to bring some of the Lord's servants to an early death before their "time to die" were cited in the cases of Abinadi (Mosiah 13:3, 7; 17:19); and Lehi and Nephi, sons of Helaman, (Helaman 5:26, 29.) Bible examples include Enoch (Moses 6:39), and Paul (2 Cor. 11:23-27; Phil. 1:23; Acts 21:13).

In conclusion, Brother Kimball says:

God can control our lives, He guides and blesses us, but gives us our agency. We may live our lives in accordance with His plan for us or we may foolishly shorten or terminate them.

I am positive in my mind that the Lord has planned our destiny. We can shorten our lives but I think we cannot lengthen them very much. Sometimes we'll understand fully, and when we see back from the vantage point of the future we shall be satisfied with many of the happenings of this life which seemed so difficult for us to comprehend. (Kimball, Spencer W.: "Tragedy or Destiny," address to the Brigham Young University Student Body, December 6, 1955, pp. 11-12.)

Chapter 30

THE PAST, PRESENT, AND FUTURE

(Section 45:1-42)

The title of this chapter suggests the functions of a prophet of God. Although there are many responsibilities belonging to a prophet in furthering the kingdom of God upon the earth, one of the principal functions is to receive revelation for the guidance of the Church. The revelation thus received may refer to the past, as an example, or illustration for present and future obedience on the part of the saints, or to clarify the scriptures previously given.

A prophet thus uses the revelations of other prophets in his understanding of the purposes of the Lord. Another purpose of the revelations received by a living prophet is to give admonitions, warnings, and advice to the people of his own generation. In other words, by the spirit of prophecy, a prophet is empowered to interpret present-day conditions for the people. He enjoys the privilege of foreseeing future events, as the Lord wills it, that the saints may be adequately warned against calamities of the future. The Lord's Preface to The Doctrine and Covenants definitely states that the revelations in that book of scripture are to constitute a voice of warning. The Prophet Joseph Smith was called by the Lord, among other reasons, for the purpose of receiving revelations because of the judgments to come in the latter days. (Chapter 3.)

Historical Background

At the time Section 45 was received by Joseph Smith, many efforts were made by the Adversary to destroy the effectiveness of the Church.

At this age of the Church [i.e., early in the spring of 1831] many false reports, lies, and foolish stories, were published in the newspapers, and circulated in every direction, to prevent people from investigating the work, or embracing the faith. A great earthquake in China, which destroyed from one to two thousand inhabitants, was burlesqued in some papers, as "Mormonism in China." But to the joy of the Saints who had to struggle against every thing that prejudice and wickedness could invent, I received the following: [D&C Section 45]. (*DHC* 1:158.)

Ol edience—Why?

Not all of the Lord's instructions nor the reasons for his giving commandments are given in one revelation. In Section 45, however, several reasons are mentioned for strict obedience to his will. The revelation begins with the fact stated, as one of these reasons, that the kingdom of God has been given to his people. (D&C 45:1.) Possession of the kingdom by the saints is the same as the attainment of salvation upon their part, but this blessing is only for those who are obedient. Because salvation is the greatest blessing obtainable to a child of God, the necessity for full obedience is apparent.

Why should one be obedient? Jesus Christ is the Creator of our earth, as well as of other worlds. He is supreme and by his power we are able to receive the benefits of an earth-life with its environment or ordered that we may live under a reign of law.

Is there anyone who is assured that he will be alive on the morrow? Death comes to all men, but when? In the words of the Savior ". . . hearken unto my voice, lest death shall overtake you; in an hour when ye think not the summer shall be past, and the harvest ended, and your souls not saved." (*Ibid.*, 45:2.) Now is the day for repentance.

If man fully understood the sufferings of Christ (who is our Advocate with the Father), as he made the atonement for us, man would be fully determined to obey

all of the Lord's commands. So intense was the suffering
of Christ that he sweat drops of blood from his pores.
(*Ibid.*, 19:15-17.) It is only through Jesus Christ that
man may receive individual salvation; consequently, he
reminds the Saints of latter days that his prayer to the
Father is in behalf of them as follows:

. . . Father, behold the sufferings and death of him who did
no sin, in whom thou wast well pleased; behold the blood of thy
Son which was shed, the blood of him whom thou gavest that
thyself might be glorified;

Wherefore, Father, spare these my brethren that believe on
my name, that they may come unto me and have everlasting life.
(*Ibid.*, 45:4-5.)

As Christ was obedient in glorifying the Father,
so, also, may we glorify the Father and the Son by our
receiving through obedience the greatest blessing of
eternal life. Everything the Father and the Son do is for
our blessing. One may well exclaim: "O how great the
goodness of our God. . . . O how great the plan of our
God. . . ." (2 Nephi 9:10, 13.) Therefore, hearken ". . . today, and harden not your hearts." (D&C 45:6.) He who
hardens his heart by disobedience is in darkness. "The
Lord Is My Light" sing his people, for Jesus is ". . . the
light and the life of the world—a light that shineth in
darkness and the darkness comprehendeth it not." (*Ibid.*,
45:7.)

There follows in this revelation another reminder
for the necessity of obedience—the Jewish people as a
nation anciently did not receive their Messiah who was
one of their own. This example from the past poses the
thought:

. . . Let it not be said a second time, that Christ has come to
"His own," even to His Church in this dispensation, but "His
own" refused to hearken to Him. (*Doctrine and Covenants Commentary*, p. 254.)

Obedience, A Challenge

In verses eleven through fourteen of Section 45, there is recounted an event of the past which the Lord says could be duplicated in this dispensation by the full obedience of his people.

Wherefore, hearken ye together and let me show unto you even my wisdom—the wisdom of him whom ye say is the God of Enoch, and his brethren,

Who were separated from the earth, and were received unto myself—a city reserved until a day of righteousness shall come—a day which was sought for by all holy men, and they found it not because of wickedness and abominations;

And confessed they were strangers and pilgrims on the earth;

But obtained a promise that they should find it and see it in their flesh. (D&C 45:11-14.)

Among the points which are brought to the reader's attention by these verses, we may think (1) verification from the Lord in this modern revelation of the historical fact that Enoch was an actual person mentioned in the Bible (Genesis 25:24); (2) the actual separation of the city of Enoch and its inhabitants from the earth; (3) the promise that the city of Enoch will return to the earth in a day of righteousness, the millennium. (In reference to Enoch's dispensation and the great events made known to him by revelation, consult Moses, chapter 7.)

The challenge to the Saints of God today is so to live that, if alive on the earth, when the millennium begins, they will as inhabitants of Zion, the New Jerusalem, be prepared to meet the people of Enoch's city when it returns to the earth. (Moses 7:62-65.) The Lord also promises that all those in the past who considered themselves to be "strangers," but were holy in their lives, seeking for a day of righteousness, might see that day "in their flesh," as resurrected beings to join with the saints of this dispensation. (*Ibid.*, 7:62-65.) Will you be numbered among those Latter-day Saints who have lived faithfully to warrant such a blessing, whether you are in mortality at the time or whether you have passed away?

Purpose of the Everlasting Covenant

In speaking of the past and the reason for obedience to the fulness of the gospel, the Savior makes known the opportunity for people to become the sons of God and to receive power to obtain eternal life. (D&C 45:8.) For this purpose the everlasting covenant has been established on the earth with all of its powers and glories. (*Ibid.*, 133:57.) This covenant is the fulness of the gospel of Jesus Christ. (*Ibid.*, 66:2.)

The Lord informs us, however, of other purposes, in fact, that there are three other reasons for which he has sent the gospel into the world. These are: (1) "to be a light to the world," that is, to show the world the way to live; (2) "to be a standard for my people, and for the Gentiles to seek to it"—the gospel will always be the means of salvation to those who accept it, and it will be an ensign to the nations through the lives of the Saints. (*Ibid.*, 115:5; Isaiah 49:22; 62:10); and (3) "to be messenger" in preparing the way before the second coming of Christ. (D&C 45:9.)

All of these purposes are important. When one thinks of the mission given to the Saints in publishing the glad tidings of eternal life through the gospel, and that all may participate in it to some extent, an enthusiasm for magnifying one's calling should be greatly heightened.

"I Will Reason With You"

In addition to showing forth strong reasons to those who come unto him (*ibid.*, 45:10), the Lord says he will prophesy as he gave forth prophecy to men in days of old.

(*Ibid.*, 45:15.) But of what shall he prophesy? Of those things which are in the minds of the Saints today and were in the meridian dispensation. His disciples during the Redeemer's earthly mission asked him what would be the signs of his coming in the clouds of heaven? In the verses which follow, from Section 45, notice that the Lord uses language in the present tense as though he were speaking directly to his discpiles of old:

as I stood before them in the flesh, and spake unto them, saying: As ye have asked of me concerning the signs of my coming, in the day when I shall come in my glory in the clouds of heaven, to fulfill the promises that I have made unto your fathers,

For as ye have looked upon the long absence of your spirits from your bodies to be a bondage, I will show unto you how the day of redemption shall come, and also the restoration of the scattered Israel. (*Ibid.*, 45:16-17.)

The *Doctrine and Covenants Commentary* interprets verse 17 as follows:

One reason for their anxiety to know the signs is here stated. The separation of the spirits from the bodies is, even to those who are Christ's own, a "bondage," which is ended only by a glorious resurrection, and they were interested in knowing by what signs they might recognize that their day of redemption was drawing near, when spirit and body should be united. The departed Saints are, we may be sure, looking for the signs of the coming of the Lord, with an intense interest as the Saints still in mortality. Jesus graciously showed them "how the day of redemption shall come, and also the restoration of scattered Israel." The two events are inseparably connected. (*Doctrine and Covenants Commentary*, p. 259.)

Continuing his prophecy of events of the meridian dispensation, Jesus said to his disciples (Cf. Matt. 24: 1-2; Luke 21:23-24):

And now ye behold this temple which is in Jerusalem, which ye call the house of God, and your enemies say that this house shall never fall.

But, verily I say unto you, that desolation shall come upon this generation as a thief in the night, and this people shall be destroyed and scattered among all nations.

And this temple which ye now see shall be thrown down that there shall not be left one stone upon another. (D&C 45:18-20.)

How literally was this prophecy fulfilled? A summary of the seige and destruction of the temple and the city of Jerusalem, including the scattering of the Jews, is given in the account of Josephus:

In the construction of this sanctuary many stones of prodigious size had been used. Josephus says some were 45 cubits long, 5 high, and 6 broad—something like 78x8x10 feet. How improbably it must have appeared that the time could ever come when one stone should not be left upon another (v. 20)! Yet, in the year 70 A.D., in the same month and on the same day that witnessed the destruction of the temple of Solomon, this temple was demolished. Roman soldiers, it is said, ploughed the ground on which it had stood.

19. *Destroyed and scattered.* Desolation came, as our Savior said would be the case, as a "thief," unexpected, not looked for. In the year 66 A.D., Cestus Gallus marched into Judea and threatened Jerusalem. He might have taken the city, but he retreated and met with defeat near Beth-Horon. The Christians in the City, remembering the words of our Lord, fled to the little city of Pella, but the Jews were fired, by their temporary success, to renewed resistance. Vespasian was then sent from Rome to crush the rebellion. He took some of the strongholds of the Country and approached Jerusalem. Internal strife prevailed there, and such horrors were perpetrated that Vespasian decided to give his army a rest, while the Jews destroyed each other. Vespasian was elevated to the throne, and his son, Titus, was left to continue the conquest. The seige began in the year 70 A.D. Soon famine prevailed. Citizens who ventured outside the walls to search for roots to eat, if seized, were crucified by the Roman soldiers. Sometimes hundreds in that awful position could be seen from the walls. A trench was dug around the City, in order to make its isolation complete. Prisoners of war were cut open, while alive, to enable soldiers to search their bodies for gold which they might have swallowed. Six hundred thousand persons died within the walls, and the dead bodies, too numerous to be buried, were left in the houses. The Zealots, a fanatical sect whose members main-

tained that God would save them at the last moment, went about murdering and urging the people to resistance. Even Titus was sick at heart at the daily horrors he witnessed or heard of. At length the temple became a fort. Titus attacked it as such. A Roman soldier, contrary to order, set fire to it. After a while the scene was one of carnage and plunder. Six thousand Jews perished in the flames. In this awful war more than a million and a half of the Jews perished, and many were sold into slavery, and thus "scattered among all nations." (*The Wars of the Jews*, VI which is summarized in the *Doctrine and Covenants Commentary*, pp. 260-261.)

As one continues reading Section 45, it is discovered that what the Lord declares therein is fulfilled in the description of the desolation given by Josephus, which came upon the Jews of the meridian dispensation:

And it shall come to pass, that this generation of Jews shall not pass away until every desolation which I have told you concerning them shall come to pass. (D&C 45:21.)

Following this prophecy, Jesus said to his disciples, according to this revelation, that they said they knew "that the end of the world cometh," meaning the destruction of the world (Pearl of Great Price, Joseph Smith 1:4, 31) which would be at his second coming, and later on the purification of the earth. Then the assurance was given that their knowledge of these things was true, and all of the prophecies would be fulfilled.

And in this ye say truly, for so it is; but these things which I have told you shall not pass away until all shall be fulfilled.

And this I have told you concerning Jerusalem; and when that day shall come, shall a remnant be scattered among all nations. (D&C 45:23-24.)

As indicated, the material of this revelation, through verse 24, pertains to the generation or dispensation of the Meridian of Time, but later verses in this chapter (D&C 45:25-42.) describe events of the generation in which we live, the Dispensation of the Fulness of Times.

A parallel between what is given in this modern revelation and the account of the Savior's instructions to his disciples of the meridian dispensation is found in the Pearl of Great Price. (Joseph Smith 1:1-20, 21-35.) The latter verses concern our own dispensation.

Dispensation of the Fulness of Times

Even as the Jews were scattered with the destruction of Jerusalem, so their descendants were to be gathered in the last days. But when would those days come? Only after the long period of apostasy from the Church established by the Christ, and then the Church restored to the earth in the last dispensation of the gospel. This restoration is described in this way:

And when the times of the Gentiles is come in, a light shall break forth among them that sit in darkness, and it shall be the fulness of my gospel. (D&C 45:28.)

Signs of the Times

As foreknown by the prophets, the restoration of the gospel would bring many great changes on the earth. In this revelation the Lord points out:

. . . in that day shall be heard of wars and rumors of wars, and the whole earth shall be in commotion, and men's hearts shall fail them, and they shall say that Christ delayeth his coming until the end of the earth. (D&C 45:26.)

Needless to state, since the return of the gospel and the Church upon the earth, wars and rumors of wars have increased upon the earth.

"Christ delayeth his coming" is another sign of this period, for men teach that Christ will not come until the end of the earth. The *Doctrine and Covenants Commentary* mentions that:

... the common doctrine of the world is that Christ will not come, until a majority of the race is converted, the Jews gathered and anti-christ conquered, and then, it is taught, come the judgment and the destruction of the Earth. It is one of the signs of the end, that men shall teach that there will be no Millennium, no personal reign of Christ on Earth. (*Doctrine and Covenants Commentary*, p. 262.)

As this revelation unfolds the future for the disciples of old (and now for us of this generation), several signs are given in rapid succession.

"And the love of men shall wax cold, and iniquity shall abound." (D&C 45:27.) As interpreted by the *Doctrine and Covenants Commentary*, p. 262, this means that because of lawlessness, the majority of men will not have genuine Christian love, which is true, unselfish, and constant. As a result, Christian unity or oneness is not to be found, but there is an abundance of cooperation based on self-interest or family connections.

When one thinks of present conditions in reference to the latter part of this verse—that iniquity or wickedness shall abound—there immediately comes to mind the extent of crime and evil practices that are present throughout the world.

Regardless of what may be said to the effect that lawlessness has always been present, the presence of organized and unorganized evil in the world in the form of sex immorality, dishonest practices in business, disrespect for human beings and life itself, are widespread today and thus they constitute one of the signs of the last days.

The coldness of men's hearts to the fulness of the gospel is another sign. With the restoration of the gospel to the earth through the Prophet Joseph Smith, the Lord said that the world will ". . . receive it not; for they perceive not the light, and they turn their hearts from me because of the precepts of men." (D&C 45:29.) Although the number of converts to The Church of Jesus Christ of

Latter-day Saints is presently increasing in the world, yet, over the time of this dispensation, the number of members of the true Church is very few compared with the population of the world. As predicted, the people of the world will reject the gospel message and thus bring upon themselves the judgment prophesied. As people reject the Lord's plan of salvation and wickedness continues to abound, the time will come when our dispensation ". . . shall see an overflowing scourge; for a desolating sickness shall cover the land." (*Ibid.*, 45:31.) Other prophecies in the modern revelations reveal, in part, the nature and the extent of such plagues. (*Ibid.*, 29:18-19.)

Amid the difficulties of the times when the foregoing events occur, the Lord makes known that his ". . . disciples shall stand in holy places, and shall not be moved; but among the wicked, men shall lift up their voices and curse God and die." (*Ibid.*, 45:32.) The disciple is one who is a true follower, and as far as this revelation is concerned, is that individual who has accepted Jesus Christ and has thus become a member of his Church. These disciples will stand in the places appointed by revelation as gathering places. (*Ibid.*, 101:16-21.)

Other signs indicating the nearness of the Lord's coming are desolations of various kinds. Amid conditions such as floods, dust storms, hurricanes, and other commotions, in which the elements give testimony of the rejection of the Lord's servants, men will continue to harden their hearts and will kill one another and curse God and die.

> And there shall be earthquakes also in divers places, and many desolations; yet men will harden their hearts against me, and they will take up the sword, one against another, and they will kill one another. (*Ibid.*, 45:33.)

When disciples of old indicated concern about these various signs, assurance was given that ". . . when all these things shall come to pass, ye may know that the

promises which have been made unto you shall be fulfilled." (*Ibid.*, 45:35.) By reference to the fig tree shoot-
ing forth its leaves as a sign of summer being at hand, so
also these various events (*Ibid.*, 45:16-33) constitute
signs by which the believer will "know that the hour is
nigh." (*Ibid.*, 45:36-38.) What is the hour spoken of? It
is the period when the times of the Gentiles shall be fulfilled.

"Times of the Gentiles Shall Be Fulfilled"

By vision, Nephi was permitted to see the time when
Jesus would manifest himself to the Jews first, and then
the Gentiles would have the opportunity to accept the
fulness of the gospel. Later, however, the Gentiles would
have this privilege first and the Jews last. (1 Nephi 13:
28-30.) Thus the first should be last and the last should be
first. (Cf. Luke 13:28-30.) As we have seen in this lesson,
the "times of the Gentiles" are ushered in with the restoration of the gospel in its fulness. (D&C 45:28-29.)
Moroni told Joseph Smith that this time "was soon to
come in." (Pearl of Great Price, Joseph Smith 2:41.)
Later in the Dispensation of the Fulness of Times, when
Jerusalem is no longer trodden down by the Gentiles, it is
to be a sign that the times of the Gentiles are fulfilled.
(D&C 45:25, 30; Luke 21:24.) This sign is to indicate
the beginning of the period of transition when the Jews
are to receive their opportunity to have the gospel taught
to them.

Purpose of the Signs of the Times and a Prophet's Answer

President Joseph F. Smith, sixth President of the
Church, had this to say concerning the purposes of these
signs of the times:

There are, in the great world of mankind, much social and
civil unrighteousness, religious unfaithfulness, and great insensi-
bility to the majesty, power, and purpose of our eternal Father

and God. In order, therefore, that he may bring the sense of himself and his purposes home to the minds of men, his intervention and interposition in nature and in men's affairs, are demanded. His aims will be accomplished even if men must be overwhelmed with the convulsions of nature to bring them to an understanding and realization of his designs. As long as conditions remain as they are in the world, none is exempt from these visitations.

The Latter-day Saints, though they themselves tremble because of their own wickedness and sins, believe that great judgments are coming upon the world because of iniquity; they firmly believe in the statements of the Holy Scriptures, that calamities will befall the nations as signs of the coming of Christ to judgment. They believe that God rules in the fire, the earthquake, the tidal wave, the volcanic eruption, and the storm. Him they recognize as the Master and Ruler of nature and her laws, and freely acknowledge his hand in all things. We believe that his judgments are poured out to bring mankind to a sense of his power and his purposes, that they may repent of their sins and prepare themselves for the second coming of Christ to reign in righteousness upon the earth. (*Gospel Doctrine*, pp. 54-55.)

What about the Latter-day Saints and the predicted judgments? President Smith wrote:

We firmly believe that Zion—which is the pure in heart—shall escape, if she observes to do all things whatsoever God has commanded; but, in the opposite event, even Zion shall be visited "with sore affliction, with pestilence, with plague, with sword, with vengeance, and with devouring fire." (D&C 97:26.) All this that her people may be taught to walk in the light of truth and in the way of the God of their salvation. (*Ibid.*, p. 55.)

Following this instruction, President Smith continues to state the belief of Latter-day Saints concerning the judgment:

We believe that these severe, natural calamities are visited upon men by the Lord for the good of his children, to quicken their devotion to others, and to bring out their better natures, that they may love and serve him. We believe, further, that they are the heralds and tokens of his final judgment, and the schoolmasters to teach the people to prepare themselves by righteous living for the coming of the Savior to reign upon the earth, when every knee shall bow and every tongue confess that Jesus is the Christ. (*Ibid.*, p. 55.)

In the original article from which this material was taken, President Smith wrote that:

. . . judgment is not an end in itself. Calamities are only permitted by a merciful Father, in order to bring about redemption. Behind the fearful storms of judgment, which often strike the just and the unjust alike, overwhelming the wicked and the righteous, there arises bright and clear the dawn of the day of salvation. (*Improvement Era*, "The Lesson in Natural Calamities," Vol. 9, p. 651.)

The President stated, furthermore, that judgments occur that the finger of God's power is manifest to call attention to:

. . . the transgressions of all mankind, that all may take warning and repent. Men who stand in the way of God's wise purposes, whether they be good or evil, must suffer in the turmoil. Thus it is that often the righteous suffer for the unrighteous; and it is not satisfactory to the thinking mind to say that therefore God is unjust: "His visage was so marred, more than any man, and his form more than the sons of men." And if, in the wisdom of God, it was so that he who is without sin should suffer for the sins of the world, why should not imperfect man, though less sinful than his neighbor, suffer with the wicked. (*Ibid.*, Vol. 9, p. 654.)

Although these calamities happen, Latter-day Saints:

. . . believe in doing all in our power to relieve distress, to aid the afflicted. and to extend to all mankind the brotherly kindness and sympathy which we ourselves crave from our fellow beings and from God. (*Ibid.*, Vol. 9, p. 654.)

Chapter 31

THE SECOND COMING OF CHRIST

(Sections 43:8-35; 45:43-75)

Our attention is directed in this chapter to the need of becoming more fully acquainted with what the revelations of the Lord say regarding the times in which we live; and also of events which are prophesied to occur near the time of the Savior's return to the earth and of his appearance.

Section 43

In Chapter 18 the first seven verses of Section 43 of The Doctrine and Covenants were discussed as setting forth the important principle that there is only one man on the earth at a time who has the right by ordination and calling to receive revelation for The Church of Jesus Christ of Latter-day Saints. In exercising this right, the President of the Church not only directs his message to the Saints but to the world, if necessary. Joseph Smith was the mouthpiece of the Lord in the opening of this dispensation of the gospel. (D&C 21:4-6.) The Lord introduced his volume of scripture, The Doctrine and Covenants, by stating that his message was to go to all the world as "the voice of warning" unto all people. His servants were to proclaim this message and, in time, all would hear that message. (*Ibid.*, 1:1-7.) In preparation for preaching the gospel, the Lord gave pertinent advice to elders or to the members of the Church. They were instructed:

. . . when ye are assembled together ye shall instruct and edify each other, that ye may know how to act and direct my church, how to act upon the points of my law and commandments, which I have given. (*Ibid.*, 43:8.)

By giving words of edification arising out of their understanding of the gospel, the elders were to become "sanctified by that which ye have received, and ye shall bind yourselves to act in all holiness before me." (*Ibid.*, 43:9.) As the result of being so instructed in meetings, and making of the commandments a part of daily living "... glory shall be added to the kingdom [Church] which ye have received ..." but negligence in these matters would result in a loss of the blessings which it was the right of the faithful to obtain. The Lord continued:

Purge ye out the iniquity which is among you; sanctify yourselves before me;

And if ye desire the glories of the kingdom, appoint ye my servant Joseph Smith, Jun., and uphold him before me by the prayer of faith. (*Ibid.*, 43:11-12.)

Joseph Smith Prophesies

The Saints have always been admonished to uphold the prophet of the Lord for therein lies safety. How closely do we follow the revelations which have come through the Prophet Joseph Smith? For example, do we, as Latter-day Saints, uphold him in what he has given us? Here are some of his prophecies:

I will prophesy that the signs of the coming of the Son of Man are already commenced. One pestilence will desolate after another. We shall soon have war and bloodshed. The moon will be turned into blood. I testify of these things, and that the coming of the Son of Man is nigh, even at your doors. If our souls and our bodies are not looking forth for the coming of the Son of Man; and after we are dead, if we are not looking forth, we shall be among those who are calling for the rocks to fall upon them. (*DHC* III:390.)

The coming of the Son of Man never will be—never can be till the judgments spoken of for this hour are poured out: which judgments are commenced. (*DHC* V:336.)

The hour spoken of in the last prophecy was predicted by John the Revelator as "the hour of his [God's] judgment. . . ." (Rev. 14:7.)

"Give as I Have Spoken"

As the Lord continued to instruct the elders who would study and take the message of the dispensation to the world in preparation for the Lord's coming, he charged them that they were sent forth to teach the children of men and not to be taught. He had given them information of things to come—of "judgments which are on the land" (D&C 88:79)—and by the power of his Spirit they were to teach. Since their instructions came from the Giver of truth, who knows all things, they were to sanctify themselves and "ye shall be endowed with power, that ye may give even as I have spoken." (*Ibid.*, 43:15-16.)

But what has the Lord spoken? What has he given which is to be carried by the elders?

Hearken ye, for, behold, the great day of the Lord is nigh at hand.

For the day cometh that the Lord shall utter his voice out of heaven; the heavens shall shake and the earth shall tremble, and the trump of God shall sound both long and loud, and shall say to the sleeping nations: Ye saints arise and live; ye sinners stay and sleep until I shall call again. (*Ibid.*, 43:17-18.)

In continuing his message, the Lord emphasized the need for missionary work to be done among the nations that all who would respond to his call might repent. The missionaries were to accept the call to service lest they be found among those who were negligent in their responsibilities. (*Ibid.*, 43:19-20.) In fact, this dispensation is the last time when the Lord's servants are to call upon the inhabitants of the earth. (*Ibid.*, 43:28.) As one reads this revelation, he discovers that the people of the Lord are to make preparations for the great day of the Lord. (*Ibid.*, 43:20-22.)

The great day of the Lord is the day when the Lord comes to reign upon the earth. Joseph Smith was informed in many revelations that this was the message of the Lord for this dispensation.

When the inhabitants of the earth do not accept the call of the missionaries to repent, the Lord will, as this revelation points out, answer his own question—"What will ye say when the day cometh when the thunders shall utter their voices from the ends of the earth?"—by saying:

How oft have I called upon you by the mouth of my servants, and by the ministering of angels, and by mine own voice, and by the voice of thunderings ... lightnings ... tempests ... earthquakes, and great hailstorms, and by the voice of famines and pestilences of every kind ... and by the voice of glory and honor and the riches of eternal life, and would have saved you with an everlasting salvation, but ye would not. (*Ibid.*, 43:25.)

The Lord's Message Literal or Figurative?

The Lord's message is to be taken literally:

It is predicted that calamity and destruction await the inhabitants of the earth if they continue to reject the Gospel and fill the cup of their iniquity. This punishment will come when "the wrath of God shall be poured out upon the wicked without measure." (*Ibid.*, 1:9.) It will come after the elders of Israel have declared their message to all the world. Then will come the testimony of wrath and indignation; the testimony of earthquakes, the voice of thunders and lightnings and tempests and the waves heaving themselves beyond their bounds. (*Ibid.*, 88:88-91.) (*Doctrine and Covenants Commentary*, p. 246.)

The Lord Shall Utter His Voice

When the judgments of the Lord come as warnings, how will he speak?

If we understand this prophecy [Section 43:23], correctly, it means that after the warning voices of the thunders and lightnings and world wars, God will again speak to the children of men. In other words, the gospel sound will be heard. The Lord will explain to men, through His servants, why the calamities have come, viz., to cause men to repent and be saved. (v. 24-27.) (*Ibid.*, p. 247.)

Section 45—Review and Prelude

The purpose of Chapter 30 was to give the reader an insight into some of the signs of the times as those events were foreseen by the Master and told to his disciples in the Meridian of Time, and then to relate the events of our own dispensation. (D&C 45:1-42.) From Section 45, beginning with verses 15 through 24, Jesus told his disciples of events to be expected during their own dispensation or generation. From verses 25 through 38 the Lord gave his disciples some signs by which they might know that in the final dispensation of the gospel the "times of the Gentiles" were about to be finished.

Should Latter-day Saints look forward to these signs of the times? Hear the word of the Lord:

And it shall come to pass that he that feareth me shall be looking forth for the great day of the Lord to come, even for the signs of the coming of the Son of Man. (*Ibid.*, 45:39.)

This prophecy would suggest that as the Lord's coming nears, there will be some devout souls who will be impressed with the doctrine of the second coming and the millennium, but, in general, the people of the world will not give heed to these biblical teachings. These devout people:

... shall see signs and wonders, for they shall be shown forth in the heavens above, and in the earth beneath.

And they shall behold blood, and fire, and vapors of smoke. (*Ibid.*, 45:40-41.)

Sign of the Son of Man

Among these signs to precede the Lord's coming, is one event which was mentioned by Jesus to his disciples in the Meridian of Time (Matt. 24:30; Luke 21:25-27), and spoken of again in this dispensation as "a great sign in heaven, and all people shall see it together." (D&C 88: 93.) What is this sign? Because all people shall see it, does it follow that it will be recognized by the world as a sign indicating that the Lord's coming is near, or will it be explained as another natural phenomenon? In February 1843, the Prophet Joseph Smith reported that a Mr. Redding had claimed he saw the sign of the Son of Man. The Prophet wrote concerning this claim:

> He has not seen the sign of the Son of Man as foretold by Jesus; neither has any man, nor will any man, until after the sun shall have been darkened and the moon bathed in blood: for the Lord hath not shown me any such sign; and as the prophet saith, so it must be—"Surely the Lord God will do nothing, but he revealeth his secret unto his servants the prophets." (See Amos 3:7.) (*Teachings of the Prophet Joseph Smith*, 280.)

Inasmuch as wickedness and unbelief will, in general, reign on the earth near the Lord's coming, the world will not accept this great sign for what it is. Among faithful Latter-day Saints, however, who are looking forward to these signs and to the leadership of the Church for guidance in such matters, they shall know what the sign is and of its meaning.

> Judah must return, Jerusalem must be rebuilt, and the temple, and water come out from under the temple, and the waters of the Dead Sea be healed. It will take some time to rebuild the walls of the city and the temple, &c.; and all this must be done before the Son of Man will make His appearance. There will be wars and rumors of wars, signs in the heavens above and on the earth beneath, the sun turned into darkness and the moon to blood, earthquakes in divers places, the seas heaving beyond their bounds; then will appear one grand sign of the Son of Man in heaven. But what will the world do? They will say it is a planet, a comet, &c. But the Son of Man will come as the sign of the coming of the Son of Man, which will be as the light of the morning cometh out of the east. (*DHC* V:337.)

A Bow in the Heavens? (Not One but Many Signs)

It is well to keep in mind that there is no one sign or event which signalizes the nearness of the Lord's second coming. Included among these signs are those which are referred to about the sun, moon, and the stars. (D&C 45:42.) But there is one sign referred to by the Prophet which, by the absence of a natural phenomenon, has considerable importance. Here are the words of the Prophet:

I have asked of the Lord concerning His coming; and while asking the Lord, He gave a sign and said, "In the days of Noah I set a bow in the heavens as a sign and token that in any year that the bow should be seen the Lord would not come; but there should be seed time and harvest during that year; but whenever you see the bow withdrawn, it shall be a token that there shall be famine, pestilence, and great distress among the nations, and that the coming of the Messiah is not far distant." (DHC V:254.)

First Appearance—to the Saints

The Lord's first appearance as part of the second coming will be to his Saints. Of such an appearance the Old Testament prophet spoke when he referred to the Lord's suddenly coming to his temple in the day when it could be appropriately asked: "But who may abide the day of his coming? and who shall stand when he appeareth? for he is like a refiner's fire, and like fullers' soap." (Mal. 3:2.) Moroni quoted part of this chapter to Joseph Smith when he visited him in 1823. (Pearl of Great Price, Joseph Smith 2:36.)

It may be concluded that this appearance to the Saints may not be generally known, except as the world is informed of it by the Saints. As partial fulfillment of this prophecy was the appearance of the Savior in the Kirtland Temple in 1836. (D&C 110:1-4.) That the complete fulfillment has reference to the temple in the New Jerusalem, yet to be erected in Jackson County, Missouri, is indicated by reason of the offering to be made by the sons of Levi. (Mal. 3:3; D&C 84:21-34; *Teachings of the Prophet Joseph Smith*, 171-173.) President Brigham Young said that:

> When Jesus makes his next appearance upon the earth, but few of this Church and kingdom will be prepared to receive him and see him face to face and converse with him; but he will come to his temple. (*Journal of Discourses* 7:142.)

In the General Conference of April 1898, President Wilford Woodruff told of his first meeting the Prophet Joseph Smith and of the Priesthood assemblage of 1833 when the Prophet prophesied that the Saints would be settled in the Rocky Mountains.

> . . . When they [the brethren present] got through the Prophet said, "Brethren I have been very much edified and instructed in your testimonies here tonight, but I want to say to you before the Lord, that you know no more concerning the destinies of this Church and kingdom than a babe upon its mother's lap. You don't comprehend it." I was rather surprised. He said "it is only a little handful [sic] of Priesthood you see here tonight, but this Church will fill North and South America—it will fill the world." Among other things he said, "It will fill the Rocky Mountains. There will be tens of thousands of Latter-day Saints who will be gathered in the Rocky Mountains, and there they will open the door for the establishing of the Gospel among the Lamanites, who will receive the Gospel and their endowments and the blessings of God. *This people will go into the Rocky Mountains; they will there build temples to the Most High. They will raise up a posterity there, and the Latter-day Saints who dwell in these mountains will stand in the flesh until the coming of the Son of Man. The Son of Man will come to them while in the Rocky Mountains.*"
>
> I name these things because I want to bear testimony before God, angels and men that mine eyes behold the day, and have beheld for the last fifty years of my life, the fulfillment of that prophecy. . . . (*Conference Report*, April 1898, p. 57.) (Italics by author.)

Some of the Saints by appointment will attend the **great council at Adam-ondi-Ahman** spoken of by the

Prophet Joseph Smith. At that time Adam will deliver up his stewardship to Christ preparatory to the "coming of the Son of Man" in glory.

Daniel in his seventh chapter speaks of the Ancient of Days; he means the oldest man, our Father Adam, Michael, he will call his children together and hold a council with them to prepare them for the coming of the Son of Man. He (Adam) is the father of the human family, and presides over the spirits of all man, and all that have had the keys must stand before him in this grand council. This may take place before some of us leave this stage of action. The Son of Man stands before him, and there is given him glory and dominion. Adam delivers up his stewardship to Christ, that which was delivered to him as holding the keys of the universe, but retains his standing as head of the human family. (*Teachings of the Prophet Joseph Smith*, p. 157.)

Another Appearance—to the Jews

Another great appearance of the Master will be at a time when the Jews are gathered to the Holy Land. When this happens the nations will be at war with the Jews, who since 1948 have had their own government in Israel (Palestine), to which the Jews are now gathering. The Prophet declares that when sorely besieged and part of Jerusalem is taken (Zechariah 14:1-2), two prophets or witnesses "raised up to the Jewish nation in the last days" will be killed and their dead bodies shall lie in the streets three days and a half. Life will re-enter their bodies, which will ascend into heaven. A great earthquake will cause the Mount of Olives to divide and the earth will tremble. (Rev. 11:1-13; D&C 77:15.) The Lord will then fight their battle. (Zechariah 14:3-9.) As the text of this chapter states:

And then shall the Jews look upon me and say: What are these wounds in thine hands and in thy feet?
Then shall they know that I am the Lord; for I will say unto them: These wounds are the wounds with which I was wounded

in the house of my friends. I am he who was lifted up. I am Jesus that was crucified. I am the Son of God.

And then shall they weep because of their iniquities; then shall they lament because they persecuted their king. (D&C 45: 51-53; See also, Zechariah 13:6; 12:8-14; 13:1.)

And thus Judah shall be redeemed by acceptance of their Savior Jesus Christ. In order for salvation to be received by any people it will be through baptism by immersion for the remission of sins and the bestowal of the Holy Ghost.

Third Appearance—in Power to the World

There follows the great and glorious coming of Jesus Christ, who subdues all enemies under his feet, "and the Lord shall be king over all the earth." This is the coming for which the righteous have prayed, that wickedness might be removed from the earth. His coming in power is described in the modern revelations as "an entire separation of the righteous and the wicked" with the wicked being consumed. (D&C 63:54; 101:23-24; 133:63-64.) This chapter reveals that the nations of the earth will be afraid:

For when the Lord shall appear he shall be terrible unto them, that fear may seize upon them, and they shall stand afar off and tremble.

And all nations shall be afraid because of the terror of the Lord, and the power of his might. Even so. Amen. (*Ibid.*, 45:74-75.)

Notice the sublime language used by President Charles W. Penrose in describing this last coming of the Christ:

. . . who can describe it in the language of mortals? The tongue of man falters, and the pen drops from the hand of the writer, as the mind is rapt in contemplation of the sublime and awful majesty of his coming to take vengeance on the ungodly and to reign as King of the whole earth.

He comes! The earth shakes, and the tall mountains tremble; the mighty deep rolls back to the north as in fear, and the rent skies glow like molten brass. He comes! The dead saints burst forth from their tombs, and "those who are alive and remain" are "caught up" with them to meet him. The ungodly rush to hide themselves from his presence, and call upon the quivering rocks to cover them. He comes! with all the hosts of the righteous glorified. The breath of his lips strikes death to the wicked. His glory is a consuming fire. The proud and rebellious are as stubble; they are burned and "left neither root nor branch." He sweeps the earth "as with the besom of destruction." He deluges the earth with the fiery floods of his wrath, and the filthiness and abominations of the world are consumed. Satan and his dark hosts are taken and bound—the prince of the power of the air has lost his dominion, for He whose right it is to reign has come, and "the kingdoms of this world have become the kingdoms of our Lord and of his Christ." (*Millennial Star*, Vol. 21, page 583, September 10, 1859.)

The New Jerusalem

One of the best descriptions of the center place of Zion in the last days when the judgments of the Lord are poured out upon the wicked is found in our text:

And it shall be called the New Jerusalem, a land of peace, a city of refuge, a place of safety for the saints of the Most High God;

And the glory of the Lord shall be there, and the terror of the Lord also shall be there, insomuch that the wicked will not come unto it, and it shall be called Zion.

And it shall come to pass among the wicked, that every man that will not take his sword against his neighbor must needs flee unto Zion for safety.

And there shall be gathered unto it out of every nation under heaven; and it shall be the only people that shall not be at war one with another.

And it shall be said among the wicked: Let us not go up to battle against Zion, for the inhabitants of Zion are terrible; wherefore we cannot stand.

And it shall come to pass that the righteous shall be gathered out from among all nations, and shall come to Zion, singing with songs of everlasting joy. (D&C 45:66-71.)

The Lord has set forth in ancient and modern times that there would be two gathering places in the last days —Palestine (Israel) and America. (Micah 4:1-2; D&C 133:12-13.)

Other Events

When the Savior comes, as indicated, a general resurrection will occur, the heathen nations shall be redeemed, and Satan is to be bound as a part of the great millennial reign of Christ. (*Ibid.*, 45:54; 43:29-35.)

Be Prepared

During his mortal ministry, the Lord spoke concerning the preparedness of believers in the last days. The parable of the ten virgins, five of whom were prepared to meet the bridegroom while the remaining five were unprepared and rejected from entrance to the marriage feast, is closed with this application: ". . . verily I say unto you, I know you not. Watch therefore, for ye know neither the day nor the hour wherein the Son of Man cometh. (Matt., 25:12-13.)

Does this parable apply to the Latter-day Saints? Definitely so. Hear the words of the Lord to the Prophet Joseph Smith:

And at that day, when I shall come in my glory, shall the parable be fulfilled which I spake concerning the ten virgins.

For they that are wise and have received the truth, and have taken the Holy Spirit for their guide, and have not been deceived —verily I say unto you, they shall not be hewn down and cast into the fire, but shall abide the day.

And the earth shall be given unto them for an inheritance; and they shall multiply and wax strong, and their children shall grow up without sin unto salvation.

For the Lord shall be in their midst, and his glory shall be upon them, and he will be their king and their lawgiver. (D&C 45:56-59.)

No one else upon the face of the earth meets the description given in these verses better than do the Latter-day Saints, for "—they have received the truth, and have taken the Holy Spirit for their guide, and have not been deceived...." (*Ibid.*, 45:57.)

Chapter 32

THE GIFTS OF THE HOLY GHOST

(Section 46)

The revelation for study in this chapter was received in the spring of 1831, the day following Section 45, which was received to sustain the members of the Church as a result of many foolish stories which were circulated about them. Section 46 was given by the Lord to correct some false ideas which were entertained by members of the Church. At this period, according to the Church Historian, John Whitmer, there were some of our number who believed that nonmembers should not be admitted to the Sacrament meeting. Some members felt this practice was contrary to the instructions of the resurrected Lord to the Nephites as stated in the Book of Mormon:

And behold, ye shall meet together oft; and ye shall not forbid any man from coming unto you when ye shall meet together, but suffer them that they may come unto you and forbid them not; but ye shall pray for them, and shall not cast them out; and if it so be that they come unto you oft ye shall pray for them unto the Father, in my name. (3 Nephi 18:22, 23.)

In the first seven verses of Section 46 the Lord gives sufficient information to the Church in this dispensation to clarify this problem, and also gives the Lord's will about the meetings of the Church. First, for the profit and learning of the Elders they are "to conduct all meetings as they are directed and guided by the Holy Spirit." (D&C 46:2.) Then follows the commandment about which there was some disputation, "Nevertheless ye are commanded never to cast any one out from your public

meetings, which are held before the world." (*Ibid.*, v. 3.)
In further clarification of this instruction, the Sacrament meeting is indicated as a public meeting:

> And again I say unto you, ye shall not cast any out of
> your sacrament meetings who are earnestly seeking the kingdom: I speak this concerning those who are not of the Church.
> (*Ibid.*, v. 5.)

This same commandment is given regarding the "confirmation meetings." (*Ibid.*, v. 6.) This meeting is our fast meeting when the Holy Ghost is conferred upon the newly baptized person. There are meetings of the Church which are to be considered as private because they are special meetings to which only certain members of the Church are invited to attend, such as auxiliary prayer or officers' and teachers' meetings.

There are in this revelation instructions regarding the member of the Church and the Sacrament meeting. Church members are welcome to this meeting, but they are counseled to make reconciliation with their fellow man against whom they have sinned before they partake of the Sacrament. (*Ibid.*, v. 4.)

"Walking uprightly before me"

One of the most important items of counsel given by the Lord appears in this revelation. It is as follows:

> But ye are commanded in all things to ask of God, who
> giveth liberally; and that which the Spirit testifies unto you
> even so I would that ye should do in all holiness of heart, walking uprightly before me, considering the end of your salvation,
> doing all things with prayer and thanksgiving, that ye may not
> be seduced by evil spirits, or doctrines of devils, or the commandments of men; for some are of men, and others of devils.
> (*Ibid.*, 46:7.)

What is there in this scripture which makes it of such great importance? Notice the several principles that are basic to the obtaining of eternal life: (a) Pray to him who giveth liberally; (b) Obtain the Spirit and accept its promptings in humility: (c) Walk uprightly before the Lord—keep the commandments; (d) Always remember that the purpose of existence is to "work out your salvation"; (e) In the spirit of prayer be grateful for blessings received. What is the promised blessing for those who practice this counsel? They shall neither be deceived by the ideas of men nor by the doctrines of devils.

Importance of Obtaining the Spirit

Learning the necessity of receiving the Spirit is of great importance to the members of the Church. The operation of the Holy Ghost in the lives of the prophets during the Old Testament period, as well as the time of the apostles of Jesus, is generally known to the membership of the Church in this dispensation. Directed by that same Spirit the leaders of the Church have counseled the Church membership throughout this dispensation, of the need to have the Holy Ghost. It is informative to know that this counsel has not only been given by the living revelators, but also by some of these brethren when they have passed beyond this life. This fact gives further strength to the place of the Spirit in guiding and assisting one on the way to eternal life. President Wilford Woodruff is on record as saying that, "One morning while we were at Winter Quarters, Brother Brigham Young said to me and the brethren that he had a visitation the night previously from Joseph Smith. I asked him what he said to him. He replied that Joseph had told him to tell the people to labor to obtain the Spirit of God; that they needed that to sustain them and to give them power to go through their work on the earth." In this same sermon, President Woodruff said that while en route to his last mission in England, Joseph Smith visited him and gave him similar instructions. In continuing his discourse on the importance of having the Spirit, President Woodruff said: "Brigham Young also visited me after his death . . . He said, 'I want you to teach the people to get the Spirit of God. You cannot build up the Kingdom of God without that.' That is what I want to say to the brothers and sisters here today." (*The Deseret Weekly*, Vol. 53, No. 21, Nov. 7, 1896, p. 643.)

Joseph Smith and Martin VanBuren

On November 29, 1839, the Prophet Joseph Smith and Elias Higbee in seeking redress for crimes committed against the Saints in Missouri, visited President VanBuren in Washington, D.C., as a part of this mission. In that interview, the president of the United States asked the Prophet wherein the Latter-day Saints differed from other religions of that day. His reply was that, "We differed in the mode of baptism and the Holy Ghost by the laying on of hands." (*DHC* 4:42.)

What did the Prophet mean by this statement? It is apparent from his teachings given upon other occasions that the possession of the gift of the Holy Ghost is received only by those who submit to water baptism and the laying of hands by one who is authorized of the Lord to officiate for him. As this chapter continues, this principle is in evidence, but here is a positive statement which establishes the principle as given by Joseph Smith:

The sign of Peter was to repent and be baptised for the remission of sins, with the promise of the gift of the Holy Ghost; and in no other way is the gift of the Holy Ghost obtained. (*DHC* 4:555.)

Baptism is a holy ordinance preparatory to the reception of the Holy Ghost; it is the channel and key by which the Holy Ghost will be administered. The gift of the Holy Ghost by the laying on of hands, cannot be received through the medium of any other principle than the principle of righteousness, for if the proposals are not complied with, it is of no use, but withdraws. (*Ibid.*, 3:379.)

It was a characteristic of the Church of Jesus Christ in the Meridian of Time that the gift of the Holy Ghost was received only by the convert to the true Church. (Acts 2:37-38; 8:12-23; 19:1-7). But what about the gifts of the Holy Ghost? Are these gifts, as enumerated in the scriptures, received by the worthy member of that Church? The answer is yes. The loss of the spiritual gifts following the death of the apostles is an evidence of the great apostasy. The absence of these spiritual gifts is admitted by many authorities on ecclesiastical history. The testimony of John Wesley, founder of Methodism, as quoted by Elder James E. Talmage in *The Articles of Faith* (p. 495), is a good example:

"It does not appear that these extraordinary gifts of the Holy Spirit were common in the church for more than two or three centuries. We seldom hear of them after that fatal period when the emperor Constantine called himself a Christian, and from a vain imagination of promoting the Christian cause, thereby, heaped riches and power and honor upon Christians in general, but in particular upon the Christian clergy. From this time they almost totally ceased; very few instances of the kind were found. The cause of this was not as has been supposed because there was no more occasion for them—because all the world was become Christians. This is a miserable mistake; not a twentieth part of it was then nominally Christian. The real cause of it was the love of many, almost all Christians, so called was waxed cold. The Christians had no more of the Spirit of Christ than the other heathens. The Son of Man, when he came to examine His Church, could hardly find faith upon the earth. This was the real cause why the extraordinary gifts of the Holy Ghost were no longer to be found in the Christian Church—because the Christians were turned heathens again, and only had a dead form left." — *Wesley's Works,* vol. 7, 89:26, 27.

Purpose of the Gifts

For what purpose does the Lord bestow his gifts upon his true followers? Because in the world there are influences that are contrary to the plan of life and salvation. As the *Doctrine and Covenants Commentary* points out:

> Note that some false doctrines come from men, while others are originated by the devil. The former may depend on human imperfection of perception or deductions. We do not always understand the Word of God correctly, and we are apt to draw hasty conclusions, and if we teach these for doctrine, we err. The latter are inspired by the adversary to deceive men. (p. 272.)

How will the gifts of the Spirit help one on the road to perfection?

> Wherefore, beware lest ye are deceived; and *that ye may not be deceived* seek ye earnestly the best gifts, always remembering for what they are given; For verily I say unto you, *they are given for the benefit of those who love me and keep all my commandments, and him that seeketh so to do;* that all may be benefited that seek or that ask of me, that ask and not for a sign that they may consume it upon their lusts. (D&C 46:8-9. Italics by author.)

The words in italics give definite information upon the question just posed. Notice that the gifts are a part of the gospel of Jesus Christ that they might be of benefit to those who love the Lord and thus keep all of his commandments. But who are these? They are the members of his Church, for they have complied with the ordinances of baptism and the laying on of hands to receive the Holy Ghost. But the member of the Church may not be keeping all of the commandments, so, what of him? The revelation states, "and him that seeketh so to do." The Lord does not condone sin, but that member of the kingdom who will earnestly strive to overcome the barriers to his salvation by sincerely endeavoring to perfect himself through the principle of repentance will receive the help necessary to aid him. (*Ibid.,* 1:31-33.) On the purpose of the gifts of the Spirit President Joseph F. Smith once said: "The gifts of the Spirit and the powers of the Holy

Priesthood are of God, they are given for the blessing of the people, for their encouragement, and for the strengthening of their faith. This Satan knows full well, therefore he seeks by imitation-miracles to blind and deceive the children of God." (*Gospel Doctrine*, p. 376.)

The Gifts of the Holy Ghost

What are these gifts of the Holy Ghost which are imparted to the members of the Church? In the Meridian of Time Paul provided a list of these gifts for the Saints at Corinth. (1 Cor. 12:1-11.) In his discussion, the apostle emphasizes the need for these gifts to remain in the Church in order that the members might be unified as a body of baptized believers. The place of these gifts with the authorized priesthood to continue the work of perfecting the lives of the members is thus indicated: "And God hath set some in the church, first apostles, secondarily prophets, thirdly teachers, after that miracles, then gifts of healings, helps, governments, diversities of tongues . . . Have all the gifts of healing? do all speak with tongues? do all interpret? But covet earnestly the best gifts. . . ." (*Ibid.*, 12:28-31.)

In closing the Nephite record by admonishing the people of our dispensation that they might know of the truth of this book of scripture and also know, by the power of the Holy Ghost, that Christ lives, Moroni also indicated some of these gifts of the Spirit. (Moroni 10: 1-19.)

The Saints of today are counseled to "always remember, and always retain in your (their) minds what those gifts are, that are given unto the church." (D&C 46:10.) These gifts, however, are not given promiscuously but "all have not every gift given unto them; for there are many gifts, and to every man is given a gift by the Spirit of God." (*Ibid.*, v. 11.)

A summary of the gifts revealed in this revelation is provided in the *Doctrine and Covenants Commentary,* as follows: "(1) knowledge; (2) faith; (3) administration; (4) recognition of the operations of the Spirit; (5) wisdom; (6) gift to instruct; (7) faith to be healed; (8) faith to heal; (9) power to work other miracles; (10) gift of prophecy; (11) gift to discern spirits; (12) gift of tongues; (13) gift of interpretation; (14) gift to discern all these gifts." (P. 274.)

Explanation of the Gifts

Gift:

To some it is given by the Holy Ghost to know that Jesus is the Son of God, and that he was crucified for the sins of the world. (v. 13.)

Explanation:

This knowledge is placed first among the special gifts because it is obtained only by revelation. To believe that Jesus of Nazareth was the Anointed One, the Messiah, and that He was crucified for the sins of the world, is not to *know* it. Knowledge is a special gift. (*Doctrine and Covenants Commentary,* p. 274.)

Gift:

To others it is given to believe on their words, that they also might have eternal life if they continue faithful. (v. 14.)

Explanation:

That faith which enables us to realize divine things and obtain life eternal is another special gift. But it is one which God is willing to bestow upon His children. (*Ibid.*)

Gift:

And again, to some it is given by the Holy Ghost to know the difference of administration, as it will be pleasing unto the same Lord, according as the Lord's will, suiting his mercies according to the conditions of the children of men. (v. 15.)

Explanation:

This is another special gift. The term, as used by Paul (I Cor. 12:5) means the different divisions of courses of the priests and Levites engaged in the temple service, and in this Revelation it may refer to the different duties and responsi-

bilities of the Priesthood in its two divisions, the
Melchizedek and Aaronic. To know this is a gift of
the Spirit. (*Ibid.*)

Gift: And again, it is given by the Holy Ghost to
some to know the diversities of operations, wheth-
er they be of God, that the manifestations of the
Spirit may be given to every man to profit withal.
(v. 16.)

Explanation: This refers to various spiritual influences at
work, for instance such as are manifested in Spir-
itism, anarchism, and the numerous other "isms."
To know whether an influence with a professedly
moral, or reformatory aim is from the Holy Spirit,
or from another source, is a special gift. (*Ibid.*)

Gift: And again, verily I say unto you, to some
is given, by the Spirit of God, the word of wisdom.
(v. 17.)

Explanation: This means a discourse or a testimony characterized by and productive of wisdom. Wisdom,
according to Philo, was the highest of the divine
attributes, and human wisdom is a reflection of
the divine. (*Ibid.*)

Gift: To another is given the work of knowledge,
that all may be taught to be wise and to have
knowledge. (v. 18.)

Explanation: Refers to the gift to instruct others. There is
a difference between wisdom, knowledge, and abil-
ity to instruct. According to Coleridge, "common
sense in an uncommon degree" is what men call
wisdom. It is almost a direct operation of intuition.
Knowledge is a carefully-stored-up supply of facts,
generally slowly acquired. The *ability* to *instruct* is
the gift to impart of this supply to others. Each is
a gift of God. (*Ibid.*)

Gift: And again, to some it is given to have faith
to be healed. (v. 19.)

Explanation: This is a gift of the Spirit, and it should be
earnestly sought for, because our Lord is willing
both to forgive sins, if we repent of them, and to

heal *all diseases* (Psalm 103:3), as long as the appointment to death has not been made. (*Ibid.*)

Gift: And to others it is given to have faith to heal. (v. 20.)

Explanation: This is also a gift. (*Ibid.*)

Gift: And again, to some is given the working of miracles. (v. 21.)

Explanation: A special divine power is needed for the working of miracles. The Prophet Joseph had this power in a very high degree. It was one of the evidences that he had the authority of the holy Priesthood. One of the numerous miracles God performed through him was the healing of one Mrs. Johnson, who, in company with others, visited his home in Kirtland, 1831. She had, for some time, been afflicted with a lame arm. She could not raise it to her head. The conversation turned on supernatural power, and someone in the company asked if there was anybody on Earth that could heal Mrs. Johnson for instance. The Prophet arose, walked over to Mrs. Johnson, took her by the hand and said, "Woman, in the name of the Lord Jesus Christ, I command thee to be whole," whereupon he left the room. Mrs. Johnson at once lifted up her arm, and the next day was able to do her washing. (*History of the Church*, Vol. I., p. 215. *Ibid.*, p. 275.)

Gift: And to others it is given to prophesy. (v. 22.)

Explanation: That is, to speak in the name of the Lord, whether of things present, past, or future. This is a special gift. The Prophet Joseph had it in the highest degree. Heber C. Kimball also had the gift highly developed. At times he could see into the future as if it were an open book. During the time of famine in Salt Lake Valley in 1847, when many subsisted on roots and hides of animals, and knew not where to obtain bread or clothing necessary, owing to the devastation by crickets, President Kimball declared in a public meeting that, within a short time, "state goods" would be sold in the streets of Salt Lake City cheaper than in

New York, and that the people should be abun-
dantly supplied with food and clothing. Many who
heard him refused to believe. He himself said he
was afraid he had missed it. But the prophecy came
true. Very soon the California gold-hunters came
through the Valley. Salt Lake City became their
resting-place, and they were glad to exchange their
goods for whatever they could get. Many of them
threw goods away, or sold them for a song, in order
to lighten their wagons and be able to make better
progress. (Whitney's *Life of Heber C. Kimball*, p.
401-2. *Ibid.*)

Gift: And to others the discerning of spirits. (v.
23.)

Explanation: What this means may be illustrated by relating a remarkable experience which the Prophet
records. On the 9th of November, 1835, a man came
to his home and introduced himself as a Jewish
minister whose name was Joshua. The Prophet
entertained him hospitably, as he always did both
strangers and friends who visited him. One day Mr.
Joshua said that he was a lineal descendant of
Matthias, and a re-incarnation of this Apostle. The
Prophet writes:

"I told him that his doctrine was of the Devil,
that he was in reality in possession of a wicked and
depraved spirit, although he professed to be the
spirit of truth itself. He said also that he possessed
the Spirit of Christ. He tarried until Wednesday,
11th, when, after breakfast, I told him that my
God told me that his god was the Devil, and I could
not keep him any longer." (*Hist. of the Church*,
Vol. II, p. 307.) Thus the Prophet had the gift to
discern spirits. (*Ibid.*, 275, 276.)

Gift: And again, it is given to some to speak with
tongues. (v. 24.)

Explanation: The Prophet Joseph says:

"Be not so curious about tongues; do not speak
in tongues except there be an interpreter present;
the ultimate design of tongues is to speak to for-
eigners, and if persons are very anxious to display

their intelligence, let them speak to such in their own tongues. The gifts of God are all useful in their places, but when they are applied to that which God does not intend, they prove an injury, a snare, and a curse instead of a blessing." (*Hist. of the Church*, Vol. V, p. 31. *Ibid.*, p. 276.)

Also of value are these instructions by the Prophet Joseph Smith concerning this gift:

The gift of tongues is the smallest gift perhaps of the whole, and yet it is one that is the most sought after. (*DHC* 5:26-32.)

I lay this down as a rule, that if anything is taught by the gift of tongues, it is not to be received for doctrine. (*Ibid.*, 4:607.)

Tongues were given for the purpose of preaching among those whose language is not understood; as on the day of Pentecost, etc., and it is not necessary for tongues to be taught to the Church particularly, for any man that has the Holy Ghost, can speak of the things of God in his own tongue as well as to speak in another; for faith comes not by signs, but by hearing the word of God. (*DHC* 3:379.)

President Joseph F. Smith once said:

I believe in the gifts of the Holy Spirit unto men, but I do not want the gift of tongues, except when I need it. I needed the gift of tongues once, and the Lord gave it to me. I was in a foreign land, sent to preach the gospel to a people whose language I could not understand. Then I sought earnestly for the gift of tongues, and by this gift and by study, in a hundred days after landing upon those islands I could talk to the people in their language as I now talk to you in my native tongue. This was a gift that was worthy of the gospel. There was a purpose in it. There was something in it to strengthen my faith, to encourage me and to help me in my ministry. . . . Paul did not seem to care much about the gift of tongues either. He said to the Corinthians: "I had rather speak five words with my understanding, that by my voice I might teach others also, than ten thousand words in an unknown tongue." (1 Cor. 14:19. *Gospel Doctrine*, p. 201.)

In 1952, President David O. McKay related the following personal experience:

The occasion was a conference held at Huntly, New Zealand, a thousand people assembled. Before that time I had spoken through interpreters in China, Hawaii, Holland, and other places, but I felt impressed on that occasion to speak in the English language. In substance I said, "I have never been much of an advocate of the necessity of tongues in our Church, but today I wish I had that gift. But I haven't. However, I am going to speak to you, my brothers and sisters, in my native tongue and pray that you may have the gift of interpretation of tongues. We will ask Brother Stuart Meha, who is going to interpret for me, to make notes, and if necessary he may give us a summary of my talk afterwards."

Well, the outpouring of the gift of tongues on that occasion was most remarkable. Following the end of my sermon Brother Sid Christy, who was a student of Brigham Young University, a Maori, who had returned to New Zealand, rushed up and said, "Brother McKay, they got your message!"

Well, I knew they had by the attention and the nodding of their heads during the talk. I said, "I think they have but for the benefit of those who may not have understood or had that gift, we shall have the sermon interpreted."

While Brother Meha was interpreting that or giving a summary of it in the Maori language some of the natives, who had understood it, but who did not understand English, arose and corrected him in his interpretations.

President George Albert Smith and Brother Rufus K. Hardy visited New Zealand several years after that event, and Brother Hardy, hearing of the event, brought home testimonies of those who were present, and he took the occasion to have those testimonies notarized. So it is the gift of interpretation rather than the gift of tongues, that was remarkable. (*Gospel Ideals*, p. 552.)

The membership of the Church is to receive blessings from God in the form of the gifts explained above (D&C 46:26), but to certain officers in his kingdom there is a gift available which is necessary that they may function in their calling. It is necessary that this gift also be sought after. (*Ibid.*, v. 28.)

Gift: And unto the bishop of the church, and unto such as God shall appoint and ordain to watch over the church and to be elders unto the church, are to have it given unto them to *discern all those gifts* lest there shall be any among you professing and yet be not of God. (v. 27. Italics by author.)

Explanation: That is the great gift which the Bishops and others whom God appoints to watch over the Church must seek to obtain, lest hypocrites should go undetected. (*Doctrine and Covenants Commentary*, p. 276.)

To have all the gifts of the Spirit is a privilege that may come to the prophet, seer, and revelator as the "head of the church." (D&C 107:92; 46:29.)

Gifts of the Holy Ghost and the Laying on of Hands

In an article written by the Prophet Joseph Smith, June 15, 1842, on the gift of the Holy Ghost, it is pointed out that sometimes people expect that at the time the Holy Ghost is conferred following water baptism, some miraculous manifestation will result. Excerpts from that article indicate an answer to this notion:

. . . more frequently there is no manifestation at all, that is visible to the surrounding multitude . . . suppose the gifts of the Spirit were immediately, upon the imposition of hands, enjoyed by all, in all there fulness and power, the skeptic would still be as far from receiving any testimony except upon a mere casualty as before, for all the gifts are not visible to the natural vision, or understanding of man, indeed very few of them are. . . . The word of wisdom, and the word of knowledge, are as much gifts as any other, yet if a person possessed both of these gifts, or received them by the imposition of hands, who would know it? Another might receive the gift of faith, and they would be as ignorant of it. Or suppose a man had the gift of healing or power to work miracles, that would not then be known; it would require time and circumstances to call these gifts into operation. Suppose a man had the discerning of spirits, who would be the wiser for it? Or if he had the interpretation of tongues, unless someone spoke in an unknown tongue, he of course would have to be silent; there are only two gifts that could be made visible—the gifts of tongues and the gift of prophecy. These are things that are the most talked about. . . . (*DHC* 5:28-30.)

The Holy Ghost and the Lord's Spirit

There is a difference between that Spirit which comes from God to fill all space—sometimes called the Holy Spirit, Spirit of God and Light of Christ—and the Holy Ghost and the gift of the Holy Ghost. The Spirit of the Lord is given to all people (D&C 84:43-48; 88:6-13), but the gift of the Holy Ghost is received by the members of the Church of Jesus Christ—those who obey the commandments. (Acts 5:32.) The following brief statement from President Joseph F. Smith is pertinent to these ideas:

The question is often asked, Is there any difference between the Spirit of the Lord and the Holy Ghost? The terms are frequently used synonymously. We often say the Spirit of God when we mean the Holy Ghost; we likewise say the Holy Ghost when we mean the Spirit of God. The Holy Ghost is a personage in the Godhead, and is not that which lighteth every man that cometh into the world. It is the Spirit of God which proceeds through Christ to the world, that enlightens every man that comes into the world, and that strives with the children of men, and will continue to strive with them, until it brings them to a knowledge of the truth and the possession of the greater light and testimony of the Holy Ghost, If, however, he receives that greater light, and then sin against it, the Spirit of God will cease to strive with him, and the Holy Ghost will wholly depart from him. (*Gospel Doctrine*, p. 67-68.)

How to Obtain the Gifts

As pointed out in this revelation the gifts of the Holy Ghost are for those who keep all the commandments or seek to do so. (D&C 46:9.) But the member of the Church must *seek* by asking in accordance with these divine instructions:

And it shall come to pass that he that asketh in the Spirit shall receive in Spirit. . . . He that asketh in the Spirit asketh according to the will of God; wherefore it is done even as he asketh. And again, I say unto you, all things must be done in the name of Christ, whatsoever you do in the Spirit; And ye must give thanks unto God in the Spirit for whatsoever blessing ye are blessed with. And ye must practice virtue and holiness before me continually, even so, Amen. (*Ibid.*, vs. 28, 30-33.)

Chapter 33

RECORDS ARE IMPORTANT

(Section 47)

A commandment that a record should be kept was given during the meeting in which six brethren met formally to organize the Church on April 6, 1830. (D&C 21: 1.) When Oliver Cowdery met the Prophet Joseph Smith for the first time in April 1829, he began to assist the Prophet as his scribe in the translation of The Book of Mormon. (D&C, Section 6.) As the companion of Joseph Smith in this work, Oliver Cowdery acted as the Church Historian and Recorder. When Section 47 was received in Kirtland, Ohio, on March 8, 1831, appointing John Whitmer, son of Peter Whitmer, Sr., as Church Historian, Oliver Cowdery's assignment ended.

John Whitmer

John Whitmer received many wonderful privileges and opportunities to become one of the truly great men of this dispensation. In addition to his call as Church Historian, he was the subject of a number of revelations —Sections 15, 26, 30, 69, 70. Some of his responsibilities in the Church were to assist in presiding over the Church in Missouri, to serve as a missionary, to help the Prophet in the compilation of the revelations in the Book of Commandments, and to assist Oliver Cowdery in superintending the printing of them.

Probably the most important responsibility placed upon him was the call as one of the eight witnesses of The Book of Mormon. With his brethren, he testified that he had seen the plates. Although John Whitmer failed to live up to his high calling, he never denied his testimony.

After his excommunication in 1838, he had the following conversation with Theodore Turley in the company of men who had sworn to kill the Prophet Joseph Smith. Turning to him, Brother Turley said:

"There are many things published that they say are true, and again turn around and say they are false." "Do you hint at me?" Whitmer asked. Turley said, "If the cap fits, you may wear it; all I know is that you have published to the world that an angel did present those plates to Joseph Smith." Then John Whitmer, in that company, made this statement, "I now say, I handled those plates; there were fine engravings on both sides, I handled them; they were shown to me by supernatural power." (*Historical Record*, p. 458, quoted in the *Doctrine and Covenants Commentary*, p. 75.)

John Whitmer, Church Historian

The call of John Whitmer as Church Historian is an example of a fulfilled desire to receive the call by revelation.

. . . John Whitmer, according to his own representations, said he would rather not keep the Church history, but observed— "The will of the Lord be done, and if He desires it, I wish that He would manifest it through Joseph the Seer." (*DHC* I:166, footnote.)

In the revelation he is informed of his appointment and his responsibility as historian. (D&C 47:3-4.) Within the year following receipt of this revelation, John Whitmer was instructed to accompany Oliver Cowdery to Independence, Missouri, and the revelations compiled as *A Book of Commandments* should be printed. In that revelation, the duties of Brother Whitmer as historian are given.

And also that he shall continue in writing and making a history of all the important things which he shall observe and know concerning my church; . . .

Nevertheless, let my servant John Whitmer travel many times from place to place, and from church to church, that he may the more easily obtain knowledge—selecting, and obtaining all things which shall be for the good of the church, and for the rising generations that shall grow up on the land of Zion, to possess it from generation to generation, forever and ever. Amen. (D&C 69:3, 7-8.)

The history of the Church written by John Whitmer was only "a mere sketch of the things that transpired." His total work consisted of eighty-five pages which included many of the revelations given while he was in office. During the period when many brethren became disaffected, he was in the Presidency of the Church in Missouri. The members of the Church in that area did not sustain him and his associates in the Presidency. Although the presiding brethren demanded that he deliver the history of the Church to them he refused. Years after his death, a copy of the history was obtained by the Church.

Church Historian's Office

The Historian's Office became recognized as a distinct part of the Church organization in 1843, when the Prophet Joseph Smith appointed Willard Richards Church Historian and General Church Recorder. Since that time the official title of Church Historian and Recorder has been used by each person succeeding him. The present Historian and Recorder is President Joseph Fielding Smith, also President of the Council of the Twelve. The first Assistant Church Historian was Elder Wilford Woodruff who received this office in October 1856. Elder A. William Lund occupies this position today.

In an article about the Church Historian's Office written by Elder A. William Lund, from which the above information was obtained, the following appears as the purpose of this office:

It is the aim of this office to gather all books, pamphlets, tracts, newspapers, records, etc., published by the Church and those written by members of the Church; those books pertaining to Western History, especially when dealing with the Mormons; also books written by non-Mormons which are friendly in their nature and those written by anti-Mormons. We have also in the Historian's Office hundreds of early records of the missions, and since 1907, all the records of births, baptisms, ordinations, deaths, and excommunications which have taken place in the Church. (*Improvement Era,* November 1956, pp. 853-854.)

Section 123 of The Doctrine and Covenants given March 1839, is a revelation setting forth the need for the Saints to assemble all anti-Mormon literature. The importance of the position of the Church Historian is indicated in this passage:

The position of the Church Historian is one of great importance. One of the epoch-making events in the history of the world took place when the Church was organized. But without a specially-appointed recorder, that event would have passed almost unnoticed, or it would have been described from the viewpoint of enemies. The development of the Church would have had no proper place in the annals of man but for a truthful historian, well acquainted with and instructed in that part of human history. The Prophet began his history on May 2nd, 1838, "to disabuse the public mind, and put all inquirers after the truth into possession of the facts, as they have transpired, in relation to both myself and the Church, so far as I have such facts in my possession" (*History of the Church,* Vol. I., p. 1), and that is the great reason for the existence of the office of the Historian of the Church. (*Doctrine and Covenants Commentary,* p. 279.)

Historical Accuracy Essential

In harmony with the desire of the Prophet to record facts relating to his life and the history of the Church that men might know the truth, these words from the Church Historian and Recorder should give us an appreciation of the place of the Church in the world:

In regard to the recording of history, the thing that is most important is accuracy. If history is not accurate, it is harmful. It has been said that history is what historians declare it shall be and many historians write with that thought in mind. Of course this is a deplorable situation, which we cannot help. You take history written 50 years ago by some writers of the North in relation to the Civil War [in the United States] and compare it with the writings of someone from the Southern States and you will find a vast difference. . . .

The most important history in the world is the history of our Church and it is the most accurate history in the world. It must be so. It is the most important to us because that history contains the hand dealings of God direct to us through revelation as it has come in the Doctrine and Covenants, in The Book of Mormon, and in any revelation that comes to us through the servants of the Lord for our guidance. . . . In our history if there are mistakes we can say as did Moroni in The Book of Mormon, "They are the mistakes of men." (Elder Joseph Fielding Smith: "History and History Recorders," *Utah Genealogical and Historical Magazine*, Vol. 16, April 1925, pp. 53-55, 58-59.)

Is it not reasonable and consistent with our knowledge of the purpose of The Church of Jesus Christ of Latter-day Saints as the only true Church on the earth that our history is the most accurate? Certainly the Lord would inspire his servants and help them make accurate records where it is necessary that the Church be a standard and a light for the world, as prophesied. (D&C 115: 5.) The prayers of the Church membership are for the upbuilding of Zion upon the earth, a necessary part of which is the keeping of records which will redound to the blessings of the people of the world who will be attracted to the gospel. The words of Wilford Woodruff, on September 15, 1856, in dedicating the Church Historian's Office building, located on the site of the present Medical Arts Building in Salt Lake City, express the desire of the faithful member of the Church:

And by virtue of the Holy Priesthood vested in us, in the name of Jesus Christ, we do dedicate it and consecrate it unto the Lord our God, and we set it apart that it may contain holy records of the Church and Kingdom of God, and we ask in the name of Jesus Christ that it may be sanctified and holy unto Thy name, and we pray that we may be inspired by the gift and power of the Holy Ghost while acting as Historians or clerks for the Church, and may we keep a true and faithful record and history of Thy Church and Kingdom and Thy servants, and may it be kept in that way and manner that it may be acceptable unto Thee, O Lord, and unto Thy servants, the presidency of Thy Church. . . .

And we ask Thee to bless us and prosper us in all things, and we pray that Thou wilt bring to our remembrance all things which are necessary to the writing of this history. And that papers and documents and all things necessary may be brought to us, to enable us to compile a right, useful and proper history (*Improvement Era*, November, 1856, pp. 795, 853.)

Instructions to the Twelve

Among the instructions given by the Prophet to the Twelve Apostles after their appointment on February 14, 1835, was the necessity of keeping a record of their official acts. The Prophet Joseph Smith expressed sorrow over the fact that decisions reached on doctrine and duties relating to the kingdom of God had not always been recorded. Consequently, "We cannot bear record to the Church and to the world of the great and glorious manifestations which have been made to us with that degree of power and authority we otherwise could, if we now had these things to publish abroad." He then proceeded to instruct the Twelve to keep a record of their proceedings, declaring it to be of infinite worth and that it would be a feast to their souls. These records would also be a means of protection against the Adversary because neglect in this regard would bring about the withdrawal of the Spirit of God. (*DHC* II:199.)

Our Acts Are Recorded

The Prophet Joseph Smith said that "Our acts are recorded, and at a future day they will be laid before us." (*Ibid.*, II:26.) In a letter written to the Church concerning salvation for the dead, and after quoting Revelation 20:12, the Prophet wrote:

You will discover in this quotation that the books were opened; and another book was opened, which was the book of life; but the dead were judged out of those things which were written in the books, according to their works; consequently, the books spoken of must be the books which contained the record of their works, and refer to the records which are kept on the earth. And the book which was the book of life is the record which is kept in heaven; the principle agreeing precisely with the doctrine which is commanded you in the revelation contained in the latter which I wrote to you previous to my leaving my place [D&C Section 127]—that in all your recordings it may be recorded in heaven. (D&C 128:7.)

The Book of the Law of the Lord

Imbued with the need to keep records, the Prophet kept a record called The Book of the Law of the Lord in which he wrote the names of those who were true to the Lord and also to himself as the Lord's anointed. Concerning one of these persons he referred to him as "A faithful man in Israel; therefore his name shall never be forgotten." (*DHC* V:125.) To be thought of and to be worthy of such a comment would be the wish of all who have a testimony of the truth restored in this dispensation.

Joseph Smith's journal or diary is the accurate history of this dispensation from the beginning to the end of the Prophet's life. It is known as the *History of the Church*, and the *Documentary History of the Church*, consisting of six volumes. The seventh volume covers the period immediately following the martyrdom of Joseph and Hyrum Smith to the sustaining of President Brigham Young and his counselors as the First Presidency on October 8, 1848. This vote ratified the action of the general conference held on the Iowa side of the Missouri River on December 27, 1847.

The Value of Journals or Diaries

Not only did the Council of the Twelve keep minutes of their official acts as a body, but many maintained journals of their personal activities. Many of these journals, together with those kept by others of the brethren, have been extremely important in giving information about their missionary labors, pioneer activities, and other aspects of our history. The number of these brethren runs into a very large number. Among these was Wilford Woodruff who assisted in bringing many wonderful happenings during and after President Joseph Smith's life to the attention of the Church. From this passage one will realize the way in which he was able to perform this function:

> There is one subject I wish to speak upon and that is the keeping of a journal with respect to the dealings of God with us. I have many times thought the Quorum of the Twelve and others considered me rather enthusiastic upon this subject; but when the Prophet Joseph organized the Quorum of the Twelve, he counseled them to keep a history of their lives, and gave his reasons why they should do so. I have had this spirit and calling upon me since I first entered this Church. I made a record from the first sermon I heard, and from that day until now I have kept a daily journal. Whenever I heard Joseph Smith preach, teach, or prophesy, I always felt it my duty to write it; I felt uneasy and could not eat, drink, or sleep until I did write; and my mind has been so exercised upon this subject that when I heard Joseph Smith teach and had no pencil or paper, I would go home and sit down and write the whole sermon, almost word for word and sentence by sentence as it was delivered, and when I had written it it was taken from me, I remembered it no more. This was the gift of God to me. . . .
>
> Another reason I was moved upon to write in the early days was that nearly all the historians appointed in those times apostatized and took the journals away with them. (Matthias F. Cowley, *Wilford Woodruff*, pp. 476-477.)

In 1866, a large number of missionaries received instructions from Elders Wilford Woodruff and Parley

P. Pratt on the necessity of keeping an accurate record
of their labors. The journals were to be full, correct and
proper.

Many important reasons for keeping an accurate
record of important events in one's life are provided in
this advice given in 1849 by Elder Orson Pratt to the
members of the British Mission.

> If every elder had, during the last nineteen years, kept a
> faithful record of all that he had seen, heard, and felt of the good-
> ness, wisdom and power of God, the Church would now have
> been in possession of many thousand volumes, containing much
> important and useful information. How many thousands have
> been miraculously healed in this Church, and yet no one has
> recorded the circumstances. Is this right? Should these miracu-
> lous manifestations of the power of God be forgotten and pass
> into oblivion? Should the knowledge of these things slumber in
> the hearts of those who witnessed them, and extend no further
> than their own verbal reports will carry them? . . . We should
> keep a record because Jesus has commanded it. We should keep
> a record because the same will benefit us and the generations
> of our children after us. We should keep a record because it will
> furnish many important items for the general history of the
> Church which would otherwise be lost. (*Millennial Star* 11:152.)

It is probably unnecessary for everyone to keep a
daily journal, but it is necessary that one keep a record
of important activities and events in one's life. We might
raise this point, if I had kept a record of the Lord's blessings to me in faith-promoting experiences, etc., I might
leave to my children a permanent record which would
impress and create in them a desire to live the gospel and
to assist them to be strong Latter-day Saints.

The private journals kept by our progenitors are
important as a part of the general history of the Church.
With this in mind President Joseph Fielding Smith said
at a general conference:

> . . . Moreover, there are many important private journals
> scattered about which we would like to obtain for preservation

and for historical purposes. We discover that when these are left in the keeping of the descendants of the pioneers, they frequently are lost, or lose their value by the time they reach the third or fourth generation, and are thrown away. If they are given to us we will file them away where they will be preserved. (*Conference Report,* April 1934, p. 20.)

Genealogical Records

Subsequent chapters will deal with the great subject of salvation for the dead, including genealogical research as a part of that material. We should at this time, however, be mindful of the need to give encouragement to each member of the family in keeping books of remembrance, life histories, genealogical pedigrees, and the maintenance of interest in genealogical research and temple activity, where possible.

Summary

Section 47 of The Doctrine and Covenants is the revelation appointing John Whitmer as Church Historian. This brother had many opportunities to remain faithful to the high callings which came to him in the Church, but he failed in keeping the faith, notwithstanding he never denied his testimony of The Book of Mormon. Later, in 1843, the Church Historian's Office became a part of the Church organization and serves today as the repository of the vital statistics and history of the Church. The history of The Church of Jesus Christ of Latter-day Saints is intended to be an accurate history because it was and is prepared by brethren who have the Spirit of the Lord to guide them in their important duties. From the beginning of this dispensation the commandment has been given that the Latter-day Saints are to be a record-keeping people to benefit themselves as individuals and also to present to the world the truths of the Dispensation of the Fulness of Times. The value of life histories prepared by the individual in contributing to the general history of the Church has also been noted. The preparation of genealogical records is of extreme importance as a part of every Latter-day Saint's responsibility. The faithful Latter-day Saint accepts the Lord's will as contained in the scriptures, and accepts the obligation to participate in its varied activities. This faithfulness will bring joy and satisfaction to the participant and to his family.

Chapter 34

THE MISSION TO THE "SHAKING QUAKERS"

(Section 49)

One of the most interesting revelations in The Doctrine and Covenants forms the basis for this chapter. Its interest lies primarily in the background out of which it was received by the Prophet Joseph Smith. Interest is not its only value, for it provides the Latter-day Saint with knowledge concerning (a) some teachings held by an unusual sect; (b) some very important doctrinal teachings which are fundamental in the fulness of the gospel; and (c) two prophecies which are in the process of fulfillment.

Leman Copley, Convert

In the Prophet Joseph Smith's journal, it is recorded that: "At about this time (March 1831) came Leman Copley, one of the sect called Shaking Quakers, and embraced the fulness of the everlasting Gospel, apparently honest-hearted, but still retaining the idea that the Shakers were right in some particulars of their faith. In order to have a more perfect understanding of the subject . . ." the Prophet inquired of the Lord and received this revelation. (*DHC* I:167.)

Ann Lee and the "Shakers'" Origin

To appreciate fully the teachings received in Section 49 of The Doctrine and Covenants, some knowledge of the origin and beliefs of the "Shakers," whose correct name was "The United Society of Believers in Christ's Second Appearing," is necessary.

At the beginning of the 18th century (1706), a group of religionists from France went to England and were known there as the French Prophets. James Wardley, a tailor, and his wife Jane, who were seceders from Quakerism came under their influence. In 1747 the Wardleys founded a society in Manchester and began to preach. They declared that Christ was soon to return to reign on the earth, and that he would come in the form of a woman. The society increased in numbers although suffering much from persecution. One of their converts was Ann Lee. She was born February 29, 1736, the daughter of a blacksmith, and was married to a blacksmith at an early age. She gave birth to four children who died in infancy. In 1758 she was converted by Jane Wardley and also began to preach. Among her claimed revelations was one regarding the nature of God described in this manner: "The duality of Deity, God both Father and Mother; one in essence—one God, not two; but God who possesses two natures, the masculine and the feminine, each distinct in function yet one in being, co-equal in Deity." This belief is the basis for the later claim that Ann Lee became the incarnation of the Christ Spirit.

Because of persecution and lack of progress in making converts, Ann Lee and eight of her followers decided to go to America. Arriving there in 1774, they established themselves at Watervliet near Albany, New York. Ann Lee saw two other Shaker communities founded before her death in 1784. The period of greatest growth of this sect was between 1792 and 1835. At one time they numbered nearly 5,000. The sect no longer exists. (Anne White and Leila S. Taylor, "Shakerism, Its Meaning and Message"; *Encyclopedia Americana* [1949] Vol. 24, p. 642.)

Gospel Doctrine Emphasized

Although Section 49 was given at the time for the principal benefit of the missionaries who were to labor with this people, the "Shakers," it should be kept in mind that this revelation is just as important for us today as for the members of the Church in the time of the Prophet Joseph Smith.

After the call of Sidney Rigdon, Parley P. Pratt, and Leman Copley to labor with this sect, the Lord declared that "I am God, and have sent mine Only Begotten Son into the world for the redemption of the world, and have decreed that he that receiveth him shall be saved, and he that receiveth him not shall be damned—" (D&C 49: 5.) Is it not required of all men that they should repent; otherwise, they shall be damned? Regardless of the group, it is the same message—acceptance of the Christ through the means appointed. But what is that way? Specifically directed to the "Shakers," the revelation stated that they were to have faith in Christ, repent of their sins, obtain a remission of sins by baptism and then receive the Holy Ghost by the laying on of the hands. (*Ibid.*, 49:11-14.)

The ordinances of water and spirit baptism, as taught in this revelation and by the Apostle Peter on the day of Pentacost (Acts 2:37-38), were not practiced by the "Shakers." They did believe, however, that "every soul must work out its own salvation by practicing the self-denials of Jesus, aided by baptisms of the Holy Spirit of Christ, an influx of the saving power of the Divine Creator." (*Shakerism, Its Meaning and Message*, p. 259.) Water baptism to them was unnecessary as a means of salvation.

The manifestation of the Spirit upon them was claimed in their worship as they sang and danced. (*Ibid.*, p. 329.)

This sect also claimed the gifts of the Spirit. It is known as the modern parent of spiritualism, which received its impetus from the Fox Sisters near Rochester, New York, in the year 1844.

In order that none might be deceived into accepting self-claimed Christs or Messiahs, the Lord definitely makes known that his Only Begotten Son has come into the world, "And they have done unto the Son of Man even as they listed; and he has taken his power on the right hand of his glory, and now reigneth in the heavens, and will reign till he descends on the earth to put all enemies under his feet, which time is nigh at hand. . . ." (D&C 49:6.)

In view of the claim that Ann Lee was the incarnation of Christ, there was to be a clear understanding on the part of everyone that the true Messiah was not on the earth at that time, but it was known that his coming was not far distant.

There have been many who have claimed that they are the Christ who has come the second time. Such claims are false, for the scriptures denote that the Savior's final coming will be attended by great disturbances of nature and the destruction of the wicked. (*Ibid.*, 101:23-24.) As indicated in Chapter 31, Jesus Christ will come to his Saints first, then to the Jewish people assembled in the Holy Land, and, finally, to the world at large. Notice in this passage how specific the Lord is concerning the claims of the "Shaking Quakers" and also of those who profess themselves to be the Messiah:

And again, verily I say unto you, that the Son of Man cometh not in the form of a woman, neither of a man traveling on the earth. (D&C 49:22.)

The Savior will not come to the earth traveling as a man, but will come to the temples erected to receive him. This was prophesied by the Old Testament Prophet Malachi, who predicted that in the last days the Lord "shall suddenly come to his temple." (Mal. 3:1-3; also Chapter 8, for further information.) Temples are houses of the Lord where holy ordinances are performed for the living and the dead and the presence of the Lord is felt by his

Spirit. (D&C 97:15-17.) In addition, it is a place "for the most High to dwell therein." (*Ibid.*, 124:27.) In 1863, President Brigham Young voiced this thought:

> . . . We build temples because there is not a house on the face of the whole earth that has been reared to God's name, which will in any wise compare with his character, and that he can consistently call his house. There are places on the earth where the Lord can come and dwell, if he pleases. They may be found on the tops of high moutains, or in some cavern or places where sinful man has never marked the soil with his polluted feet. He requires his servants to build Him a house that He can come to, and where He can make known His will (*Journal of Discourses,* 10:252.)

Revelation 49 continues to explain that when the Christ comes in his second appearance to the world, the Saints should look forth for the earth to tremble and the valleys to be exalted as the mountains are made low. (D&C 49:23.)

Deception is one of the strongest tools used by the devil to lead men from the truth. It is manifest in many ways. When the evil one can influence men in justifying themselves in committing a little sin, to "teach with their learning and deny the Holy Ghost," in setting forth teachings which are vain and foolish, he has accomplished his purposes. (2 Nephi 28:4.) On the other hand, the true prophets by the authority of the Priesthood have counseled those who will believe in ways of truth to remain steadfast, that eternal life will be their blessing. (D&C 14:7.)

The second coming of Christ will usher in the millennium, a period of peace and righteousness when the work of salvation for the living and the dead will be increased. The reign of Christ will then commence, and there shall be no laws in force except his laws, but, at the time of his coming, great changes will come to the earth in the establishing of paradisiacal conditions. (Article of Faith, number 10.) The millennium will not begin until the Savior comes to establish his government upon the earth. Implicit in the "Shaker" belief about Ann Lee was the idea that the millennium had begun.

Marriage Is Ordained of God

The "Shakers" maintained, theologically, that the highest type of Christian life was celibacy. All people will not live a life of continence, but, they claimed, "they that marry, or in any relation propagate the children of the world, serve the world, and therefore do not serve Christ; they bring forth the appropriate fruit of the world, and are therefore the world, and abide in it. To the married, Ann Lee would plainly say: "You must forsake the marriage of the flesh or you cannot be married to the lamb, or have any share in the resurrection of Christ, for those who are counted worthy to have any part in the resurrection of Christ neither marry nor are given in marriage, but are like unto the angels." (White and Taylor, *Shakerism, Its Meaning and Message*, pp. 41-42.)

On the contrary, it has been revealed to Latter-day Saints that marriage is a divinely established institution by which the faithful followers of the Christ will be enabled to receive eternal life. Anyone who teaches that a life of celibacy is in accordance with the Lord's will stands condemned before him. Notice how explicit the Latter-day revelation explains (1) that marriage is ordained of God; and (2) that it is the means by which the earth answers the purpose of its creation. (D&C 49:15-17.)

It is important to notice that this revelation confirms what was made known to Abraham and Moses relative to the plan of salvation. (Abraham 3:22-28; Moses 4:1-4.) The pre-existent sons and daughters of God were to be given an opportunity for an earth-life in which they would be able to work out their salvation with the means provided by the Father. President Joseph

Fielding Smith made this comment on these particular verses:

> ... The Lord informs us that this earth was designed, before its foundations were formed, for the abode of the spirits who kept their first estate and all such must come here and receive their tabernacles of flesh and bones, and this is according to the number, or measure, of man according to his creation before the world was made. (Compare Deut. 32:8-9.) It is the duty of mankind, in lawful and holy wedlock to multiply according to the commandments given to Adam and Eve and later to Noah, until every spirit appointed to receive a body in this world has had that privilege. Those who teach celibacy and look upon marriage as sinful are in opposition to the word and commandment of the Lord. Such a doctrine is from an evil source and is intended to defeat the plan of redemption and the bringing into the world the spirits who kept their first estate. Satan, in every way that he can and with all his power, endeavors to defeat the work of the Lord. It is his purpose to destroy the souls of men and if he can prevent them from having bodies by teaching men and women that marriage is unrighteous and sinful, or that they should not after they are married bring children into the world, he thinks he will accomplish his purpose. All who hearken to these evil whisperings and practice this evil will stand condemned before the throne of God. (*Church History and Modern Revelation,* Melchizedek Priesthood Quorum Study for the year 1947, Vol. I, pp. 209-210.)

Relative to the health of the "Shakers," a book published in 1859 is quoted by an encyclopedia as saying that they abstained from alcoholic liquors, tobacco and that their diet did not include flesh-meat or fish. (*Encyclopedia Americana,* [1957 ed.] Vol. 24, p. 642.)

The Lord revealed that meat is good for man and he that forbids to abstain from meat is not of God. (D&C 49:18-19.)

In a later revelation, it is made known that meat is to be used sparingly. (*Ibid.,* 89:12-13.)

Although the Lord has provided the beasts of the field and the fowls of the air and grains for the use of man, (*Ibid.,* 49:20), it is sinful for man to kill animals for the sake of killing: "And wo be unto man that shed-deth blood or that wasteth flesh and hath no need." (*Ibid.*, 49:21.) President Joseph Fielding Smith made this wise comment on this passage:

> It is a grievous sin in the sight of God to kill merely for sport. Such a thing shows a weakness in the spiritual character of the individual. We cannot restore life when it is taken, and all creatures have the right to enjoy life and happiness on the earth where the Lord has placed them. Only for food, and then sparingly, should flesh be eaten, for all life is from God and is eternal (*Church History and Modern Revelation*, Vol. I, 210.)

Two Prophecies

In order that the "Shaking Quakers" might know what would occur on this continent before the Lord's second coming, these two prophecies were given:

> But before the great day of the Lord shall come, Jacob shall flourish in the wilderness, and the Lamanites shall blossom as the rose. Zion shall flourish upon the hills and rejoice upon the mountains, and shall be assembled together in the place which I have appointed. (D&C 49:24-25.)

Do these two predictions have value beyond their application to the "Shakers"? Decidedly so; for, these prophecies demonstrate the prophetic powers of the Prophet Joseph Smith.

Prophecies Fulfilled

Concerning the Indians flourishing and blossoming as the rose, we learn that by 1955, it was estimated that the number of Indians in North America was several times greater than in 1907. It should also be of interest to learn that the number of Indians living within the present confines of the United States at the beginning of 15th century is estimated at 400,000. Because of disease and displacement this number was greatly decreased until the Indian was called the "Vanishing American." Since 1920, however, the Indians have increased in number until, today, there are more than it is estimated existed at the time of the discovery of America.

Rocky Mountain Prophecy

As early as 1830 the Lord indicated in a revelation that "Zion shall rejoice upon the hills and flourish." (*Ibid.*, 35:24.) This prediction is another reference to the Saints residing in the Rocky Mountains. "And this was at a time when the Rocky Mountain region was almost unknown to the people in the Eastern States." (*Doctrine and Covenants Commentary*, p. 189.)

Ten years passed away and the Lord inspired the Prophet Joseph Smith to speak more clearly about the future of the Saints "upon the hills" and of their rejoicing "upon the mountains." On August 6, 1842, Joseph Smith wrote:

I prophesied that the Saints would continue to suffer much affliction and would be driven to the Rocky Mountains, many would apostatize, others would be put to death by our persecutors or lose their lives in consequence of exposure or disease, and some of you will live to go and assist in making settlements and build cities and see the Saints become a mighty people in the midst of the Rocky Mountains. (*DHC* V, p. 85.)

All of this prophecy has been fulfilled in the sufferings and tribulations of the Saints, including the apostasies of those who could not endure to the end. Significant in the fulfillment of this prophecy is the fact that the Saints have prospered and become a mighty people in the western part of the United States.

Truth Will Prevail

In closing this revelation, the missionaries are informed that if they will repent and labor diligently, they shall not be confounded, for the Lord will be with them. (D&C 49:26-28.) John Whitmer remarks upon this incident:

> The above-named brethren went and proclaimed [the gospel] according to the revelation given them, but the Shakers hearkened not to their words and received not the Gospel at that time, for they are bound in tradition and priestcraft; and thus they are led away with foolish and vain imaginations. (John Whitmer's *History of the Church*, ms. p. 20. *DHC* I:169.)

Because these "vain imaginations" were not true, they could not prevail. The prophecies contained in this revelation continue to be fulfilled and will prevail.

Chapter 35

BE NOT DECEIVED

(Section 50)

Section 50 is one of the many informative and interesting revelations in The Doctrine and Covenants. It is different from many of the sections because of the relationship of its various ideas to the central theme—men and women may know how to detect evil powers.

Although this revelation was given because of a condition which arose in some branches of the Church during Joseph Smith's time, it is as applicable today as then. (D&C 50:1.)

As pointed out by the Lord, the instructions in this revelation are "words of wisdom." From what source is one to seek the counsel of the Lord? In another revelation, we are instructed to "teach one another words of wisdom; yea, seek ye out of the best books words of wisdom. . . ." (*Ibid.*, 88:118.) These are the books of scripture which contain the truths that guide one to salvation. Is it not the admonition of the Lord that we should live by every word that proceedeth forth from his mouth? (*Ibid.*, 84: 44.)

As indicated in verse two of our text, there are "many spirits which are false spirits, which have gone forth in the earth deceiving the world."

Historical Background

What would be the reason for a revelation which, in the introduction, points out that there are many spirits in the world seeking to deceive? The elders of the Church for whom revelation was given, were also reminded that "Satan hath sought to deceive you, that he might overthrow you." In what way did the adversary attempt to deceive? The Lord says, "Behold, I, the Lord, have looked upon you, and have seen abominations in the church that profess my name." (*Ibid.*, 50:3-4.) Here is what Elder Parley P. Pratt, one of those addressed in this revelation, said concerning this condition in some branches of the Church near Kirtland, Ohio:

> As I went forth among the different branches, some very strange spiritual operations were manifested, which were disgusting rather than edifying. Some persons would seem to swoon away, and make unseemly gestures, and be drawn or disfigured in their countenaces. Others would fall into ecstasies, and be drawn into contortions, cramp, fits, etc. Others would seem to have visions and revelations, which were not edifying, and which were not congenial to the doctrine and spirit of the gospel. In short, a false and lying spirit seemed to be creeping into the Church.
>
> All these things were new and strange to me, and had originated in the Church during our absence, and previous to the arrival of President Joseph Smith from New York. (*Autobiography of Parley P. Pratt*, p. 61, 1950 edition.)

Joseph Smith and Revelations

With Elder John Murdock and several other elders, Brother Pratt asked the Prophet to inquire of the Lord concerning these manifestations. In relating what happened when this revelation (Section 50) was received by the Prophet, there is available to us an account of the way in which Joseph Smith received some of the revelations in the Doctrine and Covenants. Following prayer, the Prophet dictated this revelation in the presence of these elders in this way:

> Each sentence was uttered slowly and very distinctly, and with a pause between each, sufficiently long for it to be recorded, by an ordinary writer, in long hand.
>
> This was the manner in which all his written revelations were dictated and written. There was never any hesitation, reviewing, or reading back, in order to keep the run of the subject;

neither did any of these communications undergo revisions, interlinings, or corrections. As he dictated them so they stood, so far as I have witnessed; and I was present to witness the dictation of several communications of several pages each. . . . (*Ibid.*, p. 62.)

In commenting upon the above testimony, Elder B. H. Roberts writes as follows:

This statement of Elder Pratt's is true in a general way, and valuable as a description of the manner in which revelations were dictated by the Prophet; and needs modifying only to the extent of saying that some of the early revelations first published in the "Book of Commandments," in 1833, were revised by the Prophet himself in the way of correcting errors made by the scribes and publishers; and some additional clauses were inserted to throw increased light upon the subjects treated in the revelations, and paragraphs added, to make the principles or instructions apply to officers not in the Church at the time some of the earlier revelations were given. . . . (*DHC* I:173, footnote.)

Satan's Attacks

In all dispensations of the gospel, Satan has attempted to thwart the purposes of the Lord for man. He has spread false teachings, overcome many by spurious gifts to simulate the genuine, and thus has weakened faith in truth and shipwrecked many souls by his deceptions. In the period of the meridian dispensation, Satan's efforts were successful in bringing about a general apostasy of the Church. His efforts to do this in the fulness of times will not succeed according to the word of the Lord (Daniel 2; D&C 65:2); but there have been and there will probably be many who will succumb to his attacks.

In order to insure the continuance of the kingdom of God in this last dispensation, the Saints have been informed through revelation to the Prophet that there are ways to detect the deceiver.

Key against Deception

To the elders addressed in this revelation (Section 50), and for any who are seeking for a standard against deception, the Lord made known an important truth:

> And that which doth not edify is not of God, and is darkness. That which is of God is light; and he that receiveth light, and continueth in God, receiveth more light; and that light groweth brighter and brighter until the perfect day. (D&C 50:23-24.)

To edify means to improve morally and spiritually. Advancement upward is the planned purpose of God for his spirit children. Through the various stages of man's eternal journey, it is the Father's plan to develop his children. In terms of the salvation of his children, the Father's work is to bring about their exaltation. But there is only one way in which this can be accomplished. It is that man will accept Jesus Christ as his Savior. No other way is possible. Therefore, those principles, teachings, and works which do not conform to the Master's gospel will not accomplish the exaltation of man. It is he who endures to the end that will be saved. Nephi understood by revelation that all salvation revolves around the Christ. (2 Nephi 31:14, 16, 20, 21.)

Having a true understanding of the gospel of Jesus Christ, man knows that the path to exaltation or eternal life is observance of the commandments of God. Whenever the scriptures speak of salvation in the kingdom of God, they emphasize the necessity of following the example of Jesus. If the instructions received do not make a person better in terms of his attainment of salvation, then they are not from God. When one understands his own position in the eternal plan of the Father as a child of God, he then is capable of receiving more light and truth through strict obedience to the principles of progression. Again, all ideas, theories, commandments which are not in accordance with the teachings of Christ do not give the edification necessary to achieve the eternal life. In the following way a Book of Mormon prophet taught the necessity of patterning one's life after the Master:

> . . . and if ye will not hearken unto the voice of the good shepherd [Christ], to the name by which ye are called, behold ye are not the sheep of the good shepherd.
>
> And now if ye are not the sheep of the good shepherd, what fold are ye? Behold, I say unto you, that the devil is your shepherd, and ye are of his fold; and now, who can deny this? Behold, I say unto you, whosoever denieth this is a liar and a child of the devil.
>
> For I say unto you that whatsoever is good cometh from God, and whatsoever is evil cometh from the devil. Therefore, if a man bringeth forth good works he hearkeneth unto the voice of the good shepherd, and he doth follow him; but whosoever bringeth forth evil works, the same becometh a child of the devil, for he hearkeneth unto his voice, and doth follow him.
>
> And whosoever doeth this must receive his wages of him; therefore, for his wages he receiveth death, as to things pertaining unto righteousness, being dead unto all good works. (Alma 5:38-42)

Jesus Christ is the light, the truth, which is to be held up before the world. It is his atonement, his works, his example, that will make possible the greatest blessing to man—eternal life. Jesus, as the resurrected Son of God, said to the Nephites: "Therefore, hold up your light that it may shine unto the world. Behold I am the light which ye shall hold up—that which ye have seen me do. Behold ye see that I have prayed unto the Father, and ye all have witnessed." (3 Nephi 18:24.) ". . . Behold I am the light; I have set an example for you." (Ibid., 18:16.)

We follow the Savior's example when we live the gospel of Jesus Christ, which is declared to be light. (D&C 45:28-29; 14:9-10.) Men and women are truly edified when they follow the truth—the gospel of Jesus Christ. The beginning of this progression to the fulness of truth comes with the remission of sins through repentance and the atonement of Jesus. The continued blessings of forgiveness result by keeping the commandments. (Mosiah 4:26-27.)

Blessed Are the Faithful

Only to the faithful who endure to the end seeking for perfection will the greatest blessings come. (D&C 14: 7.) "But blessed are they who are faithful and endure, whether in life or in death, for they shall inherit eternal life." (*Ibid.*, 50:5.) The fight against the adversary must continue unabated by striving to overcome all of the barriers to one's salvation.

Wo unto the Deceivers

The condition which existed in some branches of the Church around Kirtland resulted, in part, because of the actions of some of the members.

. . . there are hypocrites among you, who have deceived some, which has given the adversary power; but behold such shall be reclaimed. (*Ibid.*, 50:7.)

Who is the hypocrite? He is a pretender—one who feigns righteousness, goodness, and virtue, but his professsion is not demonstrated in living the gospel. This class is particularly susceptible to being overcome by the world. Those who have been deceived by the hypocrite, however, "shall be reclaimed."

But the hypocrites shall be detected and shall be cut off, either in life or in death, even as I will. . . . (*Ibid.*, 50:8.)

Those who seek to deceive, and remain unrepentant, will be revealed. They will leave the truth, and darkness will ensue. If detected in this life, they are subject to being cut off from the Church. But if they are not known in this life, by their actions they have cut themselves off from the Spirit of the Lord.

> ... and wo unto them who are cut off from my church, for the same are overcome of the world. (*Ibid.*, 50:8.)

Who is it that remains faithful? Those who walk in the light, treasuring up the Lord's word. It is those who will not be deceived. (Pearl of Great Price, Joseph Smith 1:35.) But when men and women follow the counsel of those who are not the legal administrators in the kingdom, and who do not walk in the light of the revelations of the Lord, they are overcome of the world. (D&C 50:6-9.)

The Spirit of Christ

Every man receives the light of Christ or Holy Spirit by which he may be led into truth. He receives of that Spirit in order that he may distinguish between good and evil. Mormon, the Nephite prophet, declared: "For behold, the Spirit of Christ is given to every man, that he may know good from evil...." (Moroni 7:16.)

The Lord Reasons

After recognizing the source of deception in branches of the Church, the revelation continues to admonish the elders in their responsibilities as teachers of the gospel. In order that they might understand their calling and true position, the Lord posed a series of questions to these elders. (D&C 50:10-12.) The lessons to be learned are sometimes put in question form because this method of teaching carries its own point without the necessity of further explanation. Here is the first question: "unto what were ye ordained?" The answer sets forth the calling of these elders: "To preach my gospel by the Spirit, even the Comforter which was sent forth to teach the truth:" (v. 14.) But what happened to these elders? They received "spirits which ye [they] could not understand, and received them to be of God. . . ." But the Lord asks, "in this are ye justified?" Is this question answered in the revelation? "Behold ye shall answer this question yourselves; nevertheless, I will be merciful unto you; he that is weak among you hereafter shall be made strong." (v. 16.)

Although reprimanding these elders for their inability to understand the real source of these false manifestations, they were to be made strong by the key given them in this revelation. It is: "And that which doth not edify is not of God, and is darkness." (v. 23.) In verses 17 through 21, the elders are instructed by questions and answers that they may know the important truth that it is by the Spirit of truth one may know the things of God. Therefore, in the words of the revelation: '. . . he that preacheth and he that receiveth, understand one another, and both are edified and rejoice together." (v. 22.) Understanding one another depends upon the receptivity of the Holy Ghost by both speaker and hearer. This principle was expressed by Nephi in his parting testimony to us of this generation:

> . . . for when a man speaketh by the power of the Holy Ghost the power of the Holy Ghost carrieth it unto the hearts of the children of men. But behold, there are many that harden their hearts against the Holy Spirit, that it hath no place in them; wherefore, they cast many things away which are written and esteem them as things of naught. (2 Nephi 33:1, 2.)

Ask and It Shall Be Done

He who serves as a preacher of truth, being ordained of God and sent forth, is to be respected in his calling as he becomes the servant of all. (Matt. 20:26-28.) He is, by his faith, the possessor of all things, for all things are subject to him as the Father through his Son Jesus

Christ wills it be done. But no one may exercise such powers except as he be purified and cleansed from all sin. Then, "ye shall ask whatsoever you will in the name of Jesus and it shall be done." As it was among the Nephites (Jacob 4:6-7), so it is in this dispensation: "But know this, it shall be given you what you shall ask; as ye are appointed to the head, the spirit shall be subject unto you." (D&C 50:25-30.)

A Second Key against Deception

If he who has been ordained and cleansed from sin sees a spirit manifest which is not understood by him, sincere prayer should be offered to obtain knowledge concerning that spirit.

Wherefore, it shall come to pass, that if you behold a spirit manifested that you cannot understand, and you receive not that spirit, ye shall ask of the Father in the name of Jesus; and if he give not unto you that spirit, then you may know that it is not of God.

And it shall be given unto you, power over that spirit; and you shall proclaim against that spirit with a loud voice that it is not of God—(Ibid., 50:31-32.)

But in what way would one proclaim against such a spirit? Certainly not in pride and boasting, or in taking unto oneself the honor.

Not with railing accusation, that ye be not overcome, neither with boasting nor rejoicing, lest you be seized therewith. He that receiveth of God, let him account it of God; and let him rejoice that he is accounted of God worthy to receive. (Ibid., 50:33-34.)

The necessity for prayer by those who seek further enlightenment from our Father is well expressed by the Prophet Nephi. (2 Nephi 32:4, 8, 9.)

Summary

What did this revelation do for the Church and its members at this early period (1831)? It gave to the elders a lesson in their responsibilities as servants of the Lord. It prevented the Church from being divided into factions in following false spirits. By detecting evil influences through keys given of the Lord, the members had a means of being protected from false manifestations.

Present Application

What does this revelation mean to this generation, over 130 years later? The manifestation of spirits in the way described by Elder Pratt—unseemly gestures, contortions, gibbering, and muttering, etc.—are not present in the Church today. There are religious organizations today, however, that claim these manifestations as part of the religious life of their members. In an editorial in the *Times and Seasons* the Prophet Joseph Smith wrote:

. . . there was nothing indecorous in the proceeding of the Lord's prophets in any age; neither had the apostles nor prophets in the apostles' day anything of this kind. . . . Paul says, "Let everything be done decently and in order," but here (in the cases cited in the article) we find the greatest disorder and indecency in the conduct of both men and women, as above described. The same rule would apply to the fallings, twitchings, swoonings, shaking, and trances of many of our modern revivalists. (*DHC* 4:576.)

The members of The Church of Jesus Christ of Latter-day Saints may know that, if such manifestations should arise, there is a way to detect evil spirits, and they also know that only that which lifts one up morally and spiritually is of God. The importance of prayer in one's life is plainly revealed, as well as the need to seek for perfection.

President Joseph Fielding Smith of the Council of the Twelve has given us counsel in some of the matters contained in this revelation, as follows:

The nearer we approach God, the better we endeavor to keep His commandments, the more we will search to know His will as it has been revealed, the less likely it will be for us to be led astray by every wind of doctrine, by these false spirits that lie in wait to deceive, and by the spirits of men. . . . We will be protected, and we will have the power to understand, to segregate truth from error, we will walk in the light and we will not be deceived. . . . I want to tell you there is much error in this world that is passed off as truth, and it behooves every man of us to seek God, and . . . [to] draw near unto Him, and the nearer we draw unto Him, and the more we seek to do His will the more light we shall receive and the less shall be he danger of our deception. (*Conference Report*, April 1940, pp. 98-99.)

But what of those who do not follow the counsel to draw near to the Lord?

Now the man who is dilatory, the man who is unfaithful, the man who is not willing to keep the commandments of the Lord in all things lays himself open to deception because the Spirit of the Lord is not with him to lead and direct him and show him the way of truth and righteousness, and therefore some error comes along and he absorbs it because he cannot understand and realize the difference between truth and error. (*Ibid.*, p. 99.)

Instructions to Certain Elders

The last ten verses of Section 50 consist of counsel to Joseph Wakefield, Parley P. Pratt, John Corrill, and Edward Partridge. The first three brethren are assigned to labor in the Lord's vineyard, while Brother Partridge is told that he should not restrain Brother Corrill from his appointed calling. (vs. 37-39.) Important truths were made known to these brethren in these verses:

Behold, ye are little children and ye cannot bear all things now; ye must grow in grace and in the knowledge of the truth.
Fear not, little children, for you are of them that My Father hath given me; And none of them that my Father hath given me shall be lost. (*Ibid.*, 40-42.)

All of us are to live by faith, in this life, being submissive to the Lord's will, as little children. We may increase in faith and knowledge and thereby be able to grow in the light of truth until that "light groweth brighter and brighter until the perfect day." (v. 24.)

The Prophet Joseph Smith said:

... Faith comes by hearing the word of God. If a man has not faith enough to do one thing, he may have faith to do another: if he cannot remove a mountain, he may heal the sick. Where faith is there will be some of the fruits: all gifts and power which were sent from heaven, were poured out on the heads of those who had faith. (*DHC* V:355.)

Although John Corrill was excommunicated from the Church in 1839, a question may be raised concerning verse 42 in which it is stated that "none of them that my Father hath given me shall be lost." An authoritative source suggests the following as an interpretation of this passage and also about John Corrill:

Not that the sheep cannot go astray, but the vigilance of the Shepherd is such that no wolf can slay them, as long as they remain with the flock.

... the question might be asked, "Was not John Corrill, who, in all probability was present when this Revelation was given 'lost,' although the Lord said, 'You are of them that my Father hath given me?'" It might seem like entering the field of fruitless speculation to consider that question. But it must be remembered that there are two entirely different classes of apostates. One class consists of members too weak to resist temptations and persecutions, wherefore they fall by the wayside, when the storms sweep over them. The other class deliberately join the forces of the adversary and make war upon Christ and His followers, because they love sin and hate righteousness. Who shall say that those who have fallen because of weakness will not ultimately be reclaimed by our Savior and given some degree of glory, although they may have lost their grandest opportunity? Who can say that they are "lost," in the same sense as the enemies who die in hatred? John Corrill at one time offered, with others, to give himself to the mob as ransom for the Church, but the mob refused the sacrifice. It was when the persecution raged at its worst in Missouri that he fell. (*Doctrine and Covenants Commentary*, p. 295.)

The Guarantee

The revelation closes with the promises of the Father to all those who remain faithful.

And the Father and I are one. I am in the Father and the Father in me; and inasmuch as ye have received me, ye are in me and I in you. Wherefore, I am in your midst, and I am the good shepherd, and the stone of Israel. He that buildeth upon this rock shall never fall. And the day cometh that you shall hear my voice and see me, and know that I am. Watch, therefore, that ye may be ready. Even so. Amen. (D&C 50:43-46.)

Chapter 36

TEACH WHAT THE APOSTLES AND PROPHETS HAVE WRITTEN

(Section 52)

The temporal and spiritual welfare of the Saints was the concern of the Lord as revelations and commandments were given to his Prophet. It was most important that as people accepted the gospel, they should learn the necessity of maintaining faith in the scriptures (at that time the Bible and the Book of Mormon), and the revelations received by the Prophet Joseph Smith. The revelation upon which this chapter is written points out the need to have such faith.

Section 52—Background

Information regarding the Fourth General Conference, which convened in Kirtland, Ohio, assists us to understand the purposes for which Section 52 of the Doctrine and Covenants was given. The Church had been organized for only fourteen months, yet there were about two thousand persons in attendance at the conference which lasted for about three days, beginning about the third of June 1831. In an earlier revelation (Section 44), the appointment for this conference was made, and the Spirit of the Lord was promised to be poured out upon the faithful who should meet on that occasion.

The literal fulfillment of this promise was received in many remarkable manifestations, including a number of prophecies. In the Prophet's journal it is recorded that "The Lord displayed His power to the most perfect satisfaction of the Saints." (*DHC* I:175.)

What were some of these occurrences which would call forth this evaluation of the General Conference? "The man of sin was revealed, and the authority of the Melchizedek Priesthood was manifested. . . ." John Whitmer, Church Historian, wrote concerning this, as follows:

Joseph Smith, Jun., prophesied the day previous that the man of sin would be revealed. While the Lord poured out His Spirit upon His servants, the devil took a notion to make known his power. He bound Harvey Whitlock and John Murdock so that they could not speak, and others were affected but the Lord showed to Joseph, the seer, the design of the thing; he commanded the devil in the name of Christ, and he departed, to our joy and comfort. (*DHC* I p. 175. footnote.)

The office of High Priest was conferred upon several brethren, this being the first time that this office was conferred in this dispensation. Among those ordained was Lyman Wight who prophesied:

. . . He said the coming of the Savior should be like the sun rising in the east, and will cover the whole earth. So with the coming of the Son of Man: yea, He will appear in His brightness and consume all [the wicked] before Him; and the hills will be laid low, and the valleys be exalted, and the crooked be made straight and the rough smooth. And some of my brethren shall suffer martyrdom for the sake of the religion of Jesus Christ, and seal their testimony of Jesus with their blood. He saw the heavens opened and the Son of Man sitting on the right hand of the Father, making intercession for his brethren, the Saints. He said that God would work a work in these last days that tongue cannot express and the mind is not capable to conceive. The glory of the Lord shone around. (*Ibid.*, I p. 176, footnote.)

Another prophecy uttered by Joseph Smith at this time, 1831, concerned the activity of John the Revelator. According to the Church historian, John Whitmer, "The Spirit of the Lord fell upon Joseph in an unusual manner, and he prophesied that John the Revelator was then among the Ten Tribes of Israel who had been led away by Shalmaneser, the king of Assyria, to prepare them for

their return from their long dispersion, to again possess
the land of their fathers. He prophesied many more
things that I have not written." (*Ibid.*, I p. 176, footnote.)

Thus ended a glorious General Conference, the results of which were evaluated by the Prophet in this way:

It was clearly evident that the Lord gave us power in propor-
tion to the work to be done, and strength according to the race
set before us, and grace and help as our needs required. Great
harmony prevailed; several were ordained; faith was strengthened; and humility, so necessary for the blessing of God to follow
prayer, characterized the Saints.

The next day, as a kind of continuation of this great work of
the last days. I received the following. [Section 52.] (*Ibid.*, I:176-
177.)

Missionary Appointments

Following the general conference, the Lord called
upon many elders to preach the gospel. A number of these
were to proselyte in Ohio that the Church might be
strengthened further in that area.

The names of many elders appear in Section 52 as
these men are assigned to their missionary labors. Many
of these brethren are well known in Church history and
their lives make an interesting story. Others are little
known today, but their efforts in building up the kingdom
of God in their time could have been considerable. On
the other hand, there were those who lost their place in
the kingdom because they were overcome of the world.

Important Instructions

Important for our study are some of the instructions
given to these missionaries since they are as valid today
as when they were received. Outstanding in this regard
are the following from Section 52:

(1) ". . . preaching the word by the way, saying none other
things than that which the prophets and apostles have written,

and that which is taught them by the Comforter through the prayer of faith. (v. 9. Compare verse 36.)

(2) "And behold, he that is faithful shall be made ruler over many things." (v. 13.)

(3) The pattern against being deceived (vs. 14-21.)

Satan Deceives

Unto all the elders the Lord set forth a pattern by which the Church members might not be deceived, and thus the "spirits in all cases under the whole heaven" should be known. This is the pattern certifying that Satan is a real being who seeks to deceive:

And again, I will give unto you a pattern in all things, that ye may not be deceived; for Satan is abroad in the land, and he goeth forth deceiving the nations— (D&C 52:14.)

Who is accepted of the Lord?

Wherefore he that prayeth, whose spirit is contrite, the same is accepted of me if he obey mine ordinances.

He that speaketh, whose spirit is contrite, whose language is meek and edifieth, the same is of God if he obey mine ordinances. (Ibid., 52:15, 16.) [Italics added.]

In the early period of the Church there was a need, as there is today, for the members to distinguish between those who are acceptable to the Lord and those who are not. Here in plain language the key is given to make this distinction. Christian people believe in and practice prayer. In the lives of many this is the mark of sincerity and honesty regarding their everyday actions and beliefs. Only those, however, who are sufficiently contrite, or humble enough to accept the truth as taught in the Lord's revelations through the Prophet Joseph Smith and his successors, and who obey the ordinances of water and Spirit baptism are acceptable to him. Regardless of how meek and edifying a person's language may be, he is still unacceptable to the Lord unless he obeys these ordinances.

Verily, verily, I say unto you, they who believe not on your words, and are not baptized in water in my name, for the remission of their sins, that they may receive the Holy Ghost, shall be damned, and shall not come into my Father's kingdom where my Father and I am. (*Ibid.*, 84:74.)

There are many wonderful thoughts expressed by authors, teachers, clergymen, and other people who are not members of The Church of Jesus Christ of Latter-day Saints; but the Latter-day Saint must be prepared to distinguish between true and false teachings. The standard of judging such teachings is yet to be mentioned in this chapter.

The missionaries in the early history of the Church were prepared to inform the world that the Lord had restored the Church with its principles and ordinances as they were known anciently. These brethren were to go to the world to teach and not to be taught. (*Ibid.*, 43: 15-16.)

Deceivers among Us

The Prophet wrote that there were many false spirits abroad in the Christian and pagan world. He also said that there were some in our own Church who were possessed of this same spirit because "It is made up of all those different sects professing every variety of opinion, and having been under the influence of so many kinds of spirits, it is not to be wondered at if there should be found among us false spirits." (*DHC* IV:580.)

Down through the decades men have attempted to govern the affairs of the Church by instructing or commanding the Prophet, Seer, and Revelator at the head of the Church and also the Twelve Apostles. As indicated, this began in the time of the Prophet Joseph Smith, as pointed out by Elder George A. Smith:

There was a prevalent spirit all through the early history of the Church, which prompted the Elders to suppose that they knew more than the Prophet. Elders would tell you that the Prophet was going wrong. Men who thought they knew all about this work, some of them thirty or forty years before the Lord revealed it, tried to "steady the ark." The Church was constantly afflicted with such a class of men. (*Doctrine and Covenants Commentary,* p. 290.)

More subtle ways have been and are used today by deceivers or perverters of the truth. The casting of doubt and even unbelief on the scriptures and that revelation is received by the leadership of the Church, are common ways in which these people try to undermine the Lord's work. The standard quoted above, "if he obey mine ordinances" (D&C 52:15-16), as applied to the member of the Church is not limited to baptism and the other ordinances of the gospel. It also includes other decrees of God, including instructions and rules regarding conduct.

Where to Expect False Doctrine

President Joseph F. Smith accounted for false teachings as from these two classes:

Among the Latter-day Saints, the preaching of false doctrines disguised as truths of the gospel, may be expected from people of two classes, and practically from these only; they are:

First—The hopelessly ignorant, whose lack of intelligence is due to their indolence and sloth, who make but feeble effort, if indeed any at all, to better themselves by reading and study; those who are afflicted with a dread disease that may develop into an incurable malady—laziness.

Second—The proud and self-vaunting ones, who read by the lamp of their own conceit; who interpret by rules of their own contriving; who have become a law unto themselves, and so pose as the sole judges of their own doings. More dangerously ignorant than the first.

Beware of the lazy and the proud; their infection in each case is contagious; better for them and for all when they are compelled to display the yellow flag of warning, that the clean and uninfected may be protected. (*Gospel Doctrine,* p. 373.)

False Teachings Exposed

In 1946, President J. Reuben Clark, Jr., of the First Presidency, told the people attending the April general conference of false teachings which were being entertained by some members of the Church. Because of the need for members of the Church to be aware of these teachings and the authoritative way in which President Clark answered these claims, they are given here:

I have said on other occasions, and I repeat now that there are being taught amongst us, unfortunately, doctrines which are utterly destructive, not only of Jesus the Christ, but even of God himself, and we must be on our watch that neither we nor our children be influenced, debauched, or polluted by such doctrines.

Recently a man of education (he holds a high scholastic degree), a worthy member of the Church, sent to me a statement of some of the teachings that now are somewhat rooted amongst some of our Latter-day Saints—a few only, I trust. I am going to read this statement to you and make some comment upon the points as I proceed. There are some ten points.

I wish to say to you as earnestly as I may, that, as you will see when I have read them, if they shall attain credence amongst us, particularly amongst our young people, they will destroy our faith.

The first of these statements reads:

"1. God is not an anthropomorphic being,"— that is, he does not have hands, or eyes, or feet, or ears, or a voice—
"and not a personal God, nor a Living God."

I remember when Dr. Talmage used to say something not dissimilar from what I shall say, but he made an actual quote, as I recollect which I can only summarize after these many years. It went about this way:

"Thrust God out of the back door, and he comes in at the front door as the First Great Cause. Thrust the First Great Cause out of the back door, and God enters the front door as a Great Force. Push him out as a Great Force, and he comes back in as a Great Intelligence."

No sane man who can think at all can deny in his heart the existence of God, the God of the Bible, and of the New Testament, and of modern revelation.

The next point:

"2. Man is a creature of the Universe and draws intelligence and ideas (inventions) from the Universe by being in harmony with it."

This statement is not only indefinite, but meaningless. It does, however, seem to postulate a Universe Intelligence, and thus we are back to our great concept of God.

"3. There is no such thing as supernatural experience among men—at any time in history. No revelation directly from God."

This denies all scriptures. It denies all divine manifestations to man. It denies his goodness and his mercy and his love. It gives the lie to the commonest experience of man, recognized from the savage to the most highly civilized man; indeed, it gives the lie practically to our very existence.

"4. Jesus Christ was a revolutionary leader—but not divine."

This, of course, denies the divinity of Jesus. It falls squarely within the observation of John who declared, as I have already read:

For many deceivers are entered into the world, who confess not that Jesus Christ is come in the flesh. This is a deceiver and an antichrist. (II John 7.)

"5. Joseph Smith did not see God nor really experience any supernatural phenomena. He wrote the Book of Mormon without divine assistance. He also gave revelations to suit his purpose and the situation without divine assistance."

No man can honestly read the Book of Mormon and then say that this boy Prophet wrote it himself, and the most persistent search has failed to reveal that he stole the book. There is too much in the book to have been written by a boy whom his hostile critics brand as an ignoramus, and it should be said here, he had no opportunity for consulting either the little-known sources, which hostile critics have disinterred in trying to destroy him, or the more widely-known sources of which he probably had no knowledge whatever because they were inaccessible to him. No man of his age could have had in his mind, no matter how much he had studied, merely the allusions contained in the Book of Mormon to the holy scriptures, and all that we have of his that came from him when speaking or writing normally, gives not even a suggestion of his power to compose or to utter those great gems of majestic literature which are so plentifully found in the Book of Mormon and the Doctrine and Covenants.

"6. The value of Mormonism is in its practice and in its system. Its origin need not be basic to one's belief in or acceptance of Mormonism for its value."

Many of us have heard this heresy before. No shallower view of Mormonism can be taken than is thus expressed. The achievements of our people, the growth of the Church, the people's endurance of hardship, misery, penury, persecution, and even martyrdom itself, would have been wholly impossible without the spirituality which lay behind and vitalized their whole lives. This people of ours had the Spirit of God to direct them. Take away from us that Spirit, take away the divinity which lies behind the gospel, and there is nothing left. Had our work not been divinely fathered, we would not have outlived our first ten years of life.

"7. The three-degrees-of-glory story is a myth."

That is, Paul was mistaken, the Prophet Joseph was mistaken, all who have thought and taught that glory might come to those who live righteously and die with a testimony, some of them as martyrs, were all mistaken and all they believed in was a myth. Such a concept destroys the teachings of the restored gospel. The words of Paul and the words of the Prophet Joseph were divinely inspired and are the eternal truth.

Here is another mean thrust:

"8. Temple work may occupy old people in pleasant pastime but it is absurd and foolish in its objectives."

Thus these antichrists would not only abandon the living but discard the dead, their ancestors and loved ones; nothing would be saved, indeed salvation would for no one be a reality. Every instinct of justice and mercy, every really rational concept of man and his being cries out against any concept such as this. Temple work is part of the restored gospel.

"9. The belief that man might become as God is equally foolish."

This doctrine would, of course wipe out the great truth of eternal progression. It would thus cut off from man even the hope of advancement hereafter; it violates every concept of the future brought to us by the restored gospel.

"10. Practically every theological idea advanced by Joseph Smith can be found in some ancient religion or in some current beliefs contemporary with his time."

There is truth in the conception that the restored gospel does contain among its truths beliefs held by ancient religions and by modern ones. However, the Prophet Joseph never had the opportunity, never had the books, never had the time to search out from these sources all these various truths from the paganism and the Christianity of the past. It was not humanly possible for him to do so at his age and with the meager facilities at his command. But we know how it came to be that these partial truths were found in pagan teachings of pre-Christian eras: the gospel was on the earth from the time of Adam, and from then on down, there appeared here and there in the world, among this people and that, recollections of the doctrines and principles of the gospel as they were taught to Adam. Some of the truths of the gospel have always been on the earth. (*Conference Report,* April 1946, pp. 119-121.)

The Standard of Judgment

This revelation (Section 52), in verses 9 and 36, establishes a standard which was to be used by the missionaries mentioned in this revelation. It is the same standard that has continued from the beginning and is in force today. The Lord said that these missionaries were to teach only that which the "prophets and apostles have written, and that which is taught them by the Comforter through the prayer of faith."

In 1839, the Twelve Apostles issued an epistle to the elders and members of the Church in which they set forth the same principle:

Be careful that you teach not for the word of God the commandments of men, nor the doctrines of men, nor the ordinances of men, inasmuch as you are God's messengers. Study the word of God, and preach it and not your opinions, for no man's opinion is worth a straw. Advance no principle but what you can prove, for one scriptural proof is worth ten thousand opinions. . . . When you go forth to preach, and the Spirit of God rests upon you, giving you wisdom and utterance, and enlightening your understanding, be careful that you ascribe the glory to God, and not to yourselves. Boast not of intelligence, of wisdom, or of power;

for it is only that which God has imparted unto you; but be humble, be meek, be patient and give glory to God. . . . (*DHC* III: 395-396.)

What further counsel and blessings are pronounced upon the obedient? The Twelve Apostles continued:

> And if you unitedly seek after unity of purpose and design: if you are men of humility and of faithfulness, of integrity and perseverance; if you submit yourselves to the teachings of heaven, and are guided by the Spirit of God; if you at all times seek the glory of God and the salvation of men, and lay your honor prostrate in the dust, if need be, and are willing to fulfill the purposes of God in all things, the power of the Priesthood will rest upon you, and you will become mighty in testimony; the widow and the orphan will be made glad and the poor among man rejoice in the Holy One of Israel. . . . (*Ibid.*, III:397.)

The Counsel of Contemporary Apostles

Elder Mark E. Petersen of the Council of the Twelve has authoritatively given the position of the Church regarding the need for teachers (and others) to accept the word of the Lord in the scriptures and the authorized doctrines from the Authorities of the Church. Here are some of these statements as gleaned from *Your Faith and You*:

> *Teach only true doctrine*: . . . we can go astray with views and doctrines which are not officially accepted by the Church. That brings us directly to the matter of source material. As teachers FOR the Church we must teach only the doctrines and views OF the Church. Then our source material on doctrine must be that which the Church provides. The scholars of the world, no matter how learned, are not authorities on our Church doctrine. Neither do we rest our case with the scientists or archeologists, nor with the learned pastors of other churches, nor with researchers or educators. They may be ever so well informed in their own lines, but their "lines" do not happen to be Mormonism. The Authorities of our Church are the authorities on our doctrine, and they do portray for us in simple, understandable terms the doctrines of the Church as far as the Lord has revealed them. What does the Church provide which is safe

for use as doctrine, and how may we know what it is? Books which are published by the Church. It is placed in the front of each book where it is plainly to be seen. Some of the presiding brethren write and publish under their own names and copyrights. (p. 40.)

. . . True doctrine will bring true converts when properly presented. The great importance of true conversion cannot be overemphasized. Without it there is no obedience, because unless we are converted to the laws of God, we will see no necessity for obeying them. We will never sacrifice for something to which we have not been converted. And neither will there be any salvation without conversion, and there is no obedience without conversion, and there is no salvation without obedience, then how shall we be saved? (p. 41.)

Speculation. It seems peculiar that speculative persons are not willing to accept the doctrines of the Church without endeavoring to embellish them. It seems strange, too, that such persons do not realize that in thus embellishing the doctrines of the Church, and adding some of their own, they are advocating doctrines of men, and that manmade doctrines bring condemnation from the Lord . . . . No man has any right to change the word of God, nor to add to it. That can only be done by revelation. Yet, some persons, contrary to the position of the Church, will teach . . . . manmade notions which in no way, shape, nor manner can be declared truthfully to be Church doctrine. Setting up new doctrine in this way is dangerous and wrong. It may lead to many other extremes . . . . Speculation in doctrine leads only to confusion and doubt. Speculation does not save. Neither does it convert. Then why speculate? Our work is to help bring to pass the eternal life of man. The pure, unembellished truth is required to do that. (Pp. 128, 129.)

President Joseph Fielding Smith of the Quorum of the Twelve has given us the criterion to judge truth, as that truth affects our salvation:

The key to truth. If members of the Church would place more confidence in the word of the Lord and less confidence in the theories of men, they would be better off. I will give you *a key for your guidance. Any doctrine, whether it comes in the name of religion, science, philosophy, or whatever it may be, that is in conflict with the revelations of the Lord that have been accepted by the Church as coming from the Lord, will fail.* It may appear to be very plausible; it may be put before you in such a way that you cannot answer it, it may appear to be established by evidence that cannot be controverted, but all you need do is to bide your time. Time will level all things. *You will find that every doctrine, theory, principle, no matter how great it may appear; no matter how universally it may be believed, if it is not in accord with the word of the Lord, it will perish.* Nor is it necessary for us to try to stretch the word of the Lord to make it conform to these theories and teachings. The word of the Lord shall not pass away unfilled. I realize that we are all weak, and at times may place false interpretations upon the written word, but the revelations are so clear regarding Adam, the fall, the atonement, the resurrection, the redemption of the earth when it shall again be proclaimed "good," and so many other things which fall under the ban of present-day teaching, that we need not be led astray. The theories of men change from day to day. Much that is taught now will tomorrow be in the discard, but the *word of the Lord will endure forever. (The Utah Genealogical and Historical Magazine,* October, 1930, pp. 155, 156.)

Follow the Lord's Counsel

The scriptures are the basis for understanding our relationship to God, because they reveal the word of the Lord through his inspired prophets. His prophets today make known to the Latter-day Saints the will of the Lord and receive revelation for our guidance. The Prophet and President of The Church of Jesus Christ of Latter-day Saints is the mouthpiece of God for the people who have made covenants with the Lord by baptism. Elder John A. Widtsoe wrote that the greatest or the most important prophet to us is the living prophet, because it is his responsibility to direct the people in solving the problems of the day by the inspiration of the Lord. Every prophet who has directed the Church in any generation has been the greatest prophet to that generation. The Latter-day Saint sustains the President of the Church in this way by accepting counsel from him and those who serve with him as prophets, seers, and revelators. (*Improvement Era,* November 1943, p. 689.)

But how is the member of the Church to know the

truth? It is by the power of the Holy Ghost. But who is entitled to this power? As this revelation points out, it is one who is humble (teachable, submissive to the Lord's will), prayerful, having faith in the Church Authorities, and remembering that in this life our principal concern should be to seek salvation through the gospel. This important fact was made known by the Lord when he said it was necessary to walk uprightly before him. (D&C 46:7.)

The Blessing of Obedience

We have now come to the third instruction given to the missionaries who were to teach the words "which the prophets and apostles have written" and that which is taught by "the Comforter through the prayer of faith." (*Ibid.*, 52:9, 14-21, 36.)

"And behold, he that is faithful shall be made ruler over many things." (*Ibid.*, v. 13.) As one learns to rule himself, he grows in power, and the Lord places more responsibility upon him. (Alma 12:9-11; D&C 82:3.) This life is the time for testing and trial. He who is faithful in a few things will be made ruler over many. (Luke 19:12-26.) The reward of the true disciple of Jesus is the blessing of Godhood when all things will be subject to him.

He That Is Overcome

Among the brethren mentioned in our text (Section 52) there were some who did not remain faithful to their covenants. An example is Elder Lyman Wight who was told that "Satan desireth to sift him as chaff." (v. 12.) Years later this man, as an apostle, was tried by a High Council for false teachings but he repented and was forgiven. Later, however, he left the Church and his high calling in not submitting to the counsel of his brethren.

As the *Doctrine and Covenants Commentary* states, "The Lord told him to 'beware,' but the warning was forgotten in the hour of greatest danger." (P. 305.) Some of the missionaries named in verses 22 through 34 were also overcome of the world. (*Ibid.*, pp. 307-310.)

Summary

Section 52 was received immediately following a general conference of the Church where great spiritual blessings were enjoyed by the faithful Saints. In the main, this revelation was given that certain brethren might know of their assignments in the ministry, together with important instructions on how to detect the influences of the adversary. There was a pattern given which, if known, would be a means by which the missionaries and the members of the Church would be able to determine who is a true disciple of the Lord, and thus accept him as the Lord's representative. The standard of judgment is whether or not the person obeys the Lord's ordinances, which means the first principles of the gospel, and the rules and regulations which have been given for the guidance of the Church. Regardless of the language, meekness, and other virtues which impress people, God demands acceptance of his ordinances as the proof of faithfulness. One of the important tests to be applied to those who profess approval of the Lord is whether their teachings are from the writings of the apostles and prophets, both living and dead. The final testimony comes to the faithful Latter-day Saint through the Holy Ghost which bears witness to the truths spoken by the living oracles. The President of the Church is the revelator of the Lord and the person, who, under the power of the Holy Ghost, is authorized to determine the doctrine of the Church. His associates in the First Presidency and the Council of the Twelve receive revelation for their callings as leaders of the Church, as do other officers in the kingdom of God.

Chapter 37

"THOSE THAT SEEK ME EARLY SHALL FIND ME"
(Proverbs 8:17)

(Sections 48, 51, and 54)

With the great increase in Church membership in Ohio which was initiated by missionaries sent to the Lamanites, and with the prophesied movement of our people to the frontiers of the United States, as early as December 1830 the Lord commanded his people to gather to the Ohio Valley. (D&C 37:3.) The promise of the "Law to the Church" was made at Kirtland, Ohio, at the beginning of 1831. (*Ibid.*, 38:32.) The revelation concerning James Covill (*ibid.*, Section 39) contained a promise to the Saints that "Inasmuch as my people assemble themselves at the Ohio, I have kept in store a blessing such as is not known among the children of men, and it shall be poured forth upon their heads." (Verse 15.) Subsequent events revealed that this promise was fulfilled in the wonderful endowment poured out upon the Church in the restoration of the keys of the Priesthood. (*Ibid.*, Sec. 110.) As the spirit of gathering took hold of the Saints, they began to gather in Ohio in the spring of 1831, not long after the arrival of the Prophet Joseph Smith in Kirtland. (*Ibid.*, Section 41.) Because of this gathering, the people in Ohio were concerned as to where these immigrants would locate permanently and also as to how land would be obtained for them.

Section 48

As a result, the Lord made known his will to the Prophet as recorded in Section 48. The Saints already settled in that area were to keep their land and not, at that time move farther west, for the location of the City of Zion had not been revealed. They were to save their money, however, that an inheritance might be obtained in Zion when they received the command to gather at that place. (*Ibid.*, 48:1, 4-6.) In the meantime, as the members of the Church arrived from the East, the Ohio Saints were to divide their lands with these newcomers. If this was not sufficient, other lands were to be purchased in nearby places. (*Ibid.*, vs. 2-3.)

Law of Consecration

According to Section 51, Bishop Edward Partridge was appointed to assign the Saints to their lands and to organize them as commanded. Each person was to receive his portion according to his needs; that is, "every man equal according to his family, according to his circumstances and his wants and needs." (D&C 51:3.)

The surplus above the family's needs was to be put into a storehouse for the use of the poor and needy of the Church under the direction of the bishop as the needs of the people demanded. In this way the law of consecration was partially put into practice as a preparation for the time when the City of Zion was to be built. The Colesville, New York Branch of the Church moved to Thompson, Ohio, at this time, and the Lord extended to them the "privilege" of organizing under the United Order or the law of consecration. (D&C 51:15.) As the *Doctrine and Covenants Commentary* points out, it was not a command:

> The law of the United Order was given to the Colesville Branch as a boon, a privilege. God, who knew the weakness of His people, did not, at this time, give it with the force of a preemptory command. But some day the Saints will be required to observe this law, for Zion cannot be redeemed without it. (P. 300.)

Trouble at Thompson, Ohio

These Saints from New York State, with some who were already in Thompson, Ohio, found themselves in difficulties because some of them did not keep the covenant of the United Order. As Elder B. H. Roberts observed, "It is difficult to determine with exactness in what the transgressions of the Saints at Thompson consisted; but it is evident that selfishness and rebellion were at the bottom of their trouble, and that Leman Copley and Ezra Thayre were immediately concerned in it." (*DHC* I:180.) Brother Roberts quotes Newel Knight's journal that a man by the name of Copley had a considerable tract of land in Thompson which he offered to let the Saints use in agreement with a contract drawn up for this purpose. Leman Copley, however, broke this agreement. Thereupon, Newel Knight represented the Saints at Thompson in consulting the Prophet at Kirtland concerning these difficulties.

Section 54

From these circumstances the Lord, in answering the prayer of his prophet for guidance, recognized the faithfulness of those who, in good faith, endeavored to live by the covenants which they had made. Among these was Newel Knight who was to keep the assignment already given to him. (D&C 52:32.) As always, the faithful are promised blessings commensurate with their deeds; and so, those who kept the covenant at Thompson should "obtain mercy." (D&C 54:6.) An informative observation on this point is as follows:

"They shall obtain mercy," but in the meantime they suffered through the conduct of the covenant-breakers. However, they were assured of divine comfort. There is a difference between the sufferings of those who are innocent of wrong-doing and those of wrong-doers, who must feel the tortures of an accusing conscience, in addition to the evil consequences of trans- gression. (*Doctrine and Covenants Commentary*, pp. 315-316.)

On the other hand, the rebellious—covenant-break- ers in this case—were to know that "Wo to him by whom this offense cometh, for it had been better for him that he had been drowned in the depth of the sea." (D&C 54:5.) This reminds one of the same truth uttered by Jesus con- cerning those who would offend his children. (Luke 17: 1-2.)

Newel Knight was informed in this revelation that "If your brethren desire to escape their enemies, let them repent of all their sins, and become truly humble before me and contrite." (D&C 54:3.) In speaking of the enemies that the Latter-day Saints should fear, Presi- dent Joseph F. Smith has said:

For my part I do not fear the influence of our enemies from without, as I fear that of those from within. An open and avowed enemy, whom we may see and meet in an open field, is far less to be feared than a lurking deceitful, treacherous enemy hidden within us, such as are many of the weaknesses of our fallen human nature, which are too often allowed to go unchecked, beclouding our minds, leading away our affections from God and his truth, until they sap the very foundations of our faith and debase us beyond the possibility or hope of re- demption, either in this world or that to come. These are the enemies that we all have to battle with, they are the greatest that we have to contend with in the world, and the most diffi- cult to conquer. They are the fruits of ignorance, generally arising out of unrebuked sin and evil in our own hearts. The labor that is upon us is to subdue our passions, conquer our in- ward foes, and see that our hearts are right in the sight of the Lord, that there is nothing calculated to grieve his Spirit and lead us away from the path of duty. (*Gospel Doctrine*, p. 341.)

The enemies of the Saints were not only the sins of which they were guilty, but also there were enemies who would, if possible, inflict many kinds of persecutions upon them. In order for them to "escape" from their enemies, their lives would have to conform to the commandments. This principle reminds us that escape from those who would inflict physical and mental persecution upon the Saints is, in a large measure, dependent upon how well the Saints have kept the commandments. Examples from The Book of Mormon are many; in fact, the theme of Nephite history is that blessings of prosperity and peace come to the faithful. (Mosiah, Chapters 21 and 22.)

It is a true principle that the way of happiness and escape from inward as well as outward enemies is by keeping the commandments. Full obedience to the Lord is in overcoming evil and living not as the world lives.

The Saints at Thompson were to take their journey to Missouri "unto the borders of the Lamanites" where further instructions were to be received. (D&C 54:7-8.)

Patience Enjoined

The members of this branch had come from Colesville, New York, and thus were numbered among the first to accept the gospel in this dispensation. These members had seen persecution as soon as the Church was organized. Attempts were made to prevent their joining the Church by a mob, which tore up a dam which had been constructed to back up sufficient water to allow baptisms to be performed. Some of these people were also intimidated by mobs, but they continued obediently to assist the Prophet Joseph Smith with the temporal necessities of life, as commanded by the Lord. (*Ibid.*, 24:3-4.) Patience under temptation had been exercised by them in times past, as a part of the Christian's life.

Those who solve their problems and overcome tribulations and the enemies to their souls are to be rewarded with an "eternal weight of glory"—eternal life. (*Ibid.*, 63:66.)

Seek the Lord Early—Definition

The Lord revealed that "they who have sought me early shall find rest to their souls." (*Ibid.*, 54:10.) This truth implies at least two important thoughts. The person who has come to the Lord early in life, while yet in youth, is blessed in numerous ways. He, however, who comes to the Master late in life, in mature adulthood, discovers that many opportunities for soul-growth have been missed. Nevertheless, salvation in the kingdom of God is available to all who seek the Lord and find him, whether at the beginning or toward the end of life's journey. What, then, is the difference, if all the faithful shall find the great blessing of eternal life or exaltation? Are there advantages in one's finding the Lord early?

Education for Time and Eternity

After all, what are the purposes of life as known to the Latter-day Saints? There are many purposes, but if we understand who we are, literal spirit children of God, the basis for the most important purpose is laid. We are here to be educated in the principles of truth that we may win the victory over the enemies of our goal to become as our Father and Jesus are. To the Nephites, the Redeemer said: "Therefore I would that ye should be perfect even as I, or your Father who is in heaven is perfect." (3 Nephi 12:48.) In the words of President Joseph F. Smith, the accomplishment of this objective is paramount:

The important consideration is not how long we can live but how well we can learn the lesson of life, and discharge our duties and obligations to God and to one another. One of the main purposes of our existence is that we might conform to the image and likeness of him who sojourned in the flesh without blemish—immaculate, pure, and spotless! Christ came not only to atone for the sins of the world, but to set an example before all men and to establish the standard of God's perfection, of God's law, and of obedience to the Father (*Gospel Doctrine*, p. 270.)

In seeking for gospel understanding, we are educating ourselves for eternity, the most important part of our education. The need for education in secular pursuits is understood by all Latter-day Saints. All truth received in the educative process is intended to increase our ability to live the laws of God. The preparation made in school to earn a livelihood and the actual process of providing for one's self and family are an important part of working out one's salvation. The Lord has never given a solely temporal commandment to man, but all of his laws are spiritual. (D&C 29:34-35.)

Latter-day Saints are not the only people who have emphasized the necessity to acquire an education beyond the average, but they certainly have stressed the need to receive as much as possible. The incentive for education arises out of Latter-day Saint theology. What does this have to do with the truth that he who seeks the Lord early will find rest to his soul?

Advantages of Seeking the Lord Early

It is a known fact that the young learn fast and are easily influenced. The Lord has called many of his servants when young, presumably that they might be more amenable to instruction. The call of Samuel, Israel's prophet (1 Sam. Chapter 3), and that of Joseph Smith are examples. The Spirit of the Lord does affect the lives of those older, but the inclination to investigate, to change beliefs, and to accept a new way of life are more difficult for the person who has become set in his ways. The hand of the Lord beckons all, young and old, alike. There should be no delay when the message comes. In our dispensation it has been revealed that one should "hearken unto my voice, lest death shall overtake you; in an hour when ye think not the summer shall be past, and the harvest ended, and your souls not saved." (D&C 45:2.)

What are the advantages of seeking the Lord when young?

The Young Are Teachable

Childhood is a period of intensive accumulation of knowledge. The child is trusting and must rely upon the parents to teach correct knowledge upon which true values are founded. The period of adolescence is one of thinking about the religious beliefs received earlier. The young person's concepts of God, of good and evil, while still influenced greatly by the type of guidance he has received, come in for wonderment and pondering. During all of these years, the young need guidance from wise parents imbued with the spirit of the gospel, and the impressions made through the years will remain to shape and mold character and eventually to bring that person back to a re-examination of true values, if he has departed from the path of righteousness. There is wisdom in the proverb: "Train up a child in the way he should go: and when he is old, he will not depart from it." (Proverbs 22:6.)

Habits and Attitudes

With the quality of being teachable, there is the important fact that habit and attitude patterns are established at the crucial period of character formation. The exposure of the child to home and Church auxiliary teachings in honesty, kindness, virtue, truthfulness, and other basic virtues is not to be underestimated as an advantage in successfully completing life's journey.

How important it is that habits be formed in keeping with the divine guidance found in the Word of Wisdom (D&C 89), in abstaining from the use of tobacco, alcohol, coffee, etc. How important is the practice—to make it a habit while in youth to attend Church meetings and to assume responsibilities of Church service in the Priesthood quorums for the boy and in the auxiliaries for both boy and girl. Learning to avoid temptation is an essential part of this process. The association of people who are endeavoring to do what is right contributes very much to assist the young and old in keeping the commandments of the Lord. Habits and attitudes can be changed, as amply demonstrated by thousands of converts to the Church yearly. But how many of us have heard some of these good people say, "Oh! if I had only known of the fulness of the gospel years ago. What a difference it would have made in my life."

Preparation for a Full Life

One of the major responsibilities of The Church of Jesus Christ of Latter-day Saints, as an institution, is to perfect the lives of its members. What has the Lord provided in his Church for the one who comes to him early? President Stephen L Richards in a general conference said:

I believe it is safe to say that no organization has ever made more ample and adequate provision for the care and training of youth than has the restored Church of Jesus Christ. Since its organization it has devoted a very major portion of all its efforts to the education and development of children in the home, the school and the Church. And not only has it provided almost unparalleled responsibilities that have seldom, if ever, come to young people of comparable age. This has come about, in part, through the unique organization of the Church, and, in part, through the universal concept of its membership that everyone, old and young alike, who secures a knowledge and testimony of the restored gospel thereby become a potential missionary for the dissemination of the truth to all mankind. (*Where is Wisdom?*, p. 270.)

With these thoughts before us, let us reflect upon some of the marvelous opportunities that have come to

our youth. Think of the young men ordained to the priesthood at the age of twelve. All of them are given definite
duties to perform which bring them in contact with many
people in passing the Sacrament, the collection of fast
offerings, as well as other opportunities for development
in a social situation. Furthermore, to many of the
Aaronic Priesthood members there are opportunities for
leadership, even to conducting meetings, as officers in
priesthood quorums, personal development is received
in public speaking, giving lessons, as ward or branch
teachers, and also training in the cultural arts, and
athletics sponsored by the Mutual Improvement Associations. These many privileges for personal development
provide a means of making the best use of a person's
talents and potential abilities. This type of development
helps the person to make a livelihood and also to indoc-
trinate his children in the way of truth. The very important missionary service performed by our young people
in the stakes and foreign missions contributes so much
to strengthening faith, increasing testimony, and giving
a solid background for life that its contribution to our
subject matter cannot be overestimated. Goals in life
should be established early in order to profit most. The
gospel affords all men goals based upon an eternal perspective because man is an eternal being. When the member of the Church becomes aware of the purpose of
mortality and of the reality of the future life, the foundation is laid for making decisions which bring joy and
happiness in this life and in the world to come. There can
be no real happiness without preparation for the next life.
Preparation for eternity by temple marriage with the
object of rearing a family in Latter-day Saint environment is a prime purpose of those who seek the Lord early.

Spiritual Reservoir

The longer a person is in the fold of Christ, the
greater is his influence for good among his fellow men.

Great shall be the joy of those who minister to the spiritual needs of his brothers and sisters. More joy is received in this life and in the future life for those who bring many unto the Savior. (D&C 18:10-16.)

Not only is the joy great because of the long term of service in the Lord's work but also in building up, over the years, sufficient spiritual strength to overcome temptations, surmount difficulties and the problems of daily living. One of the seemingly necessary trials confronting us mortals is the need to face times when loved ones are taken away in death. To know that there will be a reunion with such persons as spirit beings and to realize that a future happiness may be enjoyed in the resurrection, softens the sting of death. The only real comfort available in such times comes through this understanding and the testimony of the Spirit. Aided by the gifts of the Holy Ghost throughout life brings stability and strength of character to meet discouragements and trials. These gifts also help one, in this and other ways, to prepare for the eternity ahead.

We build a reservoir of strength by keeping the commandments of our Father in heaven. The Holy Ghost leads, directs, comforts, and guides us on the way to that perfect life made available through The Church of Jesus Christ of Latter-day Saints. Reliance upon this power will bring happiness. The way in which one builds up a reservoir of strength is stated in this truth:

> Draw near unto me and I will draw near unto you; seek me diligently and ye shall find me; ask, and ye shall receive; knock, and it shall be opened unto you. (*Ibid.*, 88:63)

Lessons for Young and Old

What is the lesson for members of the Church, both young and old? There is no better answer to this question than the message of the revelation we now are studying. It is:

And again, be patient in tribulation until I come; and, behold, I come quickly, and my reward is with me, and they who
have sought me early shall find rest to their souls. Even so.
Amen. (*Ibid.*, 54:10.)

Another scripture from the revelations gives this
truth:

He that seeketh me early shall find me, and shall not be forsaken. (*Ibid.*, 88:83.)

The counsel is—begin now! There is no time but the
present for young and old. The testimony of Jesus is the
anchor of one's soul. A testimony can be the foundation to
effect a mighty change in the heart. (Alma 5.)

Teach the youth of the Church especially in your
homes, your sons and daughters and grandchildren. The
testimony is a strong way to assist and help others. Faith-
promoting experiences are also long remembered. Attendance at appointed Church meetings has its effect
upon others as well as on one's self.

An example of such influence is told by President
David O. McKay, as follows:

I shall never forget, as long as I live, the impression my
mother gave me when she told the story of those two thousand
sons who went to battle under the leadership of Helaman. Think
of those boys. Hold them as a pattern, you priests, teachers, and
deacons, yes, and high priests, seventies, and elders. If two
thousand men in that ancient time could live such lives, two
thousand, nay ten thousand and a hundred thousand, men can
live it today. These were their principles, founded upon the
principle of faith, inculcated into their hearts by their mothers,
who taught them in their youth that if they prayed to God nothing doubting, their prayers would be answered. Such is their
testimony; such was the result of their mothers' teachings,
showing the influence of home on boys' lives. (Alma 53-56.)
[*Gospel Ideals*, p. 453.]

For all, and especially those who have "fought the
good fight," there remains the opportunity to enjoy the

future in contemplation of a life well spent. Encouragement is given to continue in the enjoyment of a faith built upon the assurance that all shall come to judgment to be rewarded for their love of the Savior as demonstrated in their lives. The Lord will not forsake them, and they shall find "rest to their souls"—and partake of the fulness of his glory. (D&C 84:24.)

The Final Message

The Prophet Isaiah counseled the people of his generation, as follows:

Seek ye the Lord while he may be found, call upon him while he is near. (Isaiah 55:6.)

Chapter 38

ENDURE TO THE END

(Sections 53 and 55)

Throughout all scriptures, the divine message has been—seek the Lord early and remain true to the covenants made with him. If faithful in doing this, there is no blessing which will be withheld.

Algernon Sidney Gilbert

The revelation for study in this chapter was addressed to Algernon Sidney Gilbert, who was in the Church for only four years. He became a member in the year 1830 and died June 1834. Before he joined the Church he was a merchant in Painesville, Ohio, but later in Kirtland, he was the business partner of Newel K. Whitney. It was into their store that the Prophet Joseph Smith entered and introduced himself to Brother Whitney. (Chapter 25.)

A few months after the arrival of the Prophet and his party in Ohio, Brother Gilbert requested that the Prophet inquire of the Lord concerning his place in the kingdom. Section 53 was received in reply to this request. After this revelation was received, in which Brother Gilbert was commanded to accompany the Prophet and others to Missouri, these brethren left Kirtland on June 19, 1831, for the west. By this same revelation Brother Gilbert was appointed keeper of the Lord's storehouse. Later this call was to receive "moneys, to be an agent unto the Church, to buy land in all the regions about . . . in righteousness and . . . wisdom." (D&C 57:6.) In addition, he was to establish a store, the profits of which were to be used for the building up of Zion. (*Ibid.*, v. 8.)

In July 1833, a mob of about five hundred threatened the Saints of Independence, Missouri, with whippings, the same cruel treatment which they had administered to a number of the brethren not long before this. Six of the leading brethren, including Algernon S. Gilbert and William W. Phelps, offered themselves as a ransom for the Church, even to allow themselves to be whipped to death, if necessary. These six brethren agreed that they would arrange for the Saints to leave Jackson County as soon as possible. In this transaction, Brother Gilbert and John Corrill were to remain longer than the rest of the Saints to finish the business of the Church in that area.

It is recorded that Brother Gilbert "had been known to say that he 'would rather die than go forth to preach the Gospel to the Gentiles.' " In commenting upon this remark, Elder B. H. Roberts pointed out that his refusal to preach the gospel did not arise from a lack of faith, but from diffidence and lack of confidence in his own ability to preach. In extolling Brother Gilbert's great contribution to the Church, Brother Roberts continues as follows:

He was a man of rare good sense, conservative and of sound judgment. All of which appears in the many communications drawn up in Missouri by him during the troublous times through which the Church passed in those days. Much of the correspondence between the Missouri brethren and Governor Dunklin was the work of Elder Gilbert, and it bears witness to the truth of what is here said of him. Nor did he entirely refuse to bear witness of the truth of the Gospel to others. (*DHC* II:119, footnote.)

In summary of this man's contribution, Elder B. H. Roberts gives this evaluation: "The Lord has had few more devoted servants in this dispensation." (*Ibid.*, p. 118.)

Section 53

The Prophet's inquiry of the Lord in behalf of Algernon S. Gilbert brought forth a revelation consisting of only seven verses. A significant truth to be received from that first verse is that the Lord hears and answers prayer; for he had heard and answered Brother Gilbert's prayer. In the growing kingdom of God, many had requested that their place in the Church might be known through revelation. The revelations given for the members in the early period of the Church have revealed many great truths that have given encouragement, hope, and inspiration to those who live in the decades following the Prophet's period. Elder Gilbert was assured in this revelation that the Church which he had joined was raised up by the Lord in these last days.

In order that he and all who should become acquainted with this revelation might know that the purpose of Jesus crucifixion or atonement is to offer the only means of escape from sin, the Lord revealed:

> Behold, I, the Lord, who was crucified for the sins of the world, give unto you a commandment that you shall forsake the world. (D&C 53:2.)

If Jesus gave his life that we, who receive this gift of remission of sins by acceptance of the gospel, might enjoy blessings in this life and an eternal reward of exaltation, there must be continued effort to forsake the world of sin. President David O. McKay said in a General Conference:

> Now, what do we mean by the world? It is sometimes used as an indefinite term. I take it that the world refers to the inhabitants who are alienated from the Saints of God. They are aliens to the Church, and it is the spirit of this alienation that we should keep ourselves free from. . . . (Gospel Ideals, p. 153.)

A recognition that all of us are imperfect to some degree should stimulate us to search for ways and means to overcome those imperfections, which hinder us from reaching the goal of perfection admonished by the Savior. (Matt. 5:48.)

Three verses point out Elder Gilbert's calling in the Church. (D&C 53:3-5.) The success he had in this calling has already been pointed out in the forepart of this chapter.

Important to Elder Gilbert would be the counsel given in verse six wherein he is told that his present assignment should be accepted in faith. Through his faithfulness "in the vineyard," other responsibilities would be placed upon him. The person of faith is desirous of building up Zion as much as possible.

The closing verse of Section 53 counsels Elder Gilbert that the rich rewards of heaven come to him who remains faithful to the end.

And again, I would that ye should learn that he only is saved who endureth unto the end. Even so. Amen. (*Ibid.*, v. 7.)

This same counsel has been given in other dispensations of the gospel. The Savior taught his disciples during his ministry that their labors would bring persecution upon them, but "he that endureth to the end shall be saved." (Matt. 10:22.)

As the resurrected Redeemer, Jesus expressed this fact to the Nephites:

Behold, I am the law, and the light. Look unto me, and endure to the end, and ye shall live; for unto him that endureth to the end will I give eternal life. (3 Nephi 15:9.)

On the day The Church of Jesus of Latter-day Saints was organized, the Savior revealed this same truth to the Prophet Joseph Smith as an admonition to all men, particularly addressed to the people of this dispensation. The first step in salvation is to accept Jesus Christ as one's Savior through faith, repentance, and baptism of the water and of the Spirit, as stated in the revelation:

And we know that all men must repent and believe on the name of Jesus Christ, and worship the Father in his name, and endure in faith on his name to the end, or they cannot be saved in the kingdom of God. (D&C 20:29.)

In order that there might not be any misunderstanding as to the fact that men are saved by the atonement of Christ, that revelation continues as follows:

And we know that justification through the grace of our Lord and Savior Jesus Christ is just and true; and we know also, that sanctification through the grace of our Lord and Savior Jesus Christ is just and true, to all those who love and serve God with all their mights, minds, and strength. (*Ibid.*, v. 30, 31.)

And in order that those who have become sanctified (holy) by striving for perfection will not believe that their position is secure for,

. . . there is a possibility that man may fall from grace and depart from the living God; Therefore let the Church take heed and pray always, lest they fall into temptation; Yea, and even let those who are sanctified take heed also. (*Ibid.*, vs. 32, 33.)

Meaning of "Endure to the End"

A dictionary definition of "endure" is "To continue in the same state without perishing; last; to remain firm, as under trial; to suffer or bear up patiently; to endure hardship; to withstand or bear, as pain, sorrow, or destructive force, without yielding."

What might the Latter-day Saint be required to endure? The member of the Church is susceptible to the ills which afflict mankind in general. With these ills, mental and physical, one must bear patiently. However, it is a fact that blessings of health, happiness, and even prosperity result from one's faithfulness to the gospel. We may not always recognize our faults which bring physical and mental suffering because of ignorance or unwillingness to correct our lives. The violation of health laws will bring its penalties. The Lord told Joseph Smith to: "Be patient in afflictions, for thou shalt have many; but endure them, for, lo, I am with thee, even unto the end of thy days." (*Ibid.*, 24:8.)

Elder George Q. Cannon said:

> So it is with all of us. We have great afflictions from time to time. It seems to be necessary that we should be tried and proved to see whether we are full of integrity or not. In this way we get to know ourselves and our own weaknesses; and the Lord knows us, and our brethren and sisters know us. Therefore, it is a precious gift to have the gift of patience, to be good-tempered, to be cheerful, to not be depressed, to not give way to wrong feelings and become impatient and irritable. It is a blessed gift for all to possess. (*Gospel Truth*, p. 198.)

The Latter-day Saints must also bear persecution patiently, whether physical or mental. The tauntings or ridicule of those who consider a Latter-day Saint as too religious or "fanatical" may be examples of the latter. That the disciples of the Master would receive such persecutions was said by Jesus in the Sermon on the Mount. (Matt. 5:10-12.)

In this life one must also endure or stand up against temptation in its numerous forms.

Sometimes we may become so general in our remarks on what we should do, that some of the help that can be extended to those who want to know what to do is not always given. The Latter-day Saint wants to know the answer to the question, "What must I do to be exalted?" He already knows that acceptance of the first principles and ordinances of the gospel is the beginning of the new life, but how may he keep on that road which leads to exaltation? If we say, "Keep the commandments," it has all been said, but there is the need to know the commandments. Furthermore, it is also necessary to know that there are some guideposts, which, when pointed out, draw attention to certain pitfalls that may ensnare even those who are trying to follow the Savior's teachings. It is not intended that the following suggestions in this chapter on guideposts are a complete list, but they are intended to be helpful.

Seek the Spirit

The counsel to seek for the influence of the Holy Ghost is always paramount as one desires to maintain faith unto the end. It is by that Spirit that one is able to discern truth from untruth. By that guidance there comes understanding of the way one should live. The principle of receiving more bounteously of the Spirit is set forth in this scripture:

Draw near unto me and I will draw near unto you; seek me diligently and ye shall find me; ask, and ye shall receive; knock, and it shall be opened unto you. (D&C 88:63.)

Because some members of the Church had not received the peace of mind through the Spirit, and the security that accompanies it, President Joseph F. Smith said:

There are many who, not having reached this point of determined conviction, are driven about by every wind of doctrine, thus being ill at ease, unsettled, restless. These are they who are discouraged over incidents that occur in the Church, and in the nation, and in the turmoils of men and associations. They harbor a feeling of suspicion, unrest, uncertainty. Their thoughts are disturbed, and they become excited with the least change, like one at sea who has lost his bearings. (*Gospel Doctrine*, p. 126.)

Then the President of the Church asked: "Where would you have people go who are unsettled in the truth?" The answer is plain, he said.

They will not find satisfaction in the doctrines of men. Let them seek for it in the written word of God; let them pray to him in their secret chambers, where no human ear can hear, and in their closets petition for light; let them obey the doctrines of Jesus, and they will immediately begin to grow in the knowledge of the truth. This course will bring peace to their souls, joy to their hearts, and a settled conviction which no change can disturb. They may be well assured that "he that heareth in secret will reward them openly." Let them seek for strength from the source of all strength, and he will provide spiritual contentment, a rest which is incomparable with the physical rest that cometh after toil. All who seek have a right to, and may enter into, the rest of God, here upon the earth, from this time forth, now, today; and when earth-life is finished, they shall also enjoy his rest in heaven. (*Ibid.*, pp.126-127.)

One sure way of having the sense of security which comes to the faithful is by holding fast to the "rod of iron" or the scriptures, as revealed to the prophets.

Keep on the Right Side of the Line

Another President of the Church has given solid counsel on a theme upon which he spoke often. President George Albert Smith at a General Conference related some counsel given him by his grandfather, Elder George A. Smith, as follows:

He said: "There is a line of demarcation well defined between the Lord's territory and the devil's territory. If you will remain on the Lord's side of the line, the adversary cannot come there to tempt you. You are perfectly safe as long as you stay on the Lord's side of the line. But," he said, "if you cross onto the devil's side of the line, you are in his territory, and you are in his power, and he will work on you to get you just as far from that line as he possibly can, knowing that he can only succeed in destroying you by keeping you away from the place where there is safety." (*Conference Report*, October 1945, p. 118.)

President George Albert Smith then gave the following examples to illustrate when the member of the Church is "on the Lord's side of the line": (1) by observing the Sabbath day; (2) in the observance of secret and family prayers; (3) by expressing gratitude to God for food;

(4) by loving one's neighbors; (5) by being honest in all dealings with men; and (6) in keeping the Word of Wisdom. President Smith continued:

... And so I might go on through the Ten Commandments and the other commandments that God has given for our guidance and say again, all that enriches our lives and makes us happy and prepares us for eternal joy is on the Lord's side of the line. Finding fault with the things that God has given to us for our guidance is not on the Lord's side of the line ... (*Ibid.*, p. 118.)

As always, those who find fault receive less and less of the Spirit which promotes happiness and joy. Upon this subject the counsel of the living prophets is certain. All have proclaimed the necessity for upholding those whom God has appointed as his servants. President Joseph F. Smith indicated the seriousness of not sustaining the Lord's anointed, in this way:

... And I cannot emphasize too strongly the importance of Latter-day Saints honoring and sustaining in truth and in deed the authority of the Holy Priesthood which is called to preside. The moment a spirit enters the heart of a member to refrain from sustaining the constituted authorities of the Church, that moment he becomes possessed of a spirit which inclines to rebellion or dissension; and if he permits that spirit to take a firm root in his mind, it will eventually lead him into darkness and apostasy. ... (*Gospel Doctrine*, p. 224.)

But what if the Latter-day Saint does not understand the reason for certain measures or counsel? President George Q. Cannon had this to say regarding this question:

A faithful Latter-day Saint may not be able to understand all the movements of the Church nor all the motives of the authorities of the Church in giving counsel or in taking action upon different questions; but will a man of this character censure them, assail them or condemn them? Certainly not. He will be likely to say: "I do not understand the reasons for this action;

I do not see clearly what the presiding authorities have in view in doing this; but I will wait and learn more. This I do know, that this is the work of God and that these men are His servants and that they will not be permitted by him to lead the Church astray or to commit any wrong of so serious a character as to endanger its progress or perpetuity. . . ." (*Gospel Truth*, p. 234.)

Be Teachable

The person who is submissive to the will of God as proclaimed in the scriptures and by the counsel of the Priesthood is teachable. This quality or characteristic of the Christ is known in the standard works of the Church as humility. Humility is the opposite of pride. Against this vice the prophets have spoken very frequently as they have admonished the seeker for salvation to acquire the virtue of humility. Neither poverty nor sorrow which does not have as its purpose to change one's life, should be mistaken for humility. Here are some of the prophets' teachings:

Pride goeth before destruction, and an haughty spirit before a fall. (Proverbs 16:18.)

Behold, are ye stripped of pride? I say unto you, if ye are not ye are not prepared to meet God. (Alma 5:28.)

And if ye seek the riches which it is the will of the Father to give unto you, ye shall have the riches of eternity; and it must needs be that the riches of the earth are mine to give; but beware of pride, lest ye become as the Nephites of old. (D&C 38:39.)

God resisteth the proud, but giveth grace unto the humble. (James 4:6.)

Be thou humble; and the Lord thy God shall lead thee by the hand, and give thee answer to thy prayers. (D&C 112:10.)

Religious Hobbies Are Unwise

Among some members of the Church there is a tendency to emphasize one principle or practice above another. Such a person may assume an attitude of superiority and thus become conceited and full of pride. "Saints with hobbies," said President Joseph F. Smith, "are prone to judge and condemn their brethren and sisters who are not so zealous in the one particular direction of their pet theory as they are. The man with the Word of Wisdom only in his brain, is apt to find unmeasured fault with every other member of the Church who entertains liberal ideas as to the importance of other doctrines of the gospel." He also said that,

    . . . Hobbies are dangerous in the Church of Christ. They are dangerous because they give undue prominence to certain principles or ideas to the detriment and dwarfing of others just as important, just as binding, just as saving as the favored doctrines or commandments.
    Hobbies give to those who encourage them a false aspect of the gospel of the Redeemer; they distort and place out of harmony its principles and teachings. The point of view is unnatural. Every principle and practice revealed from God is essential to man's salvation, and to place any one of them unduly in front, hiding and dimming all others is unwise and dangerous; it jeopardizes our salvation, for it darkens our minds and beclouds our understandings. . . . (*Gospel Doctrine*, pp. 116-117.)

Strive for Perfection

Enduring to the end involves effort. That person who has before him the vision of what he may become through faithfulness, has a far better chance to endure to the end than the person who is not so minded. Constant vigilance in correcting habits or thoughts which militate against the attainment of the goal of perfection, is the road to success. The Savior instructed the Nephites in the goal to which we should all strive: "Therefore I would that ye should be perfect even as I, or your Father who is in heaven is perfect." (3 Nephi 12:48. Matt. 5:48.)

These words were not said to discourage his followers in that they would consider the goal unattainable, but rather to stimulate them to make preparations, then in striving for that final perfection. It is true that we will not receive perfection in this life. We can, however, work always to that end. Elder Mark E. Petersen of the Council of the Twelve in a General Conference expressed this belief:

I believe that in many ways, here and now in mortality, we can begin to perfect ourselves. A certain degree of perfection is attainable in this life. I believe that we can be one hundred percent perfect, for instance, in abstaining from the use of tea and coffee. We can be one hundred percent perfect in abstaining from liquor and tobacco. We can be one hundred percent perfect in paying a full and honest tithing. We can be one hundred percent perfect in abstaining from eating two meals on fast day and giving to the bishop as fast offering the value of those two meals from which we abstain.

We can be one hundred percent perfect in keeping the commandment which says that we shall not profane the name of God. We can be perfect in keeping the commandment which says, "Thou shalt not commit adultery." (Exod. 20:14.) We can perfect in keeping the commandment which says, "Thou shalt not steal." (*Ibid.*, 15.) We can become perfect in keeping various others of the commandments that the Lord has given us. (*Conference Report*, April, 1950, p. 133.)

President Joseph Fielding Smith said:

If we have a failing, if we have a weakness, there is where we should concentrate, with a desire to overcome, until we master and conquer. If a man feels that it is hard for him to pay his tithing, then that is the thing he should do, until he learns to pay his tithing. If it is the Word of Wisdom, that is what he should do until he learns to love that commandment. (*Conference Report*, October 1941, p. 95.)

Reminders

As a reminder of ways in which one may keep on the road to perfection or to endure to the end, these suggestions are given: (1) Become settled in the truth by seeking for the Spirit; (2) Hold fast to the word and will of the Lord as found in the four Standard Works of the

Church; (3) Keep the commandments contained in the gospel of Jesus Christ by remaining on the Lord's side of the line; (4) Sustain the Authorities of the Church by having faith in their counsel and direction or by being responsive to instruction received; (5) Be teachable by eliminating pride; (6) Do not feel that one commandment or program of the Church is to be accepted in practice above others equally as important; (7) Work for perfection by correcting the habits or practices which stand as barriers to the realization of the goal mentioned by the Savior. Do not believe that in mortality one cannot be perfect in many ways which the Lord has commanded his children to follow.

For How Long?

Wise counsel by President Brigham Young on the subject matter of this lesson was given toward the end of his life, as follows:

There are a great many texts which might be used, very comprehensive and full of meaning, but I know of none, either in the Old or New Testament, more so than that saying, said to have been made by the Savior, and I have no doubt it was, "If ye love me, keep my commandments . . . . "

How long? For a day? Keep the commandments of the Lord for a week? Observe and do his will for a month or a year? There is no promise to any individual, that I have any knowledge of, that he shall receive the reward of the just, unless he is faithful to the end. . . . (*Journal of Discourses* 13:310-311.)

Chapter 39

THE REVELATION TO WILLIAM W. PHELPS

(Section 55)

Many men of exceptional talent joined The Church of Jesus Christ of Latter-day Saints not long after its formal organization in the spring of 1830. The Lord knew the needs of the Prophet and the men who could help him most. Among those who had indicated a desire to join the Church at this early period was William Wine Phelps who will long be remembered by the Saints because of his contribution to the hymnology of the Church. He made his impress upon the history of this dispensation in many other ways, however.

According to the Prophet's journal, William W. Phelps and his family arrived in Kirtland, Ohio, about the middle of June 1831, as the Prophet was preparing for his journey to Missouri. Because Mr. Phelps desired "to do the will of the Lord," the Prophet inquired of the Lord concerning him and the revelation (Section 55) for study in this chapter was received. (*DHC* I:184-185.)

Background of Section 55

William W. Phelps was in his fortieth year when he came to Kirtland. Before this he had been active in politics in New York State and had been the editor of a newspaper for the Anti-Masonic Party. It was while thus employed in Canandaigua, New York, only a short distance from Palmyra, that he bought a copy of The Book of Mormon which had just come off the press. With an intimate knowledge of the Bible, he and his wife compared it with The Book of Mormon. A few years later (1835), he wrote this about the influence The Book of Mormon had upon him:

From the first time I read this volume of volumes, even till now, I have been struck with a kind of sacred joy at its title page. —What a wonderful volume! What a glorious treasure! By that book, I have learned the right way to God; by that book I received the fulness of the everlasting gospel; by that book I found the new covenant; by that book I learned that the New Jerusalem, even Zion was to be built upon this continent; by that book I found a key to the holy prophets; and by that book began to unfold the mysteries of God, and I was made glad. Who can tell his goodness, or estimate the worth of such a book? He only who is directed by the Holy Ghost in all things; and has kept all his Lord's commandments blameless through life.

[The above quotation, with other biographical material in this chapter, is taken from an unpublished thesis written by Walter Dean Bowen of the Church Seminary System.]

William W. Phelps' conversion to the gospel through The Book of Mormon had given to him and his wife a desire to meet Joseph Smith. This was accomplished toward the end of December 1830. Of this event, Brother Phelps recorded his feelings as follows:

Now, notwithstanding my body was not baptized into this church, yet my heart was here from the time I became acquainted with the Book of Mormon; and my hope, steadfast like an anchor, and my faith increased like the grass after a refreshing shower, when I for the first time held a conversation with our beloved brother Joseph whom I was willing to acknowledge as a prophet of the Lord, and to whom, and to whose godly account of himself and the work he was engaged in. I owe my first determination to quit the folly of my way, and the fancy and fame of this world, and seek the Lord and his righteousness, in order to enter a better world . . . .

Such was the impression made upon Brother Phelps by the Prophet. The way had been prepared, however, by the witness of the Holy Ghost to his soul.

Section 55

Six months later, the Lord, by revelation, called upon Brother Phelps to be baptized. Significantly, he would not be chosen unless he was obedient to the commandment given. The Lord calls men, but only a relatively few are chosen because their thoughts and aspirations are upon the things of this world. The essential message of the gospel for the investigator is given in verse 1 of this revelation. (D&C 55:1.)

> Behold, thus saith the Lord unto you, my servant William, yea, even the Lord of the whole earth, thou art called and chosen; and after thou hast been baptized by water, which if you do with an eye single to my glory, you shall have a remission of your sins and a reception of the Holy Spirit by the laying on of hands;

Every convert receives a remission of sins by obedience to the commandment that his faith and repentance are sincere, with the intent that his act of obedience to baptism will be pointed to the glory of God. It is the Lord's work and glory to bring about the eternal life of man. Acceptance of the gospel requires that the person's efforts will be turned into furthering the Lord's work in every possible way.

Another important truth is indicated in this verse when it is understood in its historical background. Brother Phelps had already received a testimony of The Book of Mormon by the Holy Ghost; yet, he was told that if he was baptized in the water the Holy Ghost would be given to him by the laying on of hands. Why was it necessary for Brother Phelps (and all converts to receive this gift, if he had already received the Holy Ghost? The brief answer is as follows: The Holy Ghost which convinces the investigator of the truth will not remain with him unless baptism in water is accepted, and also the laying on of hands for the gift of the Holy Ghost. Not until the authorized servant of God bestows this gift by the power of the Priesthood does the person have the "right" to retain the blessings of the Holy Ghost. (Chapter 32.)

Phelps' Baptism

There are probably many ways that the Lord has brought great persons of talent into his work. An understanding of some teachings of the gospel was a factor in the case of Brother Phelps, although he had already received the testimony of the Holy Ghost. Of his conversion, he once wrote:

> I was not a professor at the time, nor a believer in sectarian religion, but a believer in God, and the Son of God, as two distinct characters, and a believer in sacred scriptures. I had long been searching for the "old paths," that I might find the right way and walk in it, and after a suitable time to investigate the work, and prove its truth by corresponding evidence from the old Bible, and by internal witness of the spirit, according to the rules of holiness, I embraced it for the truth's sake, and all honest men who seek a better world, will "go and do likewise," (*Messenger and Advocate,* I:115.)

Obedient to the revelation, Brother Phelps was baptized on June 16, 1831.

Because of William W. Phelps' prominence in New York State, several newspapers made note of his becoming a member of The Church of Jesus Christ of Latter-day Saints.

A General Assignment

Continuing the revelation, the promise is made that upon his baptism, Brother Phelps would be ordained an elder by Joseph Smith, and thus he would be able to preach repentance and baptism for the remission of sins. (D&C 55:2.) Following this promise the revelation reads:

> And on whomsoever you shall lay your hands, if they are contrite before me, you shall have power to give the Holy Spirit. (*Ibid.,* v. 3.)

This promise to Brother Phelps was not intended for him alone, but it is a blessing which may be participated in by any worthy elder of this Church. In itself, it is an important truth. These following two facts are worthy of consideration: (1) By revelation in this day man may know that the power to bestow the Holy Ghost was never intended only for the Twelve Apostles appointed in the meridian dispensation; and (2) There is a way by which the elder may be able to see the evidence of his ministry in the lives of those whom he serves.

How would Elder Phelps be able to know, on the basis of verse 3 of this revelation, that he had not been deceived? As long as he worthily performed his duties as an elder and the person he confirmed a member of the Church had prepared himself with an "eye single to my [God's] glory," there should be manifest in the lives of those converts the fruits of the Spirit. The Lord promised many gifts of the Holy Ghost to the sincere believer. (D&C 46:11, 26.) As these gifts were received and use made of them in healings, and other miracles, prophesyings, etc., the elder in the Church would be apprised of the power which he possessed as an elder. One may conclude that the steadfastness which Brother Phelps and many others demonstrated during their lives, aided by the Spirit, gave evidence of the promise given to faithful Priesthood bearers.

Specific Calling

The revelation addressed to William W. Phelps gave him an assignment which was suited to his special abilities. In these words, the Lord said:

And again, you shall be ordained to assist my servant Oliver Cowdery to do the work of printing, and of selecting and writing books for schools in this church, that little children also may receive instruction before me as is pleasing unto me. (*Ibid.*, 55:4.)

This is the first time in the revelations in the Doctrine and Covenants that mention is made of schools in the Church.

It should also be noted that this revelation (v. 5) commands Brother Phelps to accompany the Prophet and Sidney Rigdon to the land of the Saints' inheritance, (Missouri) where he would undertake the work assigned him. The last verse of Section 55 assigns Joseph Coe also to be a member of the company. Concerning this journey, the Prophet's history states that they traveled by wagon, canal boats, and stages to St. Louis, but from that point on, some members of the party, including Brother Phelps, "went by foot on land to Independence, Jackson County, Missouri, where we arrived about the middle of July, and the rest of the company came by water a few days later." (*DHC* I:188.)

In Jackson County, Missouri (July 1831), the Lord gave to the Prophet a revelation in which Brother Phelps was to be established as a "printer unto the church" at that place. Important in this connection is that the position of printer in that period was much more than a pressman, it also included the responsibilities of editor. It is said of such men that they had great versatility and knowledge. In Section 57 Brother Phelps is told to "obtain whatsoever he can obtain in righteousness, for the good of the saints." (v. 12.)

The Evening and Morning Star

With the call to be the printer unto the Church and work with Oliver Cowdery in publishing books for the Church, Brother Phelps purchased a printing press at Cincinnati. With the establishment of this enterprise and the issuance of *The Evening and Morning Star*, a monthly publication, the first periodical of the Church, there was great joy for the Saints, as the Prophet recorded:

. . . In July, we received the first number of *The Evening and Morning Star,* which was a joyous treat to the Saints. Delightful indeed, was it to contemplate that the little band of brethren had become so large, and grown so strong, in so short a time as to be able to issue a paper of their own, which contained not only some of the revelations, but other information also,— which would gratify and enlighten the humble inquirer after truth.

So embittered was the public mind against the truth, that the press universally had been arrayed against us; and although many newspapers published the prospectus of our paper, yet it appeared to have been done more to calumniate the editor, than give publicity to the forthcoming periodical. Editors thought to do us harm, while the Saints rejoiced that they could do nothing against the truth but for it. (*DHC* I:273.)

In this periodical appeared many of the revelations which are now found in the Doctrine and Covenants and also a chapter and parts of three other chapters of the book of Moses. It was published from the period June 1832, until the destruction of the press on July 20, 1833, at which time the Book of Commandments, the first compilation of revelations consisting of 65 chapters, was being printed. (In 1835, *The Evening and Morning Star* was re-established in Kirtland, Ohio, with Oliver Cowdery as editor.) The first issue of the *Star* informed its readers that its office was "situated within twelve miles of the west line of the State of Missouri; which at present is the western limits of the United States, and about 120 miles west of any press in the state. . . ." (*Ibid.,* p. 277.)

There also appeared in the first issue, the following counsel concerning the education of children:

The disciples should lose no time in preparing schools for their children, that they may be taught as is pleasing unto the Lord, and brought up in the way of holiness. Those appointed to select and prepare books for the use of schools, will attend to that subject as soon as more weighty matters are finished.

Since that time the Church has developed an educational system that has provided for the secular and religious education of its members.

Latter-day Saint Schools

It is a matter of much satisfaction that the date, location and name of the first school established within the present limits of Kansas City are matters of historical record. This school was founded by the Mormon Prophet, Joseph Smith, in 1832, in what is now Troost Park Lake, a site 12½ miles west of Independence. Parley P. Pratt was placed in charge of the school, that was named the "Colesville School" after the present Morman Church at Colesville, New York. (Bennion, M. Lynn: *Mormonism and Education*, Missouri Valley Historical Society, quoted by Kansas City Journal Post, March 4, 1923, pp. 17-18.)

Beginning in February 1833, and throughout that winter the School of the Prophets was held in Kirtland, Ohio. This school was organized according to revelation. (D&C 88:119-141.) President Brigham Young said that the Prophet Joseph Smith at first taught the elders the doctrine of the Church that they might teach the gospel to the world. This instruction did not give them information on how to govern their lives temporally; consequently, he taught them "how to live, that they might be better prepared to perform the great work they were called to accomplish." (*Doctrine and Covenants Commentary*, p. 567.) This School of the Prophets continued in Kirtland until the Saints left that locality. There was also a school conducted there for the teaching of languages and other subjects. In Missouri, the School of the Prophets was also held.

In Nauvoo, Illinois, the first university under Latter-day Saint supervision was organized as the "University of the City of Nauvoo" for the purpose of teaching the sciences and arts.

Wherever the Saints moved, their interest was in the education of their children. The Sunday School and other auxiliary organizations came into being as the need arose. Seminaries and institutes are a part of the Church School System for the instruction of high school and college students that they may receive religious as well as secular education on weekdays. Church-operated colleges and the Brigham Young University are also a part of this system. It can be said that The Church of Jesus Christ of Latter-day Saints from the beginning has encouraged its members to become educated better to meet the purpose of their creation. This process of learning must always serve the Church member for the purpose for which he is responsible—his temporal and spiritual salvation.

William W. Phelps' Career

William W. Phelps was a man of great ability with varied interests. Numerous were his contributions to The Church of Jesus Christ of Latter-day Saints and to the American frontier. His versatility of ability and interests is shown by the following occupations and offices held by him. He was "a printer, hymn writer, poet-journalist, newspaper editor, judge, orator, scribe, lawyer, educator, missionary, temple worker, member of the city council, member of stake presidency, pioneer, explorer, writer of books and pamphlets, topographical engineer, superintendent of schools, surveyor general, weather man, chaplain of lower house of representatives, and speaker of the house in the legislature of the State of Deseret."

In the years of 1837 and 1838 when many leading brethren apostatized, Brother Phelps was one of them. The members of the Church in Missouri withdrew the hand of fellowship from the local presidency of the Church, consisting of Brother Phelps, David Whitmer, and John Whitmer, because of disobedience to the word of the Lord.

Notwithstanding the action of Brother Phelps which

brought about his severance from the Church in the spring of 1838, the Lord still provided an opportunity for him to return to the fold in a revelation a few months later. (*DHC* III:46.) Later in the year 1838, Brother Phelps, with other former members of the Church, signed an affidavit against the Prophet in a court of inquiry. At a conference of the Church in Quincy, Illinois, March 17, 1839, Brother Phelps was excommunicated. Several years later he confessed that this affidavit was made under duress and that his part of betraying his brethren was done to save his life.

The Prodigal Returns

In June 1840, William W. Phelps wrote to the Prophet asking forgiveness for the errors he had committed in Missouri. His confession and spirit shown in this letter indicated what was said earlier in this chapter, that he had received a witness of the truth, but he permitted Satan temporarily to overcome him. He wrote as follows:

. . . I am as the prodigal son, though I never doubt or disbelieve the fulness of the Gospel. I have been greatly abused and humbled, and I blessed the God of Israel when I lately read your prophetic blessing on my head, as follows:

"The Lord will chasten him because he taketh honor to himself, and when his soul is greatly humbled he will forsake the evil. Then shall the light of the Lord break upon him as at noonday and in him shall be no darkness," &c.

I have seen the folly of my way, and I tremble at the gulf I have passed. So it is, and why I know not. I prayed and God answered, but what could I do? Says I, "I will repent and live, and ask my old brethren to forgive me, and though they chasten me to death, yet I will die with them, for their God is my God. The least place with them is enough for me, yea, it is bigger and better than all Babylon."

I know my situation, you know it, and God knows it, and I want to be saved if my friends will help me. . . . I have done wrong and I am sorry. The beam is in my own eye. I have not walked along with my friends according to my holy anointing. I ask forgiveness in the name of Jesus Christ of all the Saints, for I will do right, God helping me. I want your Fellowship; if you cannot grant that grant me your peace and friendship, for we are brethren, and our communion used to be sweet, and whenever the Lord brings us together again, I will make all the satisfaction on every point that Saints or God can require. Amen. (*DHC* 4:141-142.)

The Prophet's Greatness

In reply to this request, Joseph Smith extended the hand of forgiveness for himself and the Saints. He referred to the suffering caused by Brother Phelps and said:

... the cup of gall, already full enough for mortals to drink, was indeed filled to overflowing when you turned against us. ...

However, the cup has been drunk, the will of our Father has been done, and we are yet alive, for which we thank the Lord. And having been delivered from the hands of wicked men by the mercy of our God, we say it is your privilege to be delivered from the powers of the adversary .... Your letter was read to the Saints last Sunday, and an expression of their feeling was taken, when it was unanimously *Resolved,* that W. W. Phelps should be received into fellowship. "Come on, dear brother. Since the war is past, for friends at first, are friends again at last." (*Ibid.,* pp. 163-164.)

Elder B. H. Roberts has very well expressed the greatness of Joseph Smith in this act of charity for this brother, as follows:

When the great offense of Elder William W. Phelps was taken into account—amounting as it did to a betrayal of the Prophet and the Church in Missouri, during the troubles of the Saints in that state—this letter is remarkable. The Prophet's frank forgiveness of his erring brother, gently chiding his wrong-doing, but at the same time remembering in a large way that brother's former devotion and labors; the Prophet's willingness to have the prodigal return and occupy his former high standing among the Saints—all this exhibits a broad-mindedness and

generosity that can come only from a great soul, influenced by
the spirit of charity enjoined upon his disciples by the teachings of the Son of God. One of the surest evidences of Joseph
Smith's greatness of mind and of the inspiration of God upon
him is to be seen in his treatment of those who had fallen but
were willing to and did repent of their sins. His capacity to
forgive under these circumstances seemed boundless. (*Ibid.*, pp.
162, 163, footnote.)

Brother Phelps' faithfulness after this was evidenced in many ways during his life. His testimony of the
truth was shown when he sustained the Twelve Apostles
after the martydom of the Prophet. As a pioneer in the
West his contribution was great as already indicated in
his numerous activities.

Phelps, the Hymn Writer

Many of the accomplishments and contributions of
William W. Phelps have been forgotten by the members
or are unknown to them, but there is one contribution
made by him which will never be unknown. It was his
great gift to write hymns. It is improbable that any one
person has left his impress to a greater degree upon the
Church in this way than has Brother Phelps.

It will be remembered that Emma Hale Smith, the
wife of Joseph Smith, was appointed by revelation to
make a selection of sacred hymns, for the Lord said His
"soul delighteth in the song of the heart; yea, the song
of the righteous is a prayer unto me, and it shall be answered with a blessing upon their heads." (D&C 25:11-
12.) In this initial work of producing a hymnal for the
Church, Emma was assisted by Brother Phelps. Of the
ninety selections in that book, published in 1835, twenty-
nine were written by him. One of his first hymns, "Redeemer of Israel," which appeared in the *Evening and
Morning Star* and later in the first hymnal, continues to
be one of the most popular of Latter-day Saint hymns.

In his *Stories of Latter-day Saint Hymns*, George D. Pyper has included several of Brother Phelps' hymns, with the remark that they breathe the spirit of the period of the restoration. The one hymn sung frequently in our services and particularly on special occasions, such as conferences and temple dedications, is "The Spirit of God like a Fire Is Burning." (first named "Hosanna Hymn.") Although it was sung by the Saints before the completion of the Kirtland Temple, "the full measure of its emotional and spiritual power was not reached until it climaxed the dedicatory services of that temple, which occurred March 27, 1836." P. 88.) ". . . The chorus is a stanza of exaltation in which the Saints join with the 'angels of heaven' in the cry which embodies the most sacred shout of the Latter-day Saints, viz: 'HOSANNA, HOSANNA, HOSANNA, TO GOD AND THE LAMB!'" (pp. 88-91.)

"Now Let Us Rejoice in the Day of Salvation," known to all Latter-day Saints, was written after mobs had destroyed the printing establishment in Jackson County and also more than two hundred homes at a later date. It came out of a situation of "defeat, frustration, homelessness, suffering, privation, hunger, even—these produced a hymn that still gives hope and sustenance to hundreds of thousands who live in better times." (P. 188.)

An event which will live long in the memory of every Latter-day Saint as an evidence of the truth of Joseph Smith's testimony is his martyrdom. It can probably be said that no one has depicted this event and the feeling which a Latter-day Saint has for the Prophet more forcefully than has Brother Phelps in his epitaphic eulogy "Praise to the Man." Great is its message, and with fervor the followers of the Prophet will sing it with "joyful sadness."

Only a few other great hymns can be mentioned, such as: "Gently Raise the Sacred Strain," the theme hymn of the Salt Lake Tabernacle Choir, and also "O God, the Eternal Father," and "Glorious Things Are Sung of Zion."

W. W. Phelps' Testimony

The conversion of William W. Phelps came about from his reading The Book of Mormon. Upon meeting the Prophet Joseph Smith, he and his wife were convinced of the truth of what the Prophet had said concerning the reopening of the heavens and the revelations directing the establishment of the kingdom of God on the earth. Although there were times when he turned against the Church he had accepted as true, yet, he came through many trials and persecutions. Truly the Lord had blessed him generously with many talents which he used for the advancement of his work. He was "called and chosen" as the revelation said. (D&C 55:1.) Upon his return to the fold and until his death on March 6, 1872, in Salt Lake City, Utah, he continued firm in his testimony of the work instituted by God through the Prophet Joseph Smith. In the General Conference of April 1860, Elder Phelps

... held in his hand a copy of the first edition of that Book [Book of Mormon] and declared it to be the truth of the Almighty; he had heard the testimony of Joseph Smith and that of the chosen witnesses in relation to the Book of Mormon, and he with them wished to give his testimony to the world relative to its divine origin. He said that he knew this was the church of the living God, and that Brigham Young was the legally appointed successor of Joseph Smith, and that all who receive this testimony will be saved in the celestial kingdom, and he wished that he had a thousand tongues to speak of the great things of the kingdom to the nations of the earth. (*Deseret News*, April 11, 1860.)

Chapter 40

PUT THE KINGDOM OF GOD FIRST

(Section 56)

We have learned that the law of consecration was in effect, and that people were called to repentance because of slothfulness and selfishness. The revelation for study in this chapter is a call to repentance to certain individuals and also to classes or groups, arising principally out of a need to live the law of consecration. (Additional background information is found in Chapter 37.)

Specifically, however, Section 56 was received because of an inquiry by Thomas B. Marsh concerning his mission, due to the failure of Ezra Thayre, his companion, to perform the missionary service to which they were called by revelation. (D&C 52:22.)

With a background of rebellion on the part of Ezra Thayre, as just noted, and also because of another circumstance arising out of his failure to participate fully in the law of consecration (*ibid.*, 56:8-10), the Lord reminds those of his Church that his anger is kindled against the rebellious and the time will come when this class, the rebellious, "shall know mine arm and mine indignation, in the day of visitation and of wrath upon the nations." (*Ibid.*, 56:1.) In reference to the anger of the Lord as one of his attributes, we learn:

The Lord has, on several occasions declared His anger against the rebellious (Comp. 1:13, 5:8; 19:5, and many other passages). Those who believe in a God without passions must deny that He can feel anger, and love too, for that matter, but the Word of God is clear on this point. Sin and wickedness kindle the anger of the Lord, when persisted in. But the great difference between the divine passion and that of man is this,

that in God's anger there is no element of malice. It is the
"wrath of the Lamb." (Rev. 6:16.) [*Doctrine and Covenants
Commentary*, p. 321.]

Take up Your Cross

An important truth follows the Lord's statement regarding the rebellious, which emphasizes a need on the
part of every one who professes to be a follower of Christ.
Our salvation is dependent upon how well we follow the
Savior. He who does not do so, will not be saved in the
celestial kingdom. Thus we have this truth:

And he that will not take up his cross and follow me, and
keep my commandments, the same shall not be saved. Behold,
I, the Lord, command; and he that will not obey shall be cut
off in mine own due time, after I have commanded and the commandment is broken. (D&C 56:2-3.)

As one considers the full importance of this message,
he is reminded that man is free to choose good or evil.
Men are responsible for the choice made according to the
law under which they live. For a Latter-day Saint, as in
the case of Ezra Thayre, commandments are given with
promises of blessings commensurate with the law obeyed.
The commandments of God are really opportunities for
man to become free from barriers to attain the highest
measure of salvation. When a commandment has been
broken and not repented of, the Lord says that in his
own due time the violator will be cut off from his
kingdom.

But what does it mean to take up one's cross? Instructive in answering this question is an examination
of some scriptures which bear upon the meaning of the
verse from this revelation. It is apparent that to take
up one's cross is to follow the Savior devotedly, obediently, in service and consecration. Upon one occasion
Jesus rebuked Peter by reminding him that "If any man

will come after me, let him deny himself, and take up his cross, and follow me." (Matt. 16:24.)

By inspiration, the Prophet Joseph Smith continued this admonition as follows: "And now for a man to take up his cross, is to deny himself all ungodliness, and every worldly lust, and keep my commandments."

In commenting upon the case of Peter referred to, Elder James E. Talmage wrote:

. . .There was left no shadow of excuse for the thought that devotion to Christ would not mean denial and privation. He who would save his life at the cost of duty, as Peter had just suggested that Christ should do, would surely lose it in a sense worse than that of physical death; whereas he who stood willing to lose all, even life itself, should find the life that is eternal. (*Jesus the Christ*, p. 365.)

To be a true disciple of Christ is to follow him regardless of the cost. Freedom can come to us only by breaking the shackles of sin, of habits detrimental to eternal welfare. Is it easy to follow the Lord? The Savior knew that if man wanted to find release from the bondage of sin, he could find it by faith in him through his redeeming sacrifice for man. Are not his words as true today as when uttered centuries ago?

Come unto me, all ye that labour and are heavy laden, and I will give you rest.

Take my yoke upon you, and learn of me; for I am meek and lowly in heart: and ye shall find rest unto your souls.

For my yoke is easy, and my burden is light. (Matt. 11:28-30.)

The words of President Joseph Fielding Smith should give us food for thought on this question.

When a man confesses that it is hard to keep the commandments of the Lord, he is making a sad confession—that he is a violator of the Gospel law. Habits are easily formed. It is just as easy to form good habits as it is to form evil ones. Of course it is not easy to tell the truth, if you have been a confirmed liar. It is not easy to be honest, if you have formed habits of dishonesty. A man finds it very difficult to pray, if he has never prayed. On the other side, when a man has always been truthful, it is a hard thing for him to lie. If he has always been honest and he does some dishonest thing, his conscience protests very loudly. He will find no peace, except in repentance. If a man has the spirit of prayer, he delights in prayer. It is easy for him to approach the Lord with assurance that his petition will be answered. The paying of tithing is not hard for the man, fully converted to the Gospel, who pays his tenth on all that he receives. So we see the Lord has given us a great truth—his yoke is easy, his burden is light *if we love to do his will.* (*The Way to Perfection,* p. 150.)

Follow the Christ

During the time of Joseph Smith, the expression "to take up one's cross" was apparently not uncommon. We know that Newel Knight, a frequent attender at some of the early Church meetings, when asked to participate in prayer at these meetings, "said that he would try and take up his cross, and pray vocally during meeting." (*DHC* I:82.) How well do we members of the Church take up our cross in accepting the responsibilities of membership and the callings that come to us in our branch, ward, or stake positions? Here is what Elder Mark E. Petersen wrote about those who follow Christ:

If we are truly to follow him, we will take his advice in which he tells us to seek first the kingdom of God. He actually meant that we should give it first place in our lives. We should have "no other gods before him," neither should we have any habits, or tendencies, or desires, or practices, which are given preference to our religion. In times of decision, when we must make up our minds whether to go one way or another, let us remember this requirement of the Lord for his followers—put the kindom of God FIRST.

In doing this we may have to take steps to follow him even into some Gethsemane. When the real test comes, will we follow his example? Will we have the courage and the faith to cry out to the Father, even as he did: "Thy will be done"—"not as I will, but as Thou wilt"?

If we are his followers in this sense, we will not hesitate about honoring the Sabbath, or paying our tithing, or refraining from the use of tea, coffee, liquor and tobacco—those things which are prohibited through the Word of Wisdom. We will be honest and filled with integrity, and a temptation to make a dollar by "sharp" practices will find no response in us. We will hold morals high, and regard virtue as dearer than life itself. Those, and many other things, are to characterize his true disciples. (*Your Faith and You,* pp. 142-143.)

The first miracle in the Church resulted from Newel Knight's resolution to pray. What actually happened was that his uneasiness of mind because he did not accept the invitation to pray in a meeting, created a situation where he became possessed of a devil, causing him to request deliverance by the Prophet Joseph Smith. The Prophet replied,

"If you know that I can, it shall be done"; and then almost unconsciously I rebuked the devil, and commanded him in the name of Jesus Christ to depart from him; when immediately Newel spoke out and said that he saw the devil leave him and vanish from his sight. This was the first miracle which was done in the Church, or by any member of it; and it was done not by man, nor by the power of man, but it was done by God, and by the power of godliness; therefore, let the honor and the praise, the dominion and the glory, be ascribed to the Father, Son, and Holy Spirit, for ever and ever. Amen.

The scene was not entirely changed, for as soon as the devil had departed from our friend, his countenance became natural, his distortions of body ceased, and almost immediately the Spirit of the Lord descended upon him, and the visions of eternity were opened to his view. (*DHC* I:83.)

Newel Knight did take up his cross and obediently performed his duties as directed by revelation. He was told to remain with the Saints of the Thompson Branch (Ohio) and lead them to Missouri. (D&C 56:7.) Not long after the Prophet arrived in Missouri, this group, led by Brother Knight, arrived in that land. Subsequently, he served in other capacities in the Church in taking up his cross.

In contrast, Ezra Thayre did not take up his cross to the end. He apparently repented as admonished by this revelation (*ibid.*, v. 8) in connection with some land arrangement which was a part of the law of consecration begun as a privilege by the Thompson Saints. Later Brother Thayre also participated in the Zion's camp march and was chosen as one of the First Council of the Seventy. His continuance in faith to the end, however, did not materialize.

"I, the Lord, Revoke"

In verses 4, 5, and 6 of Section 56, the Lord revokes some of the commandments which had been given previously to Thomas B. Marsh, Ezra Thayre, Selah J. Griffin, and Newel Knight, and gave them other appointments. The revocation of a commandment might seem strange to some, in view of some scriptures which indicate that the Lord is unchangeable. (James 1:17.) In this revelation, it is stated that "Wherefore, I, the Lord, command and revoke, as it seemeth me good; and all this to be answered upon the heads of the rebellious. . . ." (D&C 56:4.)

Here we learn that He commands and revokes, as seemeth Him good; that is, not capriciously, but for good and sufficient reasons. God is a free agent. We must not suppose that His immutability deprives Him of free agency. And because He is a free agent, He can command and revoke at will. But those who make it necessary for God, because of rebellion, to revoke laws given for the benefit of His children, will be held responsible. (*Doctrine and Covenants Commentary*, p. 322.)

There is security in obeying the commandments of God. He has declared that his promises will not go unfulfilled (D&C 1:37-38), but if man rejects the law, he forfeits the opportunity to have that security which is based upon obedience. (*Ibid.*, 82:10; 130:20-21.)

In Section 56 Ezra Thayre was called to repentance because of his attempt to repudiate a land contract made with the Church at Thompson, Ohio, where the Saints were attempting to live the law of consecration. (*Ibid.*, 56:8.) If he did not repent, he was to be paid the amount involved for the use of the land by the Saints and be cut off from the Church. (v. 10.) The following verse in this revelation points up the necessity for all men to observe the law given or suffer the consequences. "And though the heaven and earth pass away, these words shall not pass away, but shall be fulfilled." (v. 11.)

The truth thus stated is particularly important at this point in the chapter because of the discussion on the revocation of commandments. Again, when men disobey, judgment follows, unless repentance is forthcoming. Although the truth that the Lord's words shall not pass away is about Ezra Thayre, there is a universal application to all men who come within the sphere of the gospel plan. In a sense, our eternal welfare is in our hands as Latter-day Saints, but only if we keep the commandments. On the other hand, if we reject the word of the Lord, the penalty is certain.

In verses 12 and 13 of the revelation, the Prophet is told that he should furnish the money to recompense Brother Thayre and payment would come to the Prophet in Missouri. Those who would assist Joseph Smith in defraying this expense by their contributions would receive land in Missouri in return—"For according to that which they do they shall receive. . . ." (v. 13.)

True Repentance

As we have already noted in this revelation, there are truths found in it which have application to members of the Church other than those to whom the revelation was specifically directed. In reference to verse 14, it is apparent that it could be applied to all Saints today, as well as in 1831:

Behold, thus saith the Lord unto my people—you have many things to do and to repent of; for behold, your sins have come up unto me, and are not pardoned, because you seek to counsel in your own ways. (*Ibid.*, 14.)

Do these words apply to the membership of the Church today? This is a question for each Latter-day Saint to ask himself or herself, not his neighbor. The answer to this question is found in an authoritative source, as follows:

"To do and to repent" are inseparably connected. Repentance is primarily a change of mind, but it is a change of mind that produces a change from wrong conduct. For instance, "A certain man had two sons; and he came to the first and said, Son, go work today in my vineyard. He answered and said, I will not; but afterwards repented and went." (Matt. 21:28, 29.) That was genuine repentance. The word in Romans 11:29, translated "repentance," means "regret," or a "change of plan," without a change of mind.

True repentance is both a change of mind and of conduct. (*Doctrine and Covenants Commentary*, p. 324.)

Is repentance a principle to be applied once, immediately before baptism, for example, or is it to be a lifetime practice?

Repentance is not accomplished once for all. It is a spiritual experience that is completed only when this earthly existence is ended. For, no matter how far advanced we may be, there is always something to better, something to improve, and the first step to improvement is repentance. The Saints always "have many things to do and to repent of," until they reach the stage of perfection. (*Ibid.*)

In this revelation concerning the Saints at Thompson, Ohio, it might be stated: "Our Lord, who told Peter, the apostle, that he had yet to be converted (Luke 22: 32), also taught the Colesville Saints [originally from Colesville, New York] "that they, though members of the Church, had many things to repent of." (*Ibid.*) Of these members in Thompson who had not organized under the law of consecration, there was need for repentance since the Lord had not pardoned them. Their besetting sin as a group was that they sought to counsel in their own ways. Is it also true today that many Latter-day Saints believe that they can use their own judgment concerning keeping the laws of God although the Lord has spoken directly against "our counsel," as we ignore his words in the revelations?

"And Your Hearts Are Not Satisfied"

Joy or happiness comes to the member of the Church who faithfully obeys the commandments of the Lord. There is no lasting joy for one who veers from the commandments after having tasted the fruit of the gospel.

Consistent with the background of this revelation where men of wealth had not fully subscribed to the fundamentals of the law of consecration, there was reason for the following condemnation:

> Wo unto you rich men, that will not give your substance to the poor, for your riches will canker your souls; and this shall be your lamentation in the day of visitation, and of judgment, and of indignation: The harvest is past, the summer is ended, and my soul is not saved! (D&C 56:16.)

Under the perfect law designed to prepare the Lord's followers for the celestial kingdom, there would be an equality of wealth commensurate with the need of the individual and his family.

It was the Prophet Benjamin of the Book of Mormon who taught his followers that to retain a remission of sins it was necessary to give of one's substance to those in need. (Mosiah 4:26.) In doing this, one is to exercise wisdom, ". . . for it is not requisite that a man should run faster than he has strength. And again, it is expedient that he should be diligent, that thereby he might win the prize; therefore, all things must be done in order." (*Ibid.*, v. 27.) An orderly way by which members of the Church may discharge their obligations to the needy is through the organized Welfare Program of the Church. Material wealth or "riches" may canker or corrupt the soul of man. (James 5:1-3.) The wealth of this world is not to be treasured above the wisdom of God, advised the Savior in the Sermon on the Mount. (Matt. 6:19-21.)

Wealth Evaluated

What is the curse of wealth with so many people? Indulgence in the pleasures of the world, the desire for wealth giving rise to dishonest ways of obtaining wealth, and a disregard for fellow men are but some of the possible evils of riches. It takes a strong Latter-day Saint to remain true to the faith when wealth comes his way. The counsel of the Savior, while in mortality and also after his resurrection, should continue to be the guiding rule to follow. It is to seek the kingdom of God first. The riches of this earth should be a means to an end. The only true criterion for the Latter-day Saint is to consider the things of this world from the point of view of eternity. Riches are designed for the building up of the kingdom of God and its members. All temporal possessions are the Lord's for we are his stewards. (D&C 104:13-17.)

An informative evaluation of wealth is as follows:

. . . Our Lord does not object to his people's being rich. It all depends on *how* they *obtain* wealth and how they *use* it. Wealth obtained by dishonesty and oppression is a curse. Wealth used for selfish purposes is a snare. Money received of the Lord, through his blessings, and used for the furtherance of His kingdom is a means of eternal exaltation. (*Doctrine and Covenants Commentary,* p. 208.)

Wo to Rich and Poor

When the Lord condemned the rich of the Thompson Branch (D&C 56:16), strong as that condemnation was, he did not censure them only, but the poor were also at fault. The main reasons for the failure of the United Order at this time were that many, in addition to the rich, did not give of their substance to the poor. Notice in verse 17 the number of reasons why the poor contributed to this failure:

Wo unto you poor men, whose hearts are not broken, whose spirits are not contrite, and whose bellies are not satisfied, and whose hands are not stayed from laying hold upon other men's goods, whose eyes are full of greediness, and who will not labor with your own hands!

Too often we associate poverty with virtue. The poor are not blessed in the sight of the Lord because they are poor. A purpose of the law of consecration was to raise the standards of those in need of temporal goods that they might more fully enjoy the Spirit of the Lord. Poverty can and often does result in the sins mentioned by the Lord in this revelation. The Welfare Program of the Church today is intended to assist the needy in maintaining the true spirit of the gospel. The poor in this revelation are charged with desires and actions which conflict with contriteness of spirit or humility and a lack of the desire to repent. What are these sins? Their "bellies are not satisfied," with their earthly possessions; therefore, their "hands are not stayed from laying hold upon other men's goods," stealing; their "eyes are full of greediness." Covetousness, envy, jealousy, or the desire for other people's goods are not uncommon vices in the world; and, also, the Lord said they "will not labor with your [their] own hands." May not this be the basis for some of the poverty in the world?

True happiness cannot be found in dishonesty, greediness, or laziness. Certainly, the fulness of the gospel is not lived when these sins remain a part of our makeup.

Blessed Are the Poor

Who are the poor, or the rich, for that matter, who are blessed? Only those who are pure in heart and who come unto Christ receive the blessings prophesied in this revelation. (D&C 97:21.)

What are the blessings for the poor who are the pure in heart? ". . . they shall see the kingdom of God coming in power and great glory unto their deliverance; for the fatness of the earth shall be theirs." (*Ibid.*, 56: 18.) Faithful Latter-day Saints, living or dead, will have the privilege of seeing the Lord come with the kingdom of heaven merging with the kingdom of God on the earth. "For behold, the Lord shall come, and his recompense shall be with him, and he shall reward every man, and the poor shall rejoice." (*Ibid.*, v. 19.) Yes, the "fatness of the earth"—its bounties, will be possessed by the pure in heart when the Savior comes, and rejoicing will be found on the earth. Those who are not counted worthy to stand in that day will be recompensed for their works of unrighteousness. (*Ibid.*, 29:11-13; Alma 41:3-6.) What shall be the final blessing for the pure in heart who have come unto Christ?

And their generations shall inherit the earth from generation to generation, forever and ever. . . . (D&C 56:20.)

The earth in its celestialized state will be the home of those who lived the celestial law. (*Ibid.*, 88:15-20.) The glories of eternity will be theirs—all knowledge with the opportunity for endless advancement. (*Ibid.*, 130:7-11.)

Chapter 41

THE CENTER PLACE OF ZION

(Sections 57; 58:1-14)

The year 1831 was an eventful one in the life of the Prophet Joseph Smith and, consequently, of the Church. Among many important developments of that year, the Prophet had come to Kirtland, Ohio, for the first time. Within six months he was in Jackson County, Missouri, arriving there in July.

With the publication of The Book of Mormon, the Saints began to speculate as to where the New Jerusalem of which the ancient scriptures prophesied would be located. The Jaredite prophet Ether was shown many events of the last days, including the fact that the New Jerusalem would be built upon the American Continent. (Ether 13:2-11.) Several centuries later, the resurrected Christ taught the same thing to the Nephites. (3 Nephi 20:22.) The Savior continued by explaining that with his Church established in the land of America in the last days, all of gathered Israel, including the Lamanites of that day, would build the city of the New Jerusalem. (*Ibid.*, 21:20-29.) The Lord said to Enoch, the seventh from Adam, that he and his city which were taken into the heavens would unite with the city of Zion on the earth at the beginning of the millennium. (Moses 7:62-64.)

Interest in the location of the New Jerusalem was shown by many Saints. One of these, Hiram Page, claimed to know the place where this holy city would be built. As a result, the Lord revealed that this location was not to be known then (September 1830), but that it would be "on the borders by the Lamanites." (D&C 28:9.)

In February 1831, the Saints were told by revelation that if they prayed for information on this subject it would be revealed. (*Ibid.*, 42:62.) In the following months it was made known that the New Jerusalem would be located in the western lands. In preparation for this, the elders were to preach the gospel and build up churches. (*Ibid.*, 45:64-66.)

At the close of the June 1831 conference held in Kirtland, the Lord said that the Saints were to assemble in the land of Missouri. (*Ibid.*, 52:2, 42-43.)

In the middle of July 1831, the Prophet rejoiced with his brethren, who had long awaited his arrival in Missouri. Upon arriving in the "promised land," the Prophet felt to exclaim: "When will the wilderness blossom as the rose? When will Zion be built up in her glory, and where will Thy temple stand, unto which all nations shall come in the last days?" (*DHC* I:189.) These questions were soon answered upon receiving Section 57 in July 1831.

Section 57 and the New Jerusalem

Verses 1 and 2 of Section 57 point out that the land of Missouri is the land for the gathering of the Saints.

Wherefore, this is the land of promise, and the place for the city of Zion. (D&C 57:2.)

After revealing that the center place of Zion was Independence, Missouri, the Lord said that the land of inheritance should be purchased "even unto the line running directly between Jew and Gentile." (*Ibid.*, 3-5.) The Jew here is the Lamanite or Indian. (*Ibid.*, 19:27; Omni 14-19.) In this sparsely settled land the Saints were advised to obtain land by peaceful means.

The remainder of this revelation gives instructions to several brethren whose appointment to these callings had been made in former revelations (namely, Sidney

Gilbert, *ibid.*, 57:6; 53:4; Edward Partridge, *ibid.*, 57:7; 41:9; 42:10; William W. Phelps and Oliver Cowdery, *ibid.*, 57:11-13; 55:4.)

The promise of revelation to guide the elders and members of the Church closes Section 57. (*Ibid.*, 57:16.) On the first day of the next month a revelation was received in which the Lord set forth his plan for the Church in Missouri.

Background of Section 58

As the Nephites knew ancient America to be the land of promise, so also do the Latter-day Saints know that within the greater promised land, the land of Missouri is "the land of Promise" where the righteous will be gathered in the troublous days preceding the second coming of Christ. (D&C 57:1-2; 45:62-75.)

A preaching service was held the first Sunday after the Prophet and his party arrived in Jackson County when two persons were baptized. (*DHC* I:190-191.)

The Beginnings of Zion

Just before Section 58 was received, the Colesville (New York) Saints, more recently from Thompson, Ohio, numbering about sixty persons, arrived in Missouri by commandment. (*DHC* I:191.) Concerning this branch of the Church and its part in the beginning of Zion, the Prophet wrote that the first log for a house was "carried and placed by twelve men, in honor of the twelve tribes of Israel." The land was also dedicated by Elder Sidney Rigdon for the gathering of the Saints. (*Ibid.*, I:196.)

From John Whitmer's "History of the Church" we learn that the Saints pledged to keep the commandments in their new land. (*Ibid.*, I:196.) A description of this part of Missouri at the time of the Prophet is found in his journal. (*Ibid.*, I:197-198.)

A Message of Hope and a Forewarning

For the Saints who had arrived in Jackson County and for those who would follow, the Lord expressed a message of hope for the future, as well as a prediction of tribulation. These messages were directly concerned with the land of Missouri.

For verily I say unto you, blessed is he that keepeth my commandments, whether in life or in death; and he that is faithful in tribulation, the reward of the same is greater in the kingdom of heaven. (D&C 58:2.)

The predictive element in this verse is strongly present. The emphasis placed upon the two propositions stated—hope and also tribulation—is announced by the use of the word "verily," which means "in very truth." Although all men are expected to live the laws of God, as they know them, the Latter-day Saint is bound by acceptance of the atonement of Christ through baptism to keep the commandments. (*Ibid.*, 18:42-43.) Throughout the scriptures, promises are made that the blessings shall be rich for those who remain worthy even unto death. In the revelation we are now studying (Section 58:2), it is stated that continued faithfulness is required even beyond mortality. That we shall be the same persons in the spirit world that we are when we leave this life, is a part of our knowledge. (Alma 34:32-34.) In that day we shall all realize that happiness results from obedience to divine law.

With counsel concerning the necessity to be faithful in tribulation, the Saints are immediately informed that the land of Missouri would not then be known as their permanent home. Granted that the Saints may not have realized the full import of the following message, yet they were forewarned:

Ye cannot behold with your natural eyes, for the present time, the design of your God concerning those things which shall come hereafter, and the glory which shall follow after much tribulation.

For after much tribulation come the blessings. Wherefore the day cometh that ye shall be crowned with much glory; the hour is not yet, but is nigh at hand. (D&C 58:3-4.)

It was not long before persecution was heaped upon the Saints in Missouri. Details of the future are wisely withheld by the Father that his people may look beyond temporary setbacks to their ultimate glory.

In a subsequent chapter we shall learn more about the reasons why the Saints were persecuted. For the present, however, two causes are mentioned, first, their religious beliefs, especially concerning the restoration of the gospel with its gifts and powers. For example, the Manifesto issued by a Missouri mob on July 20, 1833, referred to the Saints pretending to receive revelations direct from heaven and to perform miracles as the apostles and prophets of old. (*DHC* I:374-376.) Second, that in consequence of the Saints' transgressions, they were chastened and not allowed to redeem Zion at that time. (D&C 101:1-10; 103:1-4; 105:1-6.) The prediction that the Saints would pass through tribulation was fulfilled when they were driven from Missouri, then Illinois, and then to the mountains outside the boundaries of the United States.

The manner in which most of the early Saints endured "much tribulation" is a credit to their faith. The testimony of President Young concerning his own experience could be said of many others:

. . . We have passed through a great many scenes, we may say, of tribulation, though I would have all my brethren understand that I do not take this to myself, for all that I have passed through has been joy and joyful to me. . . . I have, myself, five times before I came to this valley, left everything that the Lord had blessed me with pertaining to this world's goods, which, for the country where I lived, was not a very little. (*Journal of Discourses*, 18:237.)

The ability of the faithful Latter-day Saints to pass through tribulation or trials though they may come only as the normal experiences of life, may be attributed to the hope and knowledge that "the day cometh that ye [they] shall be crowned with much glory. . . ." (D&C 58:4.) One can understand as a Latter-day Saint that the testimony of the truth restored through the Prophet Joseph Smith has given and continues to give an assurance that the Lord's word will be fulfilled. Without this divine promise, many would find it difficult to endure to the end.

Glory to Come

Ultimately to all the faithful will come blessings of eternal life. There will be a happy reunion with departed loved ones, and the joy of eternal increase with its manifold blessings of dominion and honor. But the message to the Saints of our time is that the inheritance promised in Missouri [Zion] will yet be realized. "the hour is not yet, but is nigh at hand." (D&C 58:4.) "It must be much nearer now than when this inspired line was first penned." (*Doctrine and Covenants Commentary*, page 335.)

This significant truth is found in the fifth verse of this revelation:

Remember this, which I tell you before, that you may lay it to heart, and receive that which is to follow. (D&C 58:5.)

The Lord had promised his people that after much tribulation would come the blessings of much glory. At the time, however, they were not to see the redemption of Zion. For us today, we may be assured that the prophecy is to serve as confirmation of the prophet's mission and that the fulfillment will instill in the hearts of people the desire to obey the Lord's word. In the light of these purposes, what faith should the Latter-day Saint have in the future of Zion?

Reasons for the Saints Gathering in Zion

Several reasons are given for the commandment to gather to Missouri. It is clear from this revelation that the Saints were to lay the foundation of Zion. Regardless of what would happen after the Saints began their work, the time would come when Zion would prosper in the preparations made for the return of the Savior to the earth. The redemption of Zion would come only as the people knew and fully accepted in their lives the reasons which follow:

Behold, verily I say unto you, for this cause I have sent you— that you might be obedient, and that your hearts might be prepared to bear testimony of the things which are to come. (*Ibid.*, 58:6.)

The Church of Jesus Christ is divinely directed. Strict obedience is essential for salvation. The direction of the Church requires the directing will of the Father through inspired prophets.

This important commentary is found in an authoritative source:

Obedience is absolutely necessary for the furtherance of the kingdom of God. There must be *one* directing will. This is necessary in earthly concerns—a factory, a ship, a railroad system. It is equally necessary in the kingdom of God. His will must be supreme there.

To render obedience to lawful authority, is not humiliating or degrading. Even the Son learned obedience (Heb. 5:8), before He became the author of eternal salvation. Disobedience, or rebellion, is as bad as idolatry. (I Sam. 15:23.) The Lord does not stand personally in the midst of the people to direct their affairs but He speaks to them through His inspired servants. When we obey their counsel, we obey God. Those who refuse to obey them, would refuse to obey the Lord, even if He spoke to them Himself, in person. (*Doctrine and Covenants Commentary*, p. 336.)

In verse 6 we have also another purpose in that the obedient would bear testimony of the truth revealed through the Prophet.

In addition to keeping the commandments as stated, the Saints of 1831 were to be honored in laying the foundation of Zion. (D&C 58:7.) The Prophet Joseph Smith records that on the third day of August 1831, he dedicated the temple site, a little west of what was then Independence, Missouri. As a part of this service, the 87th Psalm was read. When one thinks of the glory which will yet surround this place and the purpose of the temple prophesied centuries ago, he can well understand the Prophet's comment: "The scene was solemn and impressive." (*DHC* I:199.)

The fourth reason for the Saints coming to Zion, as given in verse 7 of this revelation, was to bear record of the land itself.

Another purpose of God in establishing Zion is given in verses 8 to 10 which was realized at some period after laying the foundation of that city.

The Day of the Lord's Power

Further information regarding the glory of the Zion of the last days is brought to our attention in verses 11 and 12 of this revelation. The interpretation of these verses indicates events which usher in the millennial reign of the Savior.

Zion will be built. The Temple will be reared. Enoch's Zion, the "Jerusalem which is above," will meet the Saints who have part in the first resurrection, and those who will be changed in the twinkling of an eye, and they will all be united. Then will come the day of God's power. The poor and the lame, the blind and the deaf will all be invited to partake of the blessings of the Millennium. The Earth will not be freed from all defects at once. The work of redemption will be gradual. (*Doctrine and Covenants Commentary*, p. 337.)

The assurance of the fulfillment of God's word brings forth the Lord's last reason for the building of Zion. (D&C 1:37-38.) It is that his testimony or law is to go forth from Zion to enlighten the world. (*Ibid.*, 58: 13.)

The Future Glory of Zion

President Brigham Young in these words referred to the time when he saw the return of the Saints to build up Zion in Missouri:

> . . .Before we were driven out of Missouri I had a vision, if I would dare to say that I had a vision, and saw that the people would go to the east, to the north and to the west; but we should go back to Jackson County from the west. When this people return to the Centre Stake [place] of Zion, they will go from the west. (*Journal of Discourses*, 11:17.)

Because of the conditions which prevented the Saints from building the temple in Zion, the Lord released the Saints from performing this important duty at that time. (D&C 124:49-51.) When the call comes from the divinely appointed servants of the Lord, the city and temple will be built as commanded for this generation. (*Ibid.*, 84: 4-5.)

Due to the driving of our people from the land of their inheritance, being thus moved out of their place, they will return to build unto the Lord the long-predicted Zion. (*Ibid.*, 101:17-19.) When this task is undertaken the Saints will be led with power. In the meantime, the Lord's people must become great and sanctified before him. (*Ibid* 105:11-13, 31-32.) The laws and commandments, including the living of the law of consecration, will be lived "after her [Zion's] redemption." (*Ibid.*, 105:34.)

When the Prophet Joseph Smith first viewed the land of Missouri, his vision was not on the then advantages of that place but upon the greatness of the Zion to be. Here is his message:

But all these impediments vanish when it is recollected what the Prophets have said concerning Zion in the last days; how the glory of Lebanon is to come upon her; the fir tree, the pine tree, and the box tree together, to beautify the place of His sanctuary, that He may make the place of His feet glorious. Where for brass, He will bring gold; and for iron, He will bring silver; and for wood, brass; and for stones, iron; and where the feast of fat things will be given to the just; yea, when the splendor of the Lord is brought to our consideration for the good of His people, the calculations of men and the vain glory of the world vanish, and we exclaim, "Out of Zion the perfection of beauty, God hath shined." (*DHC* I:198; *cf.* Isaiah 60:12-22.)

Chapter 42

ENGAGED IN A GOOD CAUSE

(Section 58:15-65)

In the year 1831, the Prophet Joseph Smith received a revelation designating Independence, Jackson County, Missouri, as the site for the city of Zion or the New Jerusalem. Hundreds of years before this the Lord had decreed that his holy city, to which the faithful would come in the last days, would shine forth as a light to beckon earth's inhabitants to accept the gospel. This city will become the capital of the world government when the Savior comes to establish his kingdom at the time of the millennium.

Although the Saints were driven from the center place of Zion, their belief in the restoration of the gospel, and their own inability, at that time, to live the gospel as required, brought about the persecutions which drove them from Missouri. (Chapter 41.)

Notwithstanding what happened in 1834 when our people were ejected from Missouri, the promises of the Lord concerning that land are still to be fulfilled. The leadership of this Church has always understood and taught that the New Jerusalem will become all that the Lord has said it would be. President George Q. Cannon, one of the apostles close to the events of Missouri, expressed the feelings of the Saints concerning these matters. After twenty years in the west, he said:

> We talk about going back to build up the centre stake [place] of Zion; it is the burden of our daily prayers. The aspirations of thousands of the people ascend in the ears of the Lord of Sabaoth [hosts] in behalf of the redemption of Zion, and that the purposes of God may be forwarded, and that the time may soon come when the centre stake [place] of Zion shall be build up and the people be prepared to go back and inhabit that land. Why do

we wish this? Because we anticipate when that day shall come that we will be that much nearer the day of triumph, the day when Jesus will come and reign among his Saints . . . we look forward to that land with indescribable feelings, because it is the place where God has said His city shall be built. It is the land where Adam, the Ancient of Days, will gather his posterity again, and where the blessings of God will descend upon them. . . . (*Journal of Discourses* 11:336-337.)

Preparations must be made for the building of Zion as commanded. The Lord revealed in this revelation (Section 58) why the Saints should go to Missouri, beginning in 1831 as well as in the future. (Chapter 41.) What is necessary today to realize the blessings of building the City of Zion? This question is answered in this chapter.

President Cannon said:

. . .We expect when that day shall come that we will be a very different people to what we are today. We will be prepared to commune with heavenly beings; at any rate, the preparation will be going on very rapidly for Jesus to be revealed. We expect that a society will be organized there that will be a pattern of heavenly society, that when Jesus and the heavenly beings who come with him are revealed in the clouds of heaven, their feelings will not be shocked by the change, for a society will be organized on the earth whose members will be prepared through the revelations of God to meet and associate with them, if not on terms of perfect equality, at least with some degree of equality. (*Journal of Discourses,* 11:337.)

Edward Partridge

Our discussion of Section 58 begins with verse 14 in which we are reminded that Edward Partridge, who received his appointment as bishop by revelation (D&C 41:9), was to place his full trust in the things pertaining to the kingdom of God. This counsel is applicable to every person who has entered covenant relationship with God. Putting one's emphasis on worldly objects to the exclusion of God's purposes is to have "unbelief and blindness of heart." (*Ibid.*, 58:15; *Doctrine and Covenants Commentary*, pp. 338-339.)

Bishop Partridge's duties were known to him. He and bishops who have succeeded him are to be judges among the Saints. He was to appoint to the Saints their inheritances—land—as it was appointed in ancient Israel. (*Cf.* Exodus 18:13.)

The bishop is "to judge his people by the testimony of the just, and by the assistance of his counselors, according to the laws of the kingdom which are given by the prophets of God." (D&C 58:18.) In order for the Lord's representative, the bishop, in this case, to understand his position as a judge, the Law of the Church (Section 42) is to be his guide in morals and plans for the welfare of the members. (*Ibid.*, 58:19.) No bishop, however should consider that he is a "ruler." The only ruler in the kingdom of God is Jesus Christ. Officiators in his kingdom are servants. (*Ibid.*, 58:20.)

The Law of the Land

Not only are the Saints of God to accept the rulership of Christ and to follow his divinely appointed servants, but they should be obedient to the laws of the land.

Let no man break the laws of the land, for he that keepeth the laws of God hath no need to break the laws of the land. (*Ibid.*, 58:21.)

The principle of law observance did not have its origin in this dispensation. Obedience to law is necessary that order and stability may exist. Judges who administered the law were known among ancient Israel. In Moses' day a just judgment was to be meted to those who transgressed the law. (Deut. 16:18; 1 Chron. 23:4.) Elder James E. Talmage pointed out how Christ acknowledged the existing laws of the land, both Jewish and Roman, although the Roman law was sometimes exercised unjustly. A strong case for obedience to law was given by Jesus when he performed a miracle to provide tax money.

When the tax-collector called for the tribute money demanded by the hierarchy, Christ, though not admitting the justice of the claim, directed that the tax be paid, and even invoked a miraculous circumstance whereby the money could be provided. Of Peter he asked: "What thinkest thou, Simon? Of whom do the kings of the earth take custom or tribute? Of their own children, or of strangers? Peter saith unto him, Of strangers. Jesus saith unto him, Then are the children free. Notwithstanding, lest we should offend them, go thou to the sea, and cast an hook, and take up the fish that first cometh up; and when thou hast opened his mouth, thou shall find a piece of money: that take, and give unto them for me and thee." (*Articles of Faith*, p. 416.) The well-known reply to those who attempted to trap the Messiah as one who stood against the ruling powers was: ". . . Render therefore unto Caesar the things which are Caesar's; and unto God the things that are God's." (Matt. 22:21.)

The apostles followed their Master's example in teaching that observance of the law of the land was necessary for the full living of the religious life. (Acts 23:1-5; Titus 3:1; Rom. 13:1-7; 1 Tim. 2:1-3; 1 Peter 2:13-17. For the application of these and other examples, consult James E. Talmage, *Articles of Faith*, pp. 418-421.)

As for our dispensation, by revelation and instruction from the leaders of the Church, the message is clear —to be a Latter-day Saint strict observance of the law of God and the law of the land is imperative. The Twelfth Article of Faith is well known to all. (*Ibid.*, page 3; Pearl of Great Price, page 60.)

Obedience to law is a test of a man's religion. As Elder Talmage expressed it:

Religion is essentially a matter of every-day life. It has as much to do with the adjustment of the individual to his material environment as with his abstract belief in matters spiritual. A man's religion should be a concrete demonstration of his conceptions concerning God and the Divine purposes respecting himself and his fellows. Anything less lacks both the form of godliness and the power thereof. . . .

Loyal citizenship is at once a characteristic and a test of a man's religion; and as to the incumbent duties of citizenship, the voice of the people, as expressed through the established channels of government, must determine. (*The Vitality of Mormonism*, 1948, pp. 180-181.)

That the Constitution of the United States was divinely established and thus to be obeyed by its citizens is a revealed part of our religion. (D&C 98:4-10; 101:76-80.)

Christ Shall Reign

Distinctive in Latter-day Saint belief is our understanding of the eventual reign of Christ on the earth. The following verse carries the same truth expressed in the Tenth Article of Faith:

Wherefore, be subject to the powers that be, until he reigns whose right it is to reign, and subdues all enemies under his feet. (*Ibid.*, 58:22.)

When the Savior returns to the earth in power, his kingdom will be established. The inauguration of his rule will bring all of his enemies under control. Some of these enemies of God and man are tyranny, despotism, other evils of Satan, and for man, the last enemy, death. (1 Cor. 15:26-28.) When the King of Kings comes, there will be no other king. (D&C 38:21-22.)

When that glorious day comes, earth's inhabitants will be governed by laws which are righteous; freedom will then be enjoyed by all.

Latter-day Saints, Law-Abiders

In order that no Latter-day Saint shall misunderstand his obligation to the law of the land and the law of the gospel, the revelation continues:

Behold, the laws which ye have received from my hand are the laws of the church, and in this light ye shall hold them forth. Behold, here is wisdom. (*Ibid.*, 58:23.)

To Be Commanded in All Things?

The next several verses of Section 58 (verses 24-33) are directed to Edward Partridge, his counselors, and Sidney Gilbert (*ibid.*, 57:6-9) to attend to their assignments in Missouri. Important instructions to these brethren are (1) that they are not to be commanded in all things; (2) they must have initiative; (3) they have power within themselves to do much good; and (4) the revocation of commandments by God and loss of blessings. As we examine these scriptures it is apparent that the Lord desires all men to know these principles because they apply to all.

For behold, it is not meet that I should command in all things; for he that is compelled in all things, the same is a slothful and not a wise servant; wherefore he receiveth no reward. (*Ibid.*, 58:26.)

The underlying principle in this scripture is that man is a free agent. In all stages of his endless life, man exercises his right of choice. Among the many prophets discoursing on this aspect of man's life was Lehi. (2 Nephi 2:16, 26-27.)

Elder James E. Talmage wrote:

The predominant attribute of justice, recognized as part of the divine nature, forbids the thought that man should receive promises of reward for righteousness, and threats of punishment for evil deeds, if he possessed no power of independent action. It is no more a part of God's plan to compel men to work righteousness than it is His purpose to permit evil powers to force His children into sin.... (*Articles of Faith*, p. 53.)

Given his free agency, why should man be compelled in all things? Man grows by exercising his right to solve his own problems. There would be no growth if man were to act only as an automaton or robot. Guidance, however, eliminates waste of time and energy.

When a person has a position in the Lord's kingdom, it is expected that he will use his initiative and not be told precisely what to do in all things. Some people do only the bare minimum required of them without exercising their talents beyond duty. He is a slothful servant lacking in wisdom who expects to be compelled in all things.

The good that men do will live after them. Their righteous purposes will bring a sure reward from the Father who knows all and will judge all men by their works. (D&C 19:3.)

Power Is within Men

Verily I say, men should be anxiously engaged in a good cause, and do many things of their own free will, and bring to pass much righteousness;

For the power is in them, wherein they are agents unto themselves. And inasmuch as men do good they shall in nowise lose their reward.

But he that doeth not anything until he is commanded, and receiveth a commandment with doubtful heart, and keepeth it with slothfulness, the same is damned. (*Ibid.*, 58:27-29.)

It is true that men should engage themselves in causes which contribute to the happiness of their fellow men. Only the Church, however, is committed to programs that advance man's joy and is able to give him happiness in the eternities to come. At the time this revelation was given, the Saints were commanded to lay the foundation of Zion. (*Ibid.*, vs. 6-7.) Counsel regard-

ing this had been given at the beginning of this dispensation. If one would seek "to bring forth and establish the
cause of Zion," and seek for wisdom *then* the mysteries
of the kingdom would be his and, if faithful, eternal life.
(*Ibid.*, 6:6-7.)

Diligent service based upon a true desire to build up
the cause of Zion is accepted by the Lord. Weak faith or
a doubting heart brings weak effort characterized as
slothful.

Is This the Work of God?

Some people believe that because blessings are not
answered on their heads, although a try may have been
made at keeping the commandments, although not fully
and only halfheartedly, the Lord's promises are not fulfilled. To such, as well as to all, the Lord addressed some
questions:

Who am I that made man, saith the Lord, that will hold
him guiltless that obeys not my commandments?
Who am I, saith the Lord, that have promised and have not
fulfilled?
I command and men obey not; I revoke and they receive not
the blessing.
Then they say in their hearts: This is not the work of the
Lord, for his promises are not fulfilled. But woe unto such, for
their reward lurketh beneath, and not from above. (*Ibid.*, 58:
30-33.)

The important question for every Latter-day Saint
is, "Am I living the commandments so faithfully that
the Lord will bless me as I am entitled to his blessings?
On the other hand, should I complain against my Maker
because of my own lack of diligence?"

The lesson to be learned by all is found in this significant comment:

The Saints sometimes fail to do their duty and to keep the
commandments of God. But they expect Him to make good to

them the promises He has given to the faithful. If He does not, they complain. They neglect their prayers; they absent themselves from their meetings; they break the Word of Wisdom; they withhold their tithing; but when sickness comes and falls like a dark, terrifying shadow across their path, they expect immediate Divine interference in their behalf, through the administration of the Elders. If their expectations are not realized, they say, in a rebellious spirit, "His promises are not fulfilled." The reply of the Lord to that is, "Their reward lurketh beneath." They must look "beneath" for their reward; they have no claim on heaven. (*Doctrine and Covenants Commentary*, p. 340.)

If the Saints have an opportunity to live a commandment to further their eternal progression and they fail, or conditions develop which do not allow them to keep that commandment, the law may be revoked, or put in abeyance, until the Saints are able to live the commandments. An example is the Law of Consecration, studied in Chapter 28. In ancient Israel, the Lord, through Moses, sought to give his people higher laws, but they refused them. As a result, a lesser law was given, and thus Israel lost its great opportunity at that time.

Further Directions Concerning Zion

The remainder of this revelation (D&C 58:34-65) deals with specific directions to some elders and also to the members of the Church concerning Zion. Counsel to these individuals is applicable to all members of the Church as a warning not to fall into similar errors.

Chapter 43

THE DAY OF REST AND DEVOTIONS

(Section 59:1-14)

On Sunday, August 7, 1831, the Prophet Joseph Smith attended the funeral of Polly Knight, wife of Joseph Knight, Sr., who had given material substance to the Prophet. (D&C 12; 23:6.) Their son, Newel K. Knight, wrote that his mother insisted upon traveling from Kirtland to Missouri, notwithstanding the fact that she was very ill. Her greatest desire, to stand on the land of Zion, was granted her. Of Polly Knight, the Prophet wrote that she was the first to die in the land of Zion, and as "a worthy member sleeps in Jesus till the resurrection." (*DHC* I:190, footnote.) By the 7th of August the land of Zion was consecrated as a gathering place for the Saints, the temple site was dedicated, and the first conference was held in Zion, this being the Fifth General Conference. The Colesville Branch members were present at this conference.

They Shall Rest from Their Labors

The Lord promised blessings to those who were to come up to the land of Zion, provided that they would have an eye single to God's glory. As Section 59:1 points out, "an eye single to my glory" requires that one keep the commandments. Consistent with this thought is the verse which follows:

For those that live shall inherit the earth, and those that die shall rest from all their labors, and their works shall follow them; and they shall receive a crown in the mansions of my Father which I have prepared for them. (D&C 59:2.)

One may reflect upon this scripture with joy, realizing that when men and women follow the Lord's plan of life here, then righteous labors will be rewarded when mortality ends.

Following the necessary sojourn in the spirit world where advancement is made toward the ultimate glory of the resurrection, a place is received in the mansions of the Father—the celestial kingdom, for those who have had their minds single to God. (*Ibid.*, 88:20-22, 66-68.)

Revelations Are Blessings

The good things of the earth are promised those who obey the gospel. This is a blessing discussed in Chapter 41 concerning Zion. In addition to these temporal blessings, the Saints are to be blessed with commandments and revelations.

And they shall also be crowned with blessings from above, yea, and with commandments not a few, and with revelations in their time—they that are faithful and diligent before me. (*Ibid.*, 59:4.)

There is the fact that one's spiritual welfare is greatly enhanced by obedience to all of God's commandments. There are some people, and their numbers are great, who believe that commandments are restrictive, little realizing that the gospel frees people from bondage. (John 8:31-32; D&C 84:40-53.) Real freedom consists of a clear conscience toward God and man.

Commandments come by revelation. Revelations also provide the faithful with hope, peace, and courage to continue on to the end.

Great Commandments

Only the Father can say that one of his commandments is greater than another. This he has done through his Son by saying that one should love God as the first

commandment and second, that one should love his neighbor as himself. (Matt. 22:37-40.) In the revelation comprising this chapter, notice the important information
given about these two great commandments.

> Wherefore, I give unto them a commandment, saying thus;
> Thou shalt love the Lord thy God with all thy heart, with all
> thy might, mind and strength and in the name of Jesus Christ
> thou shalt serve him.
>
> Thou shalt love thy neighbor as thyself. Thou shalt not
> steal, neither commit adultery, nor kill, nor do anything unto
> it. (D&C 59:5-6.)

In this revelation specific reference is made to certain commandments the violation of which clearly indicates that one does not love his fellow man. These laws
condemn stealing, adultery, murder, or anything like it.
All one needs to do to verify the importance of these laws
in relation to the second great commandment is to ask:
"Does one love his neighbor if he commits any one of
these infractions of the moral law?" (Chapters 26 and
27.)

Thanksgiving and Humility

Thanksgiving is to be shown to the Lord in all things.
For what should the Saint be thankful—life with its
opportunities to prove oneself? the fulness of the gospel that brings purpose into life? that divine direction is
received today by inspired prophets? the joy of knowing
that great blessings accrue to those who are faithful?
These and countless other blessings should be acknowledged to the Father in prayer. But this is not the only
way that gratitude is to be expressed. When one keeps the
commandments he prays, and he also loves the Father
and the Son. (John 14:15; D&C 46:7.) Prayer offered
in humility with a thankful heart assists one to continue
in the faith. Humility is the quality of being teachable, of
responding fully to the Lord's will. The humble person,

one who has a broken heart and contrite spirit, will demonstrate his gratitude for all things, and he will be made glorious. (D&C 78:19.)

The Sabbath Commandment

All of the foregoing truths from Section 59 were given in preparation for the Sabbath day commandments as follows:

> And that thou mayest more fully keep thyself unspotted from the world, thou shalt go to the house of prayer and offer up thy sacraments upon my holy day.
> For verily this is a day appointed unto you to rest from your labors, and to pay thy devotions unto the Most High.
> Nevertheless thy vows shall be offered up in righteousness on all days and at all times.
> But remember that on this, the Lord's day, thou shalt offer thine oblations and thy sacraments unto the Most High, confessing thy sins unto thy brethren, and before the Lord.
> And on this day thou shalt do none other thing, only let thy food be prepared with singleness of heart that thy fasting may be perfect, or, in other words, that thy joy may be full.
> Verily, this is fasting and prayer, or in other words, rejoicing and prayer. (D&C 59:9-14.)

Shown in the form of "thou shalt," or what is required on the Sabbath day, these commandments may be stated as:

1. "Thou shalt go to the house of prayer." For what purpose? ". . . that thou mayest more fully keep thyself unspotted from the world." Under the most favorable conditions people may fall away from the truth, but the person who goes to the appointed Church meetings will find a place of faith, of learning, of glory, of order, and verily, a house of God. (*Ibid.*, 88:119.) In the house of the Lord, as in a Sacrament meeting the communicant meets friends from whom he receives encouragement.

Sometimes members of the Church absent themselves from the Sacrament meeting because they feel that they hear the same messages often or for some other reason. President Heber J. Grant had this to say on this thought:

There are some who say they will not go to meeting because they know just who will talk and what they will say. I realize that such persons are becoming indifferent to the spiritual things of the kingdom. I know people who in the old world would go many miles to a meeting because they were in love with the gospel. They will not cross the street now because they have lost that love just as failing to eat will cause our physical frames to shrink and die. Just so sure neglect to supply our spiritual natures will bring death to them. (*Gospel Standards*, p. 98.)

2. "Thou shalt offer up thy sacraments upon my holy day." What does this mean? Sacraments and devotions are similar. Specifically, a sacrament is a ceremony wherein one makes a covenant with the Lord. For Latter-day Saints the partaking of the Sacrament constitutes a covenant-making and a covenant-renewal opportunity. When partaking of the Sacrament worthily, the member is promised the blessing of the Spirit to be with him. Here alone is sufficient reason for attending the Sacrament meeting in the true spirit of worship.

3. "This is a day appointed unto you to rest from your labors." Verse 10 of Section 59 informs us that the keeping of this commandment is essential to Sabbath worship. What does it mean to rest? Certainly it does not mean idleness. But from what are we to rest? Elder John A. Widtsoe suggested that a true rest is one in which the person has a change from the occupations of work of the weekday, however, we should devote our activities to the requirements of the Sabbath day. (*Evidences and Reconciliations* I:220-221.) But are these activities of the week in which some people must be engaged? There is necessary work to be performed, such as the feeding and care of animals on the farm, some public service industries as power, light, hospital, police and fire protection, etc. In the main, however, the person who engages in Sunday

work may find himself an inactive member of God's kingdom.

4. Thou shalt "pay thy devotions unto the Most High." As indicated earlier, devotions are similar to Sacrament as given in this revelation. What are the devotions of the Saints in meetings of the Sabbath? Instructive on this question is the following:

On the Sabbath, the Saints should be in the house of prayer and offer up their sacraments, that is, present their devotions before the Lord, in the form of songs of praise, prayer and thanksgiving testimonies, partaking of the Sacrament and contemplation of the Word of God. All this is meant by the word "sacrament" which, in its widest range, stands for any sacred rite or ceremony whereby we affirm our allegiance to our divine Lord. (*Doctrine and Covenants Commentary*, p. 351.)

In the words of President Joseph F. Smith:

Men are not showing zeal and ardor in their religious faith and duty when they hustle off early Sunday morning on the cars, in teams, in automobiles, to the canyons, the resorts, and to visit friends, or places of amusement with their wives and children. They are not paying their devotions in this way to the Most High. (*Gospel Doctrine*, p. 246.)

5. "Thou shalt offer thine oblations . . . unto the Most High." Spiritual as well as temporal offerings (which are really spiritual) are to be rendered to the Lord. An enlightening explanation of the meaning and application of "oblations" anciently and today, may be found in the *Doctrine and Covenants Commentary* page 352.

6. Thou shalt confess "thy sins unto thy brethren, and before the Lord." The following statement of Elder Marion G. Romney, delivered in General Conference, suggests an explanation:

I would assume that we are to confess all our sins unto the Lord. For transgressions which are wholly personal, affecting none but ourselves and the Lord, such confession would seem to be sufficient.

For misconduct which offends another, confession should also be made to the offended one, and his forgiveness sought.

Finally, where one's transgressions are of such a nature as would, unrepented of, put in jeopardy his right to membership or fellowship in the Church of Jesus Christ, full and effective confession would, in my judgment, require confession by the repentant sinner to his bishop or other proper presiding Church officer—not that the Church officer could forgive the sin (this power rests in the Lord himself and those only to whom he specifically delegates it) but rather that the Church, acting through its duly appointed officers, might with full knowledge of the facts take such action with respect to Church discipline as the circumstances merit.

One having forsaken his sins and, by proper confession, cleared his conduct with the Lord, with the people he has offended, and with the Church of Jesus Christ, where necessary, may with full confidence seek the Lord's forgiveness and go forth in newness of life, relying upon the merits of Christ. (*Conference Report*, October 1955, p. 125.)

7. Thou shalt "let thy food be prepared with singleness of heart." It seems that the intent of this instruction is that Sunday does not become a feast day. On this point we have the following:

Upon the Sabbath, even the food should be prepared "with singleness of heart"; that is to say, in simplicity. Our hearts, our desires, on that day should not be elaborate feasts, whereby some are prevented from having a Sabbath. A simple meal should suffice. To that extent every Sabbath should be a fast day. One bringing perfect joy. (*Doctrine and Covenants Commentary*, p. 352.)

8. "And on this day thou shalt do none other thing." This admonition seems to point out that the positive requirements of observing Sunday, as listed above, provide enough counsel on what should be done. It is also apparent to the careful reader of this revelation that the Lord did not seem at that time to catalogue the negative aspects of this law. In time, however, disobedience by the world

to the Sabbath law in making Sunday a holiday instead of a holy day, and the use of the automobile with public places of recreation open on the Sabbath became widespread, and members of the Church began to succumb to these temptations. Accordingly, First Presidencies have issued formal statements about Sabbath observance. The latest, issued on June 19, 1959, by President David O. McKay, J. Reuben Clark, Jr., and Henry D. Moyle, emphasizes the commandments given anciently and in Section 59. After quoting the modern revelation and Exodus 20:8-11, 20, the following appears:

Latter-day Saints should not permit these commandments regarding the Sabbath to slip from their minds. All during this, the Last Dispensation, the Prophets of the Lord have urged Sabbath observance upon the people. Different concepts of Sabbath observance have been urged upon us by unbelievers, partial believers, and by the thoughtless, concerned primarily with the pleasures of the world, sometimes under the guise of recreation, sometimes by activities the Lord has told us were sinful.

The Sabbath is not just another day on which we merely rest from work, free to spend it as our lightmindedness may suggest. It is a holy day, the Lord's Day, to be spent as a day of worship and reverence. All matters extraneous thereto should be shunned.

We must bear in mind all these principles. We must remember particularly actual Sabbath breaking labor which might be required from a great number of Lesser Priesthood members in any Sabbath breaking activities, including interference with their duties and attendance at quorum meetings. For all these and for many other reasons affecting injuriously the religious duties and activities of the whole Church membership. Latter-day Saints, with a testimony of the Gospel and a knowledge of the spiritual blessings that come from keeping the Sabbath will never permit themselves to make it a shopping day, an activity that has no place in a proper observance of the Holy Day of the Lord, on which we are commanded to pour out our souls in gratitude for the many blessings of health, strength, physical comfort, and spiritual joy which comes from the Lord's bounteous hand. (*Deseret News,* Saturday, June 20, 1959.)

Parental Example

The Lord established the Sabbath as a holy day that man might benefit spiritually. Unto Moses, Israel's prophet, the Sabbath was known as a sign between the Lord and Israel. (Exodus 31:13-14; Ezekiel 20:19-24.)

The counsel to keep the Sabbath holy is as applicable today as when it was given. The observance of Sunday as the Lord's Day is a fact of modern revelation. (D&C 59: 12.) The keeping of the Sabbath today will have the same effect as was promised anciently, the sanctification of the person.

How will the world know the Lord's people today? One way is by their observance of the day of rest. The testimony of the truth comes to the obedient. A witness of the gospel must be based upon the faith of the individual. Every parent should ask, "Is my attitude toward Sabbath observance reflected in the faith of my children?" In other words, if the parents break the law, will the children feel that they may disregard the Lord's commandment? Observance of the Sabbath day by the parents brings forth fruits of faith in the lives of the children and the testimony of truth through keeping the other commandments.

Chapter 44

REWARDS OF KEEPING THE COMMANDMENTS

(Section 59:15-24)

In the last chapter we learned that on the day the Prophet Joseph Smith attended the funeral of Polly Knight, the Lord gave a most important revelation for the comfort of the Saints. It was a message of hope concerning the future life where the deceased continue to find joy in activity. The Saints also learned that they would be blessed with commandments received by revelation through the Prophet. One of these commandments was the proper observance of the Lord's day of rest. Eight positive requirements of Sabbath day observance were enumerated in the lesson. An official statement by the First Presidency was also given concerning violation of the Sabbath. (Chapter 43.)

"Inasmuch As Ye Do These Things with Thanksgiving"

If we follow the commandment concerning the Sabbath day and are faithful in keeping the other commandments, our harvest will be rich. But what is expected of the member as he obeys God's will? Gratitude, yes, as we learn from verse 7 of Section 59. Then what? As a member follows the commandments in keeping the Sabbath day holy, joy is received, and rich blessings are promised. (D&C 59:15-19.) Keeping the commandments brings the favor of heaven. In the foregoing verses there is stated the purpose for which the things of the earth—food, clothing, and shelter—are provided, to strengthen one physically and spiritually. Implicit in these verses is the same thought expressed in an earlier revelation. All laws and commandments thought of as temporal are spiritual. (*Ibid.*, 29:34-35.)

The important fact is that the bounties of the earth are for all men (*Ibid.*, 49:19), but not in excess. An equitable distribution of the products of the earth is the ideal. Those who receive more of these materials are not only to use judgment in their use, but also to see that advantage is not taken of their fellow men.

And it pleaseth God that he hath given all these things unto man, for unto this end were they made to be used with judgment, not to excess, neither by extortion. (*Ibid.*, 59:20.)

Moderation and honesty are to guide man's use of God's creations provided for man's sojourn on the earth. Riches are to be used for the benefit of man. (*Ibid.*, 49:20; Jacob 2:18-19.) President David O. McKay has emphasized that life should not be centered on wealth. (*Gospel Ideals*, p. 30.) President Heber J. Grant has pointed out that riches in themselves may be blessings if used in the way the Lord intended. (*Gospel Standards*, p. 108.)

Man's Offenses

God's wrath is kindled against those who disregard his commandments when they know his will. His wrath or anger will be demonstrated at his coming in power to the world. (D&C 1:9-10.) The wicked will feel his wrath because they have brought his displeasure upon themselves due to violation of law. (*Ibid.*, 124:48.) The demands of justice will be met by all those who remain unrepentant. (3 Nephi 28:34-35.)

When the Lord stated the temporal blessings received by the faithful who obey the Sabbath, he expressed a truth which emphasizes the necessity of man's full acceptance of God's sovereignty and his dependence upon the Creator. It is:

And on nothing doth man offend God or against none is his wrath kindled, save those who confess not his hand in all things and obey not his commandments. (D&C 59:21.)

Is man to acknowledge the earth and the things of the earth for his benefit as coming from the Father in heaven? President Joseph F. Smith taught that man should acknowledge all truth from God. (*Gospel Doctrine*, pp. 5-6.) For one who has felt the divine goodness of God, as did King Benjamin the Nephite, of the Book of Mormon, the answer must be yes. He labored to serve his subjects, for which they expressed gratitude. Using this as an opportunity to show wherein the Nephites were to thank their heavenly king, he said that if men should serve God with all their hearts, they would still be unprofitable servants. (Mosiah 2:20-21.) To acknowledge the Lord as the Creator who has given man life and provided the bounties of the earth for his benefit does not seem to be for many a part of present-day belief and practice.

We should as Latter-day Saints learn a lesson from the Nephites. When the bounteous blessings of the earth are received, we are to be stewards over them, realizing that they are given to us by the Lord. A lesson that we should learn is that pride was the downfall of the Nephite nation. (*Ibid.*, 38-39.)

Obey His Commandments

The Nephites were given specific promises that if they did keep the commandments they would prosper in the land. (1 Nephi 4:14; 2 Nephi 1:20; 3 Nephi 5:22.) This same promise is given to the Saints of the latter-days. (2 Nephi 10:19; D&C 10:57.) Although one acknowledges the hand of the Lord in the blessings of life, he is still not completely acceptable to God unless he keeps his commandments. The keeping of the commandments is based upon faith in the Lord Jesus as the Savior and Redeemer. The strength of one's motivation to keep the commandments is determined, in large measure, by his attitude toward the Savior and the Father. Are we dependent upon them for life, for the opportunity to use earth's resources as stewards? Do we genuinely believe that we should give thanks to the Lord for these blessings? Is there a direct relationship between one's keeping the commandments and one's temporal and spiritual welfare? According to the prophets, as shown above, those who do not show their gratitude by keeping the commandments offend God and against them his wrath is kindled. (D&C 59:21.) The time will come when all men will confess that God is sovereign, and they will acknowledge him as the Giver of life with its opportunities for proving oneself a true disciple.

A Great Truth

One of the outstanding truths given sacred literature concludes Section 59. That all believers might know the pathway to successful living, the Lord revealed:

But learn that he who doeth the works of righteousness shall receive his reward, even peace in this world, and eternal life in the world to come.

I, the Lord, have spoken it, and the Spirit beareth record, Amen. (D&C 59:23-24.)

This truth expresses the most important promise the Father can give to any of his children. The greatest measure of salvation attainable is eternal life. When one thinks of rewards as blessings from the Father, one should remember that the Lord favors those who keep his commandments. (1 Nephi 17:35.)

Specifying "Works of Righteousness"

What are the works of righteousness required of one to receive the rewards mentioned in the text quoted above? (D&C 59:23.) One might summarize the answer by saying, "Keep the commandments!" But we don't al-

ways gain our objective by such a general statement.
When the prophets by inspiration tell the people that they
should keep the commandments, it is assumed that the
Saints are acquainted with the commandments. Not all of
us are sufficient readers of the scriptures and the works
of the living prophets to have specific knowledge of the
Lord's will. It seems necessary, therefore, that we speak
with some detail about the works of righteousness. Perhaps this restatement may serve as a review for many,
and to others it may bring a greater understanding. For
all it should be an opportunity for taking inventory of
one's own status before God. Appropriate to this thought
is the admonition that the member of the Church should
learn his duty in all diligence. (*Ibid.*, 107:99.)

Without considering the following suggestions of
works of righteousness as complete or of their importance in the order in which they are given, let us consider
some significant items.

Seeking Perfection

One of the first steps toward righteousness in the
sight of the Lord is to accept baptism in his kingdom.
(Matt. 3:15; 2 Nephi 31:5-10.) Having taken this step,
an important work of righteousness for the member of
the Church would be to continually have in mind the objective of life, that is, to strive for perfection. (Matt. 5:
48 3 Nephi 12:48.) The genuine desire for perfection suggests that the member will rid himself of all ungodliness.
(Moroni 10:32.) The most successful method of accomplishing this goal is to love the Lord with all one's heart,
might, mind, and strength. (D&C 59:9.) Develop a love
for Christ that "worketh by faith." Such love will en-
gender the same emotion toward all men, but intrinsi-
cally, it must come in the realization of one's dependence
upon Christ for all things, for what he has done in behalf
of the individual through his redeeming sacrifice. (2
Nephi 31:18-20.)

A second great step toward righteousness is to help perfect the lives of the members. In the process of working out one's salvation, interest in others is a necessary part. Instructing others in the gospel contributes to perfecting the life of the teacher as well as of the person taught.

Missionary Work—Righteousness

What other responsibilities come to a member of the Church in his acceptance of Christ? If one answers this question in terms of the purposes of the Church, the missionary program stands out before most. The individual members have the responsibility, a work of righteousness, to teach the gospel. If this is not performed, the salvation of our fellow men is upon our heads. (D&C 88: 81-82.) In addition to the formal missionary program to which one may be called, there are other opportunities for the member. Referring names of nonmember friends to stake and foreign missionaries, as well as discussing the gospel with nonmembers is one way. The keeping of a missionary in the field or contributing with others to the maintenance of a missionary is another way. By teaching the gospel in the auxiliary organizations of the Church, one may have an opportunity to perform missionary service. If the teacher, however, is to make a "convert" his attitude must be that of the missionary. Elder Mark E. Petersen has pointed out the need for conversion of members of the Church, as follows:

Conversion is all-important in the classroom. Each member of the Church must be thoroughly converted. But conversion is dependent on good teaching, and good teaching must include good doctrine. Good doctrine may be found in the official sources of the Church, and from such sources we should obtain it.

Conversion is so important to the whole future life of an individual that all care must be taken to have him converted to correct doctrine and practice and not to mistaken views of some persons, no matter how sincere. (*Your Faith and You*, p. 40.)

Labor for the Dead

The responsibility of the Church to provide the facilities for the members to discharge their own responsibility to their kindred dead is a work of righteousness. This activity is one of the most direct ways to participate in the salvation of others. One may be a "savior" of the living, but he may also become the "savior" of countless dead. This work of righteousness includes the genealogical research as well as temple service, where possible.

Service to Others

Every principle of the gospel lived, every Church activity engaged in, serves as an example for others.

This kind of service cannot be overemphasized, for "when ye are in the service of your fellow beings ye are only in the service of your God." (Mosiah 2:17.) One provides for continued works of righteousness through the Church organization by contributions of material means in the form of tithing, fast offerings, ward or branch budget, building fund, and other assessments. In a practical sense, if there is a work of righteousness that contributes to the service of others, it is the giving of one's own self in terms of such contributions.

Participation in worthy Church projects for the advancement of others, such as Welfare projects by the Priesthood members and the Relief Society members stands high among the works of righteousness. This is the organizational way that a member may, in part, retain a remission of his sins from day to day—by imparting of his substance to the needy. (*Ibid.*, 4:26-27.)

Obey Leadership

With the Church as the divine institution through which the foregoing purposes for man may be realized, it is evident that full confidence is to be shown in the counsel given by those who preside over us. Continuous revelation is received that the member may reach perfection by obedience to the Lord's will through his servants. There is salvation in no other way.

Everyday Religion

The works of righteousness are to be shown forth on all days and not only on the Sabbath. (D&C 59:11.) In the words of President Joseph F. Smith, we learn:

Now I want to tell you that the religion of Christ is not a Sunday religion. It is not a momentary religion; it is a religion that never ends and it requires duties of its devotees on Monday, Tuesday, Wednesday and all of the days of the week just as sincerely, just as strongly as it does on the Sabbath day. (*Gospel Doctrine*, p. 394.)

Rewards of Righteousness

The first reward of righteousness given in our text (D&C 59:23) is peace in this world. Certainly this peace does not mean that war will end before the second coming of Christ. (*Ibid.*, 1:35; 87:6; 97:22-23.) Peace as a reward to the righteous may be enjoyed always regardless of the turmoil, strife, and tribulation in the world. It is a peace of mind, a sense of security, a settled conviction, a joy to the soul which comes only through the Holy Ghost because works of righteousness have and are being performed. (Smith, Joseph F., *Gospel Doctrine*, pp. 126-127; Chapter 38.) Isaiah expressed it as a "quietness and assurance forever." (Isaiah 32:17.)

The second reward of righteousness and the greatest gift to be conferred by the Father upon his children is eternal life. (D&C 14:7.) The quality of living forever is possessed by the eternal spirit of man, but to live forever as a soul, that is, with the spirit and body united, through the resurrection, is known as immortality. (*Ibid.*, 88:14-16.) Immortality is conferred on all of the earth's inhabitants, but eternal life is reserved for those who become like God. (*Ibid.*, 29:43; Moses 1:39.) Eternal life or exaltation is to live in God's presence, to become like him, with the powers of spirit procreation. (*Ibid.*, 132:15-17, 19-22.) What greater blessings may one have than the assurance of well-being in this life and eternal life in the world to come?

Rewards for Sabbath observance are numerous, but these blessings come not because of Sabbath-keeping alone but also by keeping the other commandments. Thus, the Lord declared that his people are to acknowledge his hand in all things and to keep the commandments, and the rewards will be peace of mind in this world and eternal life in the world to come.

Chapter 45

TALENTS AND TESTIMONIES

(Sections 60 and 62)

The time came for the Prophet Joseph Smith and some of the brethren to leave Jackson County, Missouri. They had been there for only two months, but the foundations of Zion had been laid by dedication of the land as a gathering place for the Saints, and, also, as a site for the temple. Other instructions were given concerning the people and their settling in the promised land.

Instructions about Travel

Several elders approached the Prophet to learn what the Lord desired of them. These elders were instructed to return to their homes in the East. (D&C 60:5.) Joseph Smith, Sidney Rigdon, Oliver Cowdery, and the others were to go to St. Louis by water, whence the brethren named were to journey to Cincinnati. The rest were to go "two by two, and preach the word, not in haste, among the congregations of the wicked." (*Ibid.*, 60:8.)

"Congregations of the Wicked"

Section 60 mentions "congregations of the wicked" twice. (*Ibid.*, 60:8, 13.) The definition of the expression was given a few days later. While on the bank of the Missouri River en route to St. Louis, the Prophet and his party were met by some elders on their way to Jackson County. In the revelation dated August 13, 1831, these elders were told to declare the gospel to the inhabitants of the earth, or in other words, to the congregations of the wicked. (*Ibid.*, 62:5.) "Congregations" in these revelations are not necessarily church gatherings only, but they may be. By definition of "wicked," the student of the modern revelations understands that they are the (1) morally corrupt and (2) those who have not accepted the fulness of the gospel. (*Ibid.*, 35:12; 84:49-53.) Consequently, "congregations of the wicked" are those who have not accepted the true gospel. But these people are to have an opportunity to receive the gospel either in this life or in the spirit world. (1 Peter 3:18-20; 4:6; D&C 128:5.)

"I Am Not Well Pleased"

With the elders who had come to Missouri, the Lord was pleased, but those who lacked courage and diligence to open their mouths did not receive the same commendation. (*Ibid.*, 60:1-2.) These elders had failed to exercise their talents in behalf of the Church. Talents are natural endowments or gifts. These talents constitute our ability to make contributions to the welfare of our fellow men, through music, poetry, drama, and other arts, in mechanics, and in the professions. Some people have talent or aptitude in leadership, organization, in speech, and in getting along with people.

Since talents or gifts are natural endowments, then every person possesses them. It is also true that some people are gifted to a greater degree than others.

Source of Talents

Latter-day Saints are blessed with a far better understanding of themselves, their origin, and the answers to many perplexing situations in life than are those who do not believe in the gospel. Accepting the truth that we lived as intelligent beings in a pre-earth life and that we developed ourselves during those eternities, it follows that we had our "natural" endowments in that life. This point of view is interestingly developed in correspondence between Elder Orson F. Whitney of the Council of the

Twelve and President Joseph F. Smith. In the words of
Elder Whitney, we learn:

Spirit Memories.—Writing one day upon the subject of
spirit memories, and the influence exerted upon the affairs of
this life by the awakened recollections of a former experience,
I found myself indulging in the following reflections:

Why are we drawn toward certain persons, and they toward us, independently of any known previous acquaintance? Is
it a fact, or only a fancy, that we and they were mutually acquainted and mutually attracted in some earlier period of our
eternal existence? More than once, after meeting someone whom
I had never met before on earth, I have wondered why his or her
face seemed so familiar. Many times, upon hearing a noble
sentiment expressed, though unable to recall having heard it
until then, I have been thrilled by it, and felt as if I had always
known it. The same is true of music, some strains of which
are like echoes from afar, sounds falling from celestial heights,
notes struck from the vibrant harps of eternity. I do not assert
pre-acquaintance in all such cases, but as one thought suggests
another, these queries arise in the mind.

The Shepherd's Voice.—When it comes to the Gospel, I feel
more positive. Why did the Savior say: "My sheep know my
voice"? Can a sheep know the voice of its shepherd, if it has
never heard that voice before? They who love Truth, and to
whom it appeals most powerfully, were they not its best friends
in a previous state of existence? I think so. I believe that we
knew the Gospel before we came here, and it is this knowledge,
this acquaintance, that gives. to it a familiar sound.

Very much in the same vein, I once wrote to President Joseph
F. Smith—he at the time in Utah, and I on a mission in Europe.
Here is his reply:

President Smith's View

I heartily endorse your sentiments respecting congeniality
of spirits. Our knowledge of persons and things before we came
here, combined with the divinity awakened within our souls
through obedience to the gospel, powerfully affects, in my
opinion, all our likes and dislikes, and guides our preferences in
the course of this life, provided we give careful heed to the
admonitions of the Spirit.

All those salient truths which come home so forcibly to the head and heart seem but the awakening of the memories of the spirit. Can we know anything here that we did not know before we came? Are not the means of knowledge in the first estate equal to those of this? I think that the spirit, before and after this probation, possesses greater facilities, aye, manifold greater, for the acquisition of knowledge, than while manacled and shut up in the prison-house of mortality. I believe that our Savior possessed a foreknowledge of all the vicissitudes through which he would have to pass in the mortal tabernacle. . . .

If Christ knew beforehand, so did we. But in coming here, we forgot all, that our agency might be free indeed, to choose good or evil, that we might merit the reward of our own choice and conduct. But by the power of the Spirit, in the redemption of Christ, through obedience, we often catch a spark from the awakened memories of the immortal soul, which lights up our whole being as with the glory of our former home. (*Saturday Night Thoughts*, pp. 294-296. See also, *Gospel Doctrine*, pp. 12-14.)

Among other things from the foregoing, we understand that talents were a part of ourselves in pre-mortality, that character-traits were formed there, that abilities, such as to believe in or accept truth, are brought to this life. The great truth, allowing for environmental factors here, is that we are very much the same as we were in the pre-existence.

Improve Each Moment

Each stage of our eternal existence—pre-existence, earth-life, and the spirit world—is an opportunity stage to develop talents. We are here, but we are now body and spirit. The talents we bring with us must also become a part of the whole person. Our knowledge of the pre-earth life is presently gone, but the influence of that life is felt. Nevertheless, we are to take what we have and grow and develop. It is the use we make of our natural endowments that will determine whether we shall eventually be called a wise or slothful servant.

Although each person is what he was in pre-existence and, thus, different from others, all have talents to use in the Lord's work. It doesn't matter what we may think of our abilities; we have ability which should be used.

Parable of the Talents

The Savior gave two parables that emphasize the need to develop one's talents. The parable of the Entrusted Talent tells of the man who gave talents (goods) to his servants. To one he gave five talents, to another two, and to the last, only one. The doubling of their talents by the first two brought forth the same commendation.

> . . .Well done, good and faithful servant; thou hast been faithful over a few things, I will make thee ruler over many things: enter thou into the joy of thy Lord. (Matt. 25:23.)

These two servants had used their talents wisely, though they were different. But the servant who received one talent had buried it in the ground, fearful that it might be lost. The reply of the master was ". . . thou wicked and slothful servant. . . ." (*Ibid.*, v. 26; Talmage, James E., *Jesus the Christ*, pp. 580-584.)

Latter-day Saints may think of talents as blessings, since we have an opportunity to develop them in the Church, which provides the means for us to increase all good gifts. When we fail to take the opportunities to assist in the furthering of the Lord's work, we are slothful servants. The Prophet Joseph Smith said:

> . . . Blessings offered, but rejected, are no longer blessings, but become like the talent hid in the earth by the wicked and slothful servant; the proffered good returns to the giver; the blessing is besowed on those who will receive and occupy; for unto him that hath shall be given, and he shall have abundantly,

but unto him that hath not or will not receive, shall be taken away that which he hath, or might have had. (*Teachings of the Prophet Joseph Smith*, p. 257.)

The Gift of the Holy Ghost

Every Latter-day Saint has the privilege of receiving one or more gifts of the Holy Ghost. (D&C 46:11-12; Chapter 32.) He does not know his latent talents nor the gifts of the Spirit; consequently, he must earnestly seek after the best gifts, remembering the purposes for which they are given, that he may not be deceived. If he does this, he will exert his best efforts to advance his own salvation and that of his fellow men. (*Ibid.*, 46:7-10.)

In the case of the elders with whom the Lord was displeased because they feared man and therefore would not use their talents to preach and testify (*Ibid.*, 60:1-2), he said:

And it shall come to pass, if they are not more faithful unto me, it shall be taken away, even that which they have. (*Ibid.*, v. 3.)

One can believe that if these elders had courageously taught the gospel, the Lord would have sustained them as he told Joseph Smith he would uphold him against the Adversary. (*Ibid.*, 3:7-8.)

He who does not develop his talents and gifts is declared by the Lord to be an idler. Those who were to come to Zion in 1831 were told that they should not idle away their time, nor bury their talent. (*Ibid.*, 60:13.)

The Lord Rules

All scripture proclaims the truth that God is sovereign in this world. The revealed fact that God is all-knowing and all-powerful, that he knows the destiny of individuals and nations, makes him supreme. It is this assurance that gives to the believer the faith to put his full trust in the ultimate victory of truth. The Lord rules among the armies of the earth, and the day will come when all men shall know of his power. (*Ibid.*, 60:4.) In 1831, this truth served to bolster the courage of those who were weak in not testifying to the truth; but this is not its only purpose, for one realizes that God shapes the destinies of man and nations. God has promised peace and prosperity to those who serve him diligently, but wrath and indignation upon those people who transgress his laws. (*Ibid.*, 59:23; 39:16-18.)

The power of the Lord will be known when his fury is unleashed upon the unrepentant. (*Ibid.*, 29:17-20; 88:88-92.) When the last great conflict is ended at the close of the millennium, the Lord's power will be fully demonstrated. (*Ibid.*, 43:22-30; 88:111-116.) At the time Christ declares his work finished, his jewels, the people of God, will have been gathered together for time and eternity. (*Ibid.*, 60:4; 88:106.)

Shake Dust Off Feet

The testimony of the Spirit is powerful. Its consequences are always expressed with power. A testimony rejected leads eventually, unless repented of, to loss of great blessings. For the first time in The Doctrine and Covenants we learn about an ancient practice of testimony and its attendant power. The law is given in Section 60:15 as shaking the dust off one's feet against those who do not accept the missionary. This ceremony is to be performed in secret. The washing of the feet is a testimony against the person in the day of judgment. (*Ibid.*, 60:15; 1:8-10.) Thus the missionary has power to seal up the rebellious until the time of wrath. This was true in the Old Testament period as well as in the time of Jesus and the apostles. (Nehemiah 5:13; Matt. 10:14;

Luke 10:10-11; Acts 13:51; 18:6.) The testimony of warning is a part of the plan in this dispensation. (D&C 84:87-95; 75:20-21; 99:4.)

When should this ceremony be performed? The answer must be given at the time and according to the circumstances. The missionary is to be guided by love and patience in all things. It would seem that the elder would follow the counsel given to Hyrum Smith, that he should be directed by the Spirit in all things. (*Ibid.*, 11:12.) In the final analysis, the gospel is one of love, but there may be conditions such as persecution or violence toward the elder, that would give rise to the use of the ceremony, if directed by the Spirit.

Section 62—Testimony

It was from Section 62 that we learned the meaning of "congregations of the wicked." The Lord reminds his people that his knowledge includes an understanding of man's weaknesses and also that he knows the way that man may be rescued from falling into temptation. (*Ibid.*, 62:1.) Concerning the few elders on their way to Zion in 1831, he would have them know that they were blessed in bearing their testimonies to the world. But wherein were they blessed?

Nevertheless, ye are blessed, for the testimony which ye have borne is recorded in heaven for the angels to look upon; and they rejoice over you, and your sins are forgiven you. (*Ibid.*, v. 3.)

This passage points up the importance of being in the service of one's fellow men. In this dispensation the Lord has emphasized the need for missionary work, a service of love for fellow man. (*Ibid.*, 15:6.) When a person speaks by the power of the Holy Ghost, that Spirit testifies to the truth spoken. (2 Nephi 33:1.) When such testimonies are uttered they are recorded in the heavens.

Why should angels rejoice in this? Holy beings are concerned with the salvation of men. The testimony is a means to an end—the salvation of the testator and the convincing of others of God's truth. "Happy is the man, indeed, who can receive this soul-satisfying testimony, and be at rest, and seek no other road to peace than the doctrine of Jesus Christ." (Joseph F. Smith, *Gospel Doctrine*, p. 158.)

Service to God and Man

When one is using his talents for the salvation of men, he is serving God and advancing his own salvation. (Mosiah 2:17.) The Lord admonishes his Saints to develop their talents and use the gifts he has bestowed upon them by his Spirit. Viewed from the perspective of man's eternal nature, there is no more important work in life than to work for one's salvation and that of his fellow beings. The greatest influence that the Latter-day Saint can exert upon others is to be a living testimony of God's truth as revealed through the Prophet Joseph Smith.

In concluding this revelation the Lord reminds his servants that,

... I, the Lord, promise the faithful and cannot lie. ...
Behold, the kingdom is yours. And behold, and lo, I am with the faithful always. Even so. Amen. (D&C 62:6, 9.)

Chapter 46

THE WATERS AND THE LAND

(Section 61)

As pointed out in the last chapter, the Prophet Joseph Smith and a party of elders left Independence landing for St. Louis by canoe. In the Prophet's own words, we read:

... In company with ten Elders, I left Independence landing for Kirtland . . . . at McIlwaine's Bend, Brother Phelps, in open vision by daylight, saw the destroyer in his most horrible power, ride upon the face of the waters; others heard the noise, but saw not the vision.

The next morning after prayer, I received the following: [D&C Section 61.] (*DHC* I:202-203.)

It appears that the elders in the party were greatly humbled because of the dangerous water and because of the great noise and the horrible power of the adversary on the waters, as shown in vision to Brother W. W. Phelps. This is suggested in the opening verses of Section 61, where the Lord declares that their sins are forgiven. It continues to make known the reason for the blessing, as follows:

... for I, the Lord forgive sins, and am merciful unto those who confess their sins with humble hearts. (D&C 61:2.)

Bear Record by Testimony

These elders were permitted to travel upon the waters that they might bear record of their experiences. Some of the elders traveling by water needed to preach to the people on both sides of the river who were perishing in unbelief. (*Ibid.*, 61:3-4.)

What was there in this experience about which they could bear testimony? One important fact was the existence of Satan, the destroyer. His power on the waters were known to these brethren. They could also be thankful that the Lord was all-powerful for the benefit of the faithful. (*Ibid.*, 61:5-6.)

An outstanding example of protection to the faithful is that of Helaman's two thousand sons. (Alma 53: 10-23; 56:41-57.) True faith in God will bring preservation to a people. (Alma 44:4.)

President Wilford Woodruff, who was appointed by President Brigham Young to gather Saints living in New England and Canada, said:

. .. I did as he told me. It took me two years to gather up everybody, and I brought up the rear with a company. When I got into Pittsburg with this company it was dusk, and I saw a steamer just preparing to go out. I walked right up to the captain and asked him if he was ready to go out. He said he was. "How many passengers have you?" "Two hundred and fifty." "Can you take another hundred?" "I can." "Then," said I. "I would like to go aboard with you." The words were hardly out of my mouth when the Holy Ghost said to me, "Don't you nor your company go aboard that steamer." That was enough; I had learned the voice of the Spirit. I turned and told the captain that I had made up my mind not to go at present. That steamer started out. It was a dark night, and before the steamer had gone far she took fire, and all on board was lost. We should probably have shared the same fate, had it not been for that monitor within me. (*The Deseret Weekly*, Vol. 53, No. 21, Nov. 7, 1896, cf. *Discourses of Wilford Woodruff*, p. 295.)

The Lord Reasons

The Lord said he would reason with these elders as he had done with men in days of old. (D&C 61:13.)

A modern revelation showing forth the reasoning of the Lord with his servants is Section 50, vs. 10 through 24. (Chapter 35.)

Why did the Lord give this revelation; was it for

these few elders only? It is apparent from the following verses that the counsel concerning the waters was for all Saints in the latter days:

Behold, I the Lord, in the beginning blessed the waters; but in the last days, by the mouth of my servant John, I cursed the waters.

Wherefore, the days will come that no flesh shall be safe upon the waters.

And it shall be said in days to come that none is able to go up to the land of Zion upon the waters, but he that is upright in heart: (D&C 61:14-16.)

In the beginning the Lord saw that his creations were good. (Gen. 1:10.) The waters were blessed for the use of man. But in the last days the waters are cursed. It was John the Revelator who saw the judgment of God poured out upon the world in the last days. Among the vials of wrath, the second angel poured his vial upon the sea and every living soul died in the sea. With the release of the contents of the vial upon the rivers carried by the next angel, they became blood. (Rev. 16:3-4.)

As a part of the Plan conceived in the heavens before the world was formed, men were to learn from the prophets that judgments or calamities would visit the earth if the laws of God were not observed. Amos announced the truth that the Lord would do nothing but what he would reveal it to his prophets first. (Amos 3:7.) The Lord's objective is to save and not to destroy or curse. As pointed out in Proverbs, the Lord's object is to bless, even in chastisement. (Proverbs 3:11-12.)

Waters Cursed

Attention is called to verse 5 of Section 61 in which the brethren in Joseph Smith's party were informed that many destructions would occur on the Missouri and Mississippi rivers. It is virtually impossible to give specific data regarding the destruction on these two rivers and their tributaries since the time that this revelation was given. That the number of lives lost has been great and the property damage enormous is known. During his lifetime, the Prophet Joseph Smith mentioned great losses in lives and property damage. (*Doctrine and Covenants Commentary*, pp. 362-363.)

An informative article by Elder B. H. Roberts entitled "Joseph Smith's Prediction of Destruction upon the Waters; More Especially of the Inland Waters of North America and of Western Missouri," gives data on this subject up to 1903. (*A Comprehensive History of The Church of Jesus Christ of Latter-day Saints*, Vol. 1, pp. 275-278.)

Destructions upon the Waters

Not only were the waters of the Missouri and Mississippi cursed in the last days, but also other waters. (D&C 61:4-5.)

It states that the days would come when no flesh would be safe upon the waters except the upright in heart. (*Ibid.*, vs. 15-16.) One need only think of the great sea disaster caused by striking icebergs, collisions, burnings, tossing on rocks or other objects during peace times, to bring forcefully to one's mind destruction upon the waters. The tremendous property damage and loss of life during the last two World Wars are staggering. (*Doctrine and Covenants Commentary*, p. 365.)

A Contrast and the Lord's Assurance

In the last days the waters are cursed. Nevertheless, there would be traffic on the waters. The elders for whom Section 61 was given specifically, were to travel by water, after a little while, or by land. Other brethren were, however, to be warned about the Missouri and Mississippi rivers.

And now I give unto you a commandment that what I say unto one I say unto all, that you shall forewarn your brethren concerning these waters, that they come not in journeying upon them, lest their faith fail and they are caught in snares;

I, the Lord, have decreed, and the destroyer rideth upon the face thereof; and I revoke not the decree. (D&C 61:18-19.)

The Lord, however, gave assurance to his Saints that they would not perish by the waters, although the day would come that only the upright in heart would come to Zion by water.

Nevertheless, all flesh is in mine hand, and he that is faithful among you shall not perish by the waters. . .

Wherefore, the days will come that no flesh shall be safe upon the waters.

And it shall be said in days to come that none is able to go up to the land of Zion upon the waters, but he that is upright in heart. (*Ibid.*, 61:6, 15-16.)

Emigration to Zion in Earlier Days

To come to Zion was the desire of the Saints almost as soon as the gospel was preached in Great Britain, the first European mission to be opened. This movement of the members to assist in the building of settlements and temples in selected areas of the Western United States was encouraged by providing funds for the converts from the Emigration Fund.

The success of this emigration movement under the direction of the General Authorities of the Church is history. The pioneer period was ended with the coming of the railroad to Utah in 1869. In this same year the emigrant voyages by sailing vessels ceased, as the steamship took the place of the slower vessel. It would take from five to six weeks by sailing vessel from Europe. An interesting notable description on one of these "packet" ships was given by the noted English author Charles Dickens, who went on board the Mormon emigrant ship to testify against the Saints but came off the ship praising the character of them.

"Mr. Uncommercial" in the following is Charles Dickens:

Behold me on my way to an Emigrant Ship, on a hot morning early in June. . .

I go aboard my Emigrant ship . . . But nobody is in an ill-temper, nobody is the worse for drink, nobody swears an oath or uses a coarse word, nobody appears depressed, nobody is weeping, and down upon the deck in every corner where it is possible to find a few square feet to kneel, crouch, or lie in every unsuitable attitude for writing, are writing letters.

Now, I have been in emigrant ships before this day in June. And these people are so strikingly different from all other people in like circumstances whom I have never seen, that I wonder a-loud, "What would a stranger suppose these emigrants to be!"

The vigilant bright face of the weather-browned captain of the Amazon is at my shoulder, and he says, "What, indeed! The most of these came aboard yesterday evening. They came from various parts of England in small parties that had never seen one another before. Yet they had not been a couple of hours on board, when they established their own police, made their own regulations, and set their own watches at all the hatchways. Before nine o'clock, the ship was as orderly and as quiet as a man-of-war! . . .

"A stranger would be puzzled to guess the right name of these people, Mr. Uncommercial," says the captain.

"Indeed he would."

"If you hadn't known, could you ever have supposed—?"

"How could I!" I should have said they were in their degree the pick and flower of England."

"So should I," says the captain.

"How many are they?"

"Eight hundred in round numbers." . . . Eight hundred Mormons.

I afterwards learned that a Dispatch was sent home by the captain before he struck out into the wide Atlantic, highly extolling the behavior of these Emigrants, and the perfect order and propriety of all their social arrangements. . . . But I went on board their ship to bear testimony against them if they deserved it, as I fully believed they would; to my great astonishment they did not deserve it; and my predispositions and tendencies must not affect me as an honest witness. I went over the Amazon's side, feeling it impossible to deny that, so far, some remarkable influence had produced a remarkable result, which better known influences have often missed. (Dickens, Charles: *The Uncommercial Traveller*, pp. 200-211.)

The writer's maternal grandparents were among the more than 800 Saints described by Charles Dickens on the vessel *"Amazon"* that left London, England, on June 4, 1863. It is traditional in the family that the ship was saved from destruction by heavy storms through the prayers of the ship's passengers.

Among the many accounts of this kind, the following one concerning Harrison Burgess, a missionary to England in 1850, indicates fulfillment of the Lord's promise that they who traveled to Zion in the last days would not perish by the water:

We sailed along quite comfortably until the twenty-sixth of the month (January, 1850) when a terrible storm arose. About two o'clock in the afternoon the sea began to swell and show its power, and the vessel lay first on one side and then on the other. Water came in upon us on both sides of our ship. We lost our sails and yard-arms, and the chains in the rigging on the ship broke. In the evening, when everything looked most dismal, our president called together his counselors and all joined in prayer to the Lord to cause the winds to cease. Scarcely had the brethren ceased their supplications when there was a calm, so sudden in fact that the captain and the officers of the ship were greatly surprised, and they came and inquired of us how it was that we felt so happy and gay amid the great danger through which we had just passed. They could not realize that the Lord removed all fear from the hearts of his faithful Saints when they were endeavoring to do their duty. (*Labors in the Vineyard*, Twelfth Book of the Faith-Promoting Series, pp. 72-73.)

When the time comes for the Saints to gather to Zion, the Lord's power will be manifest in their behalf.

Land Blessed

In the beginning the land was cursed (Gen. 3:17), but in the last days it is blessed for the use of the Saints. (D&C 61:17.) The complete fulfillment of this prophecy is reserved for the millennium when the earth will be renewed and receive its condition of terrestrialization and become as a beautiful garden. Elder George A. Smith made this observation concerning the way the Lord blessed the land of Utah for his Saints:

We came to this land [Utah] because it was so desert, desolate and God-forsaken that no mortal upon earth ever would covet it; but, as Colonel Fremont reported that at the mouth of the Bear River, in the early part of August, his thermometer stood at 29 degrees Fahrenheit, three degrees below the freezing-point, which would kill grain, fruit, or vegetables, our enemies said, "You Mormons may go there and welcome," chuckling to each other over what seemed to them our annihilation. . . . The newspapers recorded the joy, and gratification felt at the utter end of "Mormonism.". . . Notwithstanding, however, the many drawbacks and difficulties encountered in the shape of drought, crickets, grasshoppers, and the cold, sterile climate, the Spirit of the Lord was hovering over the Great Basin . . . and the climate became genial and soft. (*Doctrine and Covenants Commentary*, p. 359.)

Prophetic Utterance

Verses 24 through 29 of Section 61 give instructions concerning the course the Saints were to travel en route to Zion. In the main they were to journey by land and not by these waters, the Missouri and Mississippi rivers. By the spirit of revelation they were to be led as the children of Israel were led anciently by Moses. (D&C 8:2-3.)

Section 61 Concluded

The Lord counseled his servants in their traveling to Cincinnati, Ohio, and beginning in Cincinnati, to be diligent in testimony. (*Ibid.*, 61:30-35.) In concluding the revelation, encouragement is given to these brethren by reminding them that they are little children who should be cheerful, for the Lord is with them. He has not forsaken them. (*Ibid.*, vs. 36-37.) Finally, there comes this admonition, applicable to all Saints.

Gird up your loins and be watchful and be sober, looking forth for the coming of the Son of Man, for he cometh in an hour you think not.

Pray always that you enter not into temptation, that you may abide the day of his coming, whether in life or in death. Even so, Amen. (*Ibid.*, vs. 38-39.)

"Gird up your loins . . ." is a common statement among Latter-day Saints. It means "Be Prepared." For what? The coming of the Lord. What should be one means of preparation? Praying that one will have the strength and courage to resist temptation. If so, the Saints will surely abide the day of Jesus' coming, whether in death or in life.

Chapter 47

THE SIGN SEEKER

(Section 63:1-21)

The Prophet took leave of Missouri where he had received new revelation dealing with the founding of Zion, the city of God, and numerous matters relating to the gathering of the Saints. Arriving in Kirtland the Prophet wrote:

> In these infant days of the Church, there was a great anxiety to obtain the word of the Lord upon every subject that in any way concerned our salvation; and as the land of Zion was now the most important temporal object in view, I enquired of the Lord for further information upon the gathering of the Saints, and the purchase of the land, and other matters, and received the following. [Section 63.] (*DHC* 1:207.)

Wickedness and Rebellion

Section 63 begins with the call of the Saints to listen, to open their hearts to a revelation of the Lord's word. (D&C 63:1.) All men should understand that God is angry with the wicked. Some members of the Church may be classed as stiffnecked (stubborn) and unbelieving as well as those who have not made covenant with the Savior.

The Lord's displeasure is also shown toward the rebellious. Rebellion against God's law makes a person wicked. Such people wilfully defy God after knowing his will toward them. This was true of Lucifer and the third part of the hosts of heaven. (*Ibid.*, 29:36-37.) King Benjamin in The Book of Mormon taught that rebellion against teachings received brought a withdrawal of the Spirit. (Mosiah 2:36-38.) The rebellious are condemned because of their having accepted gospel principles and then having disobeyed them. Greater responsibilities bring greater blessings, but, if not carried out, they bring greater condemnations. (D&C 1:2-3; 82:3.) The degree of condemnation is dependent upon the nature of the disobedience and the light enjoyed by the member.

The Lord's Power

God's power is understood when men realize that he controls life and is able to cast men into hell. The wicked and rebellious, knowing that they have flaunted their Maker, are fearful that death may overtake them. The ever-present question is, "What will be my situation after death?" God can do all things even to destroying the world, as well as "to cast the soul down to hell." (*Ibid.*, 63:3-4.)

The unrepentant will not escape the Lord's wrath:

Behold, I, the Lord, utter my voice, and it shall be obeyed.

Wherefore, verily I say, let the wicked take heed, and let the rebellious fear and tremble; and let the unbelieving hold their lips, for the day of wrath shall come upon them as a whirlwind, and all flesh shall know that I am God. (*Ibid.*, 63:5-6.)

In like manner the revelations describe the condition of those who do not hearken to the Lord's message. (*Ibid.*, 84:95-102; 133:71-73.) On the other hand, the Prophet Joseph Smith says that blessings of a celestial nature await those who obey the Lord's voice:

...God has in reserve a time, or period appointed in His own bosom, when He will bring all His subjects, who have obeyed His voice and kept His commandments, into His celestial rest. This rest is of such perfection and glory, that man has need of a preparation before he can, according to the laws of that kingdom, enter it and enjoy its blessings. This being the fact, God has given certain laws to the human family, which, if observed, are sufficient to prepare them to inherit His rest. (*Teachings of the Prophet Joseph Smith*, p. 54.)

Signs Shall Be Seen

As one evidence of the last days, signs are to be seen. Many types of natural phenomena are mentioned in scriptures. The ones generally known are those which are to appear in the heavens, such as the sun darkening and the moon turning to blood. (D&C 29:14; 34:9; 45:42; 88:87.) Other ocular signs will be observed. (*Ibid.*, 29:14; Pearl of Great Price, Moses 7:61.) But these are not the only signs predicted for these times. There are those who desire to have some visual demonstration, such as a miracle, to evidence the existence of God, of the divinity of his Church, of the divine calling of the Prophet Joseph Smith, and the truth of the principles of the gospel.

One desire for some "tangible" evidence of the work of the Lord in our times is the belief that the gold plates of The Book of Mormon should be on display for those who want to "know" that Joseph Smith had plates of ancient origin. These plates, if put on exhibit, would not give evidence of the truth of The Book of Mormon to those who would not accept that scripture on faith or seek for the testimony of the Spirit. Great faith would still be required to believe that these particular plates were of ancient origin or that the characters were what the Prophet claimed them to be. Disputations would probably not cease concerning these claims. Men are not converted to the gospel by such visual demonstrations. The Lord does not give man such demonstrable evidence to convert him. Faith continues as the principle to test man's allegiance to God and the only way that the rich blessings may be enjoyed. (Hebrews 11:1.) The testimony of the witnesses to The Book of Mormon condemns those who reject that testimony. (D&C 5:10-20.)

The Lord has given evidences or signs that men may understand his purposes, but these may not be so apparent to the person who is not looking for these evidences. The missionary calls signs to the attention of his hearer, such as evidence that these are the days when men are called to repentance for the last time. (*Ibid.*, 33:2-3; 39:17; 43:28; 90:2.) What are some of these signs? Among several which might be mentioned, these three stand out significantly: (1) the coming forth of The Book of Mormon. As the Old Testament prophets predicted many details about this volume, they indicated that men should know of God's work in the last days by the fulfillment of such prophecies. (Isaiah, Chapter 29; Ezek. 37:16-20.) Associated with this first sign to give evidence of The Book of Mormon is the second one; (2) the gathering of Israel, particularly the Jewish portion. (Isaiah 29:17-19, 22-23; Ezek. 37:21-28.) One of the remarkable historical events of our times is the return of the Lord's ancient covenant people, Judah, to the land of their inheritance. The establishment of this one nation, Israel, in Palestine, in 1948, serves to remind all people that with the return of Judah to the holy land, God is remembering his people as prophesied. (Jeremiah 31:31, 33; 2 Nephi 20:29-31.) He is remembering not only Judah, but others of the tribes of Israel, especially Joseph— the Indians, and also the Latter-day Saints who have been gathered from the nations. (1 Nephi 19:13-16.) (3) The third sign—a definite sign of the last days—is that of the wars, rumors of war and preparations for, together with disease, earthquakes, famines, floods, and other natural calamities that are so evident on the earth today. (Chapter 30) These three signs are some of the Lord's ways of letting man know that now is the time to repent, and that these signs are to help in man's conversion to the fulness of the gospel.

Sign Seekers in the Church

When Section 63 was received in August 1831, there were members who had come into the Church seeking signs, as there are probably some today who expect some miracle to convince them further of the truth. Concerning these members the Lord gave this message:

> And he that seeketh signs shall see signs, but not unto salvation.
> Verily, I say unto you, there are those among you who seek signs, and there have been such even from the beginning;
> But, behold, faith cometh not by signs, but signs follow those that believe.
> Yea, signs come by faith, not by the will of men, nor as they please, but by the will of God.
> Yea, signs come by faith, unto mighty works, for without faith no man pleaseth God; and with whom God is angry he is not well pleased; wherefore, unto such he showeth no signs, only in wrath unto their condemnation.
> Wherefore, I, the Lord, am not pleased with those among you who have sought after signs and wonders for faith, and not for the good of men unto my glory.

The Lord is not pleased with those who seek signs to convince them of the truth. Signs shall follow, but not always the kind of sign desired. They may be in the form of judgments because of wickedness. Those who sought for a sign in the time of Christ were classified as an evil and adulterous generation. (Matt. 12:38-39.) Sign-seekers show a lack of faith in God and, therefore, the desired sign is not forthcoming to their salvation.

Sign-Seekers, Some Examples

Some notable examples of sign-seekers are found in The Book of Mormon. Lacking in faith, they sought some visual demonstration of God's power as a convincing sign. Several centuries before Jesus' birth a Nephite named Sherem denied that there would be a Christ as Jacob, son of Lehi, and other prophets had declared. Like many modern doubters, including men of religious profession, it was claimed that "no man knoweth of such things; for he cannot tell of things to come." (Jacob 7:7.) Jacob bore a solemn witness that prophecy from a prophet of God is true and that Christ would come to the earth, but Sherem demanded a sign. (*Ibid.*, 7:11-13; read also 14-21.)

Another example of one who denied prophecy and the coming of Christ was Korihor. The prophet replied to his request for a sign that there is a God as follows:

> Thou hast had signs enough; will ye tempt your God? Will ye say, Show unto me a sign, when ye have the testimony of all these thy brethren, and also all the holy prophets? The scriptures are laid before thee, yea, and all things denote there is a God; yea, even the earth, and all things that are upon the face of it, yea, and its motion, yea, and also all the planets which move in their regular form do witness that there is a Supreme Creator. (Alma 30:44.)

An Important Principle

This reply, with other experiences, emphasizes an important principle based upon the fact that God is no respecter of persons and that all men must acknowledge him. The Lord gives the same signs to all men, but if they receive a sign without faith, it will be to condemnation.

For the faithful member of the Church there may be many "signs" received, if asked in humility and for the person's good unto the glory of God. (1 John 3:22.) Signs come by faith which brings forth righteous deeds. Men may develop faith by greater and continued acts of righteousness.

The signs received by the humble Saint are blessings received from the Holy Ghost. (D&C 46; Chapter 32.) These blessings are intended principally to prevent the member from being deceived, although they may serve to strengthen faith and bless with the power of God.

The miracle as an instrument of conversion was never intended in the gospel. It has become axiomatic with Latter-day Saints that the person converted by the miracle may require a miracle to keep him in the Church.

President Brigham Young declared:

... When the voice of the Good Shepherd is heard, the honest in heart believe and receive it. It is good to taste with the inward taste, to see with the inward eyes, and to enjoy with the sensations of the ever-living spirit. No person, unless he is an adulterer, a fornicator, covetous, or an idolator, will ever require a miracle; in other words, no good, honest person ever will. (*Journal of Discourses* 8:42.)

Sins Revealed

When the sign or miracle is granted to the faithful member of the Church for his personal benefit and the glory of God, the sign attests to the fact that the spiritual gifts are a part of the gospel. Because of the darkness of mind and sin, some members desire evidence of God's existence of the truth of the Church by a sign. In 1831 there were members who felt this same way. Commandments of moral purity had been given, but some had turned away from them. (D&C 63:13.) Among these covenant breakers there were adulterers and adultresses, a number of whom had turned away from the faith, but there were others who had not apostatized but in time they would be known. (*Ibid.*, v. 14.) The thought suggested in this and the succeeding verse (verse 15) should be understood by those who are tempted to sin or who have sinned and remain unrepentant. It is that this person shall be known and labeled in the eyes of the people.

There follows the significant fact stated in another revelation, that the thought precedes the deed of immorality. (*Ibid.*, 42:23.) The consequences of immoral thoughts for the Church member are loss of the spirit, denial of the faith, and the resulting fear because of the consequences in time and eternity. (*Ibid.*, 63:16; Chapter 27.)

Condemnation of the Sinner

President Joseph F. Smith considered that of all principles of the gospel which emphasized the attributes of justice in Deity is the fact that all men will be rewarded for their works, whether they be good or evil. (*Gospel Doctrine*, p. 69.)

In accordance with this truth, the Lord has revealed much concerning the final state of the unrepentant sinner. Language similar to what was later revealed concerning the salvation offered to those who wilfully sin with knowledge, is given in this revelation. Belief in false teachings or unbelief in the doctrines as restored to the Church in this dispensation, constitutes in the member a form of falsehood or misrepresentation of belief. The member of the Church is committed by covenant to believe the doctrine and to live the principles that the Lord has revealed. The condemnation for those who love and make a lie, and the immoral, is to receive the telestial kingdom. (D&C 63:17-18; 76:98-107.) They suffer the vengeance of eternal fire to receive the torment of conscience, which is like an unquenchable fire. (Mosiah 2:37-38.) The mental torment of those who receive the lake of fire and brimstone is described by the Prophet Joseph Smith in this way:

A man is his own tormentor and his own condemner. Hence the saying, They shall go into the lake that burns with fire and brimstone. The torment of disappointment in the mind of man is as exquisite as a lake with fire and brimstone. I say, so is the torment of man. (*DHC* VI:314.)

Because there were immoral members in the Church, some having left but others to be ferreted out if they did not repent, the membership was not justified in allowing these conditions to exist. (D&C 63:19.) The Lord has prescribed excommunication of these persons unless they speedily repent. (*Ibid.*, 42:24-26, 80-81, 87.)

The Faithful Are Justified

Those, however, who endure in faith by keeping the commandments are promised great blessings, even beyond their present comprehension.

Nevertheless, he that endureth in faith and doeth my will, the same shall overcome, and shall receive an inheritance upon the earth when the day of transfiguration shall come. (*Ibid.*, 63:20.)

Familiar to students of the scriptures is the meaning of "overcome." As used in the above verse, the person of faith becomes free of the bondage of sin by overcoming the sinful habit or impediment to his eternal progression. (Romans 6:18; 2 Peter 2:19.) They shall overcome all things and receive an exaltation in the Father's kingdom. (Rev. 21:7; D&C 84:38.)

The Day of Transfiguration

For those who have overcome through faith, an inheritance upon the earth is promised. (Matt. 5:5.) For this intent was the earth created. (D&C 88:17-20.) But before the earth is celestialized as the home of celestial beings, which is its final transfiguration, the Lord has said that the earth shall receive a regeneration (Matt. 19:28), for it will be restored to its former condition as a paradise. The Tenth Article of Faith mentions that the "earth will be renewed and receive its paradisiacal glory." Thus the earth will be restored to its former state when it is transformed to the condition before it fell to its present telestial state.

Those who endure in faith and do the will of the Lord have the promise of an inheritance on Earth after its "transfiguration." The earth is to pass through fire and become "sanctified and immortal"; it will be made like unto crystal, and be a urim and thummim, "whereby all things pertaining to an inferior kingdom will be manifest to those who dwell on it." (Sec. 130:9.) The scriptures teach us that there will be a restitution of all things (Matt. 17:11; Acts 3:21); a "regeneration" (Matt. 19:28), which begins with the millennium and will be completed when the Earth is re-born and sanctified, fit for

an abode of celestial bodies. Then those who are faithful
will have an inheritance on the glorified Earth. "Blessed
are the meek; for they shall inherit the Earth." [Matt.
5:5.] (*Doctrine and Covenants Commentary*, p. 377.)

Chapter 48

GIVE HEED TO WARNINGS AND TRIFLE NOT WITH SACRED THINGS

(Section 63:22-66)

The center place for the city of Zion (Jackson County, Missouri) had been designated by revelation. Members of the Church desired to know what they should do in relationship to it; therefore the Lord made known his purposes to his Saints. They were to gather to that place if they desired to do the will of the Lord. As stated in verses 22 and 23 of Section 63, they were not to consider this a commandment. The Lord gives revelation for the benefit of all who will obey, but he knows that some members, if commanded in all things, will bring condemnation on themselves by disobedience. Consequently, in this revelation, he leaves it up to the individual to obey his will or not to obey. Those who love the Lord will obey his will as if it were a commandment. (Matt. 7:21; D&C 84:44-45; *Doctrine and Covenants Commentary*, p. 378.)

Mysteries as Blessings

Latter-day Saints know that to meddle in the things which have not been revealed brings disappointment and sometimes loss of faith in fundamental beliefs. Speculation does not contribute to salvation. Rationalization of the scriptures may destroy faith. There are mysteries of the kingdom which may be known by all who seek in faith. (Alma 12:9-11.) These revealed truths further one's salvation, for they are essential to soul-growth. As one learns the truth contained in the revelations, it becomes "a well of living water, springing up unto everlasting life." (D&C 63:23; John 4:10-14.) It should be clear that individuals differ in their knowledge of gospel truths and the application of them in their lives. There is ample opportunity for the Latter-day Saint to learn the mysteries revealed in the scriptures.

Concerning the gathering to the land of Zion, the Saints were to learn this mystery: do not undertake the journey in haste, lest pestilence follow. (D&C 63:24.) Sickness could result by taking a long journey without proper food and suitable clothing, a lesson learned later by the American army in the Spanish-American War. (*Doctrine and Covenants Commentary*, p. 379.)

Render unto Caesar

During the ministry of Christ there came some who sought to trap him by asking him whether one should pay tribute to Caesar. His reply then and also in this dispensation stresses the necessity for the Saint to follow the laws of the land. "Render unto Caesar the things which are Caesar's." (Matt. 22:15-22; D&C 63:26; 58:21-32.) This truth is emphasized when one understands that Jesus is the Creator of the earth, yet he respects the laws of the land. The Saints who were to go to Zion were to follow legal practices in purchasing the land, although it was to be their inheritance. Only by this means would they have an opportunity to live in peace with their neighbors. Enough opposition would come to the Saints from Satan stirring up the hearts of their enemies, without their tempting them to shed blood. (*Ibid.*, 63:25-28.) When the Lord commanded the Saints to purchase the lands and there should be no shedding of blood, he was saying what had been said of old—"Thou shalt not kill." (Exodus 20:13.) In fact, what follows in the revelation is a warning to comply with the commandment to purchase the land promptly, or else they would be scourged from place to place. (D&C 63:29-31.) Elder B. H. Roberts wrote the following on this prophecy:

. . . And so the event turned out. The saints failed to respond with becoming promptness to the commandment to purchase the land of Zion; and all that was predicted in the revelation befell them. The passage then was a warning to the saints, not a threat directed at the old settlers of Jackson county; and if blood was to be shed, clearly it was to be the blood of the saints rather than that of their enemies. (*A Comprehensive History of The Church of Jesus Christ of Latter-day Saints*, 1:264.)

Wars Decreed

Immediately following this prediction of distress among the Saints because of negligence in following counsel, the Lord declares that the wicked in the world shall slay the wicked, for they lose his spirit by their unrighteousness. (D&C 63:32-33.) Destruction follows when that spirit is withdrawn from men. (2 Nephi 26:11; *Doctrine and Covenants Commentary*, p. 380.) Fear will come upon all men in that day because men will be fighting amongst themselves and the Saints will hardly escape. (D&C 63:34-35; cf, 1:34-36.) The Saints in 1831 and later, during the time of the Prophet Joseph Smith, were counseled to come to the land of Zion that they might not be engulfed in these tribulations. (*Doctrine and Covenants Commentary*, p. 380.) Those who should come to Zion were to be the faithful, serving God in righteousness and faith. It was the solemn duty of the Saints to declare a warning voice to the world that judgment awaited the unrepentant, and the only escape would be through following the will of the Lord. (D&C 63:36-37.) That the Saints would "hardly escape" was commented upon by the Prophet on September 29, 1839, as follows:

. . . Explained concerning the coming of the Son of Man; also, that it is a false idea that the Saints will escape all the judgments, whilst the wicked suffer; for all flesh is subject to suffer, and "the righteous shall hardly escape"; still many of the Saints will escape, for the just shall live by faith; yet many of the righteous shall fall a prey to disease, to pestilence, etc., by reason of the weakness of the flesh, and yet be saved in the Kingdom of

God. So that it is an unhallowed principle to say that such and such have transgressed because they have been preyed upon by disease or death, for all flesh is subject to death; and the Savior has said, "Judge not, lest ye be judged." (*DHC* IV:11.)

Instructions to Kirtland Saints

From verses 38 to 47 in Section 63, instructions are given to members of the Church in Kirtland, Ohio. Specific directions are given that the Titus Billings farm should be disposed of and some were to go to Zion. (vs. 37-39.) The money thus received was to be used for the purchase of land in Missouri. (v. 40.) Newel K. Whitney was to continue the operation of his store, and funds from this source were to be sent also. (vs. 41-44.) He was to take charge of these operations and also to act as an agent of the Church, since some members were not to go to Zion at this time. (vs. 45-46.) The counsel given in this revelation suggests a pattern for the future when the city of the New Jerusalem will be built. Only those who are worthy and receive a call to assemble in that area will have the privilege of participating actively in that endeavor. Only he who is faithful overcomes the world. Constancy in the work of the Lord brings the blessings of having overcome. (v. 47.)

"Blessed Are the Dead That Die in the Lord"

The Latter-day Saint's concept of death is stated in these words:

He that sendeth up treasures unto the land of Zion shall receive an inheritance in this world, and his works shall follow him, and also a reward in the world to come.

Yea, and blessed are the dead that die in the Lord, from henceforth, when the Lord shall come, and old things shall pass away, and all things become new, they shall rise from the dead and shall not die after, and shall receive an inheritance before the Lord, in the holy city. (D&C 63:48-49.)

Several important facts concerning the faithful dead are found in these verses: (1) Righteous works follow the faithful in building a mansion of glory. (2) The dead that die in the Lord are blessed. Death is a blessing for it opens the way to the faithful for further progression on the way to eternal life. Great blessings of communion with loved ones and the realization of having fought a good fight on the earth bring joy. (3) Those that "die in the Lord" need have no fear for the future. Uncertainty and doubt of the period after death flee from those who have and are sincerely overcoming the world. (4) The greatest blessings are not available in the spirit world because that sphere of life is only intended as temporary in preparing one for the resurrection. (5) The departed Saints look forward to the second coming of Christ when they shall rise from the grave to obtain an inheritance in the place prepared for them. Even "the holy city" (New Jerusalem)will be a part of their inheritance. (6) The faithful dead will have a resurrected body free from diesase, pain, and sorrow. This union of spirit and body in the resurrection will remain forever. Death will never again separate them.

The Millennium

In continuation of events following death of the body and the coming of the Lord in judgment upon the wicked, several ideas about the thousand year period of peace and righteousness on the earth are indicated. The present telestial condition of the earth will pass away, and a terrestrial state will prevail. Death is one of the most real events of mortality. It must come to all. Notwithstanding the millennium is known as the time when death shall not bring sorrow, death will come when man reaches the "age of a tree," which is the millennial "age of man." (D&C 101: 29-30; 63:50.) Death during this period will consist of being changed immediately from mortality to resurrection. (*Ibid.*, 63:51-52.)

Look forward to "these things"—death, spirit world, resurrection, second coming of Christ, millennium, an inheritance in the earth. In 1831, speaking as the Lord views time, the second coming of Christ was near at hand. In the assurance that his coming is nearer than at the beginning of this dispensation, Saints should follow the counsel to look forward even to "the day of the coming of the Son of Man." (*Ibid.*, 63:53.) The Lord knows that there will be many among the Saints who will not be prepared by righteous living to receive the Savior when he comes. These have been called "foolish virgins among the wise." They are foolish because they had the law, they knew of these things and yet this knowledge was taken lightly in not letting the doctrine of the second coming have an influence upon their lives for repentance. They shall, however, be separated from the righteous, for the Lord will take judgment upon them. (*Ibid.*, 63:53-54.)

That there is great need for a call to repentance is known by all who have a knowledge of the bondage of sin which holds so many people in the world. The Lord is not to be mocked by those who themselves have not received the benefit of release from sin through accepting his atonement. (*Ibid.*, 63:58; *Doctrine and Covenants Commentary*, page 384.)

Even though this condition exists today as a result of the apostasy, men should know that the Lord is all-powerful and that in time all things shall be subject unto him. (D&C 63:59-60.)

Do Not Blaspheme

Wherefore, let all men beware how they take my name in their lips—

For behold, verily I say, that many there be who are under this condemnation, who use the name of the Lord, and use it in vain, having not authority.

Wherefore, let the church repent of their sins, and I, the Lord, will own them; otherwise they shall be cut off. (*Ibid.*, 63:61-63.)

To blaspheme is to speak irreverently of God or sacred things. The name of Deity should be held in the greatest respect. To take the name of the Lord in vain has been condemned from the beginning. (Exodus 20:7; Lev. 22:32; Deut. 5:11.) Ancient Israel understood that to curse or blaspheme Deity was an offense so serious that death was the penalty. (Lev. 24:16.) But how far has the world departed from the divine injunction that the Lord's name should be used reverently? The vulgar person often delights in blaspheming the name of the Lord, consciously or designedly, to verify his oath or word. In commenting upon this practice of the world, President Joseph Fielding Smith has said:

> . . . Some individuals have become so profane that it appears almost impossible for them to speak two or three sentences without the emphasis—as they think—of a vulgar or blasphemous oath. A person is known as much by his language as he is by the company he keeps. . .
> . . . How strange it is that some people, and good people at that, think that to use some expression involving the name of the Lord, adds interest, wit, or power to their stories! How often this is seen in the moving pictures, even in shows that otherwise are commendable.
> Above all other peoples on the earth, the Latter-day Saints should hold in the utmost sacredness and reverence all things that are holy. The people of the world have not been trained as we have been in such matters, notwithstanding there are many honest, devout, and refined people in the world. But we have the guidance of the Holy Spirit and the revelations of the Lord, and He has solemnly taught us in our own day our duty in relation to all such things. (*Improvement Era,* July, 1941, p. 525.)

Sacred Things Made Light Of

The people of the world are not the only ones who make light of sacred things. In the days of the Prophet some members of the Church did so, and there are members today who do not sense its seriousness. The word of the Lord in the scriptures, the principles, ordinances, and practices of the Church are to be spoken of with care, for they are sacred. Mockery of sacred truths is blasphemy in the sight of the Lord. The Nephites in the pride of their hearts sinned grievously and lost their strength for the Spirit withdrew from them. One of their sins was "making a mock of that which was sacred." (Helaman 4:11-13.)

Two thoughts emerge from the truth that man is not to mock sacred truths. In the first place, the person who professes belief and practice and at the same time does not live the principles, is making light of sacred things. All should determine that the best life is the life of conformance to God's will. The second thought is the too prevalent poking fun at or jesting about Church teachings and practices. An editorial in a Church publication written by Elder Mark E. Petersen of the Council of the Twelve poses the following pertinent questions as well as others on this point.

How many people joke about the Word of Wisdom when in social groups?

How many joke about sobriety or the lack of it?

How many make light of our teachings on modest dress, and flaunt their standards by persistent violations?

How many make light of the dress requirements of those who go to the temple?

What is our attitude toward the Sabbath? Do we make light of it, and at times do we make fun of it as we proceed to violate it?

There follows the admonition to self-examine our attitudes on these matters, and a stern reminder of the seriousness of trifling with sacred things:

The Lord will not be made light of. He will not be laughed at, nor ridiculed, nor ignored by those who are under obligation to Him.

Self-examination on these matters can be a wholesome thing. And self-determination will be likewise. Determination of what? Determine whether we want to be in the good graces of the Lord or not. Whether we want to be "fence straddlers" or not. Whether we want to carry water on both shoulders, or not. Whether we want to be sincere or not. Whether we are willing to compromise our principles or not. Whether we are willing to sin a little for business sake or for social prestige. . . .

If we trifle with sacred things, we not only disobey, but we ridicule as well. . . .

We may do it thoughtlessly, you say. But that very thoughtlessness is itself an evidence of lack of interest, lack of concern about it all. It is itself proof positive that we are taking lightly the things of God, that we therefore trifle with them.

Without sincerity there is no salvation, regardless of any show of obedience. (*Church News Section, Deseret News,* March 29, 1958.)

Now is the day to determine to whom obedience will be given. If we have been negligent in the past, the Lord is gracious and kind to the repentant.

These things remain to overcome through patience, that such may receive a more exceeding and eternal weight of glory, otherwise, a greater condemnation. (D&C 63:66.)

Remember that that which cometh from above is sacred, and must be spoken with care, and by constraint of the Spirit; and in this there is no condemnation, and ye receive the Spirit through prayer; wherefore, without this there remaineth condemnation. (*Ibid.,* 63:64.)

Chapter 49

THE LAW OF FORGIVENESS

(Section 64:1-14)

With the designation of western Missouri as the land of Zion, and Independence, Jackson County, as the center place of the Zion of the last days, preparations were underway for the Saints to secure that land as their inheritance. In the early part of September 1831, preparations were made for Joseph Smith and Sidney Rigdon to go to Hiram, Ohio, where the Prophet was to reside at the home of Father John Johnson. Their special work was to continue in the revision of the Bible, which the Prophet had commenced while in Fayette, New York, but because of other duties the Lord had commanded him to wait until he got to the Ohio. (D&C 37:1; 45:60-61.)

Just before leaving for Hiram, the Prophet received the revelation from which this chapter is prepared. (*DHC* I:211.)

"Ye Should Overcome the World"

To the elders who were preparing to leave for Jackson County, the Lord gave the comforting message that their sins were forgiven. (D&C 64:3.) Notwithstanding that the Church was only eighteen months old and the members were all converts who had received a remission of sins through baptism, some had sinned in some things, although perhaps not grievously. (Rom. 3:10.) The thought expressed in verse 3 of Section 64, "verily I say, for this once, for mine own glory, and for the salvation of souls, I have forgiven you your sins," suggests the important truth that elders must so live to retain the remission of their sins that their own salvation will redound to God's glory and that their effectiveness in the work of the Lord will bring others to salvation. The purpose of the gospel is to make men perfect through their obedience. When an elder strives with all his heart to keep the commandments, he enjoys the Spirit that convinces others of the truth (D&C 50:21-22), and he retains a remission of his own sins. (Mosiah 4:26.) Forgiveness of sins is dependent upon how well one overcomes the world.

To enjoy the fellowship of the Spirit, one must eschew evil in all of its forms. Following the ways of the world by partaking of customs, practices, and ideas incompatible with what the Lord has revealed, brings loss of true happiness and the protecting companionship of the Holy Ghost. It is just as true today, as in 1831 when the first four verses of Section 64 were given, that the kingdom has been given to those who have received Jesus Christ in baptism, and therefore, the wonderful opportunity is theirs to receive the blessings of salvation by overcoming the world, always striving to retain a remission of sin.

The Keys of the Kingdom

The members of the Church belong to the kingdom, but only one person holds the Priesthood keys which entitle him to direct the work of the kingdom. Joseph Smith is told in this revelation that he would continue to hold the keys of the mysteries of that kingdom as he observed the commandments. (D&C 64:5.) In an earlier revelation Joseph Smith was informed that if he did not prove faithful he could appoint another in his place. (*Ibid.*, 43: 1-10; Chapter 18.) In the Prophet's case he had sinned as all men sin, although apparently not grievously. Because he had erred did not give cause for anyone to have "occasion against him without cause." (*Ibid.*, 64:6.) President George A. Smith said that throughout the history of the Church a spirit developed among many elders "to suppose that they knew more than the Prophet," and that he "was going wrong." (*Journal of Discourses* 11: 7.)

The Steps of Repentance

Throughout the revelations, repentance and forgiveness are spoken of in connection with the Church membership as a whole and also with individuals. We should keep in mind that repentance is for everyone. Sins of omission as well as commission are condemned by the Lord. An example is from Section 58 where we learn that William W. Phelps was admonished to cease from seeking to excel and become humble. (vs. 40-41.) The following verses express the law of forgiveness as it applies to the member of the Church:

Behold, he who has repented of his sins, the same is forgiven, and I, the Lord, remember them no more.

By this ye may know if a man repenteth of his sins—behold, he will confess them and forsake them. (*Ibid.*, 58:42-43.)

Several significant points are made in these verses. First, the soul that sins shall receive forgiveness, provided the repentance is sincere, and they shall no longer be remembered. Second, an important element of repentance is confession, and third, there is no repentance and consequently no forgiveness without forsaking sin.

Elder Spencer W. Kimball has outlined the steps of repentance as (1) sorrow for sin, (2) abandonment of sin, (3) confession of sin, (4) restitution for sin, and (5) doing the will of the Lord. (*Conference Report*, October 1949, p. 127.)

It is probable that at no time does one lose completely his sensitivity to sin, but the full impact of the sin in bringing one to repentance is lessened by continued sinning. When the person repents, remorse of conscience brings the urge to abandon the sin and seek the Lord's forgiveness. The principal step to forgiveness is to forsake sin. In the language of Elder James E. Talmage:

Repentance, to be worthy of its name, must comprise something more than a mere self-acknowledgement of error; it does not consist in lamentations and wordy confessions, but in the heartfelt recognition of guilt, which carries with it a horror for sin and a resolute determination to make amends for the past and to do better in the future. If such a conviction be genuine it is marked by that godly sorrow which, as Paul has said, "worketh repentance to salvation, not to be repented of; but the sorrow of the world worketh death." (2 Cor. 7:10) Apostle Orson Pratt has wisely said: "It would be of no use for the sinner to confess his sins to God unless he were determined to forsake them; it would be of no benefit to him to feel sorry that he had done wrong unless he intended to do wrong no more; it would be folly for him to confess before God that he injured his fellow man unless he were determined to do all in his power to make restitution. Repentance, then, is not only confession of sins, with a sorrowful, contrite heart, but a fixed, settled purpose to refrain from every evil way." (*The Articles of Faith*, p. 112.)

In an earlier revelation, the Lord revealed that offenses committed with public knowledge should be confessed in public, while those committed in secret should be rebuked in secret. (D&C 42:88-93.) Confession of sin is a part of repentance—confession to God in the name of the Savior, always. Those sins, however, that may affect the member's status in the Church are to be confessed to the Lord's representative, the bishop. In a commentary on Section 58, verse 43, Elder Spencer W. Kimball says:

Especially grave errors such as sexual sins shall be confessed to the bishop as well as to the Lord. There are two remissions which one might wish to have. First, the forgiveness from the Lord, and second, the forgiveness of the Lord's Church through its leaders. As soon as one has an inner conviction of his sins, he should go to the Lord in "mighty prayer" as did Enos and never cease his supplications until he shall, like Enos (of the Book of Mormon), receive assurance that his sins have been forgiven by the Lord. It is unthinkable that God absolves serious sins upon a few requests. He is likely to wait until there has been long sustained repentance as evidenced by a willingness to comply with all His other requirements. No priest nor elder is authorized to thus act for the Church. The Lord has a consistent, orderly plan. Every soul in the stakes is given a bishop who, by the very nature of his calling and his ordination, is a "judge in Israel." The bishop is one's best earthly friend. He will hear the problems, judge the seriousness thereof, determine the degree of repentance and decide if it warrants an eventual forgiveness. He does this as the earthly representative of God, the master physician, the master psychologist, the master psychiatrist. If repentance is sufficient he may waive penalties which is tantamount to forgiveness. The bishop claims no authority to absolve sins, but he does share the burden, waive penalties, relieve tension and strain and he may assure a continuation of activity. He will keep the whole matter most confidential. ("Be Ye Clean," BYU Speeches of the Year, May 4, 1954.)

To the elders (and to all members of the Church) referred to in Section 64, the Lord said that he would forgive whomsoever he would, but of us it is required to forgive all men. (D&C 64:10.) In other words, ultimate forgiveness is in the hands of the Lord, but he has promised, as indicated above, that he will, when, in addition to sorrow for sin, there is abandonment and confession of sins, by the one seeking forgiveness, forgive the sinner upon sincere repentance. Then, what more is required of the person seeking forgiveness? The next step is restitution insofar as this is possible. There are some things for which complete restitution cannot be made. The murderer and the one who takes virtue cannot restore what is taken, but there are some things that might be done to mitigate the offense. In the case of the latter, complete and full devotion to the cause of Zion in bringing souls to Christ is a part of possible restitution. "And James indicated that each good deed, each testimony, each proselyting effort, each safeguard thrown about others is like a blanket over one's own sins, or like a deposit against an overdraft in the bank," said Elder Kimball. This leads us to the final step in repentance.

Doing the Father's Will

Since every person needs to repent (1 John 1:8), some because of serious sins, we learn of another reason for keeping the commandments. The fullest measure of salvation is available to those who obey the Lord in all things, which includes repentance. (D&C 133:62.) In the Lord's Preface to the Doctrine and Covenants, we find this sublime truth:

For I the Lord cannot look upon sin with the least degree of allowance;

Nevertheless, he that repents and does the commandments of the Lord shall be forgiven. (*Ibid.*, 1:31-32.)

A Law of Forgiveness

Throughout the Savior's ministry emphasis was put upon man's relationship with his fellow man. His admonitions against murder, adultery, stealing, slander, and other vices were intended to bring peace to individuals and a reign of peace for all men. But, in general, mankind has not accepted the way of peace, and in these last days, the world is ripened in iniquity and is in need of great repentance. (See General Conference sermons by Elders Spencer W. Kimball and Delbert L. Stapley, *Improvement Era*, December 1961.)

The Lord's forgiveness is withheld until the person can also forgive his fellow men. Elder James E. Talmage forcefully brings this point to the reader's attention by reference to several instances in Jesus' teachings, including the parable of the talents (Matt. 18:23-35; *Articles of Faith*, pp. 110-111.) In commenting upon a part of the Lord's Prayer, as given in the Bible (Matt. 6:9, 12), and the emphasis given in the Book of Mormon, Elder

Kimball says, "Then in the Lord's prayer to the people in Jerusalem, he said: 'Our Father which art in heaven . . . forgive us our debts, as we forgive our debtors.' Did he not mean in the same manner and in the same degree, perhaps, as we forgive our debtors? He made it a little more clear, even, to the Nephites, for after he had said; 'forgive us our debts as we forgive our debtors' (3 Nephi 13:11) he said, 'For, if ye forgive men their trespasses your heavenly Father will also forgive you;

"But if ye forgive not men their trespasses neither will your Father forgive your trespasses.' (3 Nephi 13: 14-15; also Mosiah 26:31.) Condemnation, then, comes to you who will not forgive, probably even greater than to him who gave the offense." (*Conference Report*, October 1949, p. 128.)

Section 64 and Forgiveness

In this dispensation, the Lord has revealed, with emphasis, the law that,

> . . . he that forgiveth not his brother his trespasses standeth condemned before the Lord; for there remaineth in him the greater sin.
>
> I, the Lord, will forgive whom I will forgive, but of you it is required to forgive all men. (vs. 9-11.)

There were occasions when the disciples were guilty of offenses against one another and failed to forgive in their hearts, and for this the Lord said "they were afflicted and sorely chastened." (v. 8.) It is consistent with gospel teachings that disobedience brings unhappiness, loss of the Spirit with its many blessings, and thus afflictions follow. Sometimes we think that the blessings of the gospel and also condemnations come only in the future existence. King Benjamin taught that the Lord's blessings come bounteously in this life to those who remember him in faith. (Mosiah 2:24.) What greater blessing can be received than to have happiness here and eternal life in the world to come? (D&C 59:23.)

The living prophets have counseled the saint to follow the Savior's teachings in not setting up one's self in judgment against his neighbor. The common offenses that bring ill will, malice and hatred are ofttimes due to misunderstandings. To eliminate this possibility, the Lord admonished his followers to be the first to make reconciliation when offenses arise. The *injured* should go to the one who injured him and seek reconciliation! President David O. McKay has given us the Savior's teaching regarding forgiveness of fellow men in these words:

If we would have peace as individuals, we must supplant emnity with forbearance, which means to refrain or abstain from finding fault or from condemning others. "It is a noble thing to be charitable with the failings and weaknesses of a friend; to bury his weaknesses in silence, but to proclaim his virtues from the house tops." We shall have power to do this if we really cherish in our hearts the ideals of Christ, who said:

"If thou bring thy gift to the altar, and there rememberest that thy brother hath ought against thee; Leave there thy gift before the altar, and go thy way; first be reconciled to thy brother, and then come and offer thy gift." (Matt. 5:23-24.)

Note that Savior did not say if you have ought against him, but if you find that another has ought against you. How many of us are ready to come up to that standard? If we are, we shall find peace. Many of us, however, instead of following this admonition, nurse our ill-will until it grows to hatred, then this hatred expresses itself in fault-finding and even slander, "whose whisper over the world's diameter as level as a cannon to its mouth, transports its poison shot." Back-biting, fault-finding, are weeds of society that should be constantly eradicated. Gossip, too, brings discord and thrives best in superficial minds, as fungi grows best on weakened plants. "Bear ye one another's burdens," but do not add to those burdens by gossiping about your neighbors or by spreading slander. Diogenes was asked one day to name that beast, the bite of which is the most dangerous. The old philosopher replied: "Of tame beasts, the bite of the flatterer; of wild beasts, that of the slanderer." (*Conference Report*, October 1938, pp. 133-134.)

The law that the injured one make the first step to be reconciled with his brother does not remove the responsibility from the person who injured another to take the first step to reconciliation.

The Evil One rejoices when bitterness and hatred abound among men, for his purposes are opposed to peace and happiness. (3 Nephi 11:29-30.) When the spirit of Christ is with the Saints because they obey the commandments, President Joseph F. Smith said:

> ...we shall be a power in the world for good; we shall overwhelm and overcome all evil, all opposition to the truth, and bring to pass righteousness upon the face of the earth. For the Gospel will be spread and the people in the world will feel the influence which will be shed forth from the people of Zion, and they will be inclined more to repent of their sins and to receive the truth. (*Conference Report*, April 1915, p. 120.)

Herein lies the secret to success as individuals and as a Church. We are commissioned by covenant to work for the cause of Zion in the world. (D&C 6:6.) Our effectiveness in this is determined by the extent that we possess the Spirit of the Lord. That Spirit will not abide with those who are unforgiving of their brothers and sisters, and who carry grudges that canker their souls, that gossip and back-bite. How can we find forgiveness of our sins through repentance if we neglect the essential ingredient of repentance—namely, to extend forgiveness to our brothers and sisters which includes the elimination of criticism and gossip? We must remember that judgment lies in the Lord's hands and not in ours. (*Ibid.*, 64:11.)

He Shall Be Cast Out

The information concerning the unrepentant in Section 64 is an extension of what an earlier revelation said about "casting" the member from the Church because of disobedience to gospel principles. (D&C 41:5-6; 42:20-28.)

One of the laws given in Section 42 is the law concerning transgressors. This law provides that the unrepentant shall be brought before a Church court and, if found guilty, he shall be dealt with according to the law of God. (*Ibid.*, 42:80-83.) When the Lord said that we were not to judge our fellow man, he did not mean that judgment must not be made by the officers of his Church. The bishop is a judge in Israel. (*Ibid.*, 58:17; 65:40; 107:71-75.) It is his calling to make many judgments as to the worthiness of those who seek recommends for patriarchal blessings, temple service, priesthood advancements, etc. The penalty of excommunication or disfellowshipment is not used as a means of destroying the individual, and every effort is made to save the person before such a penalty is administered. As Elder James E. Talmage said:

The Lord hath declared that there must not be iniquity in his Church, and He has provided officers whose specific and specified duty it is to hunt out iniquity, to run it down, so that every case may be dealt with, and the afflicted ones perchance, be saved. He has not told us to cover up sin in the Church. That is not the Lord's will, nor purpose nor plan. (*Conference Report*, Oct. 1920, p. 62.)

That God May Be Glorified

Why does the Lord command that the unrepentant sinner be cast out of his kingdom?

And this ye shall do that God may be glorified—not because ye forgive not, having not compassion, but that ye may be justified in the eyes of the law, that ye may not offend him who is your lawgiver—
Verily I say, for this cause ye shall do these things. (D&C 64:13-14.)

We know what the law of the gospel demands for members of the Church who evidence by their actions that they no longer want to remain in God's kingdom. But wherein is God glorified by the application of this law? An answer to this question is found in the mission of the Church in the last days. With the restoration of the gospel the last and greatest dispensation was ushered in. This is the last time that the Lord will call upon the inhabitants of the earth to prepare for the culmination of his work. In these times when Israel is gathered to fulfill the Lord's purposes for the salvation of men, the members of the kingdom of God must show the world by their lives that this is the day of fulfilled prophecy and that there is little time remaining until his work will be completed. Ezekiel foresaw the last days when Israel would be returned to her own land and she would become clean, capable of enjoying the Lord's spirit. (Ezekiel 36: 16-38.)

> But I had pity for mine holy name, which the house of Israel had profaned among the heathen, whither they went.
>
> Therefore say unto the house of Israel, Thus saith the Lord God; I do not this for your sakes, O house of Israel, but for mine holy name's sake, which ye have profaned among the heathen, whither ye went.
>
> And I will sanctify my great name, which was profaned among the heathen, which ye have profaned among the heathen, which ye have profaned in the midst of them; and *the heathen shall know that I am the Lord, saith the Lord God, when I shall be sanctified in you before their eyes.*
>
> For I will take you from among the heathen, and gather you out of all countries and will bring you into your own land. (*Ibid.*, 36:21-24; italics added.)

How shall the "heathen" (world) know the Lord? By the lives of those who represent him as citizens of his kingdom. Is God holy or unholy? Is the Lord to be known by the lives of those who flaunt his laws in wickedness, or by the humble, sincere, faithful followers of the Prince of Peace?

We who have accepted the benefits of the atonement of Christ must seek by earnest effort the perfection which God and Christ enjoy. (3 Nephi 12:48.)

Chapter 50

"YE ARE ON THE LORD'S ERRAND"
(Section 64: 15-43)

From the last chapter we learned that Section 64 of the Doctrine and Covenants was received so that certain elders who were preparing to leave for Jackson County, Missouri, might understand the purposes of the Lord concerning themselves and the glories to be received by the faithful.

Because some of these elders lacked a forgiving spirit, the Lord revealed anew his law of forgiveness with a warning that members of his kingdom who would not repent would lose their citizenship in that kingdom by disobedience to the commandments.

Ezra Booth and Isaac Morley

As if to present an object lesson in the principles that had just been made known, Section 64 continues by referring to two individuals — Ezra Booth and Isaac Morley. The former is known as one "who was my servant," while the latter retains his membership in the Church, for "I have forgiven my servant Isaac Morley." Both of these men "kept not the law, neither the commandment. . . . They condemned for evil that thing in which there was no evil. . . ." (D&C 64:15-16.) It is evident, from the counsel concerning forgiveness in this revelation, that Brother Morley repented of his sin, while Ezra Booth decided to leave the kingdom of God. At the time of this revelation Isaac Morley was counselor to Edward Partridge, Presiding Bishop of the Church, and remained so until 1840 when Bishop Partridge died.

An indication of the depth of their conversion to the gospel and of the character of these two men is plainly apparent from the Lord's acceptance of one and his rejection of the unrepentant. Isaac Morley accepted the meaning of "Ye are on the Lord's errand." When Brother Morley accepted the gospel in 1830, his life thereafter was dedicated to the furtherance of the cause of Zion. One can believe that he accepted the commandment to sell his farm, as mentioned in verse 20 of Section 64. He is described as a man of loyalty to God's servants who was willing to consecrate all of his wealth to building up Zion while participating in numerous Church positions. (Romney, Thomas C.: *The Gospel in Action*, pp. 113-118.)

On the other hand, Ezra Booth lives in infamy in the annals of the Church. He is sometimes mentioned as an example of one who was converted by a miracle. The wife of Father Johnson was unable to raise her arm for two years. As a friend of the family, Ezra Booth, a Methodist priest, was present when the Prophet Joseph Smith and the elders administered to her, restoring her arm to instant use. Soon after this healing, Booth was baptized. President George A. Smith said that when Booth had to preach without purse or scrip, he felt that there were better ways of "earning a livelihood." The Prophet reported that when Booth learned,

> . . .that faith, humility, patience, and tribulation go before blessing, and that God brings low before He exalts; that instead of the "Savior's granting him power to smite men and make them believe," (as he said he wanted God to do in his own case) — when he found he must become all things to all men, that he might peradventure save some; and that, too, by all diligence, by perils by sea and land, as was the case in the days of Jesus — then he was disappointed. (*DHC* I:216.)

Under these circumstances Booth apostatized and, as is true with many apostates, he sought to justify himself by publishing a series of lying letters as evidence against the Church. His apostasy contributed to the organization of a mob that tarred and feathered Joseph Smith, and caused the death of one of his adopted children. (*Ibid.*, I:260-265.)

Edward Partridge at this time was guilty of "unbelief and blindness of heart." " 'Unbelief,' in this case means 'weak faith' (as in Mark 9:24), and it was, perhaps, the cause of the blindness of heart." (*Doctrine and Covenants Commentary*, p. 339.) Again, the faithful, diligent member who errs, corrects his life, and learns that the Lord is merciful and forgiving. (D&C 64:17.)

A Stronghold in Kirtland

During this period the establishment of the Church in two general areas was begun. Kirtland, Ohio, became the headquarters of the Church. With the designation of western Missouri as Zion, and the dedication of the land and the temple site, that area began its part in the growing Church. Many Saints felt the urge to assemble in Missouri. Sidney Gilbert was commanded to establish a business in Zion (D&C 64:18), while Frederick G. Williams was to retain his holdings in Kirtland that a stronghold might be maintained there. (*Ibid.*, v. 21.) This verse is a prophecy that was literally fulfilled by subsequent events. In verse 26, Newel K. Whitney and Sidney Gilbert are counseled to retain their store and their possessions so that the Lord's purposes for Kirtland might be fulfilled. After five years "any with an open heart" was free to assemble in the land of Zion. (*Ibid.*, v. 22.)

What did the Lord have in store for Kirtland in five years from then? On April 3, 1836, the Kirtland Temple became the most important edifice on the earth at the time. By the labor of the Saints, amid poverty and persecution, the Lord had commanded that this holy house should be reared to his name, that he might visit his people in that structure. It was there that the capstone of Priesthood was received by Joseph Smith and Oliver Cowdery from personages from beyond the veil. (Section 110.) The events of April 3, 1836, brought a turning point in world events by the restoration of keys of Priesthood pertaining to the gathering of Israel from the corners of the earth. As a result of this authority, Latter-day Saints have come out of the world into a life of "being on the Lord's errand." The gathering includes the restoration of the Jewish people to their homeland, long predicted by Bible and Book of Mormon prophets. (Jer. 30: 3; 2 Nephi 30:7-8.) The great missionary movement of the Church began its world-wide activity after Moses restored these keys. The bringing of the gospel of Abraham with the keys of the restoration of all things (D&C 110:12), and, finally, the keys of sealing powers for the living and the dead, with the important work of salvation for the dead by Elijah, began a tremendous activity for the salvation of man. (*Ibid.*, vs. 13-16.)

The Lord Jesus Christ visited his temple at that time to accept it as his house with the message that this would be the beginning of the blessings to be received for the benefit of his people. (*Ibid.*, vs. 1-10.) When one considers the impact of these events upon the future of the Church and the world, one can easily understand why some of the Saints were commanded to continue their daily activities in Kirtland. Their work was also to help the Saints "obtain an inheritance in the land of Zion." (D&C 64:30.)

Counsel on Debt

The members of the Church mentioned in Section 64 (and the other Saints) were counseled to keep out of debt to their enemies. (vs. 27-28.) For the Church to be in debt to those who were unfriendly might have brought failure to the cause of Zion in that area. The instructions given about retaining material possessions and keeping out of debt remind the Latter-day Saint that the Lord provides his people with counsel in their temporal affairs. As to individuals, the authorities of the Church have advised our people against the burden of debt. Elder Marriner W. Merrill told a general conference of the Church that a financier gave him the key to getting out of debt. "It was simply this: 'Stop immediately from going into debt. Don't go into debt another dollar until you get out and are free.' " (*Conference Report*, April 1899, p. 15.)

"Ye Are Laying the Foundation"

As one studies the beginning of this dispensation, he sometimes wonders if the membership of the Church realized the full significance of these words:

> And behold, I, the Lord, declare unto you, and my words are sure and shall not fail, that they shall obtain it.
> But all things must come to pass in their time.
> Wherefore, be not weary in well-doing, for ye are laying the foundation of a great work. And out of small things proceedeth that which is great. (D&C 64:31-33.)

In 1833, Wilford Woodruff met the Prophet for the first time. He attended a meeting where many of the brethren bore testimony of the restoration. Brother Woodruff said at a general conference in 1898:

> . . .when they got through the Prophet said, "Brethren I have been very much edified and instructed in your testimonies here tonight, but I want to say to you before the Lord, that you know no more concerning the destinies of this Church and kingdom than a babe upon its mother's lap. You don't comprehend it." I was rather surprised. He said "it is only a little handful of Priesthood you see here tonight, but this Church will fill North and South America — it will fill the world." Among other things he said, "it will fill the Rocky Mountains. There will be tens of thousands of Latter-day Saints who will be gathered in the Rocky Mountains, and there they will open the door for the establishing of the Gospel among the Lamanites, who will receive the Gospel and their endowments and the blessings of God. This people will go into the Rocky Mountains; they will there build temples to the Most High. They will raise up a posterity there, and the Latter-day Saints who dwell in these mountains will stand in the flesh until the coming of the Son of Man. The Son of Man will come to them while in the Rocky Mountains."

I name these things because I want to bear testimony before God, angels and men that mine eyes behold the day, and have beheld for the last fifty years of my life, the fulfillment of that prophecy. I never expected to see the Rocky Mountains when I listened to that man's voice, but I have, and do today. (*Conference Report,* April 1898, p. 57.)

It was not only the brethren of 1831 who were laying the foundation of the great work, but the Priesthood of 1833 and 1836 and of the entire period of this dispensation, even in our time of 1964. Each Latter-day Saint who accepts the "Lord's errand" is building a foundation of a great work which will eventually fill the whole earth. Every program of the Church participated in, every contribution given, every work performed with a willing heart and obedient spirit will find rich rewards in assisting the new generation to carry on in building for the ultimate victory of eternal life. Should not every Latter-day Saint feel encouraged that out of small things proceedeth that which is great? The contribution may appear small but in the aggregate it builds for the future.

"For The Tithing of My People"

We have learned that the Lord instituted the law of consecration for the benefit of the poor among the Saints in the early part of this dispensation. (Chapter 28.) Although it was lived in Thompson, Ohio, and the Saints were later commanded to practice it in Missouri, the apparent failure of the Saints to live that law was foreshadowed in Section 64. The law of tithing is known as a schoolmaster to bring people to the greater law of consecration. Elder Francis M. Lyman pointed out in a general conference that,

. . . any person who is not able to observe this law [tithing] faithfully and well will never, worlds without end, be able to observe the law of consecration. The law of tithing is a stepping stone, and it is a law that will abide forever, because a great majority possibly of the children of God will not be able to reach the higher law. (*Conference Report,* October 1899, p. 34.)

It was in July 1838, that the Lord commanded his people to observe the law of tithing. Yet, in 1831, the Saints were informed that certain judgment would come upon those who did not observe this law when it was introduced. Tithing also has the connotation of sacrifice as suggested in the following:

Behold, now it is called today until the coming of the Son of Man, and verily it is a day of sacrifice, and a day for the tithing of my people; for he that is tithed shall not be burned at his coming. (D&C 64:23.)

On the law of tithing and obedience, President Joseph F. Smith said:

"Obedience is better than sacrifice, and to hearken than the fat of rams." It is the heart and the willing mind that the Lord requires of His people, and not so much their substance. He does not need our obedience. But we need to be obedient; for it is through obedience that we will receive the reward.

So I come to the conclusion that the principal thing about tithe paying is obedience to the law, and that more good will come to us through that obedience than to anybody else. We may be worth our tens of thousands, and pay an honest tithing on our income, making our tithing a large amount; yet the good that will come to ourselves by being obedient to the law of God will be far greater in the end than the good which our substance may do to the poor. (*Conference Report,* April 1899, p. 69.)

"The Heart and a Willing Mind"

The heart is associated in scripture as the seat of emotions, and when applied to this scripture it probably means that only those who love the Lord intensely will reap the blessings.

Behold, the Lord requireth the heart and a willing mind; and the willing and obedient shall eat the good of the land of Zion in these last days. (D&C 64:34.)

The Saints of 1831 were no different from the Saints of 1964 in the Lord requiring whole-souled devotion to the labor of the kingdom.

Those who are "on the Lord's errand" all the days of their lives will not come under the condemnation of the rebellious who shall be cut off from the land of Zion, for these are not of the chosen blood of Ephraim and must be plucked out. (*Ibid.*, 35-36.) In commenting upon the context of these verses, President George Q. Cannon said:

From the beginning of this Church until the present the men and women who have been obedient to the counsel of God's servants have always been the most favored. President Brigham Young, during the lifetime of the Prophet Joseph, was always noted for his strict obedience to the prophet. Brother Joseph never made any requirement of him that he did not strictly comply with. The same may be said of the other faithful men who, during his lifetime, were associated with him. But the disobedient and rebellious have been, as the Lord said they should be, cut off. Oliver Cowdery was with Joseph when John the Baptist came to them and ordained them to the Aaronic Priesthood. He was the second apostle in the Church also, and a witness of the Book of Mormon, the angel of the Lord having shown him the plates. But he was disobedient to the prophet and he could not stand. It might be thought that he was so near to Joseph and so favored of God that it was not necessary for him to do exactly as the prophet told him; but not so. There is an order in the church of Christ which all must observe, and no one can be disbedient without bringing the displeasure of the Lord upon him. This is a principle which all should learn. (*Juvenile Instructor*, Vol. 10, 1875, p. 222.)

In the historical content of Section 64, these verses are prophetic:

Behold, the Lord requireth the heart and a willing mind; and the willing and obedient shall eat the good of the land of Zion in these last days.

And the rebellious shall be cut off out of the land of Zion, and shall be sent away, and shall not inherit the land.

For, verily I say that the rebellious are not of the blood of Ephraim, wherefore they shall be plucked out. (D&C 64:34-36.)

When the Saints were expelled from Jackson County in 1833, they had not fully subscribed to the law which the Lord had given, because of carelessness, neglect, and wickedness. Therefore, they were "plucked out" of the land, and were "sent away."

False Prophets to Be Known

The principle laid down in verses 37 through 39—the children of Zion shall judge all things pertaining to Zion —is consistent with verse 5, because Zion's inhabitants know how to detect the deceivers. False prophets are known by Latter-day Saints because of the keys against deception which the Lord has provided for their use. First, their spurious revelations are to be judged by the criteria given in Sections 28 and 43; namely, there is only one person at a time who is empowered to receive revelation for the Church. (Chapters 18 and 49.) Second, the false teachers may be judged by the standard set forth in Section 52:9, 36—by the teachings of the ancient and modern apostles and prophets in the true Church of Jesus Christ. (Chapter 36.)

The Lord declares that all things pertaining to Zion will be judged by the Church, and, eventually, the nations will be judged by the Church. In the due time of the Lord judgment will be meted out to all.

"Ye Are on the Lord's Errand"

As the early Saints were told not to be weary in well-doing for they were laying the foundation of a great work, so also they were told that their work would eventuate in the building of a Zion upon this continent that would be the admiration of the world.

For, behold, I say unto you that Zion shall flourish, and the glory of the Lord shall be upon her:

And she shall be an ensign unto the people, and there shall come unto her out of every nation under heaven.

And the day shall come when the nations of the earth shall tremble because of her, and shall fear because of her terrible ones. The Lord hath spoken it. Amen. (*Ibid.*, 64:41-43.)

To the brethren mentioned in Section 64, the Lord said that, as his agents, they were "on the Lord's errand." (v. 29.) We are all agents of the Lord and are all on his errand. By covenant we are committed through faithful, loyal devotion to build on the foundation laid in the past, eventually to terminate in the Zion that shall flourish, where the glory of the Lord will be there.

But how shall we measure up to being on the Lord's errand? Elder George Teasdale of the Council of the Twelve, suggested this idea:

We are the redeemed of the Lord. We have accepted of the principles of redemption, and consequently have been sanctified in the precious blood of Christ. Those who love God and keep his commandments represent Him and the Lord Jesus Christ. They love one another, and they are known by their works. Their faith is manifested by their works. (*Conference Report*, April 1898, p. 52.)

Chapter 51

THE KINGDOM OF GOD

(Section 65)

The Prophet Joseph Smith records in his history that on the 12th of September 1831, he moved his family to the township of Hiram, Ohio, to live at the home of John Johnson, a member of the Church. Hiram was about thirty miles in a southeasterly direction from Kirtland. From the time of his arrival until the forepart of October, the Prophet made preparations to "recommence the translation [revision] of the Bible." (*DHC* I:215.) He wrote that Section 65 of the Doctrine and Covenants is a prayer received through revelation. This is the first time in this book of scripture that a revelation is so designated. When the Kirtland Temple was ready for dedication, the Lord gave the dedicatory prayer by revelation. (Section 109.)

"Prepare Ye the Way"

An authoritative source has pointed out that the expression "Hearken, and lo, a voice as of one sent down from on high" in verse 1 suggests that like John on Patmos (Rev. 1:10-12) Joseph Smith heard a voice described as:

... a voice as of one sent down from on high, who is mighty and powerful, whose going forth is unto the ends of the earth, yea, whose voice is unto men—Prepare ye the way of the Lord, make his paths straight. (D&C 65:1.)

This same source refers to "Prepare ye the way of the Lord, make his paths straight," also found in Isaiah 40:3, as having meaning in Oriental imagery. Anciently, an Eastern ruler would send his messenger to announce his coming which would give notice to his loyal subjects that crooked paths were to be made straight and the roads to be made level. The comparison with this revelation seems clear. The Lord's messengers have been sent in this dispensation to make preparations for his second coming. Loyal subjects of his kingdom will make necessary preparations to receive their king. "When we comply with His commandments and prepare for His advent, our prayers are acceptable to Him." (*Doctrine and Covenants Commentary*, p. 398.)

"The Keys of the Kingdom"

The Lord reminded Joseph Smith that the keys of the kingdom of God had been given to man upon the earth. (D&C 65:2.) Apostles of the meridian dispensation foresaw the time when the gospel would be restored to the earth following a long period of apostasy from the true principles and ordinances of the gospel, as given by the Savior and continued by the apostles. Peter describes that time as a period of "refreshing" from the presence of the Lord, which would result because of a "restitution of all things, which God hath spoken by the mouth of all his holy prophets since the world began." (Acts 3:19-21.) This prophecy is significant because it reminds one of the numerous words of the prophets concerning our times— the coming forth of The Book of Mormon (Isa. 29; Ezek. 37:15-28): the gathering of Israel, (Jer. 3:14-18; 31: 31-33; Isa. 11:10-12); the building of a house of the Lord in the mountains (Isa. 2:2-3); the building of a temple to which the Lord would come suddenly (Mal. 3:1); and other prophecies that have been fulfilled or are in the course of fulfillment.

Paul the apostle foresaw the time when all things would be gathered together in one in the last dispensation—the fulness of times. (Eph. 1:9, 10.) The gospel would be restored by an angel to usher in that dispensation as a part of the restoration of what the prophets saw. (Rev. 14:6, 7.)

The keys of the kingdom of God were a necessary part of the restoration of all things. Without the authority of the Priesthood to administer the laws and ordinances of the gospel, there would be no validity to the plan of salvation. (John 15:16; Heb. 5:4.) The necessary keys (power to direct the work of the kingdom) had been given to Joseph Smith and Oliver Cowdery by John the Baptist (D&C Section 13; Mal. 3:1-3), and by Peter, James, and John. (D&C 27:12-13.) In the last scripture, reference is made to the committing of the keys of the dispensation in which the Lord would gather together in one all things as prophesied.

Later on in the dispensation still additional authority was to be restored that specific activities of the dispensation might be carried out. Elijah was to come, as foreknown. (Mal. 4:5, 6; D&C 2; 110:13-16.) Moses and Elias were also to be sent that functions necessary for our times might be accomplished. (*Ibid.*, 110:11-12.) Still others would bring their authorities, rights, powers, and glories to bless those who want the riches of eternity. (*Ibid.*, 128:21.)

The Prophesied Kingdom

One of the remarkable prophesies of the Old Testament relative to the setting up of the kingdom of God in the last days is found in Daniel, chapter 2. The expression in verse 45, "the stone was cut out of the mountain without hands" is also found in verse 2 of Section 65, which reads as follows:

The keys of the kingdom of God are committed unto man on the earth, and from thence shall the gospel roll forth unto the ends of the earth, as the stone which is cut out of the mountain without hands shall roll forth, until it has filled the whole earth.

An interesting statement from the Prophet's remarks concerning this prophecy in the book of Daniel was made not long before he was martyred:

... The ancient prophets declared that in the last days the God of heaven should set up a kingdom which should never be destroyed, nor left to other people; and the very time that was calculated on, this people were struggling to bring it out. ...

I calculate to be one of the instruments of setting up the kingdom of Daniel by the word of the Lord, and I intend to lay a foundation that will revolutionize the whole world. I once offered my life to the Missouri mob as a sacrifice for my people and here I am. It will not be by sword or gun that this kingdom will roll on: the power of truth is such that all nations will be under the necessity of obeying the Gospel. . . . (*DHC* VI:364-365.)

The Gospel, A Leaven

Asael Smith, the grandfather of Joseph Smith, was inspired to say: "it has been borne in upon my soul that one of my descendants will promulgate a work to revolutionize the world of religious faith." (Smith, Joseph Fielding: *Essentials in Church History*, page 29.) The influence of the restoration of the gospel and its promulgation throughout the world has been very great, and the future will see a greater influence upon the people of the world. Some of our leaders have pointed out the leavening effect of the true gospel in the world. Men's ideas of religious concepts have undergone some changes since the spring of 1820.

There may be, and probably are, other reasons for changes in the minds of men on religious principles, but if their ideas become more congenial to the fulness of the gospel then contention on these points will lessen. Before the Church was organized, and in reference to the bringing forth of The Book of Mormon, the Lord revealed that it was his purpose to decrease contention by this means. (D&C 10:61-63.) Certainly, the leavening influence of the restored gospel was not felt immediately. It takes a long time for change to come. The last sentence of the Prophet's remark quoted above suggests that the day will come when the power of truth will bring the nations to obey the gospel. That day, however, will not be in the time of wickedness (*Ibid.*, 1:11-16), but nonetheless, it is prophesied that the time will come, and it will probably be in the millennium, when "every man might speak in the name of God the Lord, even the Savior of the world." (*Ibid.*, 1:19-20.)

Daniel's Prophecy

Many Latter-day Saint leaders have referred to Daniel, chapter 2, especially verse 44, which sets forth the application of King Nebuchadnezzar's dream, as interpreted by Daniel the Hebrew prophet, but it is probably Brother B. H. Roberts in the Introduction to Volume I of the *History of the Church* (Documentary History) by Joseph Smith, who has given us the fullest account.

Briefly, the dream of the king as interpreted by Daniel (Dan. 2:37-45) indicated that Nebuchadnezzar's kingdom, Babylonia, was the first world power (the 6th and 5th centuries B.C.) mentioned, to be replaced by the Medo-Persian empire (from 538 B.C. to about 330 B.C.), followed by the Greco-Macedonian kingdom (from about 330 B.C. to 160 B.C.), with the Roman empire immediately following and ending in the fifth century A.D. In Brother Roberts' explanation he quotes a Protestant writer who believed that the kingdom of God mentioned in verse 44 was set up in the days of Christ. Brother Roberts shows very clearly that such an interpretation is incorrect, one reason being that the kingdom of God would be established in the days of the fifth phase of the dream, at the time of the breaking up of the Roman empire into many small nations or kingdoms, and not during the Roman period when Jesus ministered. (*DHC* I:

XXXIV-XL.) Each one of the foregoing kingdoms was symbolized by a part of the great image; the golden head —Babylonia; the silver breast and arms—Medes and Persians; the brazen belly and thighs—the Greco-Macedonian kingdom; the legs of iron—Roman empire; and the feet of iron and clay which eventually were broken to be replaced by the kingdom of God.

Elder Roberts points out that the kingdom of God would be a material kingdom as other kingdoms on earth and not a spiritual kingdom of Christ only, and that it would be organized in the last days.

The Fulfillment

The prophesied kingdom of God represented as a stone cut out of the mountain without hands was formally organized on April 6, 1830, and is known as The Church of Jesus Christ of Latter-day Saints. That Church has as its head the Savior with the President of the Church as his representative to guide and direct its destiny by revelation. As the Church of Jesus Christ in his day was composed of officers and organizations, so, by the restoration of the gospel and the Church as prophesied, the Church today performs its many purposes through a tangible organization. (Chapters 13 and 14.)

A Purpose of the Church

In the beginning of this dispensation, the Lord revealed that because of the apostate condition of the world he had established his organization upon the earth that man might have the means of salvation. This restoration was to prepare those who would accept his Church for the glorious coming of the Savior. The world would also, by the preaching of the gospel, have an opportunity to know of the Lord's intentions for man if he did not repent. (D&C 1). Section 65 carries this same message of preparation for the second coming of Christ. (Read verses 3 and 4.)

It is worthy of note that this and other admonitions emphasize the charge given to the kingdom of God to make known its principles and ordinances through missionary work. The first commission given to the Church was to preach the gospel. In the days of renewed emphasis upon "every member a missionary," it is well to remind ourselves of this primary responsibility of the citizens of the kingdom.

The Kingdom of Heaven

Call upon the Lord, that his kingdom may go forth upon the earth, that the inhabitants thereof may receive it, and be prepared for the days to come, in the which the Son of Man shall come down in heaven, clothed in the brightness of his glory, to meet the kingdom of God which is set up on the earth. (D&C 65:5.)

The Lord commanded his disciples to pray for the coming of that kingdom. (Matt. 6:9-13.) This counsel reminds one that by prayer the disciple is kept in remembrance of the need to further the purposes of the kingdom, as indicated above.

The kingdom of God set up on the earth will be prepared to meet the Savior as it discharges its purposes for the salvation of the living and the dead. The faithful citizens of his kingdom will perform the functions of true followers of the Master by demonstrating their love in keeping the commandments of their King. (John 14:15.)

Wherefore, may the kingdom of God go forth that the kingdom of heaven may come, that thou, O God, mayest be glorified in heaven so on earth, that thine enemies may be subdued; for thine is the honor, power and glory, forever and ever. Amen. (D&C 65:6.)

Elder James E. Talmage wrote that the expressions "kingdom of God" and "kingdom of heaven" are frequently used interchangeably. In the latter-day scriptures, particularly the one above, there is a distinctive meaning. "The kingdom of God is the Church of Christ; the kingdom of heaven is that system of government and administration which is operative in heaven, and which we pray may some day prevail on earth. The kingdom of heaven will be established when the King shall come, as come He shall, in power and might and glory, to take dominion in and over and throughout the earth. . . . The kingdom of heaven shall come, and then shall justice rule in the earth." (Talmage, James E.: *Conference Report*, April 1917, pp. 65-66; see also *Articles of Faith*, pp. 365-368.)

It Shall Stand Forever

Probably the most quoted part of Daniel's prophecy is verse 44:

And in the days of these kings shall the God of heaven set up a kingdom, which shall never be destroyed: and the kingdom shall not be left to other people, but it shall break in pieces and comsume all these kingdoms, and it shall stand for ever.

The Prophet Joseph Smith said of the Lord's work:

No unhallowed hand can stop the work of God from progressing. Persecution may rage, mobs may combine, armies may assemble, calumny may defame; but the truth of God will go forth boldly, nobly and independently, until it has penetrated every continent and visited every clime, swept over the country and sounded in every ear till the purposes of God shall be accomplished and the great Jehovah shall say the work is done. (*Scrapbook of Mormon Literature* 2:18-19.)

As early as 1831 when Wycom Clark and others broke away from the Church and organized their own church, Satan attacked God's work by influencing men to set up counter movements to the kingdom of God. As that attempt failed so will all other efforts to overthrow the kingdom of God, even though some of the offshoots may persist for a time.

Individual apostasies will not deter the kingdom. President Charles W. Penrose once said:

If you or I, or any of us, should leave the Church, the Church would still go on. Do not let us think, any of us, that the Church owes us anything. We owe a great deal to the Church, for light and truth and every principle and ordinance and authority and organization of the priesthood and of the helps and gifts that are in the Church for our comfort, our blessing, our union, and the continuation of power in the Church. They have come to us from God through the appointed authorities of the Church, and they will abide, no matter what we may do. (*Conference Report,* April 1913, p. 64.)

Conclusion

In the revelations of God to Joseph Smith there is clear indication that the Church organized in 1830 is the kingdom of God that will continue to remain God's Church, for as Daniel said, it will never be destroyed, or given to another people, but it will stand forever. The present increase in membership with the material gains of the Church in its building program, and the vitality of the convincing power of God to make people better, are indications of the progress of this work to fulfill its divine destiny. The keys of the kingdom are on the earth to bless and benefit all who want to receive the benefits of its powers for happiness here and eternal life in the world to come.

Chapter 52

THE SCRIPTURES

(Sections 66; 67; 68:1-6; 69)

In the last chapter, in addition to other items, emphasis was put upon the kingdom of God as the Church of Jesus Christ restored to the earth in fulfillment of prophecy. This Church, or the kingdom of God, will join with the kingdom of heaven to govern the nations during the millennium. The kingdom of God, as such, will eventually fill the entire earth. The first part of this chapter gives us information about those who labor in that kingdom.

Section 66—William E. M'Lellin

On October 25, 1831, an important conference of the Church convened at Orange, Ohio. The conference was highlighted by remarks of those present to consecrate all they possessed to the Lord. The Prophet Joseph Smith said that he did not have material things to consecrate but he was willing to consecrate himself and his family. (*DHC* I:219-220, footnote.)

It was on this day that William E. M'Lellin, a recent convert in attendance at the conference, requested that the Prophet obtain the Lord's will concerning him. He was told that he was blessed in turning away from his iniquities and accepting the everlasting covenant. (D&C 66:1-2.)

In the first verse of this revelation, we are informed that Jesus Christ is the "Savior of the world, even of as many as believe on my name." (See also Section 42:1.) Also of interest to us is the definition of the everlasting covenant in verse 2. This term means "the fulness of my gospel," the purpose of which is to provide men with an opportunity to "be made partakers of the glories which are to be revealed in the last days," as prophesied. (Chapter 51.)

Notwithstanding Brother M'Lellin had recently been baptized for the remission of his sins, he is told in verse 3 that he is "clean, but not all," and that repentance should be sought for those things which were not pleasing to the Lord. (D&C 66:3.) This evaluation of M'Lellin suggests a message that could probably be addressed to all the members of the Church. The scriptures aver that everyone is in need of repentance, although we know that some sin more grievously than others. (1 John 1:8; Eccl. 7:20.) The goal of the gospel is perfection. (3 Nephi 12:48.) As President Charles W. Penrose said: "We are none of us entirely perfect; but we expect to 'go on unto perfection' by keeping the will and word of the Lord" (*Conference Report*, October 1923, p. 18).

Brother M'Lellin was appointed to preach the gospel in the "eastern lands" [States] in company with Elder Samuel H. Smith, the brother of the Prophet. (D&C 66:4-8.) Promises of healing the sick and of knowing the will of the Lord were mentioned as some of M'Lellin's blessings. (*Ibid.*, v. 9.) Then the Lord reminded him that his weakness was the temptation to commit adultery. To become clean before the Lord, it was necessary that he be free of this temptation. (*Ibid.*, v. 10.) One may be reminded of the truth that the Lord does not look upon sin with the least degree of allowance, but he is willing to forgive those who sincerely overcome their weaknesses. (*Ibid.*, 1:31-33; Chapter 49.)

Although we are imperfect, and the Lord, therefore, calls imperfect people into his kingdom, he expects that persons called to advance his work will strive to overcome their shortcomings. Effective service that advances the salvation of the individual and the persons with whom he works or serves, requires that the worker have the Spirit of the Lord. (D&C 11:11-14.) Here are the words of President Lorenzo Snow on this matter:

... I feel that it belongs to me, and my brethren here, to be long suffering, kind, always ready to forgive, and to cherish the highest love for every man and woman who is trying to do the will of God. Do not be discouraged, brethren. If you cannot become perfect at once; if you see that you have weaknesses which have brought you into some trouble, do not be discouraged; repent of that which you have done wrong, by which you have lost more or less of the Spirit of God, tell the Lord what you have done and resolve in your hearts that you will do it no more. Then the Spirit of the Lord will be upon you. (*Conference Report,* October 1898, p. 56.)

The kingdom of God has imperfect workers in it who, if they are genuinely seeking to build Zion, will strive for the highest possible blessing that the Father has for his faithful children. Expressed in the revelation to William E. M'Lellin, it is achieved in instructions given in Section 66, verses 11 to 13.

Book of Commandments

When the Prophet returned from the conference at Orange, Ohio, a special conference convened at Hiram for two days. During this period several revelations were received, including Section 1, known as the "Lord's Preface" to the Doctrine and Covenants. The special business transacted at this November 1831 conference concerned the publication of the revelations which the Prophet had begun to compile in the summer of 1830. In this work he was assisted by John Whitmer, who later became the Church Historian. (*DHC* I:104; D&C 47:1.) Authorization was given for the printing of 10,000 copies of the compilation of revelations to be known as the Book of Commandments. On May 1, 1832, a general council of the Church decided that 3,000 copies should be printed. Some of the brethren mentioned in Section 70, verse 1, were appointed to prepare them for printing at the press of W. W. Phelps & Co. in Independence, Missouri. (*DHC* I:270.) In Section 69, received at the November 1831 conference, Oliver Cowdery and John Whitmer were appointed to take the revelations and certain money to the printing plant. (*DHC* I:229; D&C 69:1-2.) Further information about the Book of Commandments will be found in Chapter 2. This material tells of the destruction of the printing press, and of subsequent success in publishing the Doctrine and Covenants.

Section 67

In the Prophet's history he records that because of some conversation about revelations and language, he inquired of the Lord and received Section 67. (*DHC* I:224.) The revelation itself refers to imperfections noted by the elders at the conference, and the desire on the part of some to express the revelations better than in the Prophet's language. (D&C 67:5.) Because of these murmurings of discontent, a challenge was issued to the brethren assembled.

Now, seek ye out of the Book of Commandments, even the least that is among them, and appoint him that is the most wise among you;
Or, if there be any among you that shall make one like unto it, then ye are justified in saying that ye do not know that they are true;
But if ye cannot make one like unto it, ye are under condemnation if ye do not bear record that they are true.
For ye know that there is no unrighteousness in them, and that which is righteous cometh down from above, from the Father of lights. (D&C 67:6-9.)

In the group was William E. M'Lellin, the subject of Section 66, a schoolteacher who apparently was the chief critic of the revelations. In any case, this man felt that he was equal to the challenge and forthwith attempted to write a revelation as challenged. The Prophet's statement of this attempt gives us an insight into the character of M'Lellin as well as Joseph Smith's testimony of receiving communications from God. Here are his words:

> After the foregoing was received [Section 67], William E. M'Lellin, as the wisest man in his own estimation, having more learning than sense, endeavored to write a commandment like unto one of the least of the Lord's, but failed; it was an awful responsibility to write in the name of the Lord. The Elders and all present that witnessed this vain attempt of a man to imitate the language of Jesus Christ renewed their faith in the fulness of the Gospel, and in the truth of the commandments and revelations which the Lord had given to the Church through my instrumentality; and the Elders signified a willingness to bear testimony of their truth to all the world. (*DHC* I:226.)

In all the world there was not an individual who had the right by appointment of God to receive divine communications except Joseph Smith. The Prophet knew that "it was an awful responsibility to write in the name of the Lord."

It is true that an educated person might be able to frame words in such a manner that the language would appear to be "suitable" as a revelation, but language itself does not supply the spirit. In commenting upon this thought, Elder Orson F. Whitney said:

> It is not so easy to put the spirit of life into things. Man can make the body, but God alone can create the spirit. You have heard, have you not, of the scientist who took a grain of wheat and endeavored to make one just like it? First he separated the grain of wheat into its component parts, and found that it contained so much lime, so much silica, so much of this element and that; and then he took other parts corresponding thereto, brought them together by means of his chemical skill, and produced a grain of wheat so exactly similar to the other that the natural eye could not detect any difference beween them. But there was a difference, a vast difference, and it was demonstrated when he planted the two grains. The one that God made sprang

up, and the one that man made stayed down. Why? Because the man-made grain of wheat had no spirit — only a body, and the body without the spirit is dead. Man cannot breathe into the body of things the breath of life; that is a function and prerogative of Deity. It is not so easy to frame revelations from God. A vain boaster making ridicule of the proverbs of Solomon said: "Anybody can make proverbs." His friend answered, "Try a few," and the conversation ended. (*Conference Report,* April 1917, p. 42.)

Witnesses to the Doctrine and Covenants

Following Joseph Smith's report of M'Lellin's failure and his consequent confession to the conference, the Prophet recorded: "Accordingly I received the following": The testimony of the witnesses of the Book of Commandments, the title of the first compilation of revelations, followed. This testimony is printed in the "Explanatory Introduction" of each copy of the Doctrine and Covenants. By certifying to this statement, the elders testified that by the power of the Holy Ghost the Lord had borne witness to their souls of the truth that there was no unrighteousness in these revelations because they came from God. Since the revelations come from God, they are of utmost value to the inhabitants of the world. Section 1 of the Doctrine and Covenants states the purposes the Lord had in giving the revelations and also the benefits that may come to the world by obedience to the revelations. (Chapter 3.)

The "Explanatory Introduction" of the Doctrine and Covenants also contains the testimony of the first Quorum of Twelve Apostles of this dispensation. Their witness was given in 1835 when the second compilation of revelations was printed as the Doctrine and Covenants.

A Blessing Promised

Without disclosing the exact nature of the blessing which was offered to these elders in the November conference (D&C 67:3), the revelation continues to show how these elders might receive a knowledge of God by sight. They were told that only by stripping themselves of jealousies and fears and becoming sufficiently humble would this blessing be possible. (*Ibid.*, v. 10.) Reference is also made to the "natural man" as contrasted with the "spiritual." (*Ibid.*, v. 12.) King Benjamin of the Book of Mormon discoursed on the atonement of Christ for the salvation of man, which provides us with an important truth concerning these two conditions. (See Mosiah 3: 18-19.)

The natural man is that one who has not been influenced by the Spirit of God to change his life to become spiritual, or a saint. The characterization of a saint as one who is fully obedient to the word and will of the Lord, agrees with the many pronouncements that endurance to the end in righteousness will bring the blessings of eternal life. (Chapter 38.) To come into God's presence required that the candidate strip himself of pride, hate, cruelty, dishonesty, lying, sex offenses of thought and deed, and of other base sins of commission. Carnality in its many forms must be repented of.

The persons addressed in this revelation (Section 67) were told that they were unprepared to abide the Lord's presence or that of angels; however, if they continued in patience to perfect their lives, they would, in due time of the Lord, receive the promise of his presence. The instructions given concerning the natural man and the necessary preparation to behold God reminds one of Moses' experience in seeing him with his spiritual eyes. (Moses 1:11; D&C 67:11.)

Men may earn the perfection that warrants the Lord's presence. (D&C 88:66-68.) Perfection in many areas of living is possible in mortality as stated by Elder Mark E. Petersen:

I believe that in many ways, here and now in mortality, we can begin to perfect ourselves. A certain degree of perfection is attainable in this life. I believe that we can be one hundred percent perfect, for instance, in abstaining from the use of tea and coffee . . . paying a full and honest tithing . . . and giving to the bishop as fast offering the value of those two meals from which we abstain.

. . . in keeping the commandment which says that we shall not profane the name of God. We can be perfect in keeping the commandment which says, "Thou shalt not commit adultery." (Exod. 20:14.) We can be perfect in keeping the commandment which says, "Thou shalt not steal." (*Ibid.*, 15.) We can become perfect in keeping various other of the commandments that the Lord has given us. (*Conference Report*, April 1950, p. 153.)

Orson Hyde's Mission

Verse 1 of Section 68 is a call to Orson Hyde to preach the gospel in many lands, reasoning with the people and explaining the scriptures. This call was prophetic as subsequent events proved. Ten years later he was appointed to dedicate the land of Palestine for the return of the Jewish people to their homeland. As he made his journey to Palestine, he taught in many lands and performed his assignment on October 24, 1841. (*DHC* IV pp. 456-459.) The world today is witnessing the fulfillment of prophecies concerning the return of the tribe of Judah to that land.

How Scripture Is Made

The most important message of the forepart of Section 68 is the counsel given to these elders concerning scripture.

And, behold, and lo, this is an ensample unto all those who were ordained unto this priesthood, whose mission is appointed unto them to go forth—

And this is the ensample unto them, that they shall speak as they are moved upon by the Holy Ghost.

And whatsoever they shall speak when moved upon by the Holy Ghost, shall be scripture, shall be the will of the Lord, shall be the mind of the Lord, shall be the word of the Lord, shall be the voice of the Lord, and the power of God unto salvation.

Behold, this is the promise of the Lord unto you, O ye my servants. (D&C 68:2-5.)

It is to be noted that this counsel was directed to elders who would be engaged in a missionary work. Missionaries teaching the first principles to investigators are entitled to be moved upon by the Holy Ghost, for the diligent missionary teaches by the Spirit, and the investigator is influenced by that Spirit. (*Ibid.*, 50:22.)

There are among the General Authorities brethren who are sustained as "prophets, seers, and revelators," which gives them a special endowment in teaching the gospel to the people. President J. Reuben Clark, Jr., said that: "They have the right, the power, and authority to declare the mind and will of God to His people, subject to the overall power and authority of the President of the Church." Other members of the General Authorities are not so endowed, nor is any other officer or member of the Church. The President of the Church, as we have previously read, alone has the right to receive revelation for the Church and to give authoritative interpretations of scriptures that bind the Church. (*Ibid.*, 107:8, 65-66, 91-92.)

Scripture, then, is made by the Holy Ghost inspiring the prophets, seers, and revelators. Just as scripture was made in the past by the apostles and prophets of the Old and the New Testaments, so also is scripture being made today, when the prophets are moved upon by the Holy Ghost.

Chapter 53

THE BISHOPRIC; PARENTHOOD

(Section 68:7-35)

Four elders, one of whom was Orson Hyde, came to the Prophet Joseph Smith that they might learn the mind of the Lord concerning themselves. With the assurance that Elder Hyde and the other elders named would be sustained by the Lord in their missionary work as they faithfully fulfilled their callings, it was revealed that there should be no fear in their hearts. They were to declare their testimony of Jesus Christ as the Son of the living God who is yet to come in glory on the earth.

Missionary Message

All the faithful elders of the Church are to teach the testimony of Christ and the way that men may accept him as their Savior—by the first principles and ordinances of the gospel. As the disciples of the meridian dispensation were commanded to go into all the world with the message of faith, repentance, baptism in water, and the baptism of the Spirit, so also the elders of this dispensation are to carry the same message. (Matt. 28:19-20; D&C 68:7-9.) The promise is given that the elders so endowed with that Spirit would be blessed with signs, and they would also know of the signs of the times that herald the second coming of Christ. (*Ibid.*, vs. 10-11.)

The Saints will know the meaning of the times because the Lord has been kind to us and to all men who will believe the prophets. He who is wise in being forewarned will follow the path of safety by so living that he shall have the companionship of the Holy Ghost that gives peace, comfort, and a sense of security. The world may not recognize the signs that announce the imminence of

540   THE DOCTRINE AND COVENANTS SPEAKS

the Lord's second coming, but Latter-day Saints have reason to neither disbelieve nor fail to understand their importance.

In terms of missionary obligation President Heber J. Grant said:

> The one supreme thing that devolves upon me, upon you and upon every Latter-day Saint is the preaching of the gospel of the Lord Jesus Christ, in public and in private, and above all to proclaim the gospel in our lives, by being absolutely honest in keeping the commandments of the Lord. (*Conference Report*, October 1926, p. 6.)

The Office of Bishop

The first instruction given that bishops would be a part of the Church organization in this dispensation is found in Section 20:66-67, although these officers are mentioned as officiating in the Church during the time of the New Testament. (Phil. 1:1; Titus 1:7.)

Edward Partridge became the first bishop, his appointment being made at the time of the introduction of the law of consecration in 1831. (D&C 41:9; 57:7.) Other bishops and counselors in the bishopric, as well as agents of the Church such as Algernon S. Gilbert (*Ibid.*, 53:4) were appointed as the need arose. At this early period Bishop Partridge presided in Missouri while Bishop Newel K. Whitney officiated in a similar capacity at Kirtland, Ohio. (*Ibid.*, 72:8.)

As Paul said anciently, he who serves as bishop is in a good work. (1 Tim. 3:1.) President George Albert Smith said this about such a call:

> . . . There is no position in the Church that will bring a greater blessing to any man than the office of a bishop, if he will honor that office and be a real father to the flock over whom he is called to preside.
> . . . I have followed them and seen what their experiences were; they have a very great responsibility, and it takes a lot

of their time. But I want to say to you that there is no bishop, nor has there been a bishop in the Church, who has given the time that the Lord expected him to give in looking after the flock and teaching his people and preparing them to do the work, that has not received one hundred percent of the blessings that he labored for, and they will extend to him throughout the ages of eternity.

He may not have had wealth, may not have had distinction. He may not have had the honor of presiding over clubs and things of that kind, but if he has done his duty as a bishop, he has been hand in hand with the Father of us all, and everything that he has done to bless his kind is laid up as a treasure in heaven and nobody can take the blessing from him. (*Conference Report*, October 1948, pp. 186-187.)

Bishopric Appointments

The office of bishop and calls thereto are stated in Section 68 following the missionary call of the elders mentioned in verse 7. As the Church grew, additional workers were called to take care of the temporal concerns of the members and the Church. (*Ibid.*, 68:14.) These brethren were to be worthy high priests and appointed by the First Presidency. (*Ibid.*, v. 15.) It is explained that a high priest has authority to officiate in all lesser offices of the Melchizedek Priesthood including that of bishop which holds the presidency of the Aaronic Priesthood. (*Ibid.*, 107:13-15.) Since the Aaronic Priesthood is an appendage to the Melchizedek Priesthood, the elder or high priest may officiate in the offices of that Priesthood. (*Ibid.*, 107:10.)

Thus a ward bishop presides over the Aaronic Priesthood of his ward by reason of his ordination and setting apart as the president of the Aaronic Priesthood, and, at the same time, he presides over the Melchizedek Priesthood members of his ward, but not the quorum, because he is a high priest.

Literal Descendants

From the time of Adam into Moses' period the Higher Priesthood functioned. In the days of Moses, however, Aaron and his sons were set apart as priests in the Aaronic Priesthood which was named for Aaron. This Priesthood was conferred upon Aaron and his descendants for all time. (D&C 107:13.)

We learn in Section 68 that the seed of Aaron have a legal right to the presidency of the Aaronic Priesthood, provided the individual is the firstborn among the sons of Aaron and thus by birthright has the right of presidency. (*Ibid.*, vs. 16-17.) When no literal descendant can be found, and up to this time he has not been found, a high priest officiates as the Presiding Bishop of the Church. In the event a lineal descendant were available he would have to receive the requirements set forth in this revelation; that is, he would have to receive the same kind of call as all other officers in the Church. The claimant to this presidency would have to be designated by the First Presidency and ordained by that Presidency, if he were worthy. A further limitation is put upon such a person in that it would be necessary for him to prove his lineage or to ascertain it "by revelation from the Lord" under the hands of the Presidency of the Church. (*Ibid.*, vs. 19-21.) These provisions again remind us that the Lord's house is one of order. It would be impossible for the membership of the Church to be deceived in accepting a deceiver who would lay claim to this Priesthood. Subsequently, the Lord revealed that the literal descendant, properly appointed, could act without counselors. (*Ibid.*, 107:76.)

Another item concerning the Presiding Bishop given in Section 68 concerns the trial of that officer. Verses 22 through 24 specify that the First Presidency may try him for his membership. The ward bishop is not in the same position, since he may be tried by the presidency of the stake under whose jurisdiction he serves, because he does not hold the keys of the Aaronic Priesthood for the Church as does the Presiding Bishop.

Marriage and Parenthood

Marriage and parenthood are commanded of the Lord as necessary to fulfill the purpose of man's creation and also that of the earth. Those who maintain that marriage is not intended by God are not of him. In the fore-ordained plan of salvation, the spirit sons and daughters of God were destined to come to the earth and receive the experiences that an earth life offers. (D&C 49:15-17.) The assumption of parenthood by husband and wife entails an obligation of the most sacred kind. When one contemplates in what measure the blessings or punishments to be received by children in the eternities to come depend upon the training and teachings given by the parents, the tremendous responsibility of parenthood is better realized.

Oft-Quoted Scripture

Because of this responsibility the General Authorities through this dispensation have given emphasis to these verses:

And again, inasmuch as parents have children in Zion, or in any of her stakes which are organized, that teach them not to understand the doctrine of repentance, faith in Christ the Son of the living God, and of baptism and the gift of the Holy Ghost by the laying on of the hands, when eight years old, the sin be upon the heads of the parents.

For this shall be a law unto the inhabitants of Zion, or in any of her stakes which are organized.

And their children shall be baptized for the remission of their sins when eight years old, and receive the laying on of the hands.

And they shall also teach their children to pray, and to walk uprightly before the Lord.

And the inhabitants of Zion shall also observe the Sabbath day to keep it holy. (D&C 68:25-29.)

A summary of this commandment concerning parents and children includes the following: Parents are obligated (1) to teach their children the first principles and ordinances of the gospel; (2) to have their children baptized at the age of accountability—eight years of age; (3) to teach prayer; (4) to teach children to walk uprightly before the Lord; and (5) to teach observance of the Sabbath day.

What do these admonitions mean?

First Principles

Although faith is one of the first principles of the gospel, it is a gift that may grow as the person develops in understanding and practice of gospel principles. To nurture faith in the child, preparation must be made early when the greatest development comes to the individual. Accordingly, the parent teaches the fundamental principles of faith in Christ, of repentance, of baptism in water, and of the necessity for the Holy Ghost in the person's life. Although the Primary Association has some responsibility to prepare children for baptism, and the Sunday School assists, the first principle remains—the parents are responsible and are never relieved of this responsibility.

Baptism of Children

Section 68 sets forth in plain language that eight years is the age of accountability. Before this time the child is blameless before the Lord (*ibid.*, 29:46-47), and is saved in the kingdom of heaven. Before the age of eight, the child is of that kingdom. (Mark 10:13-16.) The two main purposes of baptism are to receive entrance into the kingdom of God, and to receive remission of sins. In the case of the child, baptism insures full membership in the kingdom, and the opportunity for the remission of sins upon repentance. (D&C 68:27.) If the person at eight or later does not accept the atonement of Christ for individual sins committed after that age, he remains in the bondage of sin. (*Ibid.*, 84:49-53.) By baptism of the water and the Spirit the door is opened for the person to have the benefits of the atonement of Christ for personal sins through sincere and genuine repentance. (Chapter 49.)

There is a class of children and adults who do not require baptism. These are the mentally deficient, for the atonement of Christ satisfies the demand of justice and redeems them without baptism. (D&C 29:49-50; Moroni 8:22; Chapter 20.)

Teach Prayer

Fundamental to belief in God and the restoration of the gospel through Joseph Smith is daily prayer. There is probably no one thing that will destroy reverence for Deity and a spiritual life more than to neglect the opportunity to pray. The investigator of the gospel is requested by the missionary to pray that he might learn the truth. The indoctrination of children in the habit of prayer will, in a large measure, keep them from error and give testimony growth. Prayer must, however, be meaningful in words and sincere in thought. The whole heart is demanded of him who seeks for divine guidance as well as the offering of gratitude for blessings received.

If you pray for your needs, then, as President Joseph F. Smith said,

... You pray with intelligence; you pray with understanding; you approach the Lord with a knowledge of what you should do, and how you should approach Him, and how you have a right to ask Him for the blessings you need, even to the laying on of hands upon the sick, praying for them, and rebuking disease, that they may be healed under the blessing of the Lord; and that the world does not possess. (*Conference Report*, April 1912, p. 8.)

"To Walk Uprightly"

Who should teach the children right and wrong, of the blessings that follow virtue, honesty, respect for authority, honor, loyalty to Church and country, attendance at Church meetings, the doctrines of the gospel, faith in the standard works of the Church, obedience to the law of tithing, Word of Wisdom, and temple marriage?

Here is what President David O. McKay says that bears upon this question:

You may think me extreme, but I am going to say that a married woman who refuses to assume the responsibilities of motherhood, or who, having children, neglects them for pleasure or social prestige, is recreant to the highest calling and privilege of womankind. The father, who because of business or political or social responsibilities, fails to share with his wife the responsibilities of rearing his sons and daughters, is untrue to his marital obligations, is a negative element in what might be and should be a joyous home atmosphere, and is a possible contributor to discord and delinquency. (*Gospel Ideals*, p. 477.)

Sabbath Day Observance

As always, the best teaching is by example. How can the parents expect the child to observe the commandments, including the keeping of the Sabbath day holy, and at the same time desecrate that day themselves? The importance of observing this holy day is given emphasis in Section 59 (Chapter 43), and also in this section, verse 29. Although given about the instruction of children, the admonition is for all the inhabitants of Zion.

The Riches of Eternity

The condition of some of the Saints in Zion (Missouri) in 1831 is depicted as idle, greedy, and with their children growing up in wickedness. (D&C 68:30-31.) We cannot put ourselves back in 1831, but there was a need for the instructions given then concerning parents and children as outlined in this revelation. With the stepped-up opportunities for wickedness resulting from the automobiles, movies—in and out of the home—false philosophies and theories, the youth of today and the parents may now have greater need for attention to this revelation than in 1831.

The counsel of the Lord based upon the perspective of the eternities is: seek earnestly for the riches of eternity (D&C 68:31), and you shall find joy and peace in this life and eternal life in the world to come, for I "shall lead thee by the hand, and give thee answer to thy prayers." (*Ibid.*, 112:10). Remember, "These sayings are true and faithful; wherefore, transgress them not, neither take therefrom." (*Ibid.*, 68:34.)

Chapter 54

MISSIONARY SERVICE

(Section 71)

Following the four November 1831 conferences, Oliver Cowdery and John Whitmer left for Jackson County, Missouri, in obedience to revelation. (D&C Section 69.) Joseph Smith resumed the revision of the Bible with Sidney Rigdon acting as scribe. (*DHC* I:238.) A month before this, Ezra Booth, mentioned in Chapter 50, apostatized and set out to bring harm to the Prophet and to the Church. His efforts to do both of these apparently met with partial success. In the first instance, it was some of his efforts and his participation in mob action against the Prophet that brought physical harm to the Prophet. (*DHC* I:261-265.) His attack against the Church and its members was made in a series of nine letters published by the *Ohio Star* (Ravenna, Ohio). They consisted of slanderous denunciations and falsehoods concerning Joseph and the Church. (Section 71.)

In view of these efforts of Satan to thwart the work of the kingdom, the Prophet and Sidney were called by revelation to preach the gospel in the regions adjacent to Kirtland. (D&C 71:1-3.) An indication of the message delivered by these two missionaries on this special mission from December 1831 until the 10th of January 1832 is given in the Prophet's journal. He said it was a vindication of the cause of the Redeemer, that the day of vengeance was coming upon this generation, and that prejudice and darkness caused some to persecute the true Church. Much of the bigotry caused by the apostate's letters was allayed through this mission.

The revelation counseled these brethren to confound their enemies both in public and private, with the promise that their opponents would be shamed. (*Ibid.*, v. 7.) It is worthy to note that when the Lord's servants are attacked, it is tantamount to attacking the Lord. (*Ibid.*, v. 8.)

Preach the Gospel

The commandment to participate in debate was given to the Prophet because of the unusual circumstances noted above. The Lord, on the other hand, had counseled his servants to preach the first principles, to obtain the Spirit that it might convey the truth to the hearer, and thus make known the message of the dispensation. (D&C 33; 34; 42:12-17.)

An experience of the Prophet in October 1833 is an excellent example of the present counsel of the General Authorities that missionaries should not indulge in debate or argument, but they should preach the simple principles by the Spirit.

While in Canada with Sidney Rigdon at the house of Freeman Nickerson's brother, the latter desired to match his Bible learning with that of the Prophet in an attempt to disprove Joseph Smith as a prophet. One night the opportunity came when Freeman Nickerson placed the Bible on the table and said, "There! Now, go to it!" The Prophet took up the challenge by telling the simple but powerful and convincing account of the restoration of the gospel. The Spirit of the Lord was so manifest in his testimony that opposition no longer remained. By the aid of Freeman's brother, meetings were held that resulted in fourteen baptisms, including the Nickerson who was determined to show the Prophet wrong. (Evans, John Henry: *Joseph Smith an American Prophet*, pp. 86-88.)

Lack of Success in Opposition

The Lord's work was not restored to fail. As pointed out earlier (Chapter 51) the kingdom of God is on the earth in the form of the Church, and the Lord has planned that it shall never be destroyed nor given to another people, but it shall stand forever. (Daniel 2:44.) In Section 71, an aspect of this foreknown eventuality is given in verses 9 and 10:

> Verily, thus saith the Lord unto you—there is no weapon that is formed against you shall prosper;
>
> And if any man lift his voice against you he shall be confounded in mine own due time.

It is apparent that this assurance of defeat for those who lift their voices in opposition to the Prophet includes not only the experiences of the missionaries of 1831-32, but of any time. To speak against the Prophet of this dispensation is the same as warring against the Church which he established, and also against God.

Published opposition was not the only "weapon" used against the Prophet and the Saints. Physical persecution has been a common means of attempting to thwart the purpose of the Lord. Despite the adversary's "weapons," the work of God has rolled on until today the voice of opposition is largely submerged by the prophesied, inevitable progress of successful endeavors.

The missionary today can be as confident of victory as those to whom the foregoing revelation was given. The testimony of President Heber J. Grant concerning those who have fought against the Lord's work is appropriate in this regard:

> Our enemies have never done anything that has injured this work of God, and they never will. I look around, I read, I reflect and I ask questions, where are the men of influence, of power and prestige, who have worked against the Latter-day Saints? Where is the reputation for honor and courage, of the governors of Missouri and Illinois, the judges, and all others who have come here to Utah on special missions against t h e Latter-day Saints? Where are there people to do them honor? They cannot be found. . . . Where are the men who have assailed this work? Where is their influence? They have faded away

like dew before the sun. We need have no fears, we Latter-day Saints. God will continue to susutain this work; he will sustain the right. If we are loyal, if we are true, if we are worthy of this Gospel, of which God has given us a testimony, there is no danger that the world can ever injure us. We can never be injured . . . by any mortals, except ourselves. (*Conference Report*, April 1909, p. 11.)

Commandments Are True

Obedience to truth is the prescription for happiness here and eternal joy in the life to come. The Lord admonished the Prophet and Sidney Rigdon to keep the commandments for they are true. (D&C 71:11.) The knowledge of truth is given by the Spirit which the missionary is counseled to receive and to teach by. President Joseph F. Smith stated the importance of adhering to the truth in these words:

Our hope of salvation must be founded upon the truth, the whole truth, and nothing but the truth, for we cannot build upon error and ascend into the courts of eternal truth and enjoy the glory and exaltation of the kingdom of our God. That cannot be done. (*Conference Report*, October 1917, p. 3.)

Chapter 55

STEWARDSHIPS; A REVIEW

(Sections 70 and 72)

During the first twelve days of November 1831, four special conferences were conducted by the Prophet Joseph Smith. A part of the proceedings of some of these conferences has already been noted in Chapter 52. One of the principal orders of business concerned the publication of the revelations into a volume to be known as the Book of Commandments. At this time the Prophet gave an evaluation of the revelations, which is worthy of notice by all people. His first point was that they were the foundation of the Church in the last days. The Prophet also said that these revelations were of such great benefit to the world because they brought eternal life within the reach of everyone who was willing to live by every word which the Lord had revealed. When one thinks of this fact, he immediately remembers that: first, divine directions were given to organize the Church, with the powers of the Priesthood restored for this purpose. Second, these revelations point out the clear pathway of salvation with its principles and ordinances to lead the faithful to exaltation. Third, they also give an understanding of man's purpose in life, with specific directions on how covenants may be kept inviolate. Fourth, the Lord's will is revealed regarding present world conditions and what one may expect in the future. Fifth, the great blessing of how to achieve joy in this life through physical and spiritual well being is indicated. These and other contributions to man's knowledge give abundant support to the Prophet's evaluation.

The first conference that convened in November voted, after approving the printing of the revelations, that

... they prize the revelations to be worth to the Church the riches of the whole earth, speaking temporally. The great benefits to the world which result from the Book of Mormon and the revelations which the Lord has seen fit in His infinite wisdom to grant unto us for our salvation, and for the salvation of all that will believe, were duly appreciated. . . . (*DHC* I:235-236.)

Following this statement the Prophet wrote that Section 70 was received upon his inquiry.

Section 70

Several elders were named in verse 1 of Section 70, and their responsibilities regarding the revelations to be printed were outlined in verses 2 through 9. In addition to taking care of the revelations, they were to see to their printing and distribution. The books were to be sold, and the surplus was to be placed in the hands of the bishop and placed in the Lord's storehouse to be consecrated to the faithful inhabitants of Zion.

In the minutes of the conference it was recorded that four of the brethren named in this revelation—Oliver Cowdery, Martin Harris, John Whitmer, Sidney Rigdon —had, from the beginning, labored with the Prophet; consequently, they, with the families of several others, according to the laws of the Church, were worthy of an inheritance from the bishop in Zion. (*DHC* I:236.)

Stewardships

The brethren mentioned in Section 70 were told that their obligation in caring for the revelations, as given above, referred to as a stewardship. As stewards, these elders were to discharge their responsibilities to the letter. The importance of caring for their stewardship in this manner is thus indicated:

And an account of this stewardship will I require of them in the day of judgment. (D&C 70:4.)

The application of this truth, when applied to all members of the Church in what the Lord has given them, is discussed by President Brigham Young, in these words:

... What is our duty? It is our duty to improve upon every blessing the Lord gives to us. If He gives us land, improve it; if He gives us the privilege of building houses, improve it ... if He gives us the privilege of gathering together, let us sanctify ourselves. In His providence He has called the Latter-day Saints from the world, has gathered them from other nations, and given them a place upon the earth. Is this a blessing? Yes, one of the greatest the people can enjoy, to be free from the wickedness of the wicked, from the calamities and clamor of the world. By this blessing we can show to our Father in Heaven that we are faithful stewards; and more, it is a blessing to have the privilege of handing back to Him that which He has put in our possession, and not say it is ours, until He shall say it from the heavens. (*Journal of Discourses* 2:304-305.)

All of us are stewards over the things of this earth which are ours legally, but, in fact, they are the Lord's. (Mosiah 2:20-26.) An accounting of what we do with these blessings, including offices in the Church, will be required of us in the day of judgment. During the period when Section 70 was given and for some time later, all members of the Church were under obligation to abide by the law of consecration. This exempted no one. (D&C 70: 10-11.) Under this law, all were to be equal, but the equality was not of a dead-level nature. Each was to receive according to his needs and circumstances. (*Ibid.*, 14-18; 42:32; 51:3.)

Worthy of His Hire

When the Lord instructed his Seventy, who were to precede him into the village where he would preach, he counseled them to receive such assistance as was needful from those who would offer it. (Luke 10:1-8.) Jesus taught the Seventy that "the labourer is worthy of his hire." (*Ibid.*, verse 7.) This truth has been given in this dispensation, and under the law as stated, those who work for the welfare of their fellow Church members are to receive in accordance with their needs. This law not only applies to those appointed to administer in the temporal but also in the spiritual concerns of the Church. (D&C 70:12-13.) It will be recalled that soon after the Church was organized, a revelation was received giving the three branches of the Church the opportunity to provide material support to the Prophet Joseph Smith, since he was required to tend to his duties as the Prophet. (*Ibid.*, 24: 3-4.) Remuneration for services or temporal assistance has been given to certain groups at different times during this dispensation. (*DHC* I:220.) What may be termed the law of remuneration was also revealed in Section 42, verses 70 through 73, and mentioned in 43:13. Where individuals must give of their full time to accomplish their callings which would not allow them to make a livelihood otherwise, a just remuneration is allowed. In the main, however, the male members of the Church function in the Priesthood without benefit of monetary help. All Church members are expected to contribute of their time, talents, and material possessions for the advancement of the kingdom of God. The spiritual rewards of such service are known to all those who have thus participated.

Section 72

The Prophet and Sidney Rigdon undertook a mission as commanded. (Section 71.) While in Kirtland, Ohio, several elders and members raised questions which apparently required the Lord's answer; whereupon, Section 72 was received. (*DHC* I:239.)

When the Prophet had arrived in Kirtland, almost one year before this, the Lord revealed that Edward Partridge should be appointed as the bishop unto the Church.

(D&C 41:9-10.) Not long after that Bishop Partridge and others, including Joseph Smith, went to western Missouri, where the bishop was to take up his duties under the law of consecration. (*Ibid.*, 58:7, 14-15.) The temporal and spiritual needs of the Church in Kirtland were such that the Lord appointed a bishop in Kirtland. The appointee was Newel K. Whitney. (*Ibid.*, 72:2, 8.) An interesting story of his call is related by his grandson, Orson F. Whitney, an apostle of this dispensation:

Newel K. Whitney, staggering under the weight of the responsibility that was about to be placed upon him, said to the Prophet: "Brother Joseph, I can't see a Bishop in myself."

No; but God could see it in him. He was a natural Bishop— a first class man of affairs. Probably no other incumbent of that important office, the Presiding Bishopric, to which he eventually attained, has been better qualified for it than Newel K. Whitney. But he could not see it, and he shrank from the responsibility. The Prophet answered: "Go and ask the Lord about it." And Newel did ask the Lord, and he heard a voice from heaven say: "Thy strength is in me." That was enough. He accepted the office, and served in it faithfully to the end of his days—a period of eighteen years. (*Conference Report*, June 1919, pp. 47-48.)

The duties of Bishop Whitney were set forth as: (1) to receive an accounting of the stewardships of the elders in that area; (2) to keep the Lord's storehouse; (3) to receive funds; (4) to administer to the wants of the elders; (5) to render an accounting to Bishop Partridge in Zion of those who were unable to pay for what they received of the Church. (D&C 72:5-13.)

Although Bishop Whitney was required to look after the stewardships of the elders in that area, each steward would have to give an accounting of his own stewardship, in time and in eternity. (*Ibid.*, v. 3.) Agreeable to the law that obedience brings forth the blessings of heaven (*ibid.*, 130:20-21), we are told that

. . . he who is faithful and wise in time is accounted worthy to inherit the mansions prepared for him of my Father. (*Ibid.*, 72:4.)

An Application

As one looks at the foregoing list of responsibilities of the bishop in Kirtland and thinks of their application to the present-day ward bishop he sees the same or similar duties to this office. Verse 12 of Section 72 states that the bishop is to take care of the poor and needy. The calling of the bishop was well explained by President Joseph F. Smith as not only taking care of the poor, the sick and the afflicted, but also these duties:

. . . It is also the duty of these presiding officers [bishopric] in the Church to look after the spiritual welfare of the people, to see that they are living moral, pure and upright lives, that they are faithful in the discharge of their duties as Latter-day Saints, that they are honest in their dealings with one another, and with all the world. It is their business to see that spiritual light exists in their hearts, and that the people under their presidency and direction are living the lives of Saints, as far as it is possible for men and women in the mortal body, beset by the weaknesses and imperfections of mankind, can be Saints. Great responsibility rests upon these, and we have to work in the Church, in this relation, a vast corps of efficient men who are laboring diligently for the welfare of mankind. (*Conference Report*, October 1904, p. 3.)

Conclusion of Section 72

Further information was given about the operation of the law of consecration with special emphasis upon the necessity for members of the Church in Kirtland, going to Zion, to take with them a certificate showing that they were worthy members. (D&C 72:16-26.) The same procedure is followed today in what is known as the membership certificate.

The conclusion of this revelation suggests that wise stewards are to follow the counsel given in the revelation. (*Ibid.*, vs. 25-26.) In the ultimate sense, the member who follows the words of the Lord will place the interests of the Church first. Brigham Young's life of dedication to the cause of Zion is a splendid example of the faithful steward.

Brigham Young is a striking illustration of wise management. In September, 1833, he came to Kirtland, absolutely destitute, a widower with two children to take care of. He had borrowed a pair of shoes and some other articles of clothing, and he had spent every dollar he had on missionary labors. Of the thirty or forty Elders who came to Kirtland that fall, he was the only one who remained there during the winter. The others went wherever they could obtain higher wages than in Kirtland. He went to work for Brother William F. Cahoon, one of the trustees of the Temple. As wages, Brother Cahoon divided what little he had with Brigham Young. But, when the work was done, the balance due was paid, and it was subsequently found that none of those who had left Kirtland for higher wages had been able to save as much as he had. He stayed in Kirtland till the year 1837, and then he practically abandoned property valued at $5,000. In Nauvoo he also left some houses, and came to Utah without a farthing, except a span of horses, a carriage and harness, all of which had been given him in payment for a house in Nauvoo. See *Journal of Discourses*, Vol. XI pp. 295-6; Brigham Young was a wise steward, because he always placed the interests of the Kingdom of God first. (*Doctrine and Covenants Commentary*, p. 428.)

Do we individually meet the requirements of the wise steward?

What of the Past?

Section 72 was the last revelation received during the year 1831. It was the most fruitful year in terms of the number of revelations received as shown in the "Chronological Order of Contents" in the forepart of each copy of the Doctrine and Covenants.

A review of the sections will indicate that, because of the growth of the Church during the latter part of 1830 and the year 1831, many problems arose in this fast-growing Church. At the beginning of the year, the Lord took cognizance of the poverty of the Saints and promised that he would give his "law" which, if lived, would bring temporal relief to the citizens of his kingdom and would prepare them for spiritual unity. This would result in the blessing of each person enjoying equally the bounties of the earth. (Section 38.) Officers were added to the Church, such as the High Priests of the Melchizedek Priesthood; the bishop, the presiding officer of the Aaronic Priesthood; and a Church Historian. (*Doctrine and Covenants Commentary*, p. 205; D&C Sections 41, 72, and 47, respectively.) The promised "law" (Section 42) included commandments regarding (1) preaching the gospel; (2) moral conduct; (3) consecration; (4) administration to the sick; (5) sundry duties; (6) remuneration for services; and (7) the law concerning transgressors.

The fundamental principle that only one man may receive revelation for the Church, while others may receive individual guidance was also given. (Section 43.) There followed the great revelations on signs which would precede the Lord's second coming and the events associated with that coming. (Sections 43 and 45.)

A series of revelations contains the keys against being deceived, for the benefit of Church members of 1831 and in subsequent years. These sections include counsel on the benefits accruing to members because of receiving the gift of the Holy Ghost, with the many gifts that strengthen one against deception. (Section 46.) Due to the presence of a sect known as the Shaking Quakers (Chapter 34), to whom the Lord directed missionary work, the Saints were given enlightenment on the purpose of the earth, the necessity of marriage, the keys against false Christs and other impostors, with the ultimate movement of the Church to the Rocky Mountain area. (Section 49.) A lesson is learned in Section 50 when manifestations of false spirits seek to deceive the unwary. Direction is provided to test false teachings out of the Church as well as in it. (Section 52.)

In counsel given to individuals who sought for guidance, there are some universal truths enunciated which point up these three facts: (1) those who seek the Lord early will find rich benefits that prepare them for a full and long life here and for the blessings of eternity (Section 54); (2) exaltation is earned by enduring to the end through constancy in living the commandments (Section 53); (3) to take up one's cross involves a large number of commitments by the covenant child of God. (Section 56.)

The anticipation of the Saints in knowing the location and the destiny of the prophesied New Jerusalem is realized. The objective to work for the establishment of Zion upon the earth is made known. (Sections 57 and 58.)

The Sabbath day observance and the rich benefits to be received by the obedient is made known during this period. (Section 59.)

A promise of "much tribulation" (Section 58), and a warning concerning the waters of the last days was also received. (Section 61.) Instructions to missionaries in exercising their talents and bearing testimony, also form a part of the year's counsel. (Sections 60 and 62.)

There is renewed the fate of the sign seeker; and counsel against falling into lightmindedness toward sacred things is given emphasis. (Section 63.)

The sections of this year's study complete the year's revelations—forgiveness and repentance, the ultimate triumph of God's work, further additions to our knowledge of Church organization—the bishopric, and, finally, the responsibility of parents in the rearing of their children.

In commenting upon the revelations received during the year 1831, the *Doctrine and Covenants Commentary* gives some important observations that bear testimony of the truth received by Joseph Smith.

There is a wonderful feature connected with these Revelations—their *Unity*. Although neither the Prophet Joseph nor his associates had any pre-arranged plan regarding the work in which they were engaged, every Revelation fits into its place perfectly, as does each separate stone which the skillful architect lays in the walls of his magnificent cathedral, and as we follow the development from Section to Section, we perceive that there is a plan so grand, so beautiful, and so well adapted to human needs, as to leave no room for doubt concerning its divine origin. Each Revelation, considered by itself, though full of beauty, may be but a stone detached from the building to which it belongs, but seen as a part of the entire structure, it speaks with convincing eloquence of the wisdom, power, and love of the Divine Builder of the Church, our Lord Jesus Christ. (p. 429.)

As one takes into consideration the foregoing evaluation and brief summary of the revelations received in the year 1831, the following general contributions emerge:

1. A set of moral laws, which, if adopted, would bring peace to man, individually and collectively
2. A socio-economic order that would answer man's basic needs in life and assist him to find advancement along the way to perfection
3. The important element of *order* so necessary for the perpetuity of the government of God
4. Basic principles to be applied by the member that he may not be deceived by false teaching and theories and misinterpretation of scripture
5. Goals for this life
6. Warning against the attainment of these goals without tribulation
7. Knowledge of and guidance in meeting the problems and issues of a world in trouble, because of increased wickedness.
8. Implementation of Church organization to meet the circumstances

BIBLIOGRAPHY

I. Latter-day Saint Scriptures

The Bible (King James translation)
The Book of Mormon (1920 edition)
The Doctrine and Covenants (1921 edition)
The Pearl of Great Price (1921 edition)

II. Books

Bennion, M. Lynn, *Mormonism and Education*, 1939.
Bowen, Albert E., *The Welfare Plan*, 1946.
Bowen, Walter Dean, *The Versatile W. W. Phelps*, Brigham Young University, 1958. Unpublished master's thesis.
Cannon, George Q., *Gospel Truth*, compiled by Jerreld L. Newquist, 1959.
Cowley, Matthias F., *Wilford Woodruff*, 1909.
Dickens, Charles, *The Uncommercial Traveler*, 1868.
Documentary History of the Church of Jesus Christ of Latter-day Saints, Six Volumes, (*Edition* beginning 1902)
Evans, John Henry, *Joseph Smith An American Prophet*, 1942
Farrar, F. W., *Eternal Hope*, 1878.
Grant, Heber J., *Gospel Standards*, 1941.
Jenson, Andrew, *L. D. S. Biographical Encyclopedia*, Vol. I, 1901.
Labors in the Vineyard, Twelfth Book of the Faith-promoting Series, 1882.
Lee, Harold B., "The Sixth Commandment," *The Ten Commandments Today*, 1954.
McKay, David O., *Gospel Ideals*, 1953.
Nibley, Preston, *Witnesses of the Book of Mormon*, 1946.
Petersen, Mark E., *Your Faith and You*, 1953.
Pratt, Parley P., *Autobiography of Parley P. Pratt*, 1874 ed.
Pyper, George D., *Stories of Latter-day Saint Hymns*, 1940.
Richards, Stephen L, *Where Is Wisdom?*, 1955.
Roberts, B. H., *A Comprehensive History of the Church of Jesus Christ of Latter-day Saints*, Vol. I, 1930.
Roberts, B. H., *New Witness for God*, Volume II, 1926.
Romney, Thomas C., *The Gospel in Action*, 1949.
Skousen, Cleon, "The Eighth Commandment," *The Ten Commandments Today*, 1954.
Smith, Hyrum M. and Sjodahl, James M., *The Doctrine and Covenants Commentary*. Revised under the direction of the First Presidency of the Church by Joseph Fielding Smith, Harold B. Lee, and Marion G. Romney, 1951.

Smith, Joseph Fielding, *Church History and Modern Revelation*, Series 1, 2, 3, and 4, 1947-1950.
Smith, Joseph Fielding, *Doctrines of Salvation*, 3 Volumes. Compiled by Bruce R. McConkie, 1954-1956.
Smith, Joseph Fielding, *Essentials in Church History*, 1924.
Smith, Joseph Fielding, *Gospel Doctrine*, 6th Edition, 1943.
Smith, Joseph Fielding, *Teachings of the Prophet Joseph Smith*, 1942.
Smith, Joseph Fielding, *The Way to Perfection*, 1940.
Smith, Luck Mack, *History of Joseph Smith by His Mother*, 1945.
Talmage, James E., *The Articles of Faith*, 1950.
Talmage, James E., *Jesus the Christ*, 1916.
Talmage, James E., *The Vitality of Mormonism*, 1919.
Taylor, John, *Mediation and Atonement*, 1950.
White, Anna and Taylor, Leila S., *Shakerism, Its Meaning and Message*, 1904.
Whitney, Orson F., *Life of Heber C. Kimball*, 1945.
Whitney, Orson F., *Saturday Night Thoughts*, 1921.
Widtsoe, John A., *Discourses of Brigham Young*, 1925.

III. Newspapers and Periodicals

Church News, May 11, 1946; March 29, 1958.
Conference Reports of The Church of Jesus Christ of Latter-day Saints, Annual and Semiannual.
Deseret News, April 11, 1860; January 20, 1959.
Deseret Weekly, Vol. 53, November 7, 1896.
Dispensation of the Fulness of Times, Part I, YMMIA Manual, 1899-1900.
Evening and Morning Star, 1832.
Historical Record, Volumes 5-8, Church Encyclopedia, Book I, 1889.
Improvement Era, November 1909 - December 1961.
Journal of Discourses, Vols. 1-26, 1854-1886.
Juvenile Instructor, Vol. 10, 1875.
Kimball, Spencer W., "Be Ye Clean," Brigham Young University Speeches of the Year, May 4, 1954.
Kimball, Spencer W., "Tragedy or Destiny," address to Brigham Young University student body, December 6, 1955.
Messenger and Advocate, Vol. I.
Millennial Star, Vol. II, 1849; Vol. 21, 1859; Vol. 26, 1864.
Relief Society Magazine, Vol. VI, March 1919.
Scrapbook of Mormon Literature, Vol. 2, (no date).
Utah Genealogical and Historical Magazine, April 1925, October 1930, October 1934.

Index By Sections of the Doctrine and Covenants Speaks

INDEX

A

Aaron, 162, 542.
Aaronic priesthood, restored, 63-71, 107, 140, 541, 542, 543, 559.
Abinadi, 280.
"Abominable" doctrine, 99-100; Lord's answer to, 100-101.
Abraham, 15, 162, 179, 215, 341, 514.
Abortion, 255-256.
Acts, 5, 7, 12, 17, 63, 68, 145, 169, 241, 278, 280, 313, 338, 439, 469, 489, 522.
Adam, 15, 36, 69, 92, 162, 173, 176, 237, 304, 426, 436, 542 and the devil, 178; fall of, 178-182.
Adam-ondi-Ahman, 303.
Administration, gift of, 316.
Administration to sick, law of, 230, 272, 281, 545-546, 559.
Adultery, 253-255, 447, 537.
Adversary, 468, 472, 550.
Age of accountability, 544.
"All things common," 261, 262-263.
Alma 4, 20, 73, 75, 76, 103, 112, 130, 190, 191, 218, 232, 233, 253, 257, 277, 350, 372, 385, 424, 472, 486.
Amazon, 477-478.
Ammon, 217.
Amos, 4, 474.
Amulek, 73, 257.
Angels, 28, 29, 30, 43, 60, 65, 70, 91, 100, 161, 188, 215, 231, 341, 470, 473, 518, 536.
Anthon, Charles, Prof., 55.
Apostasy, 2, 6, 199, 258, 290, 313, 496, 512, 529, 533; spirit of, 186-192; universal, 11.
Arguments against further revelation, 2-4.
Articles of Faith, tenth, 440, 489; 442, 503, 505, 528.
Articles &of Faith, tenth, 440, 489; twelfth, 439.
Ascension, 5.
Atonement, 93, 102, 103-105, 113, 130, 138, 180, 182, 208, 216, 283, 379, 496, 510, 536, 545.
Autobiography of Parley P. Pratt, 192, 195, 196, 347.

B

Babylon, 24, 27.
Bailey, Raymond T., 147.
Ballard, Melvin J., 61-62.

Baptism, 63-64, 69-70, 95, 106, 107, 114, 118-120, 131, 200, 205, 255, 305, 312, 314, 322, 338, 362-363, 364, 371, 390, 402, 421, 429, 458, 500, 539, 543; of children, 544-545; requirements of 119-120.
"Be Ye Clean," BYU Speeches of the Year, 1954, 503-504.
Benjamin, 257, 422, 456, 481, 536.
Bennion, M. Lynn, 407.
Bible, 3, 4, 5, 6, 8-9, 22, 29, 30, 196, 199, 231, 236, 280, 285, 359, 400, 505, 514, 521, 548, 549.
Bidamon, Lewis Crum, Major, 146.
Billings, Titus, 494.
Bishop, 264, 265, 437-438, 556; judge in Israel, 503, 509; office of, 540-541, 557, 559; Presiding, 542-543; to discern all gifts, 322.
Bishopric, the, 539-547.
Bishop's storehouse, 266, 260-271, 375, 553, 556.
Blackmail, 246.
Blaspheme, to, 496-499.
Blessings, 82, 84, 220-221, 224, 232, 532, 536, 546, 556; elder's, 404; in 278, 369, 431, 443, 446, 447, 449, 454, 455, 482, 486, 507, 514, 517, service, 25; loss of, 297; mysteries as, 491-492; of death, 494-495; promise of, 415, 456, 488; to the poor, 425.
Book of Commandments, 13-14, 21, 325, 348, 406, 532, 533, 535; publication of, 552.
Book of the Law of the Lord, 331.
Book of Mormon, 9, 13, 16, 20, 25, 38, 39, 40, 41, 43, 44, 45, 52, 53, 82, 85, 92, 97, 105, 107, 118, 137, 142, 148, 158, 161, 196, 197, 198, 216, 217, 231, 233, 252, 278, 280, 309, 329, 359, 378, 400, 413, 422, 455, 481, 484, 503, 505, 514, 522, 524, 536, 553; fundamental teachings of, 111-116; gold plates of the, 9, 483; publication of, 426; purposes of, 111; sign-seekers in, 485-486; translating of, 54, 57, 63, 79, 80, 89, 110, 194; witnesses to, 56, 188, 325, 483, 518.
Bounties of men, 455.
Bowen, Albert E., 19, 73, 262.
Booth, Ezra, 511, 512, 548.
Breastplate, 57.
Brigham Young University, 408.

Brotherly kindness, 48, 50.
Burgess, Harrison, 478.
Burglary, 245.

C

Caesar, render unto, 492-493.
Cahoon, William F., 558.
Cain, 240.
Campbellites, 196, 226.
Cannon, George Q., 235, 250, 392, 395, 436, 437, 517.
Canon of scripture, 2.
Capital punishment, 243.
Carter, Simeon, 197.
Celestial Kingdom, 85, 86, 93, 182, 413, 415, 422, 446, 482.
Celibacy, 341, 342.
Century's Change in Religion, The, 98.
Cestus Gallus, 288.
Charity, 4, 48, 95, 410.
Chastity, 49.
Children, baptism, 543-545; death of, 181-182; education of, 406-408, 546, 560; habits and attitudes of, 381-382; mentally retarded, 545; of Israel, 61, 479; opportunities for, 383; teach, 121-122, 380, 381-382, 544, 546, 560.
Christ, see Jesus Christ.
Christian churches, 2, 6.
Christianity, 6, 9.
Christy, Sid, 321.
Chronicles, 1; 6, 145, 438.
Chronicles, 2; 6, 63, 84.
Church Historians Office, 327-329, 334, 559.
Church History and Modern Revelation, 116, 342, 343.
Church News, The, 133, 499.
Church of Jesus Christ, 5, 6, 9, 11, 313, 526; re-establishment of, 63.
Church of Jesus Christ of Latter-day Saints, 1, 14, 16-18, 25, 26, 33, 35, 60, 61, 76, 83, 90, 108, 110, 138, 139, 153, 154, 155, 159, 195, 211, 232, 243, 268, 274, 296, 311, 325, 334, 355, 363, 373, 378, 384, 403, 408; converts to, 291; everyday religion, 461; gifts given to, 315-324; law of the, 228-230; membership responsibilities of, 118-126, 134, 159, 502, 540; objectives of, 222; officers appointed, 159-160, 229; ordinances of, 124; organized, 108-109, 116, 118, 390, 526; purpose of the, 526-527; records of, 124, 325-335; repentance for the, 421; responsibilities of, 46, 382.

Church Welfare Plan, The, 19, 73, 262.
Church School System, 408.
Citizenship, 440.
Civil War, 223, 329.
Clark, J. Reuben, Jr., 132, 22, 239,
Clark, J. Reuben, Jr., 132, 222, 239, 264, 270, 365, 452, 538.
Cleveland, Sarah M., 149.
Coe, Joseph, 405.
Coleridge, 317.
Colossians, 6, 49, 208.
Columbus, 206.
Commandments, 389, 395, 402, 433, 434, 446-447, 522, 560; keep, 312, 314, 324, 356, 378, 392, 398, 420, 428, 429, 433, 443, 488, 501, 505, 520, 527, 540, 551; loss of, 420, 441; obey the, 323, 419, 422; of God, 349; of the Sabbath, 448-453; rewards for keeping, 454-462; to purchase land, 492-493.
Common consent, law of, 123, 124-125, 228, 560.
Common property, 262, 271.
Communism, 265.
Comprehensive History of the Church of Jesus Christ of Latter-day Saints, 475, 493.
Condemnations, 482.
Conference Report, 61-62, 87, 223, 242, 258-259, 264, 271, 303, 334, 356, 368, 394, 395, 451, 502, 506, 507, 508, 509, 515, 516, 517, 520, 528, 529, 531, 532, 535, 536, 540, 541, 545-546, 550-551, 556, 557.
Confidence games, 246.
Congregations of the wicked, 463-464, 470.
Consecration, law of, 230, 260, 263-266, 267, 375, 414, 419, 420, 422, 424, 434, 444, 516, 530, 540, 554, 556, 557, 559.
Constitution of the U.S., 440.
Conversions, 459-460.
Converts, 90-91.
Copley, Leman, 336, 338, 376.
1 Corinthians, 4, 6, 49, 135, 149, 208, 256, 278, 315, 316, 321, 440.
2 Corinthians 280, 503.
Corrill, John, 356-357, 388.
Courage, 446.
Covenant-breakers, 376, 377.
Covenants, 131, 133-134, 449.
Covetousness, 424.
Covill, James, 207, 211, 374.
Cowdery, Oliver, 13, 17, 18, 25, 31, 35, 55, 59, 61-62, 72, 75, 79, 80, 87, 89, 92, 142, 148, 154, 156, 162, 188,

M

Malachi, 9, 30, 33, 65-66, 68, 247, 302, 339, 522.

Man, destiny of, 27; fall of, 112-113, 189-190; natural, 536; power in, 442-443; serve God, 112; spiritual existence, 174-178; temporal existence, 174-178, 260-261.

Manifestations, false, 347, 351, 353, 354, 355-356.

Mark, 67, 85, 135, 256, 273, 278.

Marsh, Thomas B., 185-188, 414, 419.

Marriage, 341, 543, 560; temple, 383, 546.

Marvelous work, 44-45, 72.

Material riches, 72-74, 423.

Matthew, 5, 17, 26, 64, 66, 67, 82, 85, 134, 135, 165, 210, 216, 228, 243, 256, 258, 278, 301, 307, 353, 390, 397, 415, 421, 423, 439, 447, 458, 467, 469, 489.

Matthias, 168.

McKay, David O., 49, 132, 258-259, 321, 385, 389, 452, 455, 507, 546.

Medical aid, 275.

Meditation and Atonement, 104, 130-131.

Meha, Stuart, 321.

Melchizedek Priesthood, 69, 70, 71, 88, 107, 140, 360, 541, 559.

Membership in Church, magnify calling in, 143-144; reasons for, 138-139; reponsibilities of, 118-126.

Mentally retarded, children, 545; death of, 183.

Meridian of Time, 2, 5, 9, 11, 17, 67, 130, 208, 216, 262, 272, 287, 289, 300, 301, 313, 315, 522, 539.

Merrill, Marriner W., 514.

Messenger and Advocate, 71, 403.

Methodism, 313.

Micah, 307.

Military service and killing, 241-243.

Millennial Star, 188, 305-306, 333.

Millennium, 69, 164, 168-173, 285, 340, 426, 433, 436, 479, 489, 495-496, 525, 530.

Ministry, calls to, 83, 89; of angels, 28-29, 299; qualifications for, 48-50.

Miracles, 278, 430, 483, 485, 512; first, 418; gift of power to work, 316, 319, 486.

Missionaries, 144, 200, 225, 469, 470, 541, 560; Instructions to, 361-362; message to, 539-540; set apart, 232-233; to preach gospel, 230-236, 368, 372; to the Lamanites (In-

dians), 194.

Missionary systems, 90-91, 94-95; work, 298-299, 459, 470, 484, 514, 527, 538, 539, 540, 548-551.

Missions, 46-47; Lamanite, 196-198; rewards of calls to, 83-84.

M'Lellin, William E., 530-531, 532, 533-534, 535.

Moral conduct, law of, 230, 237-259, 447, 559, 561; statutes of, 239.

Morality, 49; double standard, 238; single standard, 238, 253-254.

Mockery of sacred things, 497-499.

Moderation, 455.

Morley, Isaac, Capt., 227, 511, 512.

Mormon, 40, 48, 49, 183, 244, 277, 352.

"Mormonism," 211, 367.

Mormonism and Education, 407.

Moroni, 12, 13, 22, 29-30, 33, 37, 42, 48, 49, 69, 107, 110, 129, 182, 183, 224, 161, 164, 277, 293, 302, 315, 352, 458, 545; coming of, 29-30, 33; description of, 29.

Moses, 3, 32, 36, 61, 69, 79, 116, 159, 176, 179, 181, 237, 240, 280, 285, 341, 406, 436, 438, 444, 453, 462, 479, 483, 514, 523, 536.

Mosiah, 49, 50, 103, 257, 278, 280, 350, 378, 423, 456, 460, 471, 481, 488, 501, 506, 554.

Mother's love, 93; opportunities for, 124; responsibilities of, 120-121.

Mount of Olives, 304.

Mount Sinai, 237.

Mount of Transfiguration, 32.

Mount Zion, 34, 170.

Moyle, Henry D., 452.

Murder, 240-241, 447; penalty of, 242-243.

Murdock, John, 146, 347, 360.

Mysteries, 491-492.

N

Nathan, 248.

Natural man, 536.

Nehemiah, 469.

Neighbors, do not speak evil about, 238, 560.

1 Nephi, 40, 76, 84, 166, 169, 206, 216, 293, 456, 484; small plates of, 40, 252.

2 Nephi, 4, 39, 41, 43, 57, 93, 103-104, 106, 130, 181, 194, 205, 224, 231, 253, 278, 280, 284, 340, 349, 353, 441, 456, 458, 470, 484, 493, 514.

3 Nephi, 82, 88, 104, 116, 194, 216, 224, 278, 309, 350, 379, 397, 426, 455, 506, 508, 510, 531.

temporal, 74, 408; work of, 68.
Samuel, 248, 380, 432.
Sanctification, 115, 391.
Satan, 20, 36, 41, 81, 97, 103, 109,
130, 154, 155, 161, 172, 179, 184,
240, 252, 307, 315, 372, 409, 492,
528; activities of, 41, 548; evils of,
440; existence of, 473; plan of,
250-251; power of 37, 100; tactics
of, 39-41, 348-349; to deceive, 346-
349, 362-363.
Saturday Night Thoughts, 466.
Savior, 17, 24, 34, 49, 60, 71, 76, 98,
130, 163, 199, 219, 256, 386, 397,
399, 426, 432, 526, 539; birth of,
109; coming of, 168-172, 307, 425,
440, 526; teachings of, 507. See
also Jesus Christ, Redeemer.
School of the Prophets, 407.
Schools, Latterday Saint, 407.
Scrapbook of Mormon Literature,
528.
Scriptures, canon of, 2; making of,
530-538.
Sealing, power of, 22-23.
Security, 539.
Seer, 116, 156, 157, 160, 363, 538.
Seraphic hosts, 215.
Sermon on the Mount, 82, 256, 423.
Service, 45-46, 84, 94; auxiliary, 47;
law of remuneration of, 230, 267,
555; missionary, 46-47, 83-84, 144;
to God and man, 471; to others,
460, 470; qualifications for, 48-50.
*Shakerism, Its Meaning and Mes-
sage*, 337-338, 341.
Shaking Quakers, mission to, 336-
345, 559.
Shalmaneser, 360.
Shepherd's voice, 465.
Sherem, 485-486.
Sick, law of administration to, 230,
272-281, 531, 545-546.
Sign of the Son of Man, 300-301.
Sign seekers, 484-487, 560.
Signs of the times, 170-171, 290-295,
300-302, 483-487, 539, 559.
Sin, 93, 104, 106, 130, 253, 314, 389,
414, 442, 496; condemned, 26; confess, 450-451, 502-503, 504; forgiveness of, 134-135, 255, 472, 501-
510; freedom from, 416; of abortion, 255-256; remission of, 63-64,
70, 120, 200, 205, 305, 312, 389,
402, 422, 460, 500, 501, 531, 543,
545; revealed, 487; safeguard
against, 256-257.
Skousen, W. Cleon, 244, 247.
Smith, **Asael, 524.**

Smith, Emma Hale, 57, 89, 127, 146-
153, 226, 411.
Smith, George A., 186, 187, 191, 227,
363, 394, 479, 501, 512.
Smith, George Albert, 132, 321, 394,
395, 540.
Smith, Hyrum, 15, 25, 72, 80, 81, 83,
89, 108, 140, 141, 185, 331, 470.
Smith, John, 16.
Smith, Joseph, 1-2, 6, 8, 13, 21, 22,
25, 72, 75, 78, 79, 80, 81, 82, 86, 87,
88, 89, 97, 105, 121, 126, 137, 138,
141, 154, 161, 184, 186, 204, 226,
240-241, 264, 268, 274, 279, 291,
301, 319, 463, 467, 471, 482, 488,
501, 528, 555; Angel Moroni visits,
28-30, 43, 69, 164; appoints Historians, 327-335; baptism of, 64;
call of, 24, 25, 282, 483; compiling
the D&C, 13-16, 532-533; dedicates
temple site, 433; duties of, 116-
117; evaluates revelations, 552;
faith in God, 232-233; first L.D.S.
school founded by, 407; first vision, 10-12, 26, 36, 98; goes to
Hiram, Ohio, 500, 521, Kirtland,
481, St. Louis, 472, 556; greatness
of, 410; history of, 57; integrity of,
17-18, 38; Lord's mouthpiece, 155-
157, 296; martyrdom of, 412;
meets Oliver Cowdery, 52-53; mob
action against, 548; ordained, 107-
108; organizes Church, 108-109,
161-162; performs first miracle,
418; proof of plates, 58-59; rebuked by Lord, 37-38; receives gift
of the Holy Ghost, 309-326; receives Law of the Church, 237, 249,
260; receives the Priesthood, 31-32,
35, 63-71, 158-159, 518, 523; receives Sacrament revelation, 127-
136; reveals move to Rocky Mountains, 305, 344; revelation to
Thomas Marsh, 185-188; revelation
to wife Emma, 146-153; revising
Bible, 219, 548; Saints told to uphold, 297; sends mission to Lamanites (Indians), 196-198; sends mission to Shaking Quakers, 336-345;
speaks to Relief Society, 144; theological teachings revealed to, 98;
testimony, 8, 111, 303, 534, 561;
told to magnify office, 143; trans-
lates gold plates, 37, 55; vision in
Kirtland Temple, 218; visits Pres.
Van Buren, 312; W. W. Phelps
meets, 401; way revelations were
dictated by, 347-348.
Smith, Joseph F., Pres., 19, 31, 35,